This is the best book that I know of on the subject of Satan and demons. It is practical and pastorally wise. It frequently warns against erroneous teachings and practices. It contains thoughtful explanations of many dozens of Scripture passages. It takes seriously the Bible's teachings about the reality of demonic influence in our world today. It gives practical, calm guidelines for prevailing in spiritual warfare through the power of Christ. And every section ends with a brief personal history told by someone who has experienced genuine deliverance from demonic oppression. Highly recommended.

Wayne Grudem, PhD, distinguished research professor of
theology and biblical studies, Phoenix Seminary

Spiritual warfare is not something that the weird and wacky are dialed into. It is what is actually waging around all of us. Sam Storms gives us a clear and thoroughly biblical view of our real enemy and shows us how to walk in the victory that is already ours in Christ.

Matt Chandler, Village Church

I know of no one who combines a rigorous, intellectual approach to theology and biblical exegesis with an overtly, unabashedly charismatic supernaturalism the way Sam Storms does. He is truly unique. *Understanding Spiritual Warfare* is his latest treasure. It is theologically astute, biblically careful, and spiritually and experientially inspiring and enriching. Storms's book is chock-full of authentic testimonies of demonic activity and deliverance. No one can read this book and walk away with a cavalier attitude toward the reality of evil spirits. And as a scholar-pastor, Storms is careful throughout the book to provide practical wisdom and advice for cultivating a balanced and workable approach to dealing with the demonic. This is now the best book on the subject in print. It is my honor to endorse it enthusiastically.

J. P. Moreland, distinguished professor of philosophy, Talbot
School of Theology and author of *Kingdom Triangle*

The spiritual realm is real, which means that spiritual warfare is also real. The enemy is actively working to destroy our lives, along with the lives of those we love. Yet where can we go to find a reliable guide to this crucially important topic? We need a teacher who is grounded in the Word, full of the Spirit, and with years of experience in practical, hands-on ministry. Dr. Sam Storms is the man for the job, and here in one volume he tackles the most controversial topics, taking us into the unseen realm and showing us how we can live out the fullness of our victory in Christ. Regardless of your theological beliefs (Sam is an amillennial Calvinist; I'm a premillennial Arminian), if you embrace the Word and Spirit and want to put Satan and his minions under your feet, this book will be your go-to guide.

Dr. Michael L. Brown, author of *Jezebel's War with America*,
host of the *Line of Fire* radio broadcast

UNDERSTANDING
SPIRITUAL
WARFARE

UNDERSTANDING SPIRITUAL WARFARE

A COMPREHENSIVE GUIDE

SAM STORMS

ZONDERVAN
REFLECTIVE

ZONDERVAN REFLECTIVE

Understanding Spiritual Warfare
Copyright © 2021 by Sam Storms

Requests for information should be addressed to:
Zondervan, *3900 Sparks Dr. SE, Grand Rapids, Michigan 49546*

Zondervan titles may be purchased in bulk for educational, business, fundraising, or sales promotional use. For information, please email SpecialMarkets@Zondervan.com.

ISBN 978-0-310-12086-5 (audio)

Library of Congress Cataloging-in-Publication Data

Names: Storms, C. Samuel, 1951- author.
Title: Understanding spiritual warfare : a comprehensive guide / Sam Storms.
Description: Grand Rapids : Zondervan, 2021. | Includes bibliographical references and index.
Identifiers: LCCN 2020048332 (print) | LCCN 2020048333 (ebook) | ISBN 9780310120841 (paperback) |
    ISBN 9780310120858 (ebook)
Subjects: LCSH: Demonology. | Devil—Christianity. | Spiritual warfare.
Classification: LCC BT975 .S76 2021 (print) | LCC BT975 (ebook) | DDC 235/.4—dc23
LC record available at https://lccn.loc.gov/2020048332
LC ebook record available at https://lccn.loc.gov/2020048333

Material from *Practicing the Power: Welcoming the Gifts of the Holy Spirit in Your Life* by Sam Storms. Copyright © 2017 by Sam Storms. Used by permission of Zondervan. www.Zondervan.com.

Adapted material from *Tough Topics: Biblical Answers to 25 Challenging Questions* by Sam Storms, © 2013. Used by permission of Crossway, a publishing ministry of Good News Publishers, Wheaton, IL 60187, www.crossway.org.

Adapted material from *Tough Topics 2: Biblical Answers to 25 Challenging Questions* by Sam Storms (Fearn, Ross-shire, UK: Christian Focus, 2015), used with permission.

Cover design: *Jesse Owen / 10AM Design*
Cover image: © *Alev Takil / Unsplash*
Interior design: *Denise Froehlich*

Printed in the United States of America

21 22 23 24 25   /LSC/   10 9 8 7 6 5 4 3 2 1

Dedicated to
Kendra, Lesli, and Ann

With profound appreciation for your efforts in building the ministry of Inner Healing and Deliverance at Bridgeway, and for the love and tender care you display toward the men and women who have found freedom, joy, and healing through your prayerful commitment to showing them the unchanging love and life-changing power of Jesus Christ.

Contents

Foreword

There are a lot of books out there on spiritual warfare, but none are quite like this. I have been looking for one "go to" book that I could recommend to people on this important topic, and this will be it.

Sam Storms approaches spiritual warfare with the heart of a pastor, the skill of a biblical exegete, a sensitivity to the work of the Spirit, and the wisdom of a leader who has had significant experience in this arena. The result is a book that is truly well-balanced on this theme and very helpful.

Many of us know Sam as a biblical and theological scholar. I first became personally acquainted with Sam when we both served on the executive committee of the Evangelical Theological Society. He served as president of that scholarly society in 2017 and was elected to that role because of widespread recognition of his past scholarly contributions. Sam has written a number of books on a wide array of topics, but all of his work reflects scholarship done in the service of the church. All this to say that Sam approaches this topic with a great deal of scholarly credibility. Throughout this book, Sam provides a careful, yet concise, explanation of the key biblical texts related to spiritual warfare. Whereas many volumes on spiritual warfare are heavy on stories, practices, and traditions, this book starts with the Bible and reveals the meaning and relevance of what Scripture says.

But many will know Sam as pastor. He has served in a pastoral role for forty-six years. For the past twelve years, he has served as lead pastor at Bridgeway Church in Oklahoma City. It is abundantly clear throughout this volume that Sam brings with him the compassion of a shepherd who is concerned about taking care of his flock. He wants his sheep to experience a pastoral touch that will bring healing to their wounds and release from the claws of the enemy.

Sam also writes this book with the conviction that God can powerfully and mercifully intervene into peoples' lives today to bring healing and deliverance through the ministry of the Holy Spirit. This is evident in many of the personal stories sprinkled throughout the book from people who have been touched by the prayer ministry of Bridgeway Church. I personally worry that too many Christians and churches put up a stop sign (or a yield sign) when it comes to the work of the Holy Spirit. Because of past excesses and sometimes crazy stuff attributed to the Holy Spirit, many believers have perhaps grown too cautious about embracing the work of the Spirit. Yet if we believe in the reality of the work of the enemy, we need to believe in the work of the Spirit of God. Spiritual warfare can only be done in the power of the Spirit since we are not able to stand against the enemy in our own strength.

The prevailing naturalistic worldview in which many of us were educated in our K–12 years and beyond has profoundly influenced our ability to accept and understand the nature of the spirit realm. Yet if we accept the authority of the Bible, we must reckon with the fact that the theme of the demonic is present from Genesis to Revelation. Yet for many Christians, the demonic is not a *functional* part of their worldview. This book will help us grapple with what the Bible teaches on the topic and will show that we are not setting aside our intellect and rationality to accept this aspect of biblical teaching.

I appreciate Sam's emphasis on the fact that believers are not automatically immune to attack from the demonic realm. There are too many Christians who think that a force field descended around them when they became a Christian and the evil one cannot harm them in any way. That is a dangerous position to hold. Sam shows that we have the power and authority in the Lord Jesus Christ to deal with demonic attack and intrusion, but that this must be appropriated in cooperation with the Holy Spirit.

In the twenty or so years that I taught a course on spiritual warfare at my Christian university, I always stressed the need for developing a prayer ministry in the context of the local church. Having a team of people who are knowledgeable about spiritual warfare, care for people, and are attune to the work of the Spirit is sorely needed in our churches. Sam has helped to develop and equip such a team at his church. And, as the stories in this volume demonstrate, the ministry is helping many people.

This book is a great starting point as a resource for equipping such a team in your church. It is also a great guide for someone wanting an overall orientation to what spiritual warfare is all about. I am grateful that Sam Storms had the vision for writing this book. I pray that the Lord uses it to strengthen, heal, and help his church. To God be the glory.

CLINTON E. ARNOLD
dean and professor of New Testament
Talbot School of Theology (Biola University)

Acknowledgments

There are several people who were instrumental in the production of this book. I want to begin by thanking Ryan Pazdur, Elizabeth Vince, and Chris Beetham, at Zondervan, for their incredibly helpful editorial suggestions and encouragement.

I would also like to express profound gratitude to the elders, staff, and congregation at Bridgeway Church who not only provided me with the time and opportunity to write this book but also have devoted themselves to creating an atmosphere and spiritual culture at Bridgeway that facilitates and promotes the exercise of all God's precious spiritual gifts.

There are several men and women whose stories appear scattered throughout this book. They have graciously allowed me to tell briefly of what they experienced and how God worked powerfully in their lives to bring deliverance and transformation. Although their names have been changed, the substance of their testimonies is in their own words. I continue to stand in awe of their spiritual courage in facing head-on the ways in which the enemy of our souls assaulted them, but I am even more greatly moved and grateful for the kindness of Jesus Christ, through the power of the Holy Spirit, in facilitating their new-found freedom!

SAM STORMS

Introduction

Both the complexities of spiritual warfare and the controversies the topic provokes have made me hesitant to write this book. It has taken several years for me to overcome my reluctance and finally put words on a page.

Two things contributed to my decision to write this book.

First, no matter how hard we may try, it is quite simply impossible to ignore the vast amount of material in both the Old Testament and New Testament that speaks of Satan, demons, and Christian men and women's incessant battle with the temptation and oppression they try to impose on us. The only justification for avoiding these many biblical texts is to argue that the word "Satan" does not point to a living, personal being striving to undermine the spiritual flourishing of Christians and to destroy the kingdom of Christ. No, the argument is that "Satan" is simply a symbol, or perhaps a poetic metaphor that refers to all manner of evil, both moral and natural. At most, it refers to what people in ancient times once believed, but we today are far too intellectually sophisticated and technologically savvy to embrace such outmoded and superstitious ideas. Both Satan and demons were a part of a worldview that has long since lost its usefulness and cogency. This is the twenty-first century, for heaven's sake.

As you read this book, you will quickly see that we cannot so easily dismiss the plethora of biblical assertions concerning the reality of Satan and his demonic hordes. If we determine that the Bible's worldview is no longer relevant, then we must equally apply such a verdict to Christ's incarnation, the miracles he performed, his death and bodily resurrection, together with the hope of salvation and his second coming to consummate history as we know it. The biblical worldview, put simply, is God's worldview. And notwithstanding the many industrial and scientific advances we've come to enjoy in our day, I have more confidence in God's inspired verdict on what is real and not real than I do in the opinions of the most educated and allegedly enlightened minds of this or any other century.

We cannot claim to believe in the divine origin and inspiration of the Bible while so casually dismissing its extensive and unambiguous teaching on Satan's existence and activity. Simply put, I've written this book because I believe that what the Bible says about this invisible enemy is true.

My second reason for writing is directly related to what I've been doing for the past forty-six years. I'm a local church pastor, and on almost a daily basis I encounter men and women of all ages who are sorely oppressed, tormented, and tempted by demonic powers. But the good news is that I've also witnessed firsthand their deliverance, their freedom from the enemy's influence, and the joy, peace, and spiritual flourishing that comes with experiencing the victory that Jesus died and rose again to give us.

In what follows, you'll read numerous personal accounts of such victories, together with practical guidance on how you, too, can extinguish the "flaming darts" (Eph. 6:16) of the "cosmic powers" and "spiritual forces of evil" (Eph. 6:12) that so often bombard your life.

Although the subtitle of this book uses the word "comprehensive," there are undoubtedly some issues that I must address only briefly. The wide array of topics and the seemingly endless controversies that surround them unavoidably impose on me certain limitations. Still, though, I've done everything possible to address the most pressing and urgent issues with which most Christians wrestle, as well as the questions they so frequently ask.

Theological Approach

You may already be asking yourself, "What approach, theologically speaking, does Storms take in this book?" That's a perfectly reasonable question to ask. There are, after all, numerous models and perspectives on spiritual warfare circulating in the broader body of Christ. On the one hand, there are more progressive (dare I say liberal?) perspectives that, as noted above, minimize the problem by delegitimizing the very existence of Satan and his demons. Proponents of this perspective would argue that the problem of evil is more structural and systemic than personal. That is to say, they argue that the principalities and powers mentioned in Scripture are not living, thinking, conniving spirits but the interior structures of society, be they political, governmental, social, educational, etc., that exist to maintain power and control over the marginalized and weak in our world.

This is not a view I embrace. Although I will on occasion disagree with his approach to spiritual warfare, the late David Powlison of the Christian Counseling and Education Foundation (CCEF) puts it well, and I am in complete agreement with him on this point:

> [We need to know] that "Satan" is not merely a personification of impersonal forces (like "Mother Nature"). Evil comes in person, a perverse covenant lord aiming to command our disloyalty to the true King. The devil is a purposeful, intelligent, malevolent personal agent. As an immoral being, he is potent, culpable, and doomed. To react against Jesus is to live in the image of this devil, obeying his desires and loving darkness (John 3:19; 8:44). Behind the webs of deception spun by individuals and ideologies, a liar works. Behind the violence and violation done by evildoers, whether individual or institutional, a murderer works.[1]

On the other hand, there are the many Bible-believing evangelicals who do not in the least deny the existence of Satan and demons. However, their approach to facilitating the spiritual freedom of the oppressed is markedly different from the view that I will take in this book. Their approach is largely related to the cessationist view of spiritual gifts many evangelicals (such as Powlison) embrace. According to this view, the more overtly miraculous gifts of the Spirit are no longer available to the church, God having sovereignly withdrawn (or at least ceased bestowing) them shortly after the death of the apostle John, likely toward the end of the first century AD.

I am unapologetically a functioning, practicing charismatic, and the remainder of this book will give you a sense for how I believe the gifts of the Spirit operate today. So, in the interests of giving you a fair warning, I do believe in speaking in tongues, the gifts of prophecy and discerning of spirits, divine healing, and the ministry of casting out demons and providing, in

---

1   David Powlison, "The Classical Model," in *Understanding Spiritual Warfare: Four Views*, ed. James K. Beilby and Paul Rhodes Eddy (Grand Rapids: Baker Academic, 2012), 91.

God's grace and power, deliverance for those who are either demonized or oppressed or sorely harassed by the enemy.

If that is off-putting to you, I hope that you will at least dig into the pages that follow to hear a perspective that I believe will be of great benefit to your spiritual life and perhaps also to those who come your way. If you are at least mildly intrigued by this, I welcome you to walk with me through this challenging dimension of Christian life and ministry.

Personal Testimonies

Scattered throughout the pages of this book are real-life testimonies of men and women who have experienced deliverance from demonic oppression and now walk in the joy and freedom of inner spiritual healing, and in the case of some, physical healing as well. Each has given permission for their story to be told, although their names have been changed. Each of them spent eight weeks going through an extensive time of ministry that was launched here at Bridgeway Church. Each session, each week, often would last up to two hours. It involved digging deeply into each individual's past and present experience. These were not counseling sessions, although we highly value that aspect of ministry for God's people. It was a highly intensive, carefully constructed sequence of prayer, confession, repentance, and affirmation of the truth of God's Word as it applied to the lives of those who chose to walk down this path. I trust that you will be greatly encouraged to hear of how the Holy Spirit facilitated the healing and freedom of so many, and how he can do the same for you.

PART 1

LEARNING ABOUT THE DEMONIC

CHAPTER 1

A Surprising Encounter with the Demonic

S am, there's a lady behind the sound booth chanting and invoking evil spirits. I think she may be demonized."

That's not what I expected to hear on the first day of our weekend conference. My family and I had arrived in Kansas City only a month earlier (in August of 1993). The move from our church in Ardmore, Oklahoma, where I had served as pastor for eight years, to the home of the somewhat infamous "Kansas City prophets" had progressed smoothly enough. But that was about to change quite dramatically.

I made my way to the back of the auditorium, to the sound booth, and sure enough, there she was. I couldn't quite make out what was happening, but a lady whom I had never seen before had constructed something of an altar, around which she methodically danced, all the while chanting in a language I couldn't understand. I thought it best to leave her alone. Perhaps it was a harmless expression of her unique style of worship. After all, I was new to the church and didn't want to make an unpleasant scene at the first conference where I had been put in charge. As much as I tried to persuade myself that her intentions were good and godly, I knew deep within that trouble was afoot.

As I spoke with a few of my fellow pastors about what to do, I noticed that this lady had left her "shrine" and was now sitting on the back row, her eyes and attention fixed on the man sitting in front of her. The next thing I knew, Sherry Doyle, sister of our senior pastor, Mike Bickle, had taken up a seat directly next to this lady. I had only known Sherry for a few weeks, but I had come to recognize in her a mature gift of spiritual discernment. If anyone could determine if the lady was demonized and a threat, it would be Sherry.

It didn't take long. As soon as I looked up, Sherry was making a beeline for me. "Sam," she said through quivering lips, "that lady over there is seriously demonized." Before I could respond, the man at whom this lady had been staring was walking toward me, his eyes pleading for help.

"She's chanting at me in backwards tongues," he blurted out. Now, I don't know what backwards tongues is supposed to sound like. I had a difficult enough time deciphering legitimate forward tongues! In any case, I had no idea what to expect as the lady made her way in my direction.

What happened next was a first for me. But as you'll discover later on in this book, it wasn't the last time I would have an encounter with the power of the demonic. When she came within about ten feet of me, I suddenly felt enshrouded in a fog of sorts.

We often scoff when Luke Skywalker in *Star Wars* speaks of "The Force" and its abiding presence in and through all elements of the universe. But in a sense, this is the best language I have for what touched me. The lady never made physical contact with me. She never came closer than three to four feet from my body. But a "wall" of energy or power—what felt like liquid air—engulfed me. It wasn't something that a person could see or touch, but it was undeniably tangible and real. It was wave upon wave of what felt like a wind of wickedness. It actually pushed me backwards a step or two.

My mind went blank. My thoughts were jumbled and chaotic. I couldn't connect two thoughts. I couldn't speak. It was as if my tongue weighed a ton and my lips were glued shut. I was disoriented and dizzy. Nausea set in. The closer she moved toward me, the closer I came to vomiting.

There had been instances in the past where I discerned or sensed in my spirit that demonic forces were present. But this was something altogether new to me. This wasn't a case of a mental or psychological awareness. I *physically* felt something *non-physical*.

It was then that I felt Sherry grip my arm and pull me away. "Did you feel that?" she asked. "When I sat down next to her, I got dizzy and lightheaded, and thought I was going to throw up." I was glad to know that I wasn't alone in this experience.

With the help of others, we regained our composure and escorted the lady into a back room, where we attempted to ask a few questions and get some idea of what she was up to. We weren't very successful. The situation worsened until we had to call the police to have her escorted out of the building.

After her unceremonious departure, I quickly regained my emotional and mental balance and tried to make sense of what had just transpired.

If you are wondering, as I often have, why God would have permitted this experience, there are at least two reasons. First, it was an especially effective way of confirming in my heart the reality of the supernatural realm. What had always been a staple of my theological convictions suddenly invaded my experience in an undeniably tangible way. But second, and perhaps even more important, it was God's way of alerting me to the consequences of entering spiritual battle unprepared. Ephesians 6:12–18 and its emphasis on the necessity of adorning ourselves with the full armor of God suddenly became more relevant and urgent than I had ever imagined.

Two days later, on Monday morning, fifty or so people were gathered at our office building for our regular intercessory prayer meeting. My wife, Ann, was sitting at the front desk serving as the church receptionist. Suddenly, in walked the lady. Ann was immediately overwhelmed with what she described as the worst stench she had ever had the displeasure of smelling. Without a word, the lady walked past her and into the prayer room. Before I even saw her, I was overcome by the smell. It literally filled the room. It permeated the halls of the office building and up to the second floor. I had never before, nor have I since, smelled anything so putrid. If you had asked me before that day, "Do demons have an odor?" I probably would have laughed. But the answer to the question is most assuredly yes—and it is far from pleasant.

We didn't waste any time, but immediately escorted the lady into one of our pastoral offices. I and two others on our pastoral staff began investigating who she was and what she wanted from us. We learned she had been involved for several years in a vast array of occultic practices, from witchcraft to Earth worship. We carefully and prayerfully explained the gospel of Jesus Christ to her and watched in amazement as her countenance changed. We took authority in the name of Christ over every demonic spirit and commanded, in that same name, that every demon leave and be consigned to the abyss.

This ministry of deliverance lasted for at least an hour, perhaps longer. Surprisingly, there was little resistance from either the lady herself or the demons she carried. No shouting, no physical convulsions, no obscenities. The power of the Holy Spirit pierced her heart and awakened her soul to the beauty and glory of Jesus Christ, crucified and raised from the dead.

It's hard to say whether either the deliverance or conversion of this lady was finalized that day. Perhaps it was the beginning of both, but of this I can testify with all sincerity: this lady was set free of demonic bondage and darkness and was transferred into the kingdom of the Son of God! Not long after her conversion, she joined our church, where she and her family became faithful and supportive members. Such is the demon-defeating, Christ-exalting power of the Holy Spirit, to the glory of God the Father.

Some may be inclined to believe that what I experienced was perhaps due to lack of sleep or fatigue or something I ate. But why would Bible-believing Christians be skeptical of such events? If we trust the Scriptures as God's inspired and infallible revelation, the reality of a spiritual enemy who seeks to disrupt and disorient us should hardly come under suspicion.

Others may insist that I was susceptible to the sort of nausea and dizziness I encountered because of an imbalanced hankering for some super-natural experience. It was a momentary, self-induced hallucination of sorts that I mistakenly interpreted as a demonic attack. If that is your conclusion, I doubt if anything I say will convince you otherwise.

I am not the first to argue that our beliefs must be rooted in and fully consistent with Scripture. No experience alone, no matter how intense or disorienting, should be the foundation or rationale for our theological con-victions. However, at the same time, experiences such as mine do serve to bear witness to the truth of what Scripture teaches. Nothing that I felt on that day is inconsistent with what we see in God's written Word. In fact, it only served to confirm what I already believed to be true about the demonic from reading the Bible.

I'm not suggesting that every Christian will have a similar experience—nor am I suggesting that you should go looking for one. But the reality of the supernatural realm is not always holy and helpful. It is often demented and destructive.

I had come into immediate contact with the domain of darkness. And it is this realm of supernatural wickedness that I intend to explore in this book. My aim isn't to stir up the fires of sensationalism or hyper-spirituality. I intend, rather, to educate and equip you for a battle in which you've been engaged for quite some time, whether you know it or not. We call it spiritual warfare. So, let's begin.

CHAPTER 2

Confronting the Reality of Spiritual Warfare

I once dated a demon. Well, sort of. I mention this only because it is one reason why some of you may struggle with what I'm going to say in this book. I graduated from Duncan High School in Duncan, Oklahoma. We were affectionately, or in some cases, derisively known as the Duncan Demons. The "demon" in question, whom I briefly dated, was our female mascot, who at each football or basketball game would dress up in a red suit with horns and a long tail.

It is that image of a demon or perhaps even the devil himself that leads a lot of people to scoff and mock at the idea that such spiritual beings exist in reality. In his classic work *The Screwtape Letters*, C. S. Lewis portrays for us a senior demon by the name of Screwtape giving advice to a young upstart demon named Wormwood. Said Screwtape to Wormwood:

> I do not think you will have much difficulty in keeping the patient in the dark [by the "patient" he means you and me]. The fact that "devils" are predominantly *comic* figures in the modern imagination will help you. If any faint suspicion of your existence begins to arise in his mind, suggest to him a picture of something in red tights, and persuade him that since he cannot believe in that . . . he therefore cannot believe in you.[1]

It's really quite stunning when you stop to think about it. People don't make fun of the existence of God. Even atheists acknowledge that a good

---

1   C. S. Lewis, *The Screwtape Letters* (New York: Collier, 1982), 33 (emphasis original).

case can be made for the existence of a sovereign, spiritual, supernatural being we call "God." And no one, of course, who believes in God would deny that he has created people called "human beings" who are capable of both good and evil. Most who believe in God also affirm the existence of good, holy spiritual beings called "angels." So why do so many resist the idea of evil, unholy spiritual beings called "demons"?[2]

In September 2013, *New York* magazine conducted an interview with the late Supreme Court Justice Antonin Scalia. What caught the editors of the magazine by surprise wasn't any particular political or legal opinion of Scalia. What threw them into a virtual tizzy was that Scalia confessed that he believes in a literal, personal devil.

So, what do *you* believe? I have no problem at all believing in the existence and activity of a sizeable group of fallen, evil angels that the Bible calls demons. I read it everywhere in Scripture, and I've had my fair share of very real personal encounters with a few. But how important is this for you and me today, when other matters like the unpredictable stock market and the price of oil and sickness and disease and political upheavals are upon us? Is it really wise or helpful to spend time talking about demons and the devil? Yes, it is. I would go so far as to say that few things are more important, especially given what we've been seeing and experiencing in churches all across America.

There is no mistaking the teaching of Scripture on this one point: as there is a kingdom of God, so too is there a kingdom of Satan. And the two are embroiled in open conflict. Jesus himself spoke of Satan's kingdom in his response to those who charged him with casting out demons by the power of Satan himself:

> "And if Satan casts out Satan, he is divided against himself. How then will his kingdom stand?" (Matt. 12:26)

---

2   Having said that, it must be noted that 74 percent of cultures surveyed in a world ethnographic research project displayed a belief in the existence and activity of spirits and the reality of demonic possession or demonization (see Erika Bourguignon, "Spirit Possession Belief and Social Structure," in *The Realm of the Extra-Human: Ideas and Actions*, ed. A. Bharatic [Paris: Mouton, 1976], 19). This study is dated 1976. Perhaps the percentage of belief or disbelief has changed in the last forty-five years. In this regard, see especially Craig S. Keener, *Miracles: The Credibility of the New Testament Accounts*, vol. 2 (Grand Rapids: Baker Academic, 2011), 788–856.

The apostle Paul spoke of the "authority" of Satan, sometimes rendered his "dominion" (see Acts 26:18; cf. Col. 1:13). Simply put, Satan operates in the spiritual realm with authority and power, and it is precisely from bondage to this darkness that Christ has set us free.

Far too many Christians think far too little and lightly of the extent of Satan's influence in our world. We treat Satan's existence and activity in much the same way we think about gravity and breathing—we hardly give these things a second thought. Precisely. We know that gravity is real and largely accounts for why the physical universe is as it is and operates in the way it does. But no one pauses before putting a foot forward and consciously thinks, "Well, I hope gravity is still real. If it isn't, I may either fall on my face or float upwards to heaven." Likewise, no one pauses between each breath we breathe and analyzes what is happening. Sadly, and dangerously, many Christians treat Satan and his demons in much the same manner. Whether through arrogant presumption or outright neglect or even a fear of being laughed at by others, people ignore the spiritual realm. They live as if it didn't exist, or if it does, it has little to no bearing on their daily routines.

Recognizing Satan's Global Influence

The apostle John provided us with an alarming wake-up call in his first epistle:

> We know that we are from God, and the whole world lies in the power of the evil one. (1 John 5:19)

The contrasts here are striking. Whereas the "whole world" is subject to Satan's powerful influence, we who are God's children are "in him who is true" (1 John 5:20). As John Stott explains in his commentary on John's letters, "John wastes no words and blurs no issues. The uncompromising alternative is stated baldly. Everyone belongs either to 'us' or to the 'world'. Everyone is therefore either *of God* or *under the control of the evil one*. There is no third category."[3] *Everyone belongs to someone!*

We must never overlook the fact that the apostle John wrote this

---

3   John Stott, *The Letters of John: An Introduction and Commentary* (Grand Rapids: Eerdmans, 1996), 196.

statement after the cross of Christ, after the resurrection, after Christ had been exalted to the right hand of the Father, after "all rule and authority and power and dominion" had been put in subjection "under his feet" (Eph. 1:21–22), and after Pentecost and the outpouring of the Holy Spirit. The defeat of our enemy is an accomplished fact, but his presence and activity in opposition to us and the kingdom of Christ will not be terminated until the second coming of our Lord at the close of history.

This passage in 1 John 5 and others like it forever shatter the illusion of neutrality, the idea that so-called "good" people who are not Christians are neither for God nor for Satan, are neither in God's kingdom nor in Satan's. The fact is, all people, young and old, male and female, belong to one of two kingdoms: the kingdom of light or the kingdom of darkness. If people are not "in Christ," they are "in the power of the devil"—even if they have no visible, sensible awareness of being in the devil's grip. Thus, not to serve God is to serve Satan, whether you are conscious of it or not.

We must not overlook the profound implications of that simple preposition "in." It points to the fact that the whole world languishes in helpless passivity. The world and all its inhabitants who are not "in" Christ live under the influence, power, and authority of Satan. They face each day in his grip and subject to his dominion (cf. John 12:31; 14:30; 16:11; 17:15; Acts 26:18; 2 Cor. 4:4; Eph. 2:1–2). When we apply this notion to the "whole world," we see the extent of Satan's sway. He exerts an insidious influence on the financial world, business and industry, athletics, the stock market, the banking system, political institutions and parties, entertainment, the internet, education, the family, the home, the neighborhood, civic clubs and social service organizations, and country clubs.

We must reckon with a global satanic influence.

I recognize that this is a stunning, shocking revelation. It takes your breath away to consider the implications of such an assertion. This frightening revelation could easily instill fear and dread were it not for another assertion that John makes in the same epistle:

> Little children, you are from God and have overcome them, for he who is in you is greater than he who is in the world. (1 John 4:4)

The apostle John assures Christians that they have a spiritual and theological victory over false prophets and heretics. These false teachers have not succeeded in deceiving us; we know the truth and have rejected their lies. Why? How? Because "he who is in you is greater than he who is in the world."

Having contrasted Christians ("you") with the heretics ("them"), he now compares the spiritual forces who are *in* the respective antagonists. Yes, Satan is great, but God is greater! Yes, Satan is powerful, but God is infinitely more powerful! The "he" who is in the Christian is God the Father (1 John 4:4, 12–13); God the Son (1 John 2:14; cf. 2 Cor 13:5; Gal 2:20); and God the Holy Spirit (1 John 2:20, 27). And let me be clear that John does not say greater are "you" but greater is *he*. It isn't you, but *God in you* that brings the assurance of victory.

People often respond to the call to spiritual arms in one of two ways: either with obsessive preoccupation (focusing on 1 John 5:19 to the neglect of 1 John 4:4) or with complacent indifference (focusing on 1 John 4:4 to the neglect of 1 John 5:19). C. S. Lewis famously declared,

> There are two equal and opposite errors into which our race can fall about the devils. One is to disbelieve in their existence. The other is to believe, and to feel an excessive and unhealthy interest in them. They themselves [i.e., the demons] are equally pleased by both errors, and hail a materialist or a magician with the same delight.[4]

It matters little to the devil whether you attribute the totality of evil to him or none at all. In what follows, I will do my best to avoid both extremes and present what I believe is the biblical perspective on our conflict with the enemy of our souls.

Twelve Reasons Christians Are Ignorant of Spiritual Warfare

The question still lingers: Why are so many Christians oblivious to the reality of spiritual warfare? And if they understand the reality of it, why are they so complacent and ill-prepared for the fight? Here I want to identify at least a dozen reasons.

---

4 Lewis, *The Screwtape Letters*, 3.

1. Ignorance of the Bible

Many Christians simply do not know what or how much the Bible says on the subject, and they have not been acquainted with the tactics of the enemy. Paul's statement in Ephesians 6:12 highlights the ramifications of this ignorance for the Christian life, even in its most routine and seemingly mundane affairs:

> For our struggle is not against flesh and blood, but against the rulers, against the powers, against the world forces of this darkness, against the spiritual forces of wickedness in the heavenly places. (NASB)

I find it remarkable that this was written by a man like Paul, an individual whose life was seemingly a constant battle against *flesh-and-blood people*: Pharisees, angry mobs, Roman authorities, false apostles, disloyal followers, and so on. Yet, according to Paul, his war was not ultimately against them but against the unseen demonic forces behind all human opposition to the gospel. Our own war is against these same unseen forces. Ignorance of this fact has contributed greatly to most Christians' lack of preparedness.

2. Belief That the Bible Is Irrelevant

Some regard much of what the Bible says as irrelevant for our day. Believing in Satan and demons, they argue, is like believing in the Loch Ness monster and Bigfoot. They argue that the Bible simply cannot speak into our highly advanced, technologically sophisticated world. No reasonably educated person in the twenty-first century would rely upon an outdated, pre-scientific book to formulate their worldview, they argue.

An obstacle related to this is the ludicrous and comical way our culture portrays Satan and his demons. It is difficult to get people to take the devil seriously when both the church and modern society trivialize him. What an advantage we give Satan when we underestimate him! On the other hand, movies like *The Exorcist* and so many more of the horror genre today depict our enemy in such grotesquely offensive ways that people instinctively dismiss the reality of his existence and activity.

3. The Victory of the Cross

Other Christians are unprepared for spiritual warfare because they believe that, since Jesus's victory was so complete and comprehensive, we need only rest passively in the security of our position in Christ rather than aggressively apply it on a daily basis. It is true, of course, that the victory Jesus secured in his death and resurrection has forever sealed the eternal fate of Satan and his demonic hosts. But *protection against demonic attack is not automatic.* Simply being a Christian does not insulate you from demonic oppression. The "flaming darts of the evil one" (Eph. 6:16) continue to target Christians and require our diligent resistance.

John Gilhooly speaks for many today when he says, "Even though it seems that angels and demons are active today, there is less reason to expect the type of activity among angels and demons that we see in the gospel accounts."[5] Yet consider the apostle Paul's declaration in Ephesians 6:12 that our primary opposition comes from demonic beings. Consider the prevalence of demonic activity portrayed in the book of Revelation (see chapters five and six). Scripture provides substantial evidence that Gilhooly's conclusion is misguided. We have every reason to believe that angels and demons are no less active today than they were in the first century.

4. The Fear of Imbalance

Some Christians do nothing to prepare for spiritual warfare because they believe that *any* depth of study on the subject betrays a preoccupation with the demonic and is thus imbalanced. Sadly, many Christians are either so cynical when it comes to demonstrations of spiritual power or have lived so long in the utter absence of such experiences that any manifestation at all is profoundly unsettling to them. In other words, to those who have seen virtually nothing, any expression of concern for the demonic seems like too much. Likewise, to those who have seen a lot, a little seems like none at all.

5. The Fear of Sensationalism

As Clinton Arnold has argued, some Christians believe that "stressing spiritual warfare might lead to an unbalanced, experience-oriented theology centering on the spectacular."[6] The fanatical excesses of some within the broader Pentecostal-charismatic world have exerted an unhealthy influence on many

---

5   John R. Gilhooly, *40 Questions about Angels, Demons, and Spiritual Warfare* (Grand Rapids: Kregel Academic, 2018), 20.
6   Clinton E. Arnold, *3 Crucial Questions about Spiritual Warfare* (Grand Rapids: Baker, 1997), 26.

who have determined to distance themselves from anything remotely connected to the supernatural realm. As a self-identifying charismatic, I can understand this concern. But the abuses of some should never justify our turning a blind eye to the pervasive reality of the spiritual enemies that oppose us.

6. Insulated Lifestyles

Some good, solid, stable, buckle-on-the-Bible-belt, middle-class American people who have lived relatively docile and decent lives find it hard to believe that any of this is necessary, helpful, or relevant to them. "Surely Satan is more concerned with the widespread slaughter of the unborn and the spread of voodoo in Haiti than he is with my day-to-day life," they argue.

This all-too-common mindset reveals how ignorant most Christians are of the nature and extent of spiritual warfare. Satan touches our routine struggles in life no less than the Mt. Carmel confrontations we read about in Scripture. Clinton Arnold agrees:

> Spiritual warfare is all-encompassing. It touches every area of our lives—our families, our relationships, our church, our neighborhoods, our communities, our places of employment. There is virtually no part of our existence over which the Evil One does not want to maintain or reassert his unhealthy and perverse influence.[7]

The conflict between the kingdom of God and the kingdom of Satan influences how we use our money, what we watch on TV or online, how we raise our kids, which tone of voice we use to speak to our spouses, how we use our time, and how we talk about our bosses when they aren't listening. Indeed, it touches every aspect of our lives.

"Ok, ok," the complacent Christian might argue, "So Satan cares about my day-to-day life. Still, I've never encountered a demon or felt attacked by one. So why rock the boat?"

To this I would respond that our relative lack of awareness of demonic forces does not constitute proof of their nonexistence or lack of activity. It more likely points to the success of our spiritual enemies in lulling us into a dangerous slumber.

---

7   Ibid., 27.

7. Belief That Christians Can't Be Demonized

A principal reason for Christians' passivity and indifference to spiritual warfare is their belief that a Christian cannot be demonized. This conviction has lulled many into inactivity and a false sense of spiritual security. I will address this issue in considerable depth later on, but even if we conclude that a born-again believer cannot be indwelt by a demonic spirit, the demonic spirit's *attack* of the Christian remains a threat to which we must give our undivided attention.

8. The Paralyzing Fear of Fanaticism

As noted earlier, the excesses and extremes of certain deliverance ministries have evoked a disdain that often leads Christians to outright deny the reality of spiritual warfare. Lasting images of angry, sweat-drenched faces shouting at the seemingly helpless victims of demonic possession, together with the oft-related physical gyrations and hysterical reactions of those who are the focus of this so-called "ministry," have done irreparable damage to legitimate attempts to bring freedom to those who are truly oppressed by the enemy.

Related to this is the fear that those who actively engage in spiritual conflict are emotionally unstable and theologically illiterate. I'm not condoning emotional instability or theological ignorance, but what does that have to do with whether spiritual warfare is a genuine threat? The issue is not what kind of people believe and engage in spiritual warfare. The issue is whether it is biblically true. That some are inclined to find a demon behind every bush doesn't mean there aren't any at all. And the fact that these people make an embarrassing spectacle of so-called "deliverance" sessions doesn't mean there aren't victims of spiritual oppression who genuinely need to be delivered and set free.

9. Compartmentalization

Others insist that spiritual warfare pertains largely, if not exclusively, to such things as ritualistic sacrifice, seances, Ouija boards, tarot cards, and serial killers. That is precisely what Satan would love for you to believe. Anything that contributes to the lowering of your spiritual defenses is welcome news to our enemy.

10. Western World View

Perhaps the most significant reason spiritual warfare is not of immediate concern to many Christians relates to their worldview. Spirit beings, whether angels or demons, are not a *functional* part of how they view the world and the way they live.

According to the predominant view of the Western world, every effect has a physical cause. In other words, if you can't see it, touch it, taste it, smell it, or hear it, it probably doesn't exist. All phenomena can or eventually will be explained or accounted for scientifically. Reality is material and mechanical, such that *if* there *is* a spiritual realm, it has no relation to or impact upon the physical realm. Philip Johnson has defined this sort of scientific naturalism as "a story that reduces reality to physical particles and impersonal laws, portrays life as a meaningless competition among organisms that exist only to survive and reproduce, and sees the mind as no more than an emergent property of biochemical reactions."[8]

The biblical worldview, on the other hand, is thoroughly supernatural. God controls physical phenomena and all so-called natural laws. Angels do his bidding (see Ps. 103:20–21). Demons actively and energetically oppose his kingdom. Miracles, physical healing, and gifts of the Holy Spirit are essential elements that constitute *reality*. Clinton Arnold explains:

> The issue is often framed as a choice between accepting a modern scientific worldview or devolving into a gullible, uncritical acceptance of a primitive, prescientific worldview. Of course, this is not an issue of being scientific or not. It is an issue of whether we accept the predominantly naturalistic assumptions of certain understandings of science. It is in no way incompatible with the scientific method to give credence to a belief in a personal God—or, conversely, to believe in the evil spiritual dimension.[9]

Many Christians remain *functional deists*. They don't deny that God exists or that there is a spiritual realm in which angels and demons are active. They simply live as if neither God nor spiritual beings of either sort

---

8   Philip E. Johnson, *Reason in the Balance: The Case Against Naturalism in Science, Law & Education* (Downers Grove, IL: InterVarsity Press, 1995), 197.
9   Arnold, *3 Crucial Questions*, 24.

have any genuine, influential interaction with them. God isn't dead, but he might as well be. Angels and demons might exist, but what does that have to do with my life?

11. Mission-Field Mentality

If there is such a thing as spiritual warfare, some would argue, it happens only on the mission field in the non-Western world. People say that "demons are only operative in areas of the world where the gospel has not yet reached or where idolatry is still prevalent. They infer that Satan is just not as active in the Christian West."[10] Nothing could be further from the truth.

12. The Insidious Power of Pride

There is, finally, the undeniable fact that to acknowledge the existence and activity of Satan and the threat that he and his demons pose for all people often threatens one's reputation and acceptance in the broader academic community. The secular, anti-supernatural mindset is a phenomenon that has infiltrated not only the non-Christian world. Its influence is felt in the church and the Christian academy as well. If angels and demons are discussed at all, they are merely a topic for theoretical speculation. To allow them into the routines of everyday life is to risk laughter and mockery. In simple terms, the affirmation of the biblical worldview relative to angels and demons carries a social stigma that not many are willing to endure. Acceptance with one's peers and the pressing emotional need to be respected and held in high regard often becomes a more powerful incentive than orthodoxy.

I can recall a lengthy conversation I had with one of my distant relatives. He was an incredibly intelligent man whose vocabulary made the rest of us feel like first graders. We were at a family reunion when he heard me mention angels and demons. His face scrunched up with an obvious look of disdain, or perhaps it was embarrassment that someone to whom he was related would believe such obvious nonsense. I later came to believe that it was probably more fear than anything else, that is, the fear of being seen with or related to someone who embraced what could only be considered a relic of anti-intellectual religious fundamentalism. And that would not go over well among the academic and highly educated elites whose respect he coveted.

---

10 Ibid., 25.

"You do believe in the existence of God, don't you?" I asked.

"Of course," he replied.

"And you believe that God is a spiritual being who created the universe, right?"

"Yes."

"And you believe that this God of the Bible created human beings who, because of his grace, will live forever with him in the new heavens and new earth. Correct?"

"Of course," he said without hesitation.

"Well, then, why would you find it so difficult to believe that this spiritual being called God, the one who created all of humanity, might also create a large number of spiritual beings whose purpose would be to serve him and carry out his will? And since you believe that we human beings rebelled against our Creator and fell into sin and wickedness, why would you struggle to believe that many of these other spiritual beings (angels) would do the same thing?"

He had no answer, and the conversation quietly ended.

LACY'S STORY

Before going through inner healing and deliverance at our church, I suffered every day from intensely painful tension headaches, as well as tension in my right shoulder. I was also struggling with panic attacks. It became my normal, and I thought it was just something I was going to live with forever. Then, when I started this prayer ministry, I learned how unforgiveness can affect so much in our lives physically, emotionally, and spiritually.

God showed me I had some deeply rooted unforgiveness towards an individual in my life. God is so gentle. When he asks you to step in obedience into something like forgiveness, he gives you what you need in order to do it. I remember knowing I needed to forgive this individual, but in my human nature I really didn't want to. However, when I did forgive him, released him from my own punishing of him, and actually blessed his life as well, I felt such a joy come over me.

My headaches and tension have not come back since I forgave him. And I no longer suffer from panic attacks. Praise God! I had to release what I was holding onto as unforgiveness (and I thought I had a right to hold onto it) so that God could heal me and take care of that individual as well. I'm so incredibly thankful for God's working through inner healing and deliverance to shine his light on the dark and hidden places in my heart that I didn't even realize needed to be lit up.

CHAPTER 3

Who Is Satan and How Does He Act?

I don't enjoy writing about my enemy.[1] It disturbs me to provide him with even the slightest publicity. But he is our enemy and we need to know as much as possible about his character and tactics. I am reminded of a scene in the World War II movie *Patton*. Patton's intelligence service has intercepted a German radio transmission bearing news of the impending attack by Germany's most decorated military leader, Field Marshal Erwin Rommel. On the morning of the battle, Patton is awakened by his aides. A book lies open on his nightstand. It's title: *The Tank in Attack* by Erwin Rommel. As Allied forces spring their surprise, and quite successful, assault on the enemy, Patton smiles as he peers through binoculars at the carnage of battle. "Rommel," shouts Patton, "you magnificent [expletive deleted]. I read your book!"[2]

How do you win a battle? You read the enemy's book. Familiarity with his tactics and knowledge of his ways are essential in waging a successful war. It's true in military warfare. It's true in spiritual warfare as well. Patton gained an immeasurable advantage by learning in advance of being attacked where, in all likelihood, Rommel would concentrate his strike. He studied Rommel's personality, his strategy in previous battles, his philosophy of tank

---

1   This chapter has been adapted in large measure from my chapter in *Tough Topics: Biblical Answers to 25 Challenging Questions* (Wheaton, IL: Crossway, 2013) entitled "What Can We Know about Satan?" and is used here with permission.

2   Franklin J. Schaffner, dir., *Patton* (Los Angeles, CA: Twentieth Century Fox, 1970).

warfare, all with a view to anticipating and countering every conceivable move. Satan doesn't have a book. But he's in ours.

The Bible clearly and repeatedly says that Satan exists. Let's learn more about who he is and the threat he poses.

Where the Battle Began: A Brief Study of Genesis 3

Genesis 3 contains the first appearance of Satan in Scripture. The conflict we read about here is important not simply because it was the first encounter between Satan and the human race, but because it is *paradigmatic of virtually all subsequent encounters* as well. This is not simply the beginning of spiritual warfare—this is the *essence* of it.

The Serpent's Attack

Evangelicals disagree on the precise nature of the "serpent" in Genesis 3. Some point out that it is twice compared to other members of the animal kingdom (Gen. 2:19–20; 3:1, 14–15). Yet it is also quite clearly the instrument of Satan (see John 8:44; Rom. 16:20; Rev. 12:9; 20:2). Michael Heiser argues that the "serpent" in Genesis 3 is not a "mere animal" but rather "a divine being that is cast as creaturely."[3] He writes:

> Most readers will acknowledge that the serpent (Heb: nāḥāš) was not simply a member of the animal kingdom. This conclusion seems obvious, since the New Testament identifies the serpent as Satan or the devil (Rev 12:9). The devil is certainly not a zoological specimen (2 Cor 11:14; cf. Matt 4:1–11; John 8:44). Put simply, if we agree with the New Testament that a supernatural being (Satan) tempted Eve in Eden, then by definition the serpent must be more than a mere animal. We can only oppose this conclusion if we reject the New Testament assessment. Ancient readers—without the New Testament—would be able to draw the same conclusion, though they didn't necessarily use the same vocabulary. They of course knew that animals did not talk, and so when that sort of thing was encountered in

---

3   Michael S. Heiser, *The Unseen Realm: Recovering the Supernatural Worldview of the Bible* (Bellingham, WA: Lexham, 2015), 82. He goes on to say that the serpent "was an image commonly used in reference to a divine throne guardian" (ibid., 88).

storytelling, they knew supernatural power was at play or a divine presence had taken center stage.[4]

Ultimately, the precise nature of the serpent is not our primary concern, but rather what he did in leading Adam and Eve astray. Several factors give us insight into the nature of his attack. He clearly possesses preternatural knowledge as seen from his statement to Eve: "Did God really say . . ." How does the serpent know about the prohibition concerning the forbidden fruit? He also claims to know more about the fruit than God has revealed. He openly impugns God's character and motives by telling Eve, contrary to what God had said, "You shall *not* surely die." He implies that God is selfish or deceitful, or both.

The fact that the serpent/Satan approaches Eve rather than Adam points to his craftiness. Whereas some have suggested this was because the temptation had a sexual component, the best explanation is "that the serpent demonstrates his cunning by accosting the person who indirectly learned of the prohibition and who was, therefore, more vulnerable. . . . The serpent directs his attack against the one who, at least as far as the biblical narrative is concerned, had not actually heard God give instructions regarding the biblical fruit."[5]

The serpent's cunning is also revealed in his tactics. Rather than launching an overt invitation to sin, he asks what on the surface appears to be an innocent question: "Did God *really* say, 'You must not eat from any tree in the garden?'" (3:1 NIV). He speaks of "God" rather than "Lord God" (the latter being the way God is otherwise described in the context). Does this suggest an unfriendly, perhaps rebellious, attitude on the part of Satan?

The serpent also exaggerates the extent of the prohibition and thereby suggests that God has placed unreasonable and unfair limitations on Adam and Eve. Sydney Page argues that the question Satan asks "casts aspersions on God's character and implies that it is the serpent, not God, who has the couple's best interests in mind. Underlying the question is the assumption

---

4   Michael S. Heiser, *Demons: What the Bible Really Says about the Powers of Darkness* (Bellingham, WA: Lexham Press, 2020), 62.

5   Sydney H. T. Page, *Powers of Evil: A Biblical Study of Satan and Demons* (Grand Rapids: Baker, 1995), 17. I'm greatly dependent on Page for this treatment of Genesis 3, and I highly recommend his book.

that a created being has the right to pass judgment on the Creator."[6] The serpent/Satan disguises his true intent—to convince humans to follow him in forsaking creaturely dependence on the Creator and to form their own opinion about truth without appeal to God's revelation—by putting before Eve what seems to be a blessing: "become like God."

The Curse

The two-fold curse pronounced on the serpent/Satan tells us much about him. The first element in the curse is found in Genesis 3:14: "Because you have done this, cursed are you above all livestock and above all beasts of the field; on your belly you shall go, and dust you shall eat all the days of your life." Page points out that the curse teaches "that the crawling of snakes and the way they flick out their tongues, as if eating, have symbolic value. Having exalted himself so as to sit in judgment of God, the serpent is condemned to crawl on his belly; having led astray those who were created from dust (2:7), he is condemned to live in the dust."[7] Boyd points out that "crawling on one's belly and 'eating dust' (something snakes do not do) were idiomatic ways of referring to defeat and humiliation in ancient Semitic culture (e.g., Mic. 7:17). Such references clearly refer to the loathsome behavior of snakes, but they do so metaphorically."[8]

The second part of the curse is in Genesis 3:15: "I will put enmity between you and the woman, and between your offspring and her offspring; he shall bruise your head, and you shall bruise his heel." The "offspring" of the woman is obviously the human race. If the serpent is indeed Satan, then surely his "offspring" cannot be limited to ordinary snakes but must encompass spiritual beings of a similar nature, i.e., angelic beings who, like Satan, fell from their original place of goodness.

This text raises several questions. First, who is the "he" in the phrase "he will crush your head" (v. 15)? The antecedent of "he" is "offspring," a word that can have either an individual or collective reference. If it refers to an individual, the Messiah may be in view. If it is collective, the people of God are in view. The recipient of the blow ("he will crush *your* head") is clearly an

---

6   Ibid.

7   Ibid., 19–20.

8   Gregory A. Boyd, *God at War: The Bible and Spiritual Conflict* (Downers Grove, IL: InterVarsity Press, 1997), 157. Although I find Boyd's commitment to open theism highly objectionable, his insights on the reality of spiritual warfare are often quite helpful.

individual. The collective sense is supported by Romans 16:20, but the language in Genesis 3 is too ambiguous to be dogmatic. Second, does the curse describe a decisive victory over the serpent or simply a perpetual conflict? Both actions ("crush" and "strike") are described with the same Hebrew verb (best translated "strike"). Still, though, the ultimate victory of the woman's seed is implied for "the simple fact that the struggle is divinely ordained. If God instituted the conflict, we may presume that he will bring it to a resolution."[9] Second, since a blow to the "head" is more likely to be fatal than one to the "heel," victory for the woman's seed is suggested. Either way, the text emphasizes the battle, not its ultimate outcome.

What We Learn about the Enemy

There is nothing in the text to suggest that the serpent/Satan gained any new power or unique authority over the world because of Adam and Eve's sin. In fact, the only thing Satan is portrayed as experiencing as a result of this event is *cursing*! However, one must still explain those texts that speak of Satan as exercising authority over the kingdoms of the earth and this fallen world (see Matt. 4:5–6; John 12:31; 14:30; 16:11).[10] In addition, there is no support here for the so-called "serpent-seed" doctrine, according to which the serpent/Satan had sexual relations with Eve. Support for this idea has been mistakenly derived from Paul's use of the words "pure virgin" in 2 Corinthians 11:2 and his reference to Satan's "deception" (seduction?) of Eve.

Debates aside, this narrative provides us essential insight into some of Satan's tactics. First, it shows that Satan will always claim to know more about God than God himself has revealed. He will claim to have special insight into

---

9   Page, *Powers of Evil*, 22.

10   Heiser believes that Satan's authority is related to God's assignment of a variety of angels ("the sons of God") to rule over "the nations" of the earth (Deut. 32:8–9). This rule was corrupted by the sinful actions of these "gods" (Psalm 82:1–8) and was overcome by the life, death, resurrection, and exaltation of Christ (Matt. 28:18–20). He writes: "In effect, Satan was offering Jesus rule over the nations abandoned by Yahweh at Babel (Deut 32:8). That judgment was never intended to be permanent. When Yahweh raised up his own 'portion' (Deut 32:9) starting with the covenant with Abraham, he told the patriarch that it would be through his offspring that all the nations would ultimately be blessed (Gen 12:3). Jesus was the specific fulfillment of that promise . . . Had Jesus failed in the wilderness temptation, the plan to bring the nations back into the family of Yahweh also would have failed. The nature of this temptation and the implications of its outcome presume . . . that the rebellious gods of the nations were affiliated with the original rebel of Eden and, in some sense, under his authority. When the Gospels have Satan offering the kingdoms of the world to Jesus in exchange for worship, they presume this affiliation and authority" (Heiser, *Demons*, 186).

God's motives for a command or a prohibition that God himself has kept secret. In other words, he will sow seeds of doubt in your mind concerning God's goodness; he will lead you to believe that God has ulterior motives in what he has designed that will deprive you of blessings you might otherwise experience. "God is not telling you the *whole* truth. He can't afford to," Satan will argue.

Second, this passage shows us that rarely, if ever, will Satan confront you as Satan. He will almost always approach you indirectly, disguised as someone or something more likely to win your trust (such as when Peter opposed Jesus's going to Jerusalem in Matthew 16). He will come to you through something you hear or see, perhaps a movie; a lecture by a brilliant, articulate, but pagan professor; through a well-meaning friend; or as an angel of light. After all, if you knew it was Satan, you'd be less inclined to listen or say yes.

With this brief introduction to the character and ways of Satan, we are now prepared to delve more deeply into who this being is and his efforts to thwart the purposes of God and the Church.

Satan's Fall and Activity

The first thing to remember about Satan is that he, like all other angels, was created at a point in time (Col. 1:16; John 1:1–3). Satan is not eternal. He is a finite creature. He is, therefore, *God's* devil. Satan is *not* the equal and opposite power of God (contra *dualism*). His power is not infinite. He does not possess divine attributes. In sum, he is no match for God! At most, Satan is the equal and opposite power of the archangel Michael.

If he was originally created as an angel, how did Satan come to fall? Two Old Testament passages have been interpreted as descriptions of Satan's original demise: *Isaiah 14:12–20* and *Ezekiel 28:11–19*. As Sydney Page points out, both passages are "part of a funeral dirge lamenting the death of a pagan king. In both, the king is portrayed as having come to ruin because he exalted himself beyond what was appropriate. Although the form of the two texts is that of a funeral dirge, the sorrow at the passing of the monarch is not genuine. Both passages virtually drip with sarcasm. In reality, the tyrant's death is welcomed."[11] The question is, do these laments allude to Satan and his pre-temporal rebellion? In the following sections, we'll examine these passages in greater depth.

---

11 Page, *Powers of Evil*, 37.

Isaiah 14:12–15

Isaiah 14:12–15 appears in a passage that is specifically identified as a taunt of judgment against the king of Babylon (vv. 3–4). It reads:

> How you are fallen from heaven,
>> O Day Star, son of Dawn!
>
> How you are cut down to the ground,
>> you who laid the nations low!
>
> You said in your heart,
>> "I will ascend to heaven;
>
> above the stars of God
>> I will set my throne on high;
>
> I will sit on the mount of assembly
>> in the far reaches of the north;
>
> I will ascend above the heights of the clouds;
>> I will make myself like the Most High."
>
> But you are brought down to Sheol,
>> to the far reaches of the pit.
>
> Those who see you will stare at you
>> and ponder over you:
>
> "Is this the man who made the earth tremble,
>> who shook kingdoms,
>
> who made the world like a desert
>> and overthrew its cities,
>> who did not let his prisoners go home?"
>
> All the kings of the nations lie in glory,
>> each in his own tomb;
>
> but you are cast out, away from your grave,
>> like a loathed branch,
>
> clothed with the slain, those pierced by the sword,
>> who go down to the stones of the pit,
>> like a dead body trampled underfoot.
>
> You will not be joined with them in burial,
>> because you have destroyed your land,
>> you have slain your people.

> May the offspring of evildoers
>> nevermore be named! (Isaiah 14:12–20)

The taunt may be directed at one particular Babylonian king (most likely Sennacherib) or perhaps "at the whole Babylonian monarchy personified as a single individual."[12] Clearly, though, the mocking lament portrays and celebrates the demise of an *earthly* and *human* power that both opposes and oppresses the people of God.

The language used in verses 12–14 is certainly compatible with what we know of Satan's character, but may well be a use of poetic language to describe an earthly king. Many of the terms used here ("Day Star," "Dawn") have been found in texts dealing with ancient pagan mythology. Page notes that "the mythology was probably rooted in the observation of the brilliant rise of the planet Venus (the 'morning star') in the early morning sky and its rapid fading with the rise of the sun."[13] If this is true, Isaiah would be utilizing (without endorsing) motifs common in pagan mythology to describe the downfall of an earthly ruler.

Others have argued that whereas all this may be true, we can still see in this description of an earthly opponent of God (the Babylonian king) his model and heavenly inspiration (Satan). But is that what Isaiah had in mind when he wrote it? "Lucifer" (literally, "shining one" or "Day Star" in v. 12) is called a "man" in verse 16 and is compared with other earthly kings in verse 18. "Lucifer" was first used in the Latin vulgate to translate the Hebrew word (*helel*) and eventually made its way into the King James Version. According to Boyd, "Isaiah is simply comparing the king of Babylon to the planet Venus, the morning star. It rises bright at dawn and climbs to the highest point in the sky, only to be quickly extinguished by the brightness of the rising sun. Thus, Isaiah says, shall be the career of the presently shining king of Babylon. He appears on the stage of world history as the brightest star, ascending higher and higher. But in the end he shall quickly disappear in the light of the sun."[14]

---

12 Ibid., 38.

13 Ibid., 39.

14 Boyd, *God at War*, 158.

Ezekiel 28:11–19

The second passage we'll examine is Ezekiel 28:11–19. It reads:

> Moreover, the word of the LORD came to me: "Son of man, raise a lamentation over the king of Tyre, and say to him, Thus says the Lord GOD:

"You were the signet of perfection,
    full of wisdom and perfect in beauty.
You were in Eden, the garden of God;
    every precious stone was your covering,
sardius, topaz, and diamond,
    beryl, onyx, and jasper,
sapphire, emerald, and carbuncle;
    and crafted in gold were your settings
    and your engravings.
On the day that you were created
    they were prepared.
You were an anointed guardian cherub.
    I placed you; you were on the holy mountain of God;
    in the midst of the stones of fire you walked.
You were blameless in your ways
    from the day you were created,
    till unrighteousness was found in you.
In the abundance of your trade
    you were filled with violence in your midst, and you sinned;
so I cast you as a profane thing from the mountain of God,
    and I destroyed you, O guardian cherub,
    from the midst of the stones of fire.
Your heart was proud because of your beauty;
    you corrupted your wisdom for the sake of your splendor.
I cast you to the ground;
    I exposed you before kings,
    to feast their eyes on you.
By the multitude of your iniquities,
    in the unrighteousness of your trade
    you profaned your sanctuaries;

so I brought fire out from your midst;
     it consumed you,
and I turned you to ashes on the earth
     in the sight of all who saw you.
All who know you among the peoples
     are appalled at you;
you have come to a dreadful end
     and shall be no more forever."

Again, verses 1–11 refer to the "prince" or "ruler" of Tyre (a Phoenician port city located 125 miles northwest of Jerusalem). Verses 2, 9–10 clearly indicate that he is human, not angelic. The historical setting is the siege of Tyre by Nebuchadnezzar from 587–574 BC. The king of Tyre during this period was Ithobaal II.

Verses 12–19 refer to the "king" of Tyre, suggesting to some that verses 12–19 refer to a supernatural power behind the human ruler of verses 1–11.[15] However, this word ("king") is used elsewhere in Ezekiel of *earthly* rulers (17:12; 19:9; 21:19; 24:2; 26:7; 29:2–3, 18; 30:10, 21; 31:2; 32:2, 11), leading most to believe that the "prince" of verses 1–11 and the "king" of verses 12–19 are one and the same ("prince" and "king" being synonymous). On the other hand, the "king" of verses 12–19 seems to be portrayed in terms that go beyond what is true of any earthly king ("perfection," "in Eden," "created," "cherub," "holy mountain of God," "blameless").

The identification of this king as an "anointed cherub who covers (guards)" in verse 14 is considered the strongest evidence that the reference is to Satan. Others have pointed out, however, that the Hebrew text may just

---

15 For example, Daniel Kolenda argues that "as Ezekiel unfolds his prophecy, he clearly switches into another mode and begins to speak of a supernatural being" (*Slaying Dragons: A Practical Guide to Spiritual Warfare* [Lake Mary, FL: Charisma House, 2019], 14). A similar view is taken by Mark Hitchcock in *101 Answers to Questions about Satan, Demons & Spiritual Warfare* (Eugene: Harvest House, 2014), 26–34. In like fashion, Heiser contends that "Ezekiel 28 shifted from the prince of Tyre to a divine figure in Eden. That shift informed us that the writer was using a story of cosmic, divine rebellion to, by comparison, portray the arrogance of the earthly prince. After verse 11 [Isaiah 14:11], Isaiah 14 shifts to a divine context with clear links to Ezekiel 28" (*Unseen Realm*, 84). In other words, "The figure to whom the king of Babylon is being compared [in Isaiah 14] is a divine being fallen 'from heaven' (v. 12)" (ibid., 85). Again, Heiser believes "that, while each prophetic taunt/lament is directed at a human king, both passages draw on a primeval tale of a *divine* rebellion to portray the respective kings the way they do" (*Demons*, 67).

as easily be translated, "*with* a cherub." Even if the king is explicitly called a "cherub," it is more likely a reference "to the splendor of the king" and is here used metaphorically and not ontologically.[16] Also, it is difficult to understand how dishonest or unrighteous trade and the desecration of sanctuaries (v. 18) could have been involved in the fall of Satan.

How, then, are we to understand the reference to the garden of "Eden" in verse 13? One view is that the king of Tyre is being compared to Adam. "Perhaps the king believed himself to be the re-embodiment of the first man, and Ezekiel is using arrogant claims made by the king himself to set his defeat in sharper relief. . . . In effect, Ezekiel would be holding the king's pretensions up to ridicule by charging that, whatever claims he might make about his relationship with the primeval period, there is at least one similarity—like Adam, he stands under divine judgment for rebelling against his Creator."[17]

Others, such as Lamar Cooper, contend that the description of the king of Tyre in Ezekiel simply cannot be exhausted by reference to this one earthly figure. He writes:

> Overlaid in these prophetic messages [in 28:1–19] are many elements that extend beyond the characteristics of the city or the king. . . . Ezekiel presented the king of Tyre as an evil tyrant who was animated and motivated by a more sinister, unseen tyrant, Satan. . . . The sinister character of the mastermind behind God's enemies is not always recognized. The real motivating force behind the king of Tyre was the adversary, the satan, who opposed God and his people from the beginning (28:6–19).[18]

---

16 Gilhooly, *40 Questions*, 111.

17 Page, *Powers of Evil*, 42.

18 Lamar Eugene Cooper Sr., *Ezekiel*, New American Commentary (Nashville: Broadman & Holman, 1994), 268–69. Another who sees a double reference in both passages, that is, a description of both a human leader and a supernatural inspiration standing behind him, is C. Fred Dickason (*Angels: Elect and Evil* [Chicago: Moody, 1995], 135–45). Graham Cole is more cautious, but contends that "the extravagance [in which the human leader is described] is so suggestive that these descriptors are not exhausted by reference to the king of Babylon (Isaiah 14) or the king of Tyre (Ezekiel 28)" (*Against the Darkness: The Doctrine of Angels, Satan, and Demons* [Wheaton, IL: Crossway, 2019], 92). Cole then concludes that "the presence of such exaggerated language in Isaiah 14 and Ezekiel 28, the NT identification of pride as the devil's sin, with the support of the majority of early church fathers, combine to strengthen the contention that Isaiah 14 and Ezekiel 28 contain a double reference: earthly rulers and the devilish usurper" (93).

Satan or an Earthly King?

I suppose we will have to settle for a measure of uncertainty as to whether either of these texts actually describes Satan's fall. But this raises another question: *When* did Satan fall? The Bible gives no clear answer to this question. Some have argued that it could not have been prior to the sixth day of Genesis 1, since everything in God's creation until that time is said to have been "very good" (Gen. 1:31). However, this declaration may pertain only to the material creation in view. Perhaps Satan's rebellion predates Genesis 1:1. Others insist that it occurred only just before he approached Eve in the garden. We simply don't know.

Satan's Names

We learn much about the character of our enemy from the names by which he is designated in Scripture. In the following paragraphs, we'll explore in greater depth some of the most common titles.

Satan

The title *Satan* is used fifty-two times in the Bible. The Hebrew word literally means "the adversary," the one who opposes (see Zech. 3:1–2). This is the word's meaning in Numbers 22:22, 32; 1 Samuel 29:4; 2 Samuel 19:22; and 1 Kings 5:4; 11:14, 23, 25. In Psalm 109:6 it has the sense of "accuser" or "prosecuting attorney."

The use of "Satan" in the book of Job is especially instructive. Here, the phrase "sons of God" (1:6) refers to the angelic host (cf. Job 38:7), which constitute the heavenly council—God's courtiers surrounding the throne, ready to obey his every command (see also 1 Kings 22:19 and Dan. 7:9–14). With them was "*the Satan.*" Everywhere that the Hebrew word behind this translation appears in Job, it has the definite article ("the").[19] Hence, it is a title, descriptive of his function and character.

Satan was at a loss concerning Job's loyal obedience to God.[20] Job was

---

19 See Job 1:6–9, 12; 2:1–4, 6–7.

20 An increasing number of scholars do not believe that the devil is the same as "the Satan" in Job. Tremper Longman III refers to the idea that they are identical as a "marginalized view" while, at the same time, understanding "the Satan" to be an angelic "emissary" sent "to carry out his [God's] will" (*Confronting Old Testament Controversies: Pressing Questions about Evolution, Sexuality, History, and Violence* [Grand Rapids: Baker, 2019],

a puzzle to him. He didn't doubt that Job was obedient and upright. There was no mistaking his godliness. But the devil just couldn't bring himself to believe that anyone would want to be holy for nothing. The only thing left is to launch an assault against Job's motives. Whereas he could hardly question Job's righteousness, he did wonder about the reason for it. His diabolical conclusion was that Job served God for what he could get out of him. Job's piety, reasoned the devil, must be a calculated effort to milk God of his gifts. *Take away the pay and he'll quit the job*, he thought. Satan was persuaded that worship must be fundamentally selfish, that it is nothing more than a man-made device to flatter God into generosity. If God's generosity were cut off, thought Satan, Job's praise would turn to cursing.

In sum, Satan accuses God of having bought Job's loyalty with health and wealth: "Job doesn't serve you for free. Don't flatter yourself, God! No one else does either." In effect, he says: "He doesn't love you for *who* you are but only for *what* you've given him." In other words, it isn't Job that Satan accuses, but God! The question that Job will face, the question we all face is this: "Is God worthy to be loved and deserving of our obedience for who he is, irrespective of all other considerations?" Is Job sufficiently dedicated to remaining loyal if no benefits are attached? Satan says no. He accuses God of being a deceptive fraud and Job of being a selfish hypocrite.

Note also how abrupt and rude Satan is in the book of Job. Under traditional court etiquette in the ancient Near East, an inferior avoided using personal pronouns when addressing a superior. Courtiers would say, "my lord" instead of "you," and "your slave" instead of "I/me." But not Satan. On top of using personal pronouns, he also uses an imperative verb, as if to command God what to do ("stretch out your hand and touch all that he has," Job 1:11).

We should also note in verse 12 that Satan has no power or authority beyond that which God grants or permits. It is God who sets the boundaries for what Satan can do. Thus, *when given permission by God*, Satan is able to

---

166). See also David J. A. Clines, *Job 1–20*, Word Biblical Commentary (Dallas: Word, 1989), 19–22; and Heiser, *Demons*, 76–78. However, I concur with Michael Brown (*Job: The Faith to Challenge God: A New Translation and Commentary* [Peabody: Hendrickson Academic, 2019]), who concludes that "while it is overly simplistic to say that the Adversary of Job 1–2 is the devil of the New Testament, it is not inaccurate to say that they are the one and same being, with the devil of the New Testament being the full manifestation of the Adversary of the Old Testament" (341). See his complete defense of this view in "Who Was the Adversary?" *Job*, 337–42.

exercise tremendous destructive influence on nature, nations, and individuals. This would also indicate that there is an ongoing restraint by God put on Satan and what he can do.

The Devil

Our enemy is also called the "devil," a word that is used thirty-five times in Scripture and that literally means "slanderer" or "accuser" (*diabolos*; see Luke 4:2, 13; Rev. 12:9, 12). In other words, it is the devil's aim to defame. He is a constant source of false and malicious reports. He lies to God about us (Rev. 12:10; but cf. Rom. 8:33–39; 1 John 2:2), to us about God (Gen. 3; Matt. 4), and to you about yourself (Eph. 6:16). Particularly, he seeks to undermine and subvert your knowledge of who you are in Christ.

Prince of Power of the Air

One particularly instructive title for Satan is the *ruler or prince of the power* (literally, "authority") *of the air* in Ephesians 2:2. The word translated "power" or "authority" denotes the realm or sphere or empire of the devil's influence (such as demonic hosts; see Col. 1:13). The word "air" could refer to the literal atmosphere around us (hence the abode of demonic spirits), or it could be synonymous with "darkness" (cf. Luke 22:53; Eph. 6:12; Col. 1:13), or it could be a reference to the nature of the demonic hosts: they are unearthly, spiritual, and not human. Some insist that it could involve to some degree all these ideas and be "another way of indicating the 'heavenly realm,' which, according to Ephesians 6:12, is the abode of those principalities and powers, the 'world-rulers of this darkness' and 'spiritual forces of wickedness,' against which the people of Christ wage war."[21] The word does not have the modern sense of "moral atmosphere" or "world of opinion and ideas."

The next phrase has been rendered in several different ways. It could be: "the prince of the power of the air (which is) the spirit that is now working…" The "air" would thus be the spiritual atmosphere controlling unbelievers. Or it could be: "the prince of the power of the air, (the prince being) the spirit which is now working…" Others suggest that we render it, "the prince of the power of the air, [the prince of] the spirit which is now working…" That is to say, Satan is the ruling lord or prince over the evil principle (such as spirit,

---

21 Peter T. O'Brien, *The Letter to the Ephesians* (Grand Rapids: Eerdmans, 1999), 160.

mood, temper, disposition) that operates in the lost (cf. 1 Cor. 2:12 and "spirit of the world").

What is most important, however, is that Paul says Satan is "working" (*energeō*) in the "sons of disobedience" (cf. Mark 3:17; Luke 10:6; 16:8; 20:34; Acts 4:36; Eph. 5:8; 1 Pet. 1:14), a word used earlier of God's activity in the world (Eph. 1:11) in general and in the resurrection of Jesus in particular (1:20). Here it refers to Satan's supernatural activity by which he exerts a negative influence over the lives of unbelievers. This does *not* mean that all unbelievers are demon possessed. It does mean that "the whole world lies *in the power of* the evil one" (1 John 5:19).

Paul clearly says that Satan is working "*now*" in unbelievers. In other words, although the readers of this epistle and other Christians were in bondage to Satan in the *past*, this does not mean Satan's power ceased to exist. It is yet at work in the present in and among all who remain in unbelief.

The Greek preposition translated "according to" (*kata*) must mean something more than simply that the lost live "in conformity with" or "after the manner of" the devil, as if Paul were saying unbelievers live like the devil lives. The idea is that in some way they have come under the controlling influence of Satan. Paul speaks in Romans 8:4 about believers walking "according to" (*kata*) the Spirit (cf. 2 Cor. 10:2) rather than "according to the flesh," again with the idea of controlling influence.

Other Names for Satan

Satan is also called *the god of this age* (2 Cor. 4:4; but see Ps. 24:1; 89:11) and *the evil one* (Matt. 6:13; 13:38; John 17:15; 1 John 2:14; 5:18). There are several reasons to conclude that the final petition in the Lord's Prayer is a reference to Satan. The use of the adjective "evil" (*poneros*) with the definite article "the" in Matthew 13:19, 38; John 17:15; Ephesians 6:16; 2 Thessalonians 3:3; 1 John 2:13–14; 3:12; and 5:18 clearly refers to Satan. This petition is probably an allusion to Jesus's own encounter with Satan in the wilderness. Jesus's point is that we can expect to encounter the tempter in much the same way he did. Finally, the word translated "from" is *apo*, used predominantly with persons, not things.

Satan, also named Beelzebul and Belial, is the *prince or ruler of demons* (Matt. 10:25; 12:26–27; Luke 11:15; 2 Cor. 6:15). The name or title "Beelzebul" has been taken to mean "lord of dung" (god of filth), "enemy," "lord of the dwelling" (the dwelling of demons), and "lord of the flies," a title given to one of the pagan gods of the Philistines, brought over into Judaism as a name for Satan.

He is *the destroyer* (Rev. 9:11), where the Hebrew word "Abaddon" could mean ruin or destruction, and the Greek term "Apollyon" exterminator or destroyer. Finally, Satan is *the tempter* (Matt. 4:3; 1 Thess. 3:5), *the accuser* (Rev. 12:10), and *the deceiver* (Rev. 12:9; 20:3). He is a liar and a murderer (John 8:44; either an allusion to the murder of Abel by Cain or to the fall in Genesis 3; cf. 1 John 3:11–12), and a master of misrepresentation (2 Thess. 2:9; 2 Cor. 11:14–15).

Other names or descriptive titles for Satan include *Lucifer* (see above), the *old serpent* (Rev. 12:9, 15, an obvious allusion to Genesis 3; cf. 2 Cor. 11:3; Rom. 16:20), and the *great dragon* (Rev. 12:3, 7, 9, 17). He is a terrifying, destructive beast. He is also the *ruler or prince of this world* (John 12:31; 14:30; 16:11). Scripture does not make clear how it is that Satan came to exercise such authority over the world, although it is likely that he became such as people, through their sin, granted him power.

There is no denying the fact that Satan is quite powerful, but he is not omnipotent (see Matt. 4:5, 8). Similarly, he is extremely intelligent, but not omniscient (an attribute predicated of God alone in Scripture). Finally, he is active (Job 1:7; 1 Pet. 5:8), but not omnipresent. Although he can exert a global influence through the activity of his many demons, Satan himself cannot be in more than one place at a time. Simply put, if he is present in Rome, he cannot simultaneously be present in New York.

Satan's Activities

Satan has a plan. Although sinful, he is not stupid. He does not act haphazardly or without a goal in view. Paul states clearly in 2 Corinthians 2:10–11 that Satan has "designs"—a strategy, an agenda—to undermine unity in the church in that city (and no doubt in every city, yours included!). This is similar to what the apostle says in Ephesians 6:11 concerning the "schemes" (literally, *methodia* = method) of the devil. In other words, he is cunning and wily and employs carefully orchestrated stratagems (cf. Eph. 4:14) in his assault against Christian men and women and the local church. Satan energizes and gives shape to worldly value systems, institutions, organizations, philosophical movements, political, social, and economic systems. Satan sets his goals and then utilizes and exploits the most effective means, while avoiding all obstacles, to reach his diabolical ends. I've identified numerous examples of what Satan seeks to do, so let's look briefly at each.

(1) He works in active opposition to the gospel.

Paul says that he blinds the minds of the unbelieving lest they should see the glory of the gospel and be saved (2 Cor. 4:4). There are two factors in spiritual blindness: fleshly, sinful resistance to the truth on the one hand, and satanic/demonic hardening or blinding on the other. Before we ever arrive on the scene with the gospel, Satan is exerting a stupefying influence on the mind of the unbeliever. In other words, we face more than merely intellectual obstacles. We face supernatural opposition. How does Satan do it?

Sometimes he distracts them when an opportunity to hear the gospel is at hand through untimely interruptions, useless daydreaming, an intrusive telephone call, an emergency of some sort, the sudden remembrance of a job or other responsibility that needs immediate attention, or perhaps the appearance of a friend (Acts 13:7b–8). He often stirs up hostility and suspicion in the person's mind concerning the competency and integrity of the individual presenting the gospel. The unbeliever suddenly imputes sinister motives to the Christian: "He's in it for the money," or "She only wants to gain control over me," or "He's just looking for another notch on his Bible so he can boast to others of one more convert," etc. Sometimes the unbeliever will excuse the unbelief by questioning the educational and academic credentials of the believer ("He is so uneducated." "What does she know anyway?").

He stirs up the non-Christian to distort what is being said into something the speaker never intended (Jesus and the Pharisees in John 2:19–21; 6:48–52; 7:33–36; 8:51–53). He stirs up their minds to draw false conclusions or implications from the gospel that make it seem absurd (e.g., doctrine of Trinity = three gods; the doctrine of grace = you can believe and live like hell). He inclines their minds to link the Christian with people who've disgraced Christianity in the past, giving him an excuse to reject what is being said (guilt by association). "All you Christians are just like those hucksters on TV! You're in it for the gold and the glory!" He puts in their minds all sorts of questions and convinces them that if they can't get completely satisfying answers, Christianity can't be true. Right in the middle of witnessing to someone, she suddenly blurts out questions like "What about evil?" "What about all the hypocrites in the church?" "What about the heathen in Africa?" "Why is there only one way? It seems egotistical." "Why are there so many denominations?"

Just as the gospel is beginning to make sense, Satan stirs up pride or produces feelings of independence and self-sufficiency: "I don't need a religious crutch. I'm my own person!" Before serious consideration is given to the message they've heard, Satan snatches the seed of the gospel (Matt. 13:4, 18–19) from their mind. How does he do it? Perhaps on the way home from church the car breaks down, or the conversation turns to politics or sports, or a sexy billboard diverts attention, or something on the radio captivates his mind. Satan might suddenly prompt him to place a higher value on things he might lose if he were to become a Christian: friends, fame, money, fleshly pleasures, approval of others (cf. John 9). Satan stirs up feelings of hopelessness: "Not even this will work. There's no hope. My life is a lost cause. Not even Jesus can help."

Consider what Paul says in 1 Thessalonians 2:18—"we wanted to come to you—I, Paul, again and again—but Satan hindered us." Paul doesn't say by what means Satan opposes and undermines missionary endeavors, but we may assume he disrupts travel plans, works on the minds of state officials to delay or deny the issuing of visas, inflicts illness, provokes military conflict, etc. When given permission to do so, Satan can adversely influence the weather (see Job 1:18–19). Perhaps, then, Paul was prevented from visiting Thessalonica due to threatening conditions such as heavy rain or flooding or excessive heat. Neither does he tell us how he was able to discern whether it was God or Satan who was responsible for a change in plans (cf. Acts 16:6–7). Perhaps we shouldn't try, but instead simply acknowledge that God can even use Satan's schemes to accomplish his purposes.

But we shouldn't leave this passage without noting Paul's response to Satan's interference in his itinerary. Only a few verses later Paul tells the Thessalonians that he is praying "earnestly night and day" for the opportunity to "see" them "face to face" and "supply what is lacking in [their] faith" (1 Thess. 3:10). We are never helpless when Satan attacks, but like Paul, we must turn to prayer and ask for God's sovereign intervention.

(2) He is often, but not always, the source of sickness (Acts 10:38; Matt. 8:16; Mark 9:17–18; Luke 13:10–17).

We must never embrace the view that every physical affliction is directly the result of the influence of Satan or a demon. Still, Peter's words in Acts 10:38

are highly instructive. There he describes the ministry of Jesus and in particular, how "he went about doing good and healing all who were oppressed by the devil." On one day Jesus entered a synagogue and encountered "a woman who had had a disabling spirit for eighteen years. She was bent over and could not fully straighten herself" (Luke 13:11). His response to the ruler of the synagogue who objected to his healing someone on a Sabbath day was straight to the point: "And ought not this woman, a daughter of Abraham whom Satan bound for eighteen years, be loosed from this bond on the Sabbath day?" (Luke 13:16).

DEMONIC ATTACK

In our second year in Kansas City, our nine-year-old daughter Joanna invited a friend over to spend the night. There was no indication that anything dangerous was at hand, nothing to alert us to an impending spiritual encounter.

That night Ann, my wife, had a frightening dream. She saw a hideous demonic spirit kick in the front door of our house and begin to make its way down the hall toward the bedrooms. This "spirit" had long flowing and disheveled hair and flailed its arms wildly, as if preparing to harm someone.

Instead of entering our bedroom, it made its way into Joanna's room, where she and her friend were sound asleep. Ann knew instinctively in the dream that a spiritual attack of some sort was being launched against the girls. The spirit proceeded to bite both girls somewhere near their midsection, and then disappeared. Ann woke up, trembling, and immediately began to pray for protection over the girls as well as our entire family.

The next morning, she went in to awaken the girls, both of whom were not feeling well. Joanna's friend complained of a pain on her rib cage. Ann lifted her shirt and discovered a large, swelling bite mark, much like one would receive from a black widow spider or brown recluse. Joanna also complained of not feeling well. When Ann lifted up her shirt, she discovered on her shoulder and rib cage what we would later be told was a case of shingles. The doctor who examined her was more than a little surprised because shingles was not common in nine-year-old girls.

Perhaps some will say that we were not justified in drawing a direct cause-and-effect relationship between Ann's dream of the demonic spirit and the girls' physical condition. But as we prayed and processed the meaning of it all, it became increasingly clear that the dream was a call for us to intercede in prayer for the young girls of our church. There were circumstances in our local fellowship that alerted us to the fact that a number of young girls were under spiritual attack from the enemy. Needless to say, we prayed fervently and are confident that this was God's way of averting further problems.

(3) He can inflict death as well as provoke the paralyzing fear of it (Heb. 2:14; See Job 1:13–19; John 10:10).

His sinister and cruel destruction of Job's family should not put us in perpetual fear, as it is only by God's sovereign permission that Satan can exert this sort of mortal blow. Jesus reminds the Christians in Smyrna that "the devil is about to throw some of you into prison," and as a result, some of them will die (Rev. 2:10).

(4) He plants sinful plans and purposes in the minds of men (Acts 5:3; John 13:2; Matt. 16:21–23).

It is instructive to observe that in the case of Acts 5, "it is not through some act of terrible depravity, but through an act of religious devotion, that Satan brings about the downfall of Ananias and Sapphira.... It is sobering to think that the very good that God's people attempt to do can be their undoing."[22]

(5) On occasion, Satan will himself indwell a person.

Satan "entered into" Judas, according to John 13:27, language that is reminiscent of demonization (Luke 8:30, 32–33). It is important to note, however, that Judas's motive was also greed, and nowhere is he exonerated from his action simply because he was indwelt by the devil.

---

22 Page, *Powers of Evil*, 132.

(6) He sets a snare or trap for people (perhaps with a view to exploiting and intensifying their sinful inclinations).

In 1 Timothy 3:6–7 Paul speaks of the danger of falling "into the condemnation of the devil," and in 2 Timothy 2:25–26 he speaks of people experiencing "the snare of the devil," having been "captured by him to do his will." Thus Satan is able to exploit any blemish on the reputation of a Christian leader. In the latter text Paul speaks of individuals who have been led astray through false teaching. Satan thus strives to hold people captive to do his will by deceiving them to believe what is false and misleading. If nothing else, this text emphasizes how crucial sound doctrine is. More on this important point later.

(7) He tests or tries Christians.

Consider Satan's "sifting" of Peter in Luke 22. Clearly, Satan is unable to act outside the parameters established by the will of God. He must first ask permission from God. Satan's intent in "sifting" Peter was obviously malicious.[23] He wanted to destroy Peter by inciting him to deny Jesus. But God's intent in permitting Satan to do it was altogether different. God's purposes with Peter were to instruct him, humble him, perhaps discipline him, and certainly to use him as an example to others of both human arrogance and the possibility of forgiveness and restoration. The point is simply that often we cannot easily say "Satan did it" or "God did it." In cases such as this, both are true (with the understanding that God's will is sovereign, supreme, and overriding), but their respective goals are clearly opposite. Page's comments concerning this incident are important:

> Luke 22:31–32 reveals that Satan can subject the loyalty of the followers of Jesus to severe tests that are designed to produce failure. So intense are the pressures to which Satan is able to subject believers that the faith of even the most courageous may be found wanting. Satan is, however, limited in what he can do by what God permits and by the intercession of Jesus on behalf of his own [cf. Rom. 8:34; Heb. 7:25; 1 John 2:1]. Furthermore, those who temporarily falter can be restored and, like Peter, can even resume

---

23 It should be noted that Satan evidently obtained permission to test all of the disciples. Observe Jesus's use of the plural "you" (meaning all the disciples) in Luke 22:31.

positions of leadership. It is implied that Satan cannot gain ultimate victory over those for whom Jesus intercedes.[24]

(8) He attacks married believers in their sexual relationship (1 Cor. 7:5).

Paul approves of the decision by married couples to refrain from sexual relations to devote themselves to prayer, but only for a season. To abstain entirely for a prolonged period of time exposes oneself to unnecessary temptation (i.e., lust and the satisfaction of one's sexual desires outside the bonds of marriage). Again, we see here an example of how the enemy takes an otherwise godly intention and exploits it for his own nefarious purposes.

(9) He exploits our sinful decisions, most likely by intensifying the course of action we have already chosen (Eph. 4:26–27).

Note that Satan is not credited with nor blamed for creating the anger in the first place. We are responsible for it. Satan's response is to use this and other such sins to gain access to our lives and to expand and intensify our chosen course of behavior.

There are numerous additional activities of our enemy that I mention below without further commentary. For example, Satan incites persecution, imprisonment, and the political oppression of believers (1 Pet. 5:8–9; Rev. 2:10). He is the accuser of the Christian (Rev. 12:10; see also Zech. 3:1–2), performs signs and wonders to deceive the nations (2 Thess. 2:9–11), and seeks to silence the witness of the church (Rev. 12:10–12). If one of the primary ways Satan is defeated is by our witness, he will go to any lengths necessary to mute our testimony.

In 2 Corinthians 2:10–11 we find another instance in which Satan seeks to exploit the otherwise good intentions of the church. Certain people in Corinth, ostensibly to maintain the purity of the church, were reluctant to forgive and restore the wayward, but now repentant, brother. This harshness would give Satan an opportunity to crush the spirit of the repentant sinner and drive him to despair, most likely resulting in his being forever cut off from the church.

Satan also promotes false doctrine (2 Cor. 11:1–3; 1 Tim. 4:1–3; Rev. 2:24), manipulates the weather (when given permission to do so by God; Job

---

24 Page, *Powers of Evil*, 124.

1:18-19; and perhaps Mark 4:37–39), and influences the thoughts and actions of unbelievers (Eph. 2:1–2). And, as we have come to expect, he confronts us with various temptations (2 Sam. 24:1; 1 Chron. 21:1; 1 Thess. 3:5; more on Satan's tactics of temptation later in the book).

An Enemy Destined for Defeat

I refuse to conclude this chapter by leaving in your mind the ways in which Satan appears to succeed in his opposition to the gospel and the Christian. So, let's simply remember that "the reason the Son of God appeared was to destroy the works of the devil" (1 John 3:8). There is nothing Satan does that Jesus cannot reverse and overcome. He is God's devil, and he is a defeated enemy. So simply remember this: "Submit yourselves . . . to God. Resist the devil, and he will flee from you" (Jas. 4:7).

KATHERINE'S STORY

My journey through inner healing and deliverance began a few weeks before a women's retreat at our church called "Drawn Away." The Lord revealed to me that I was suffering under the destructive influence of several word curses. This, together with unbiblical generational patterns in my family, opened the door into my life for several evil spirits. Following a time of intercessory prayer on a Sunday morning, I was introduced to a lady whom the Lord used to open the way to much-needed healing and deliverance for me. Within a few weeks, I was meeting once a week with three godly women in a safe, secure environment. I wasn't sure what to expect or what I would experience, but I felt the wave of the Lord taking hold of me, and so I rode the wave.

I grew up in Edmond, Oklahoma, and my story begins at age five, when my parents divorced. At the age of six, I was raped and molested by a family member, which led to various emotional, mental, and family relationship struggles. I remember feeling anxious, numb, helpless, withdrawn, and depressed from the time I was about seven years old. I was also subjected to spending time with the perpetrator, as he was a part of the family.

As I grew older, there was a lack of parenting and direction in my life. I started smoking, using drugs and alcohol, and turned to sexual relationships to fill the void in my heart. Three times over the course of ten years I tried to kill myself. At times I ate or exercised or used drugs compulsively. I subjected myself to extreme perfectionism but could never live up to my standards. My entire life became one massive effort at self-preservation. I can only describe it as "internal chaos," much like looking at a bowl of spaghetti. Hoarding, secretiveness, manipulation, anger, jealousy, striving, disorder—these are only a few of the useless tools I have been using to cope. I'm now thirty-nine years old.

Under the direction of these ladies, I walked through forgiveness, ungodly beliefs, inner vows, generational patterns and word curses, and deliverance. I was surprised at where the Lord took me on some occasions. For example, he showed me that the music I listened to as a teenager had affected my life and professional career in very damaging ways (because of demonic influences). He also led me to remember that I had had a stepsister whom I loved when my mom remarried. We subsequently fled our home due to violence from that stepfather, and I never saw my sister again. The Lord helped me to understand that this experience was deeply traumatic. He also helped me see how the generational patterns of alcoholism, infertility, and pride, among others, had adversely affected and controlled my life. For me, the most beneficial part of this time was learning to identify my ungodly beliefs and replace them with godly beliefs. It was incredibly powerful to write out the false beliefs I'd been carrying around for decades and replace them with God's Word. I am still practicing this on a daily basis. Asking myself, "What does God say about this?" is an instant double-edged sword of the Spirit at my fingertips.

The three women who were committed to facilitating my deliverance listened to my darkest secrets, watched me weep many bitter tears, and interceded for me in prayer through several hours of ministry. I received words of encouragement, Scripture, and visions from the Lord through them, all of which are priceless to me in my ongoing recovery.

Now I find myself taking steps on my own and clearly desiring growth and healing on a daily basis. I am no longer a victim. I am a "lovely overcomer." Some things were changed or healed instantly—other things are still in an ongoing healing process. But the freedom and pure, holy desire I feel in my heart are God's seal on *his* work. Now I hope to use my experience to help others walk through inner healing and deliverance. The Lord is gracious, and I know he will open that door in his time.

CHAPTER 4

What Are Demons and How Do They Act?

It's all too easy to forget that Satan and demons are angels—fallen angels, mind you, but angels, nonetheless.[1] I am constantly amazed (and disappointed) by the widespread skepticism among professing Christians when it comes to the existence and activity of angels, both holy and fallen. If you believe that the Bible is the inspired Word of God, you must reckon with the pervasive presence of angels and demons described therein. The word "angel" (*angelos*) occurs in thirty-four of the sixty-six books of the Bible: 108 times in the Old Testament, and over 165 times in the New Testament, which is 273 times in the Bible.

All angels, both good and evil, were created at some point in time (Ps. 148:2–5; John 1:1–3; Col. 1:16). They are not eternal beings. Each angel is a direct creation; they did not descend from an original pair as we did, nor do they procreate as we do (Matt. 22:28–30). We don't know when angels were created, but they were likely created before the events of Genesis (see Job 38:4–7).

The Fall

God does not directly create evil; therefore, the fallen angels must have been created righteous and upright and subsequently rebelled. No text explicitly

---

1   Three texts confirm. Jesus himself referred to "the devil and his angels [*angelois*]" (Matt. 25:41). See also 1 Peter 3:22 and Revelation 12:7.

describes the original rebellion or fall of countless angels, but we can justifiably conclude that this must have occurred.[2]

I often hear people ask: Can holy or good angels continue to rebel if they so choose? Michael Heiser contends that "there is no scriptural indication in either the Old or New Testament that the ability to rebel against God's authority was 'turned off' at any time. Consequently, they can still conceivably fall. But one would suspect that, given the fate of divine rebels recounted in Scripture, those who remain faithful would be much less inclined toward rebellion."[3] He also points to the words of Eliphaz in Job 15:

> What is man, that he can be pure?
>   Or he who is born of a woman, that he can be righteous?
> Behold, God puts no trust in his holy ones,
>   and the heavens are not pure in his sight;
> how much less one who is abominable and corrupt,
>   a man who drinks injustice like water! (Job 15:14–16)

This text is not necessarily an assessment of the potential for angels who are in God's presence to rebel. It is more likely a reflection on the past sins of those "holy ones" who aligned themselves with Satan in his fall. Furthermore, there is a world of difference between saying that angels retain the potential to rebel and that they actually do. No text clearly asserts the latter. And what are we to make of Paul's reference in 1 Timothy 5:21 to "the elect angels"? Michael Heiser is certainly correct to say "that the designation is designed to contrast these angels with members of the heavenly host in rebellion against God (i.e, 'fallen angels')."[4] They are, he concludes, "good angels in service to the Father and the Son."[5]

But does the qualifying adjective "elect" suggest that they are secure in their relationship to and service on behalf of God and thus unable to fall? Is this a way of referring to all angels who did not fall with Satan in his

---

2   No, Revelation 12:4 does not describe the original, pre-temporal rebellion and fall of Satan and his demons. For more on this text, see chapter 7.

3   Michael S. Heiser, *Angels: What the Bible Really Says about God's Heavenly Host* (Bellingham, WA: Lexham Press, 2018), 32.

4   Ibid., 157.

5   Ibid.

rebellion? If so, were they elect before his fall? Or were they in some sense "chosen" only after the fall of those whom we now refer to as demons? Or are these angels a smaller "select" or special group, such as the cherubim and seraphim, who are assigned the unique responsibility of keeping watch over the conduct of church leaders or church affairs in particular (note the context in which they appear)? William Mounce contends that "by 'elect angels' Paul means those angels whom God chooses to do his special tasks (cf., e.g., 1 Cor. 4:9; 1 Tim. 3:16; Rev. 2:1) and who will be part of the final judgment."[6] Does this mean there might be non-elect angels, angels who are holy and have remained faithful to God but might, at some point in the future, choose to follow Satan in his rebellion? That is highly speculative. Given the fact that nowhere in the Bible are angels portrayed as "falling" or "rebelling" or "sinning" subsequent to the creation of humanity, I'm inclined to conclude that all angels who remained faithful to God are now preserved holy and cannot fall.[7]

Characteristics of Demons

Demons, in the same way as holy angels, display all the characteristics that we associate with personality (albeit deviant expressions of personality). There is no reason to believe that they lost such capacities because of their sin. Thus, Scripture portrays them as possessing intellect, emotion, will, self-consciousness, and self-determination. Do demons experience conviction of conscience as a result of their sin? Nothing suggests they do, although they are clearly aware of their impending and inevitable judgment (Matt. 8:29). All angels are intelligent but not omniscient (1 Pet. 1:12; Mark 13:32), experience

---

6   William D. Mounce, *Pastoral Epistles*, Word Biblical Commentary (Nashville: Thomas Nelson Publishers, 2000), 316.

7   Some may point to Genesis 6:1–4 (and the three New Testament allusions to this incident in 1 Pet. 3:18–20; 2 Pet. 2:4; and Jude 6) as counter evidence. But each of these texts more likely describes sins committed in time by those angels who, at some point in the past, had already fallen in their moral rebellion against God. In other words, these texts do not speak of certain angels who sinned for the first time, but of those who had previously joined Satan in his rebellion and on these specific historical occasions engage in particularly heinous immoral acts for which they are "kept in eternal chains under gloomy darkness until the judgment of the great day" (Jude 6). Thus, only a small number of those who originally fell with Satan are in these texts described as having "left their proper dwelling" (Jude 6).

emotion (Job 38:7; Matt. 8:29; Luke 15:10; Rev. 4–5), and exercise their wills (1 Pet. 3:20; 2 Pet. 2:4).

We know that angels and demons are *spirit* beings in that they are immaterial or incorporeal. They have no flesh or blood or bones. They are, as Hebrews 1:14 declares, "ministering *spirits*." However, although they are spirits, they are not omnipresent (see Dan. 9:21–23; 10:10–14 where we find both spatial movement and temporal limitations). They are always in only one place at any one time.

Possibility of Redemption

Is it possible for fallen angelic beings (demons) to be redeemed? Not likely. There is no record of such anywhere in Scripture—and neither is there any record in Scripture of demonic repentance. Whenever we read about the impact of the cross on demons, it is always portrayed as judgment, never salvation. Nowhere do we read of justification, forgiveness, redemption, adoption, or regeneration being true of any angelic being. Hebrews 2:14–17 declares that whereas Jesus "partook" of human flesh and blood, "it is not angels that he helps" but rather "the offspring of Abraham" (see also Rev. 5:8–14).

Classes or Categories of Demons

In his writings, Paul uses six terms to describe the demons, thus perhaps hinting that there are at least six classes or categories of demonic beings (Eph. 1:21; 3:10; 6:12; Col. 1:16; 2:10, 15; Rom. 8:38). The categories include:

1. Principalities or rulers (*archē*; a ruler must have someone or something over which to exercise dominion; see Eph. 1:21; 3:10; 6:12; Col. 1:16; 2:10; Rom. 8:38).
2. Authorities (*exousia*; again, authority, by definition, demands a subordinate; see Eph. 1:21; 3:10; Col. 1:16).
3. Powers (*dunamis*; Eph. 1:21; Rom. 8:38). In Mark 9:29 Jesus refers to a type of demon that "cannot be driven out by anything but prayer." The point seems to be that some demons are stronger and more powerful than others, implying a hierarchy or differentiation based on spiritual strength.

4. Dominions (*kuriotēs*; again, "lordship" or "dominion" over what, whom, and where? See Eph. 1:21; Col. 1:16).
5. Thrones (*thronoi*; this word is used of angels only in Col. 1:16).
6. World rulers (*kosmokratōr*; used of angels only in Eph. 6:12).

The fact that there are different classes or categories or types of demons would imply some form of organization. If all demons are of the same type or rank or carry the same authority, why are they described in such a variety of terms?

Demons in the Old Testament[8]

Sons of God

The only place in Scripture where demons may be thought of as having physical form is the controversial text in Genesis 6:1–4.[9]

> When man began to multiply on the face of the land and daughters were born to them, the sons of God saw that the daughters of man were attractive. And they took as their wives any they chose. Then the LORD said, "My Spirit shall not abide in man forever, for he is flesh: his days shall be 120 years." The Nephilim were on the earth in those days, and also afterward, when the sons of God came in to the daughters of man and they bore children to them. These were the mighty men who were of old, the men of renown.

The identity of the "sons of God" is debated. Some argue that the "sons of God" were humans, the godly male descendants of Seth, whereas the "daughters of men" were ungodly female descendants of Cain. There are a number of reasons why this view is unlikely:

1. The phrase is not "daughters of *Cain*" but "daughters of *men*," which seems more likely to describe daughters of men in general.

---

8 The following discussion is adapted from my book *Tough Topics* (151–65) and is used here with permission.
9 The following discussion of Genesis 6 is adapted from my book *Tough Topics 2: Biblical Answers to 25 Challenging Questions* (Fearn, Ross-shire, UK: Christian Focus, 2015), 69–71, and is used here with permission.

2. Surely not all the daughters (female descendants) of Cain are to be thought of as significantly more evil than other females in the earth.

3. Whereas the phrase "sons of God" is used to describe the nation as a whole, it is never used in the Old Testament to refer to a particular group within humanity noted for their piety.

4. The phrase "sons of God" *is* used in Scripture specifically to refer to celestial beings.

5. As Heiser notes, "there is no command in the text regarding marriages or any prohibition against marrying certain persons. There are no 'Jews and Gentiles' at this time."[10]

Another view is that the "sons of God" were men of nobility (kings, rulers, princes) who, driven by lust, married outside and well below their rank and status (their sin was polygamy). But as Oropeza observes, "it is not clear . . . why God would abhor polygamy enough to destroy the entire earth by the flood. Long after the flood, the Israelites engaged in polygamy without incurring God's displeasure."[11]

The most likely view is that this text describes a massive intrusion of the demonic into the domain of humanity. This interpretation was dominant in the patristic period until Augustine (354–430) suggested "sons of God" instead referred to Seth's descendants. I think this view is the more likely one for several reasons:

1. The phrase "sons of God" is used elsewhere in Scripture to refer to angelic beings (Job 1:6; 2:1; 38:7; Ps. 29:1; 89:6; and probably Deut. 32:8).[12]

2. The contrast between "sons of *God*" and "daughters of *men*" suggests that the former should be distinguished from human beings. The contrast is most naturally taken to be between beings who are not human and beings who are.

---

10 Heiser, *The Unseen Realm*, 95.

11 B. J. Oropeza, *99 Answers to Questions about Angels, Demons & Spiritual Warfare* (Downers Grove, IL: InterVarsity Press, 1997), 61. Heiser concurs: "But on what logical basis would multiple marriages between kings and women bring the world into chaos, necessitating God's judgment in a catastrophic flood?" (*The Unseen Realm*, 96 n. 8).

12 Although we should not give it too much weight, it is worth noting that the phrase "sons of God" was understood to refer to angels in the earliest known exposition of Genesis 6, that is, in 1 Enoch 6–11.

3. Jude 6–7 implies that these angels' sin was sexual in nature.

The most frequently cited objection to this view is Matthew 22:30, where Jesus implies that angels and demons do not marry or procreate. But in Matthew 22 Jesus is describing the *heavenly* behavior of *holy* angels, *not* the *earthly* immoral misbehavior of *evil* angels. Also, the point of Matthew 22 is that angels do not intermarry with *each other*—they are not a race that propagates itself. But they still might seek sexual interaction with *humans*. We should also remember that in Genesis 18–19 angels appeared in human form, ate solid food, and were pursued by the homosexual community of Sodom and Gomorrah. Clearly, "an angel's involvement in sexual activity was not foreign to the Pentateuch's world of thought."[13] When we add to this that the New Testament portrays demons as longing to inhabit human bodies, it suggests that Genesis 6 may be describing not so much demons *per se* but *demonized humans*—humans in whom demons are dwelling. Page summarizes as follows:

> The sin had a sexual nature, yet it was not simply a sexual sin. More fundamentally, it was a sin of rejecting the order created by God and violating distinctions he had instituted between the various kinds of creatures he had made. Not content to live within the parameters established by Yahweh, the angels formed unnatural unions with human women. The ancient Israelites may well have preserved this story because they saw in it a warning to shun the fertility religions with their sacred marriages between gods and humans.[14]

Oropeza suggests that the "sons of God" were not demonized humans but "incarnated demons" (for lack of a better term).[15] He then asks: "If angels really did manifest themselves in human form, how is it that they were able to duplicate the human DNA structure necessary to produce offspring (if indeed our current understandings of human structuring are correct)? Even if angels are supernatural and were intelligent enough to do so, creating

---

13 Page, *Powers of Evil*, 49.

14 Ibid., 53.

15 Heiser also appears to embrace this view. See *Unseen Realm*, 92–109.

human life seems to be a work that is reserved only for God."[16] He goes on to suggest that perhaps "the sons of God saw the wickedness of humans and asked God to clothe them with bodies so that they could come to earth to teach men laws and morals.... It was at this time that angels descended from heaven to earth. After they were clothed with human flesh, however, they fell to the same passions as do all humans, and so they gave themselves over to the lusts of the flesh, desiring earthly women."[17]

I believe that Genesis 6 describes the "sin" mentioned in 1 Peter 3, 2 Peter 2:4, and Jude 6. Subsequent to their fall from heaven, and as an expression of their moral depravity, an unspecified number of demons either inhabited (took up residence in) human bodies and contracted marriage relationships with the "daughters of men," or in some mysterious way not explained in Scripture were given or somehow assumed physical form and engaged in sexual relations with women. Thus we are reading about a case either of demonized men or what might be called "humanized" demons entering into marriage with women and contributing greatly to the increase of depravity and corruption in the earth (Gen. 6:5–7). These demons were, at some later time, consigned to permanent imprisonment until the day of final judgment.

Idols

Several texts indicate that the idols the Israelites worshipped during their time of rebellion were in fact demons. Visible images are but fronts for invisible demonic spirits:

> They sacrificed to demons that were no gods; to gods they had never known, to new gods that had come recently, whom your fathers had never dreaded (Deut. 32:17).

They served their idols,
  which became a snare to them.

---

16 Oropeza, *99 Answers to Questions*, 64.

17 Ibid., 64–65. Based largely on a wide range of Second Temple Jewish texts (extrabiblical, noninspired documents, especially *1 Enoch* and *Jubilees*), Michael Heiser argues that this is the origin of those entities we know as demons in the New Testament. "Specifically, the disembodied spirits released at the death of the giants [i.e., the Nephilim], the offspring of the union of the sons of God and mortal women, are the demons known in Second Temple texts and the New Testament Gospels" (*Demons*, 112 n. 4).

They sacrificed their sons
>   and their daughters to the demons;
they poured out innocent blood,
>   the blood of their sons and daughters,
whom they sacrificed to the idols of Canaan,
>   and the land was polluted with blood. (Ps. 106:36–38; cf. Ps. 96:4–5)

Texts such as Leviticus 17:7 and 2 Chronicles 11:15 refer to worship of "goat demons" or "goat idols" (literally, "hairy ones"; cf. the "satyr," a Greek mythological figure that is half goat and half man). In various passages in Leviticus, this word is used to refer to a male goat (Lev. 16:7–10, 15, 18, 20–22, 26–27). Some interpreters believe these passages indicate that demons assumed the shape or form of goats (Josh. 24:14; Ezek. 20:7). Others suggest that the references here are simply to goat idols (common in Egypt), behind which were demonic spirits. Whatever the interpretation, the goat head is still a common symbol or representation of Satan in modern occultic activity.

Evil Spirits

When we look at 1 Samuel 16:14–16, 23; 18:10; 19:9, we discover that each of these texts describes "an evil spirit" that comes "from God" or is sent by God.[18] Is this a reference to a good angel who is sent to afflict someone with evil, or is it a demon whose very character is evil who is used by the sovereign God to accomplish his purposes? The latter seems most likely. We must remember that demons are subject to the will of God just like good angels. The apostle Paul's "thorn in the flesh" was inflicted upon him by a "messenger from Satan," but just as surely this messenger was doing God's will (2 Cor. 12:7).

The spirit is described as having "terrorized" Saul. The precise nature of this suffering is not specified, but surely it was both physical and emotional. On two occasions the presence of this spirit led or induced or somehow prompted Saul to become violent and make an attempt on David's life (1

---

18 According to Heiser, "the term translated 'evil' in this phrase (lemma: *ra*) often does not speak of moral disposition or character, but something contemptible (Gen 41:20, 27; Jer 24:2, 3, 8; 49:23; Ps 112:7; Deut 22:14, 19; Neh 6:13) or harmful (Gen 19:19; Deut 7:15; 28:35, 59). Thus by 'evil spirit' the writer may mean that God was the source of an undesirable mental affliction or psychological disposition. As it relates to these and other gospel passages, the 'evil spirit' may therefore be some sort of physical malady or mental illness" (*Demons*, 197).

Sam. 18:10–11; 19:9–10). What, if anything, does this tell us about the relationship between demonic affliction and human sin? Note well that Saul himself acknowledges the sinfulness of his attempts to kill David, even though it was in some way prompted or stirred by the evil spirit (see 1 Sam. 24:16–21 and 26:21). Also, the sending of the evil spirit from God is portrayed as an act of divine judgment. It was in response to Saul's disobedience.

MUSIC AND DEMONS

We should take special note of the fact that the evil spirit left Saul whenever David played his harp (1 Sam. 16:16–23). This is a healthy reminder that music has more than simply a psychological or emotional effect on people. It also has the power to drive away, frustrate, and defeat demonic forces: "And whenever the harmful spirit from God was upon Saul, David took the lyre and played it with his hand. So Saul was refreshed and was well, and the harmful spirit departed from him" (1 Sam. 16:23).

We are told back in 1 Samuel 15:11 that God said: "I regret that I have made Saul king, for he has turned back from following me and has not performed my commandments." The result of Saul's sin is that the Spirit of God "departed" from him (1 Sam. 16:14). Recall that in the Old Testament the people of God were not permanently indwelt by the Spirit. But God would temporarily anoint kings and prophets and others with the Holy Spirit so they might be equipped and empowered to fulfill the calling on their lives.

The question is this: Why or how did David's music have this effect? Why did the demonic spirit depart from Saul such that he was refreshed and made well every time David played on the lyre? There's no indication that David sang. He played instruments. Others might have also played and nothing would happen. Why? What was so special about David? Why did *his* music carry such power? The answer is in verse 18b—"and the LORD is with him." There may well have been other musicians in Saul's court who were more skilled than David. But something about David empowered his music to pierce through the soul of Saul. The Holy Spirit evidently infused the melodies and harmonies of David's music with supernatural power that agitated the demons and drove them into retreat.

If God had not been "with" (in a sense, the Old Testament equivalent of being filled with the Spirit) David, his music might have been entertaining and sweet and enjoyable to hear, but it would not have carried the power to drive a demon from Saul's soul and bring spiritual refreshment to him. There were probably others who were more skilled on the lyre than David, but in the absence of God their music would have left any demonic spirit firmly entrenched.

In other words, music played or sung by those who love God and are filled with God's Spirit and who devote their talents to the glory of God irritates and agitates the enemy! This is why we often recommend to people who are under spiritual attack or are suffering from depression to constantly play both instrumental and vocal worship music, whether they are at home or in their car or at the office. Music devoted to God's glory, played or sung by a person in whom the Spirit dwells, creates a spiritual atmosphere that is repellent and offensive to Satan and his hosts. There's nothing magical in this. Demons don't dislike music. It isn't that they are offended by someone playing or singing off key. It is the presence of God in and with the one playing/singing that accounts for this powerful impact.

We read in 2 Samuel 22:1 that "David spoke to the LORD the words of this song on the day when the LORD delivered him from the hand of all his enemies, and from the hand of Saul." It would appear, then, that David prophesied through singing. Even music written, played, or sung by an unbeliever can be used in this way if it is in the hands of a Spirit-filled, Christ-exalting believer. You don't have to be the one playing or singing. You don't have to be musically gifted in the least. The issue is whether or not God is "with" you.

Let's look at another example. It is found in 2 Kings 3:15. The king of Israel was desperate to hear the word of the Lord regarding what would happen if he were to engage the Moabites in battle, so he sent for Elisha. Elisha then said, "'But now bring me a musician.'

And when the musician played, the hand of the LORD came upon him." The result is that Elisha prophesied.

Why did Elisha want someone to play music? It would appear that, in a manner of speaking, music clears away the interference between heaven and earth. Perhaps an analogy is the way a rainstorm can clear the air of dust particles and make your radio more receptive to a distant station. Anointed and godly music creates a spiritual atmosphere in which God's voice can more readily be heard. It eliminates distractions and enables the heart to focus on God.

Elisha wanted to be quiet and calm before the Lord. He wanted to become emotionally and spiritually and mentally in tune with and sensitive to what God would say. Sometimes it's important to put oneself in a mood that is more conducive to receiving and understanding divine revelation.

We see in 1 Samuel 10 that people would often prophesy while playing instruments, in this case the harp, tambourine, flute, and lyre. We also read in 1 Chronicles 25:1 that "David and the chiefs of the service also set apart for the service the sons of Asaph, and of Heman, and of Jeduthun, who prophesied with lyres, with harps, and with cymbals." Others are said to have "prophesied with the lyre in thanksgiving and praise to the LORD" (1 Chron. 25:3).

In what sense, if at all, can it be said that the instruments themselves prophesied? Or was it that the individuals verbally prophesied to the accompaniment of their instruments? Or are we to understand that the music served to open lines of communication and enabled the prophets to accurately hear the word of the Lord?

I've often been asked why we play background instrumental music when we pray for people. Are we just trying to create a mood and manipulate someone's emotions? *Yes*, we are trying to create a mood or atmosphere conducive to engaging with God and hearing his voice, and I make no apology for that. But *no*, we are not trying to manipulate anyone. We are simply seeking to minister effectively to people by acknowledging that the Holy Spirit is pleased to make use of music to soothe their hearts, to put them at ease emotionally, and to open their souls to God.

"Male Goat"

Isaiah 13:21 and 34:14 (cf. Lev. 17:7) are especially instructive about demons. In other texts, the word used here simply means "male goat" (the sort presented as a sin offering). It is likely, however, that in the two texts from Isaiah it refers to demons. As Page notes, "in both cases, the word appears in a prophecy of the destruction Yahweh will bring to an enemy of Israel. Chapter 13 describes the devastation of Babylon, and chapter 34 paints a similar picture for Edom. Both passages envisage a time when Israel's enemies will be utterly destroyed, when their centers of power will no longer be inhabited by humans but become a dwelling place for the denizens of the desert. The *se'irim* are included among the future inhabitants of these waste places."[19]

LILITH

Many believe that Revelation 18:2 is an allusion to Isaiah 13:21. In the former text we read, "Fallen, fallen is Babylon the great! She has become a dwelling place for demons, a haunt for every unclean spirit, a haunt for every unclean bird, a haunt for every unclean and detestable beast." Here again we see the association of demons with desolate places abandoned by humans.[20] In Isaiah 34:14, another word occurs that probably refers to demons. It is the Hebrew word translated *Lilith*, rendered "night monster" by the NASB, "night creature" by the NIV, and "night bird" by the ESV.

In Babylonian demonology, Lilith could refer to several things: a child-stealing witch; Adam's first wife, before Eve, believed to be the mother of all demons; or a night demon that prowled about in dark and desolate places. In postbiblical times, Lilith became the topic of much speculation in Judaism. "She came to be regarded primarily as a demon who seduced men in their dreams, who murdered young

---

19 Page, *Powers of Evil*, 69.

20 "In the temptation narratives Jesus confronts Satan in the wilderness. In Luke 8:29 we are told that the Gerasene demoniac was driven into the desert by a demon. And in Matthew 12:43–45 and its parallel Luke 11:24–26 the unclean spirit who has been cast out 'passes through waterless places.' These texts are illumined by the Jewish belief that the wilderness, being beyond the bounds of society, is the haunt of evil spirits (see Lev 16:10; Isa 13:21; *1 Enoch* 10:4–5; Tob 8:3; 4 Macc 18:8; *2 Apoc. Bar.* 10:8). The idea dominated later Christian monasticism" (Heiser, *Demons*, 23).

children, and who was a special threat at childbirth. More recently, she has emerged as a positive symbol for Jewish feminists."[21] Some have argued that the reference to "the terror of the night" in Psalm 91:5 is an allusion to Lilith.

INCUBUS AND SUCCUBUS

Although not biblical terms, the purported existence of demonic spirits known as *incubus* and *succubus* needs to be addressed. Incubi (from the Latin, *incubare*, "to lie upon") are said to be demons who take on the shape or form of men to seduce sleeping women; as succubi they assume the shape or form of women to seduce men. Since demons are incapable of producing either semen or eggs, there is no reproductive fruit from such encounters (unless Gen 6:1–4 is the exception, as noted earlier). Their motivation is primarily to humiliate and corrupt their victims. Most often the alleged victim feels physically immobilized and thus raped. However, it is not uncommon for the demon to *deceive* the victim into thinking that he/she was a *willing* partner, thereby intensifying the feelings of deep, personal shame and self-loathing. Many also often find it difficult to develop a healthy sexual relationship with their spouse. In the final analysis, there is no way to know with any degree of certainty whether such demons exist and whether they engage in this sort of nefarious activity.

The Divine Assembly and the Heavenly Host

In Psalm 82 God is portrayed as presiding or ruling over the divine assembly. He accuses the "gods" of failing in their duty to protect the poor and powerless and condemns them to death (v. 7). Who are these "gods"? Some argue they are human beings or judges who are called "gods" because they represent God when they issue their verdicts. More likely this is a reference to supernatural beings. Several things indicate this. The setting of the psalm (see v. 1) is the

21 Ibid., 73.

heavenly council or divine assembly. The terms "gods" (v. 1) and "sons of the Most High" (v. 6) more naturally refer to celestial beings. In verse 7 it is said they will die like men, which assumes they are not human (otherwise, there is no purpose for the comparison with humans). And the idea that celestial beings have been given responsibility for the administration of justice in particular nations is found elsewhere in the Old Testament, such as Deuteronomy 32:8–9.

It may not be wise to draw too sharp a distinction between celestial beings and earthly human rulers, for "the psalmist may well have believed that the celestial 'gods' exercised their influence on earth through terrestrial rulers."[22] Thus, I conclude that the "gods" of Psalm 82 are fallen angels, originally assigned as patrons of various nations, who shirked their responsibility and abused their powers. Page explains:

> The text is silent about the circumstances of their fall from innocence, but obviously these are fallen beings whose sin had a devastating impact on human society. The angels stand accused of aiding and abetting the wicked in their exploitation of the poor and powerless. Indeed, the plight of the marginalized in society was exacerbated by the actions of these gods. So great was their influence that verse 5 says, "All the foundations of the earth are shaken." When justice is perverted, the very structure of the cosmic order comes under attack, threatening chaos. Obviously, the psalmist saw the promotion of inequity and the absence of compassion as grievous sins that are not due to human moral deficiencies alone. So great is the evil of social injustice that it can only be accounted for by the activity of cosmic forces opposed to God.[23]

In Isaiah 24:21–22 we read of a time when God will punish "the host of heaven, in heaven." In support of the interpretation that this is a reference to fallen angels, note the contrast in verse 21 with earthly rulers or kings. These demons are thus in some way allied with the kings of various nations; they are "patron" angels of earthly nations and are involved in the sins mentioned in Psalm 82:5. The word translated "powers" (*saba*) is used elsewhere in the Old Testament to refer to angels (1 Kings 22:19).

---

22 Ibid., 58.
23 Ibid., 59.

1 Kings 22:19–23 (2 Chron. 18:18–22) is a fascinating passage. Ahab was seeking to form an alliance with Jehoshaphat, king of Judah, whereby they might together attack Ramoth-Gilead, which was under Aramean control. Jehoshaphat insisted that they first consult a prophet to get God's perspective. Ahab, on the other hand, gathered 400 of his prophets, who told him to attack Ramoth-Gilead and he would be victorious. Jehoshaphat consulted with the prophet Micaiah, who told him of a vision he had of a meeting of the heavenly council. In the vision, God asked who would go to entice Ahab into attacking Ramoth-Gilead. A "spirit" (angel?) volunteered to be a "a lying spirit in the mouth of all his [Ahab's] prophets" (v. 22). God agreed. The spirit went forth, Ahab heeded the voice of the prophets, and went forth into the battle where he eventually died.

The scene in Micaiah's vision is similar to that in Job 1—a heavenly council at which the angels are all present. Some have argued that the "spirit" was in fact Satan, but there is no indication of this in the text. The spirit is portrayed as simply one among many others. There is no evidence of some superior or special position. Was this a fallen spirit, a demon? Probably. This spirit performs an evil function: prompting Ahab's prophets to speak lies. Although the spirit is not Satan himself, there are undeniable parallels between 2 Chronicles 18:18 and Job 1. Also, the passage seems to draw a distinction between the spirit inspiring Ahab's prophets and the one inspiring Micaiah (see v. 24). "The implication is that Micaiah and Ahab's prophets could not both have received their messages from the same source. There are, of course, two distinct sources, but it is Micaiah who has the right one. After all, it is his prophecy that comes to pass."[24]

Perhaps most important of all is the fact that even this demonic spirit is absolutely subject to the will of God. Micaiah is clear that it was God who "put a lying spirit in the mouth of all these your prophets; the Lord has declared disaster for you" (v. 23). Thus God can and often does use demonic spirits to fulfill his purposes. Whether God or the devil put the lying spirit into the prophets, God is always ultimate. A close parallel with this passage is the account in Judges 9:23 where God sent an evil spirit to provoke discord between Abimelech and the people of Shechem.

24 Ibid., 79.

Demons in the New Testament

Much of the Jewish literature dating from the New Testament era focused on identifying demonic spirits by name (such as Raux, Barsafael, Artosael, and Belbel). Aside from a single reference to Satan as Belial (2 Cor. 6:15), the apostle Paul does not identify any demonic being, but there are three terms he typically uses to describe them. The first is *daimōn* or *daimonion* (demon), used sixty-three times (fifty-four of which are in the Gospels). Then there is *pneumata*, most often translated "spirits" (cf. Luke 10:17 with 10:20). Also, "unclean spirits" is used twenty-one times, half of which are in Mark (see Luke 11:19–26), and "evil spirits," which is used only eight times in the Gospels and Acts (cf. Luke 8:2). Finally, demons are also called *angelos*, translated "angel" (see Matt. 25:41; 1 Pet. 3:22; Rev. 12:7). I should also point out that the term "devils" is technically incorrect. *Diabolos* is never used in the New Testament of demons, but only of *the* devil, Satan.

Additional Characteristics and Activities of Demons

Several things in particular should be noted in addition to what was mentioned above.

What Demons Are Like

Although demons are rarely named in the New Testament (see Luke 8:30), it is reasonable to conclude that each has a name (holy angels have names: Michael, Gabriel). Demons can speak to and communicate with humans (Luke 4:33–35, 41; 8:28–30; Acts 19:13–17). They are intelligent (Luke 4:34; 8:28; Acts 19:13–17) and formulate and propagate their own doctrinal systems (1 Tim. 4:1–3; see my discussion of this in the next chapter).

DOCTRINES OF DEMONS

Distortions and misrepresentations of the truth are not always the product of merely human misunderstanding or miscalculation. Paul believes that often they are demonically inspired. This does *not*

mean, however, that everyone who disagrees with you on any particular point of doctrine is an unwitting tool of a demon! On the other
hand, it is entirely possible that certain false doctrines that well-
meaning Christians hold may be demonically energized. Together
with 1 John 4, we see that demons are extremely active in promoting
falsehoods in the church. According to 1 John 4, behind false prophets (such as those who deny the incarnation of Christ) are supernatural agents of the enemy.

Demons have emotions and experience a variety of feelings (Jas. 2:19;
Luke 8:28). There are also differences or degrees in their strength (Mark 9:29)
and sinfulness (Matt. 12:45). Like the holy angels, demons can appear to us in
various forms, both spiritual and physical (Matt. 4; Rev. 9:7–10, 17; 16:13–16).
If holy angels can visit us without our knowing it (Heb. 13:1–2), there is every
reason to believe that demons can as well.

Demons appear at present to be in one of three places. They are either
active in the earth, confined in the abyss (Luke 8:31; although this confine-
ment may not be permanent, see Rev. 9:1–3, 11), or permanently confined/
imprisoned in hell/tartarus (2 Pet. 2:4; Jude 6; and possibly 1 Pet. 3:18–20).
The verb *tartaroō* ("to send to hell") occurs only in 2 Peter 2:4 in the New
Testament, but is found frequently in Greek mythology where it refers to
the depths of the underworld. There is a textual problem in verse 4. Some
manuscripts say they were committed to "pits" of darkness, while others say
"chains" of darkness. It has been suggested that since Peter's language is necessarily figurative, he need not be interpreted as saying that these demons
are permanently confined but only significantly restricted in what they can
do in the earth. I find this latter suggestion highly unlikely.

What Demons Can Do

Demons can infuse their victims with superhuman strength (Acts 19:16;
Mark 5:3) and like the holy angels, can move swiftly through space (Dan.
9:21–23; 10:10–14). Normal physical barriers do not restrict their activity (a
"legion" [6,000] of demons inhabited one man and later 2,000 pigs). Demons
can also physically assault someone and/or cause physical affliction. Luke

9:39 (Matt. 17:15) speaks of a demon's *seizing* a young boy. He is thrown to the ground or into fire or water, together with other violent symptoms. In Matthew 9:32–34 a man's inability to speak is attributed to a demon (cf. 12:22–24; Luke 11:14–15). However, there are several cases in the Gospels of Jesus healing blindness or the inability to speak that are *not* attributed to demonic influence (Matt. 9:27–31; 20:29–34; Mark 7:31–37; 8:22–26; 10:46–52; Luke 18:35–43; John 9:1–7).

Demons inspire and energize the false wisdom of the world that all too often infiltrates the church and poisons interpersonal relationships in the body of Christ. In James 3:13–18 he describes two kinds of wisdom: that which comes from heaven, and that which is characterized as "earthly, unspiritual, demonic" (*daimoniōdēs*). "James clearly considered the arrogant, sectarian spirit of his opponents to be demonic."[25]

Demons animate and energize all non-Christian religions and all forms of idolatry (1 Cor. 10:14–22). In Galatians 4:3, 8–9, Paul refers to the "elemental things" (NASB) of this world, literally, the *stoicheia*, to which both Jews and Gentiles were held in bondage prior to their conversion to Christ. Many believe this term is a reference to demonic powers, and I will address this subject at length in the next chapter.

DEMONS AND JESUS'S CRUCIFIXION

Although we can't be certain on this, demons may have been responsible, in part, for the crucifixion of Jesus. In 1 Corinthians 2:6–8 Paul refers to the "rulers of this age" (vv. 6, 8) who "crucified the Lord of glory." Some insist this is a reference to the *human* rulers of the day, such as Annas, Caiaphas, Pilate, etc. Others argue that the evidence points to *demonic* powers. Evidence supporting this latter view is two-fold.

The term "ruler" is used elsewhere by Paul of Satan (Eph. 2:2 NIV). It is also used this way by Jesus (John 12:31; 14:30; 16:11). However, it is also used of human rulers in Romans 13:3. Second, these "rulers" are said to be "doomed to pass away." The latter is a transla-

25 Page, *Powers of Evil*, 230. More on this in chapter 7.

tion of the verb *katargeō*, a term used later in 1 Corinthians 15:24 of Christ's ultimate defeat/destruction of the principalities and powers. This verb is never used by Paul for the ultimate doom of unbelieving humanity. It is also used in Hebrews 2:14 for the defeat of the devil by Christ.

If the "rulers" refer to demonic forces, then we must conclude, with Arnold, that "Paul held the demonic rulers responsible for Christ's death. He assumes that these powers of Satan were working behind the scenes to control the course of events during the passion week. It was not a part of Paul's purpose to explain exactly how these demonic rulers operated. At the very least we can imagine they were intimately involved by exerting their devious influence in and through Judas, Pilate, Annas and Caiaphas, and by inciting the mob. Demonic victory over God's plan by putting Christ to death failed. The powers did not apprehend the full extent of God's wisdom— how the Father would use the death of Christ to atone for sin, raise him victoriously from the dead and create the church. Least of all did they envisage their own defeat!"[26]

Demons and Cosmic Warfare

Demons engage in cosmic-level warfare with the holy angels (Rev. 12:1–12). New Testament scholars have generally acknowledged that there are four levels of spiritual conflict or warfare: (1) the conflict between God and Satan (Heb. 2:14; 1 John 3:8); (2) the conflict between the elect angels and the evil angels (Rev. 12; Dan. 10); (3) the conflict between Satan and the saints (either *direct* [a sensible, often tangible encounter between intelligent evil beings and the believer; Ephesians 6], or *indirect* [the inescapable conflict from simply living in a world that lies in the power of the evil one (1 John 5:18–19), a world shaped by the values, ideologies, and institutions energized by Satan]);

---

26 Clinton E. Arnold, *Powers of Darkness: Principalities & Powers in Paul's Letters* (Downers Grove, IL: InterVarsity Press, 1992), 104. Heiser concurs with Arnold and provides persuasive arguments (*Demons*, 246–48). Note, however, that an equally strong case can be made that the "rulers" here are human, earthly rulers.

and (4) the conflict between Satan and the unsaved (2 Cor. 4:4; Acts 26:18; Col. 1:12–13; Eph. 2:2; Matt. 13:1–23)—although "conflict" is probably not a good word insofar as the unbelieving world willingly sides with Satan, even though they may not know they do. As for level-two warfare, more will be said about this when we address the defeat of Satan and his hosts.

One thing that we see in Revelation 12 is that Michael and his elect angels are more powerful and stronger than Satan and his demonic hosts (v. 8). Why? Because of the cross and resurrection of Jesus! Two other texts substantiate this point.

The first is 2 Peter 2:10–11, where the false teachers mock or "blaspheme" "the glorious ones" (literally, "glories" = evil angelic beings = demons), something not even the elect angels do. Elect angels are "greater in might and power" than evil angels. The explanation for this superior strength isn't by virtue of creation—it isn't inherent within them. Rather, it is by virtue of the victory of the cross and resurrection and exaltation of Jesus.

Why would false teachers speak disdainfully of demons? Richard Bauckham explains:

> The most plausible view is that in their confident immorality the false teachers were contemptuous of the demonic powers. When they were rebuked for their immoral behavior and warned of the danger of falling into the power of the devil and sharing his condemnation, they laughed at the idea, denying that the devil could have any power over them and speaking of the powers of evil in skeptical, mocking terms. They may have doubted the very existence of supernatural powers of evil.[27]

The second text is Jude 8–9. Here we see that Michael, though greater and more powerful than Satan (2 Pet. 2:11; Rev. 12:8) because of Christ's victory, did not pronounce a judgment against his rival. There is no reference in the Old Testament to this dispute. It comes from Jude's reconstruction of the lost ending of the *Testament of Moses* (first century BC; see Deut. 34:1–6). According to the *Testament of Moses*, Michael was sent by God to Mount Nebo to remove Moses's body to its burial place; before he could do so, Satan, making one last effort to gain power/authority over Moses, tried to

---

27 Richard J. Bauckham, *Jude, 2 Peter*, Word Biblical Commentary (Waco, TX: Word, 1983), 262.

obtain the body (hoping, perhaps, to make it an object of worship among the Israelites [idolatry] or at least to deprive Moses of the honor of burial by the archangel). It was a legal dispute, as Satan sought to prove Moses unworthy of honorable treatment by accusing him of murder (Ex. 2:12). Michael, not tolerating such slander, appealed to divine authority and said: "The Lord rebuke you" (Jude 9).

This is *not* designed to teach us to show reverence for the devil. Rather, the point is that Michael, unlike the false teachers, did not presume to be a law unto himself but referred the matter to the proper moral authority: God. Again, Richard Bauckham explains:

> The point of contrast between the false teachers and Michael is not that Michael treated the devil with respect, and the moral is not that we should be polite even to the devil. The point of the contrast is that Michael could not reject the devil's accusation on his own authority. Even though the devil was motivated by malice and Michael recognized that his accusation was slanderous, he could not himself dismiss the devil's case, because he was not the judge. All he could do was ask the Lord, who alone is judge, to condemn Satan for his slander. The moral is therefore that no one is a law to himself, an autonomous moral authority.[28]

This does *not* mean that we, as Christians, are forbidden to rebuke or verbally resist or pronounce judgment against demonic beings. Neither unbelievers (the false teachers) nor even the holy angels have the authority we have received by virtue of our being in Christ. In Christ, with his authority, we both can and must resist and rebuke the enemy (see Luke 10:1–20; Acts 5:16; 8:7; 16:16–18; 19:12). Jude makes no attempt to extend to Christians the restriction placed on Michael.

No Match for Christians

It seems only right to bring this chapter to a close with the same note of victory over demons that we saw in the previous chapter in relation to their leader, Satan. The defeat of the hosts of hell does not come by our efforts

---

28 Ibid., 61.

or energetic shouting or wild gesturing or by turning up the volume when we worship as if demonic spirits cannot tolerate loud music! Paul was clear and to the point when writing to the Colossians 2:15: "He [God the Father, or perhaps the Son] disarmed the rulers and authorities and put them to open shame, by triumphing over them in him [that is, in Christ, or perhaps in "it," the cross]." The good news is that we have been granted authority "over all the power of the enemy" (Luke 10:19). Satan and his henchmen are powerful, but they are no match for those who go forth in the name of Jesus (Luke 10:17)!

SUSAN'S STORY

For as long as I can remember, I've had stomach and back pain. The stomach pain began as early as second grade and the back pain as a teen. By the time I was in graduate school, I had neck pain, heart palpitations, vision and hearing loss, daily stomach/digestive problems and then the headaches began. I had full body inflammation and was tested for autoimmune disease within the last year. Over the last three years the headaches had become daily and I had an indentation in the right side of my head. My headaches always became worse on Sundays. I knew anytime I was going to meet with the Body of Christ, study God's Word, or go to a continuing education class, I would have a headache. Along with the physical pain, I was experiencing anger, bitterness, and loss of joy, for what I thought was no reason. I was still living life "normally," homeschooling my children, working, seeking the Lord, but just couldn't get past these circumstances. I felt like I was going to be like Paul and just have to deal with the thorn that tormented.

This past summer we joined a new community group at our church. Guess what? Every Wednesday I had a headache. Some nights were so bad I couldn't see straight. Two lovely ladies from our group approached me one evening, as they noticed I was in pain. This started my journey through deliverance. And I am so incredibly grateful. Hope was restored after the first meeting with them!

The first meeting we talked about forgiveness and repentance. I already noticed a difference. Headaches were fewer and I was finding more free time in my day to get cleaning done and rest! Next, we talked about ungodly ties. I listed several, but one really stood out. I had an ungodly tie to alternative healthcare/supplements. Revealing that was an eye-opener. I had been controlling my kids' and my health. I had done everything in my own power to keep them safe and healthy. I had taken on the task of figuring out what was "wrong" with me and not trusting a doctor or God to help me.

Next time we met we talked about generational patterns and spirits. So much was revealed! Doors in my extended family had been opened for asthma, premature death, illness/infirmities, among other familial patterns. When those were recognized and called out, I had heaviness leave me immediately. It was incredible! I had been walking around with what felt like a cloud of darkness and pressure for so long that I had forgotten what it was like to feel normal. When the demonic spirits were identified and commanded to leave, I had an immediate spinning and lightheaded sensation come over me. We prayed it off until it was gone, and the indentation in my head was healed! I felt it expand, and the Lord kept saying "expansion." To be free from this pressure in my head is wonderful. I have had fewer than five headaches since then, and when I do, I just pray through them or they are very minor.

Word curses and inner vows were discussed at our next session. I have made several inner vows, unknowingly, and have also had many curses spoken over me. Those curses typically weren't meant for harm, but I have held on to them for years. Many were against my health. One inner vow I had made was to not get my hopes up. This has impacted my view of Jesus healing me. I had decided to not get my hopes up and just live with pain. I didn't realize I had done it, but I had given up hope in the Lord's power to heal. That's why I had been trying to do it all myself. Protect my kids, heal my body, "fix" others, etc. I must do it all if God won't do it supernaturally. During our prayer time together, I felt demons encircling my head and binding together. I had pressure around the right side of my head, but they left in the name of Jesus! They are gone and may not touch the future generations! Some of the issues I was seeing in my kids changed that very week! Confusion and distraction with schoolwork was so much better. My son's breathing and skin issues changed! So much freedom!

We then addressed a number of ungodly beliefs and strongholds in my life. It has changed the way I talk, especially to my children. I want to speak life to myself and to them. I had so many ungodly beliefs about being stuck in illness and pain. I had many judgmental beliefs too. I've replaced them with the truth and am noticing a change in my home and work environment! This past week I've noticed my inflammation is down. My seasonal depression that usually rears in early October is gone. Stomach pain and digestion issues that required supplements is much better. I am feeling the Lord's presence in a sweet, physical way.

In our most recent meeting, we addressed inner healing. The Lord revealed I had been holding on to a hurt from my daughter's birth. It was a deep wound that caused frustration, anger, disappointment, and a lot of fear. It was a life-changing event that caused me to want to be in control of all things related to my children and increased my fears. Fear of the unknown, fear of man, fear of the medical world, fear of my kids not knowing Christ. In his sweetness, he showed me how he spared her life through a C-section. I am still in awe of his goodness through that! I repented and asked forgiveness for my feelings and especially fear. So much fear left! He has replaced the fear and my wanting to be in control with joy and rest! I'm excited for this new chapter full of joy! I haven't experienced that in a long time.

I know there is more to come in the days ahead. I also know this is a new way of life, and I have so many great tools to combat the enemy. And I KNOW this is now a life of freedom and deliverance and intimate relationship with Jesus! How can you not share this goodness with others?!

CHAPTER 5

The Demonic in the History of the Church: Part One

When the late Supreme Court Justice Antonin Scalia revealed to the reporters at *The New Yorker* that he believed in a literal, personal devil, the reporters asked, "Isn't it terribly frightening to believe in the Devil?" Here is the substance of what Scalia said:

> You're looking at me as though I'm weird. My God! Are you so out of touch with most of America, most of which believes in the Devil? I mean, Jesus Christ believed in the Devil! It's in the Gospels! You travel in circles that are so, *so* removed from mainstream America that you are appalled that anybody would believe in the Devil! Most of mankind has believed in the Devil, for all of history. Many more intelligent people than you or me have believed in the Devil.[1]

I realize that some of you, in the course of your Christian life, may have struggled with the idea of a literal, personal spiritual being of unimaginable wickedness called the devil or Satan. My wife was one of those people when we first started dating. She had been raised in a very liberal, mainline denominational church in Tulsa, Oklahoma, and thought such ideas were ridiculous. Her ideas were in error, but she was not alone in believing them.

In fact, many people have mistakenly minimized the presence and activity of both Satan and his demons throughout the course of the present church

---

1   Casey Cep, "The Devil You Know," *New Yorker*, October 17, 2013, www.newyorker.com/books/page-turner/the-devil-you-know.

age, that season in God's purposes that extends from the Day of Pentecost to the Second Coming of Christ. In this chapter, we'll explore why that is and how it has affected the modern church's perception of Satan.

Satan and the Early Church

Those who doubt Satan's activity in the present age often argue that, while we find a proliferation of deliverances during the ministry of Jesus, we find very few cases of demonic deliverances in Acts and the Epistles. This argument, however, is inaccurate. Acts and the Epistles contain numerous references to Satan and his demons.

For instance, in Acts 5:1–11 Satan "has filled" the "heart" of Ananias "to lie to the Holy Spirit" (v. 3). In Acts 5:16, those "afflicted with unclean spirits" were being healed and set free by Peter. And in Acts 8:7, as Philip ministered in Samaria, "unclean spirits, crying out with a loud voice, came out of many who had them." Although no explicit reference to Satan or demons is found in the narrative of Acts 8:9–25, "it is not improbable that the appearance of a magician [named Simon] implies satanic opposition to the Spirit's work in Samaria."[2]

When Peter explained the ministry of Jesus to Cornelius, he concentrated on how "God anointed Jesus of Nazareth with the Holy Spirit and with power" and how he "went about doing good and healing all who were oppressed by the devil" (Acts 10:38). Paul described Elymas the magician as a "son of the devil" (Acts 13:10), perhaps to identify the source of his power as a "magician" (Acts 13:8). Then there is the deliverance by Paul of a slave girl in Philippi. She had been demonized by a "spirit of divination" (Acts 16:16), to which Paul spoke: "'I command you in the name of Jesus Christ to come out of her.' And it came out that very hour" (Acts 16:18).

That the demonic were still very much at work and so, too, the deliverance ministry of Paul, is seen in Acts 19 where "the evil spirits came out of" those who touched the handkerchiefs and aprons that "had touched his skin" (vv. 11–12). Although the itinerant Jewish exorcists failed in their efforts to drive out demons, Luke makes it clear that there were yet many "who had evil spirits" (Acts 19:13; see also vv. 15–16). In fact, Paul summarizes the calling he had from Jesus as specifically focused on opening the eyes of the Gentiles "so that they may turn from darkness to light and from the power of Satan to God" (Acts 26:18).

Satan and Demons in the Book of Revelation

The book of Revelation, and the age it describes—the church age in which we all live—is permeated by intense satanic and demonic activity. Examining a few of Revelation's letters to churches will give us some insight into Satan's specific activity in church history.[3]

Smyrna's Synagogue of Satan

The first reference to Satan in Revelation is found in our Lord's letter to the church at Smyrna. Smyrna was a proud and beautiful city and regarded itself as the "pride of Asia." The people of Smyrna were quite sensitive to the rivalry with Ephesus for recognition as the most splendid city of Asia Minor.

Of the seven churches, only Smyrna and Philadelphia receive no complaint from the Lord. There is only commendation, encouragement, and a promise of eternal life. Perhaps the reason there is no cause for complaint is that Smyrna was a suffering church. The letter is devoted almost exclusively to an account of their past and present trials, a warning of yet more persecution to come, and a strengthening word of encouragement from the One who knows all too well the pain of scorn and death.

Among the many reasons Smyrna suffered was the great antagonism that existed within the Jewish community toward the church. This no doubt stemmed in part from their conviction that to worship a crucified carpenter from Nazareth was foolishness. Worse still, it was blasphemy (see especially 1 Cor. 1:18–25). There was also undoubtedly a measure of bitterness at the loss of so many from their ranks to the new faith. The Jews were known to inform the authorities of Christian activities, the latter being perceived as treason. Jewish opposition to the church at Smyrna is the focus of Revelation 2:9 where Jesus refers to those "who say that they are Jews and are not, but

---

3   For a discussion of the many theories surrounding the book of Revelation, see my book *Kingdom Come: The Amillennial Alternative* (Fearn, Ross-shire, UK: Christian Focus, 2015), 387–422.

are a synagogue of Satan." Clearly, in one sense, these people *are* Jews, the physical descendants of Abraham, Isaac, and Jacob, who met regularly in the synagogue to worship. Yet, in another sense, inwardly and spiritually, they are *not* Jews, having rejected Jesus and now persecuting and slandering his people.

One can hardly think of a more derisive description than to be called "a synagogue of Satan" (Rev. 2:9; see also 3:9). Evidently Satan was the ultimate source behind their denial of Jesus and their persecution of the Christians in that city. Jesus explicitly lays blame for the imprisonment and martyrdom of many in Smyrna on "the devil" (Rev. 2:10). We must remember that imprisonment in Roman communities like Smyrna wasn't technically considered a punishment. Prisons were used for one of three reasons: (1) to compel and coerce obedience to the order of a magistrate; (2) to keep the accused confined pending the trial date; or (3) to detain the guilty until the time of execution. The words "unto death" in Revelation 2:10 indicate that the third is in view.

There's simply no escaping the fact that some of them would die because of Satan's hatred of the gospel. Yet Jesus does nothing to prevent it. He doesn't alleviate their poverty nor publicly vindicate his people in the face of those who hurled their indignant slander. And when Satan moves to incite their imprisonment and eventual execution, the Lord chooses not to intervene. There are certainly numerous instances in biblical days and in the history of the church when it was otherwise (see Heb. 11:32–34). But not always (see Heb. 11:35–38).

But we must also note that there are *divinely imposed limits* on how far Satan can go in his efforts to destroy us. For the Christians at Smyrna, not unlike the situation with Job, the enemy is given a long leash. But he can only go as far as God permits. Satan is unable to act outside the parameters established by the will of his Creator. In this case, he will instigate their incarceration, but only for "ten days" (Rev. 2:10).

How can I say that Satan is limited in what he can do if some of those he throws into prison end up getting killed? That's a good question. Just as there was a divinely imposed limitation on what Satan could perpetrate, there was a divinely ordained purpose for it: to "test" them (v. 10). In giving them over to the devil for imprisonment, and for some, death, God had not forsaken his people. This was not a sign of his disdain or rejection, but a means by which to test and try and refine and purify their trust in Christ. I find it incredibly instructive that *what Satan intended for their destruction, God designed for their spiritual growth!* Satan's intent was to undermine their faith, not to "test" it. Yet God orchestrated the entire scenario as a way of honing and stabilizing and solidifying the faith of the church in Smyrna.

Another encouraging thing for us to note is that the death Satan inflicts results in life for the believer. In verse 10b Jesus encourages the Smyrneans to remain faithful unto (physical) death and he will give them "the crown of life." Jesus reminds them of this because he knows that the power to persevere comes from a vibrant faith in the certainty of God's promised reward. Those who do not love "their lives even unto death" (Rev. 12:11) are granted a "life" that infinitely transcends anything this earthly existence could ever afford. Jesus does not call for faithfulness unto death without reminding us that there awaits us in the future a quality and depth of true and unending life that far outweighs whatever sacrifice is made in the present. Even satanic opposition can and will be turned by God into an ultimate victory for those who "are called according to his purpose" (Rom. 8:28).

There is every reason to believe that the global persecution of the church in our day and the multiple martyrdoms we regularly see are likewise the work of Satan and his demons. Whether it be the beheading of believers by members of ISIS or the burning to death of a pastor and his family in some remote village of India, Satan's strategy is still the same. He aims to undermine our confidence and faith in God's goodness. But his efforts will ultimately fail, as God's people, by God's grace, remain "faithful unto death" (Rev. 2:10).

Pergamum: Satan's Throne

My wife and I lived for eleven years in Kansas City, Missouri, known as "The City of Fountains." We also lived four years just outside of Chicago, "The Windy City." Paris, France, is called "The City of Lights," and New York is often described as "The City That Never Sleeps." We have friends who live in Las Vegas, infamously (but justifiably) referred to as "Sin City," and the list could go on. From what Jesus says in his letter to the church in Pergamum, the Christians there may well be described as living in "Satan's City." "I know where you dwell," said Jesus, "where Satan's throne is" (Rev. 2:13a). Later in the same verse he refers to Pergamum as the place "where Satan dwells" (Rev. 2:13b).

Why did Satan choose Pergamum as his earthly base of operation? We know that it was one of the largest cities in the ancient world, with a population of 190,000. But it wasn't primarily for either political or economic achievements that Pergamum was famous, but for religion. Pergamum was the center of worship for at least four of the most important pagan cults of the day.

Upon entering the city, you'd see the gigantic altar of Zeus, which was erected on a huge platform some 800 feet above the city, looking down on its inhabitants like a great vulture hovering over its prey. Many have sought to identify "Satan's seat" or "throne" (v. 13) with this altar. Amazingly, a reconstructed form of this altar is on display in the Pergamum Museum in Berlin.

Pergamum was also the center for the worship of Athene and Dionysus. However, the most distinctive and celebrated cult of all was dedicated to the worship of Asclepios (or Aesculapius). Often referred to as "Savior" (*sotēr*) in Greek mythology, Asclepios was the son of Apollo and was thought to have been the very first physician. You may recall that the symbol adopted by the U.S. Department of Health, Education, and Welfare (renamed The Department of Health and Human Services in 1979) is the staff of Asclepios, which has a serpent coiled around it.

But beyond the worship directed at these pagan deities was the fact that Pergamum was the acknowledged center in Asia Minor for the imperial cult of Caesar. In 29 BC this city received permission to build and dedicate a temple to Augustus, three years before Smyrna was granted a similar privilege. Perhaps more than any of the other six cities, the people of Pergamum were devoted to the worship of Caesar.

Were it not for the fact that "greater" is he who is in us "than he who is in the world" (1 John 4:4b), it would be frightening to hear that Pergamum is "where Satan dwells" (Rev. 2:13b). Although this may simply be synonymous with "Satan's throne" (v. 13a), it's possible that this is another way of saying that evil was present in Pergamum in a particularly powerful and concentrated way. Could it be that Satan had in some sense made Pergamum the focus of his earthly base of operation?

To those believers immersed in an explicitly satanic atmosphere of idolatry and wickedness, Jesus says: "I know where you dwell!" To a people struggling by grace to remain faithful when those around them revel in faithlessness, Jesus says: "I know where you dwell!" To a church that must, at times, have felt abandoned and alone and given over to the enemy, Jesus says: "I know where you dwell!" We have already seen that our Lord "knows" the churches, for he walks among them (Rev. 2:1). In this letter, however, Jesus declares that his knowledge extends not only to the works that Christians do (as in Ephesus) and to the suffering they endure (as in Smyrna) but also to the environment in which they live. "I know where you dwell." Jesus is fully aware of the pagan surroundings and pressures his people face. And that applies no less to you today than it did to the Christians in first-century Pergamum.

Whereas it is true that "the whole world lies in the power of the evil one" (1 John 5:19b), Pergamum was especially vulnerable to Satan's influence. In some sense, this was his city. Pergamum was the center of his authority, the place of his throne, the focal point of his activity and interests. There must have been an almost tangible sense of his presence, a heaviness in the air, an oppressive spiritual atmosphere that was unmistakable and inescapable.

There have been times and places when I was keenly aware of an extraordinary spiritual darkness, all physical evidence to the contrary. A city, for example, can be outwardly prosperous, socially vibrant, and culturally sophisticated while an underlying demonic energy animates and defiles its life and ethos. We shouldn't be surprised that our enemy might choose to concentrate his efforts in particular geographical areas or at unique and critical moments in history. It's all part of his strategy to undermine Christian faith and promote the kingdom of darkness.

Thyatira: The "Jezebel Spirit" and the Deep Things of Satan

Thyatira was the least known, least remarkable, and least important of the seven cities to receive a letter from the Lord (perhaps its only claim to fame was that Lydia had lived there; see Acts 16:11–15). But it is in this letter that we hear about what many now call "the Jezebel spirit" as well as what Jesus refers to as "the deep things of Satan."

After reading in Revelation 2:18–19 of the splendid spiritual qualities in Thyatira, it is genuinely tragic to discover that moral compromise was present in the church. "I have this against you," said Jesus, "that you tolerate that woman Jezebel, who calls herself a prophetess and is teaching and seducing my servants to practice sexual immorality and to eat food sacrificed to idols" (Rev. 2:20).

Who Was Jezebel?

Jezebel's identity is debated. Some have suggested that Jezebel is none other than Lydia herself (Acts 16:14), who, if it were true, had badly fallen from the initial spiritual heights we read about in Acts 16. However, there is nothing at all in the biblical text to suggest this identification. A few Greek manuscripts include the possessive pronoun "your" (Rev. 2:20), on the basis of which it is argued that Jezebel was the wife of the senior pastor in Thyatira. But even if the pronoun is original, it probably refers to the corporate church in Thyatira, since the preceding four uses of the singular "your" in Revelation 2:19–20 clearly do so. Jezebel may be a veiled reference to the pagan prophetess *Sibyl Sambathe*, for whom a shrine had been built just outside the walls of the city. This is doubtful for two reasons: first, she is spoken of in rather definite terms, implying that a distinct historical personality is in mind and not merely a shrine to a pagan goddess; and second, the text suggests that the individual was actually a member of the church (externally, at any rate) of Thyatira and under the jurisdiction and authority of its leaders.

The most likely interpretation is that, in view of the opportunity granted to her for repentance, Jezebel was a female member of the church who was promoting destructive heresies and leading many into moral compromise. She was a real person, but the name "Jezebel" is probably symbolic. Note the parallel in the letter to Pergamum in which the Nicolaitans are subsumed under the name of an Old Testament figure: Balaam. The name "Jezebel" had, in fact, become proverbial for wickedness. Thus, this disreputable, so-called "prophetess" was as wicked and dangerous an influence in Thyatira as "Jezebel" had been to Israel in the Old Testament.

Note also that she "calls herself a prophetess" (Rev. 2:20). I can't imagine Jesus using this language if her prophetic gift was of the Holy Spirit. Some contend she was a born-again believer who had simply gone astray, but I suggest that her behavior and beliefs are an indication that whatever claims she made to being saved and prophetically gifted were spurious. This isn't to say she didn't have a supernatural power, but such powers need not always be from God (see Matt. 7:21–23; Acts 16:16–18; 2 Thess. 2:9–10).

THE OLD TESTAMENT CONTEXT OF JEZEBEL

According to 1 Kings 16:31, Jezebel was the daughter of Ethbaal, king of the Sidonians, who married Ahab, king of Israel. Largely because of her influence in seeking to combine the worship of Yah-weh with the worship of Baal, it is said of her husband that he "did more to provoke the LORD, the God of Israel, to anger than all the kings of Israel who were before him" (1 Kings 16:33). Hardly an endearing legacy! Jezebel was responsible for the killing of Naboth and confiscation of his vineyard for her husband (1 Kings 21:1–16). She sought the death of all the prophets of Israel (1 Kings 18:4; 2 Kings 9) and even came close to killing Elijah (1 Kings 19:1–3). Her death came as a result of being thrown from a window where she was then trampled by a horse. When an attempt was made to recover her body for burial, it was discovered that the only thing left was her skull, her feet, and the palms of her hands. According to 2 Kings 9:36–37, dogs had eaten her flesh, in fulfillment of a prophetic word from Elijah:

> When they came back and told him, he said, "This is the word of the LORD, which he spoke by his servant Elijah the Tishbite, 'In the territory of Jezreel the dogs shall eat the flesh of Jezebel, and the corpse of Jezebel shall be as dung on the face of the field in the territory of Jezreel, so that no one can say, This is Jezebel.'"

Although the first Jezebel had been dead for over a thousand years, her "spirit" had found new life in this woman of Thyatira. She may even have been the leader or hostess of a house church in the city.

The complaint of the Lord lies in the unhealthy degree of toleration granted this woman. When it is said, "you tolerate that woman Jezebel," the implication is that the church in general did not accept her teaching nor adopt her lifestyle. But the subsequent mention of her "lovers" and children in verse 22 indicates that a number in the community did so. These would have formed a distinct group within the church, and the church as a whole was content for them to remain.

Whereas it is probable that one individual lady is in view, others have suggested that the reference to "the woman" and "her children" sounds strangely similar to the phrase "the elect lady and her children" in 2 John 1. In 2 John this refers to the church community as a whole and to the individuals who are each a part of it. Perhaps, then, "Jezebel" is not a single person but a collective reference to a *group* of false prophets and prophetesses in Thyatira. Whether one or many, the presence of such a corrosive and corrupting influence in the church, in *any* church, simply cannot be allowed.

Jezebel obviously presumed on God's grace and interpreted his longsuffering as approval or endorsement of her sinful ways, or at least his indifference toward her chosen paths. There may have been a definite time in the past when, through some means, whether a prophetic word or direct encounter or perhaps through John, he issued this woman a warning, no doubt repeatedly. Whatever the case, the culpability of the false prophetess is evident. She "refuses" to repent. She clearly knew what was at issue and chose voluntarily to remain in her sin.

Was Jezebel a Christian?

This raises an important theological and practical question: *Was Jezebel a Christian?* My earlier comments would indicate I believe her to be unsaved, and thus some may react in horror that I raise the possibility that she might be born again. On first glance, the nature of her sin and her refusal to repent point to an unregenerate heart. But there are other factors to be considered.

For example, her judgment is said to come in the form of personal sickness, disease, or physical affliction of some sort. Jesus says, "I will throw her onto a sickbed" (Rev 2:22), language that is reminiscent of the discipline imposed on the *Christians* at Corinth who had persistently abused the Eucharist (see 1 Cor. 11:30–32). And before we too quickly conclude that someone born again could not commit such sins as are described in this passage, we should note that she is specifically charged with "teaching and seducing *my servants* to practice sexual immorality and to eat food sacrificed to idols" (Rev 2:20, italics mine). Note: Those whom Jesus calls "my servants" are guilty of "sexual immorality" and eating "food sacrificed to idols."

Of those who participate with her in these sins, Jesus says, "I will strike her children dead" (v. 23). The text could literally be translated, "I will kill with death," a proverbial statement that means "to slay utterly." Although this sounds more severe than what we might call "divine discipline" of a wayward believer, is it so different from how God dealt with Ananias and Sapphira in Acts 5?

The fact that they are called her "children" does not mean they are the actual physical progeny of her many sexual infidelities. They are, rather, men and women in Thyatira who had so identified with her sin that they are best described as younger members of her family. In other words, "those who commit adultery with her" (Rev 2:22) and her "children" (v. 23) are the same people. This also raises the question of whether or not the "sexual immorality" in view is literal/physical or a metaphor of spiritual unfaithfulness and idolatry, perhaps especially manifest in unhealthy and illicit compromise with pagan culture.

The evidence is mixed. On the one hand, I can't dismiss the possibility that literal sexual promiscuity is involved. After all, it is rare for one to embrace idolatry without yielding to sexual temptation (see Rom. 1:18–32). So it may be a false dichotomy to insist that she be guilty of *either* sexual immorality *or* religious idolatry. They seem so often (always?) to go hand in hand. On the other hand, since there were surely at least some female followers of Jezebel, the "adultery" they are said to have committed "with her" would likely, at least in their case, be metaphorical for spiritual infidelity.

Jesus says they must repent of "her" works—since they have joined "with her" in this sin, to repent of what she did is to repent of what they, too, did. If they do not, Jesus will "throw" them "into great tribulation." The precise nature of this "tribulation" is not specified, but it would surely involve, at minimum, physical illness that in the absence of repentance would culminate in physical death.

So, was Jezebel a true Christian or not? I think the answer is no, she was not.

First, the fact that she is designated by a name that is linked historically to a woman of almost unimaginable wickedness and perversity suggests that she, too, is utterly unregenerate and devoid of spiritual life. Second, having said that, I must also say, reluctantly, that Christians *can* fall into grievous and horrific sin. As noted, Jesus here says that his "servants" have joined with Jezebel in her works. The divine response of our heavenly Father to his backslidden children isn't eternal judgment but firm and loving discipline (see especially Hebrews 12). If that discipline is not met with heartfelt repentance, it may well lead to physical (not spiritual) death. This was certainly the case with Ananias and Sapphira (Acts 5) as well as the believers in Corinth. It would appear also to be the case with some of those in the church at Thyatira.

These are difficult matters that cannot be ignored, treated casually, or dismissed with cavalier dogmatism. Having said that, I am confident of two things. First, our Lord *will* deal with unrepentant sin. He himself declares in Revelation 2:23, "I will give to each of you according to your works." It may not happen immediately (longsuffering as he is), but in the absence of heartfelt conviction and repentance, it will most assuredly happen. Second, although we may not have the discernment to know infallibly who is and is not saved, "the Lord knows those who are his" (2 Tim. 2:19).

How Did She Act?

How is it that this woman called "Jezebel" came to exert such incredible power over the lives of Christians in Thyatira? What accounts for the authority she possessed to convince the followers of Jesus to abandon their commitment to ethical purity and engage in sexual immorality and other forms of compromise with the surrounding culture? There's no indication that she held an ecclesiastical office. She wasn't an elder or pastor or apostle. But she did claim to possess the gift of prophecy. Jesus said she "*calls* herself a prophetess" (Rev 2:20, italics mine).

Is Jesus suggesting she only claimed to have this gift but in fact did not? Or did she have a genuine spiritual gift but abused it in ways inconsistent with New Testament guidelines on how it was to be exercised? If Jezebel was *not* a Christian, as I have argued, it is most likely that she exercised a supernatural "prophetic-like" ability that was energized by demonic power rather than the Spirit of God. That this was (and is) distinctly possible is evident from Matthew 7:21–23 and Acts 16:16–18 (and perhaps 2 Thess. 2:9–10).

I want to suggest that it was possibly (probably?) through this alleged "prophetic" ability that Jezebel gained power and authority in the church at Thyatira and adversely influenced a number of Christians there. It's not difficult to see how this could (and does) occur.

The Jezebel Spirit

A brief word is in order about my use of the phrase "*spirit*" of Jezebel or "Jezebel spirit," language that, although not strictly biblical, has been bandied about in charismatic circles for generations, but perhaps is not as familiar to those in mainstream evangelicalism. I've read numerous articles, books, and listened to an equal number of sermons on the so-called "Jezebel spirit." To be honest, I haven't found them very helpful. In most cases they are speculative meanderings that show little concern for the biblical text.

Let me be brief and simply say that the word "spirit" is used here in one of two ways: either (a) of the *human* spirit, perhaps an attitude, disposition, habit, or set of characteristics displayed by a particular individual, or (b) of those whose supernatural "prophetic" ability is energized by a *demonic* spirit. In either case, regardless of the animating force, a person with a "Jezebel spirit" is one who displays the insidious, manipulative, and evil tendencies manifest in this woman of Thyatira.[4]

So what kind of person do I have in mind, and what is it that they do? All too often we hear of individuals using their authority or position in the local church as well as their supernatural gifting (whether it be of God or the enemy) to manipulate others into behavior they would not normally embrace. I'm burdened by the number of instances in which even Christians who are prophetically gifted use their endowment to expand their sphere of influence for personal profit or are afforded unwarranted privileges in the local church.

Virtually everyone is aware of some situation in which a Christian has used a spiritual gift, whether teaching, administration, pastoring, or another of the *charismata* to gain illicit control and influence within the wider body of Christ. So it should come as no surprise that someone who legitimately possesses the gift of prophecy might abuse it to enhance their status or broaden their liberties or even seek monetary gain.

The most heinous abuse of a "prophetic" gift is when appeal is made to special "revelatory" insights in order to justify immorality (or, at minimum, to ignore it). Similarly, because of the "wonderful contribution" that a person has made to the kingdom, he or she is virtually untouchable and rarely held accountable to the normal rules of ethical behavior that govern all other Christians. Anyone who "hears" God with such regularity and alleged accuracy, so they contend, is unique, extraordinarily anointed, and therefore so highly favored of God that they needn't worry about the temptations that

---

4   The use of the word "spirit" in Scripture is diverse. For example, we did not receive from God a "spirit of slavery to fall back into fear" (Rom. 8:15). The woman in Luke 13 suffered from "a disabling spirit" (literally, "a spirit of weakness" or "infirmity"; obviously a demon that had caused her illness). We also read of "the spirit of jealousy" (Num. 5:14), "a spirit of skill" (Exod. 28:3), "the spirit of wisdom" (Deut. 34:9), "a spirit of confusion" (Isa. 19:14), "a spirit of gentleness" (1 Cor. 4:21), and "the S/spirit of wisdom and revelation" (Eph. 1:17; most likely the Holy Spirit). Clearly, then, on occasion, a demonic being is in view, while in other texts it can refer to an attitude, a principle, an emotional state of being, the third person of the Godhead, and in most instances the spirit of a human being.

average Christians face or the tendencies of the flesh against which we typically wage war on a daily basis.

On occasion, a person with a Jezebel spirit will claim to have "revelation" that trumps Scripture (although they would rarely, if ever, put it in such stark terms; a person with this "spirit" is subtle, if nothing else). Because such "words" from God are direct, immediate, and can't be explained by appeal to what one knows by natural means, they are falsely perceived as carrying greater authority than the inspired text itself. Or it is "revelation" that allegedly provides a superior and formerly unknown interpretation of Scripture that makes it possible to circumvent (or at least treat with casual disdain) the Bible's doctrinal precepts and ethical commands.

A person with a "Jezebel spirit" is one who appeals to his or her "spirituality" or spiritual gifting to rationalize (or again, at minimum, to overlook) sensuality. Often they don't even believe it to be sinful or illicit, but are so blinded by pride, the praise of men, and sensational supernatural experiences that what may well be inappropriate for mainstream believers is, in their case, permissible. It's just one of the perks.

Religious prestige is thus employed to foster sexual liberty. Under the pretense of anointed "ministry," a person exploits his or her platform and power to gain sexual favors or to lead others into similar behavior. This person is generally unaccountable to the leadership of the church, believing that the pastor and elders are "un-anointed" or insufficiently gifted to appreciate the level of supernatural spirituality at which he or she operates on a daily basis. Eventually a double standard emerges: one set of strict, biblical guidelines to govern ordinary Christians and the exercise of their gifts within the body, and a lax, minimal, or more flexible list of expectations by which the "Man/Woman of God" is to live. Needless to say, it's a prescription for moral disaster.

Make no mistake, the Jezebel who lived in Thyatira undoubtedly appealed to her prophetic gift (and "anointing") to excuse her sexual immorality. She was using her power to manipulate others into sensuality and idolatry. You may wonder why anyone would yield to such obvious unbiblical counsel, no matter how "gifted" the individual might be. It's not that difficult to understand. Some of you may be unaware of how mesmerizing and enticing the prospect of supernatural activity can be. When one witnesses what one believes is a genuine supernatural or miraculous event, otherwise normal theological defense mechanisms often fail to operate. Discernment is cast aside, lest it be viewed as a critical spirit or the response of a cynic. No one wants to be perceived as stiff-necked and resistant to the voice of God or the manifestation of his power. So, it is hard for some to resist and challenge the "ministry" of a recognized (or "alleged") prophet in the church.

The spirit of Jezebel was not unique to the church in Thyatira. It is alive and well in the body of Christ today. One need only read the latest headlines. It is an insidious, yet subtle, spirit. It is destructive yet enticing. It typically gains momentum among those who are so fearful of quenching the Spirit (1 Thess. 5:19) that they fail to rein in the flesh.

The solution is not to repudiate the prophetic altogether, or any other spiritual gift, for that matter. Rather, we must become good Bereans, "examining the Scriptures daily" (Acts 17:11) to see if these things are of God or not. In sum, we would do well to heed Paul's counsel: "Do not despise prophecies, but test everything; hold fast what is good. Abstain from every form of evil" (1 Thess. 5:20–22).

The Deep Things of Satan

In the midst of this horrific situation, Jesus commends those in Thyatira "who have not learned what some call the deep things of Satan" (Rev. 2:24). This intriguing phrase calls for explanation. Some believe it to be a sarcastic reversal of the claims of Jezebel and "her children." They claim to know "deep [spiritual] things" when in fact what they know comes from and concerns the devil himself. In other words, the phrase "of Satan" is a sarcastic addition by Jesus designed to tell the faithful in Thyatira the true nature of their ideas and experience. Those of Jezebel may actually have used the words "of God," which Jesus deliberately alters to make the point.

Others suggest that the "deep things of Satan" is a reference to their insistence that in order to appreciate fully the depths of grace and of God (cf. 1 Cor. 2:10) one must first plumb the depths of evil and the enemy. They would claim that, because of their spiritual maturity and superiority, they need fear nothing from the devil. In any case, it's stunning to realize that people who profess to know Christ and attain to positions of authority and influence in the church can be proponents of satanic doctrine and practitioners of ethical compromise. What we desperately need today, as they did then, is an increase of (back)bone density, a strengthening of resolve to hold fast the line of orthodoxy, and a courageous commitment to that holiness of life that will assuredly evoke disdainful accusations of being narrow-minded and puritanical.

LINDA'S STORY

Knowing that the Lord speaks to me and knowing *how* he speaks is intricately tied into my deliverance. I was having persistent, almost daily, migraines. I knew it was from anxiety; I had been diagnosed with general anxiety disorder after two panic attacks. I had to limit how much I was around people because my jaw would grow so tense that I couldn't speak well. Torturous and suicidal pictures flashed through my mind and would leave me drained, depressed, and relationally distant. I began to believe the lie that I was my own worst enemy. One day a mentor was praying for me and said, "You have very vivid pictures. I think this is the Lord speaking to you, and you should pay attention to them and pray about them." I looked at her dumbfounded. That began a whirlwind of beautiful, intense healing.

Dialoguing with the Lord about the pictures led to great freedom and increased ability to pray effectively. One day I had a picture of layers of wispy, transparent fabric settling over me. Attached to the fabric were thin, fiberglass-like spears. As the layers settled on top of each other, the pain from the shards became acute, and my ability to see became greatly obscured. The day I received this picture was life changing because I understood the nature of the attack against me. I began to ask the Lord to show me the different layers burdening me, and he did. As he revealed them, he showed me how to pray about or respond to each one.

Soon afterward, I heard him say, "Your muscles have been dancing to the tune of the tormentors. I'm going to train them to rest and dance to the sweet melody of the Spirit's voice." Additional understanding came. It had been unclear to me why my quiet times were fraught with anxiety. Praying or reading the Bible seemed to increase my apprehension, confusion, and doubt. This made no sense to me whatsoever! It did not fit into the paradigm of ANY Bible teaching I had learned.

A numbing reprieve would come when I watched TV or listened to books;

I became spiritually anemic. With my new confidence in the Holy Spirit's willingness and ability to make things clear, I asked him about it. He gave me the following picture. I'm in a dark room alone. In the corner there is a TV. Vulture type birds swoop down upon me and harass me. When I begin watching the TV, the creatures fly to their perches on the wall and leave me alone. From this picture I saw what was happening spiritually. Satan was not threatened when I watched TV. However, when I began to pray or read Scripture, he went on full attack. Though I was submitting to God daily, I was not resisting the devil because I didn't know I was under assault.

My prayers turned from machine-gun shots of confession/petition/thanksgiving/praise to elongated discourses with the Healer. When anxiety would descend, I would ask the Spirit to guide me, take authority in Christ and rebuke the evil behind it. Many times, he gave me beautiful pictures to replace the anxious thoughts. Also, there were significant times when I would rebuke specific evil spirits and then feel my muscles liquify. This was no mental placebo. I had tried multiple techniques through the years to force my muscles to relax. I was shocked to see him untangle the mess in my mind. I had spent years trying to figure it out, and through his Spirit, he made it make sense. He showed me how to pray, led me to specific Scriptures and uncovered the evil. The migraines quit. I no longer needed my prescribed antidepressant. I began praying with people, and the Lord led me to begin a prayer group that meets weekly. It's all him. He sustains me, and under his banner I walk.

CHAPTER 6

The Demonic in the History of the Church: Part Two

There's been a persistent trend to downplay how actively present Satan and his demons are throughout the entire course of the church age in which we live. Some try to diminish the extent to which our invisible enemies are launching their attacks. But as we saw in the seven letters to the churches of Asia Minor (Revelation 2–3) and as we will now observe in the description of church history leading up to the Second Coming of Jesus, Satan and his hordes, if anything, have expanded their nefarious attempts to destroy mankind and the church in particular.

In the book of Revelation, the apostle John repeatedly describes the commonplaces of church history spanning the time between the two comings of Christ. By "commonplaces" I mean the conditions, circumstances, situations, and environments in which people find themselves between the two comings of Christ. As he finishes one section, concluding with the Second Coming of Christ and the end of history, he circles back around to start all over again at the start of the game. Once he concludes yet another journey, he circles back around and recapitulates the same period of time from yet another vantage point.

The Fifth Trumpet Judgment of Revelation 9:1–11

It is with the fifth trumpet judgment in Revelation 9:1–11 that we encounter a massive display of demonic activity in the earth. There is no mistaking that the locusts released from the abyss or the bottomless pit are demonic spirits whose purpose is to torment and destroy the lives of unbelieving men and women. We know this because they come out of the "bottomless pit" or "abyss" (vv. 1–3).

The Greek word translated "bottomless pit" or "abyss" (*abyssos*) is used nine times in the New Testament, seven of which are in Revelation (9:1, 2, 11; 11:7; 17:8; 20:1, 3). The word literally means "without depth," boundless, or bottomless. Here the shaft of the abyss is portrayed as blocked by a door to which God alone has the key. The demons whom Jesus expelled entreated him "not to command them to depart into the abyss" (Luke 8:31). Here in Revelation 9 the bottomless pit appears to be the abode of the demonic hosts. The idea of a "pit" with a "shaft" that is "opened" or "locked shut" ("sealed") by a "key" held by an angel is obviously figurative language.

The "angel of the bottomless pit [abyss]" in verse 11, that being who exercises authority over the demonic hordes dwelling there (he is called their "king"), the one called "Abaddon" and "Apollyon," is certainly evil and is most likely Satan himself. As disturbing as this portrayal of demonic activity may be, and as much as you may be inclined to look away and ignore it, please don't. John's vision is designed to let us see beyond the material realm to the spiritual dynamics that alone make sense of what is happening in our society.

"Smoke" emerges from the abyss when it is opened so that the sun and air are darkened by it (cf. Joel 2:10, 31; 3:15; also Exod. 10:15—in these texts such darkening is a sign of judgment). Smoke here likely points us to the deception and moral darkness in which most of our world is languishing. Demonic beings are here portrayed as "locusts" to whom "authority" or "power" "was given." This use of the passive voice is typical both in Revelation and in the rest of the New Testament. We see it again in Revelation 9:4 ("they were told") and in verse 5 ("they were allowed"). These verbs in the passive voice point to divine activity. In other words, it is God (or the risen Christ) who has commissioned and authorized them. This authority is likened to that possessed by "scorpions." People greatly fear scorpions because of their venomous sting, which is extremely painful and sometimes lethal.

The literal plague of locusts in Exodus 10:12–15 (the eighth of ten) also brought darkness on the land. There we read that "they ate all the plants in the land and all the fruit of the trees that the hail had left. Not a green thing remained, neither tree nor plant of the field, through all the land of Egypt" (v. 15; see Deut. 28:38; 1 Kings 8:37; 2 Chron. 6:28; 7:13; Ps. 78:46; 105:34–35; Joel 1:4; 2:25; Amos 4:9; 7:1–2; Nah. 3:15). But here the locusts are commanded not to harm the "grass . . . or any green plant or any tree" (Rev. 9:4). They are commanded only to hurt unbelievers—those who don't have the seal of God by which one might be protected from such a plague. This is an encouraging reminder that God has taken steps to protect his people against the devastating impact of these plagues, be they literal or symbolic. God's people will never, ever suffer God's wrath! This also proves yet again that the 144,000 in Revelation 7 and 14 who are "sealed" on their foreheads must refer to all God's people, Jewish believers in Jesus and Gentile believers in Jesus. It would be wholly inconsistent with the character of God that he would protect only 144,000 Jewish believers from this horrid demonic attack and leave all the millions of other believers in Jesus to suffer this torment.

There is an additional two-fold limitation on their activity. First, they are not allowed to kill anyone (in contrast with Rev. 9:15–20), but only to "torment" them (which sounds similar to what God allowed Satan to do to Job). Second, the torment will last for only "five months." Some take this literally but have no explanation for why such an odd number should be chosen. More likely the five months alludes to the five-month life cycle of the locust. Or "five" may simply be a round number meaning "a few." We can't be certain.

The "torment" they inflict is likened to that of a scorpion when it stings a man. Scorpions are a metaphor for punishment in 1 Kings 12:11, 14. The word "torment" is used in Revelation for spiritual, emotional, or psychological pain (see 11:10; and perhaps 18:7, 10, 15). It comes as no surprise that John describes the suffering inflicted by demons as like that inflicted by scorpions, given the fact that Jesus himself referred to demons as "scorpions" (and "serpents") in Luke 10:19.

The anguish of those tormented by the demonic hordes is any form of psychological or emotional suffering (physical too?) that provoked in them a desire for death. Yet they are unwilling actually to commit suicide, for surely if someone truly wants to die, they can find the means to end their life. John appears to be describing that emotional and psychological depression, frustration, anger, bitterness, and sense of futility and meaninglessness and lack of value that drives people to the point of utter despair. They prefer death to life but lack the courage to take their own lives, perhaps for fear of the unknown beyond the grave. All of this, says John, is the result of demonic activity (cf. Heb. 2:14–15), like unto that of a plague of locusts unleashed into the earth!

Perhaps John is describing the horrid realization in the human heart that one's belief system is false, that one's philosophy is vain, that one's values are empty, that one's destiny is bleak, and thus that one lacks purpose in living, that one is thus helpless and hopeless. Contrast this with the "peace of God, which surpasses all understanding" (Phil. 4:7) granted unto believers who bring their burdens and anxieties to God in prayer.

People without Jesus are desperate to find meaning and dignity and happiness in any number of ways: complex philosophies, self-indulgent hedonism, the New Age movement with its endless remedies for what ails the human soul, reincarnation, radical feminism, political agendas, homosexuality, drugs, sexual immorality, materialism, self-ism, etc. Demonic "locusts" lead them into such pursuits, all of which are, at the end of the day, empty and lifeless.

The description of these demonic spirits (Rev. 9:7–11) reflects what we see in Joel 1–2 where a plague of locusts devastates Israel's land. There, as here, a trumpet is sounded to herald their arrival (Joel 2:1, 15). There, as here, the locusts are said to have "the appearance of horses" (Joel 2:4) prepared for battle. This judgment in Joel is itself based on the plague of locusts in Exodus 10. However, whereas the locusts in Exodus were literal (though they certainly symbolized something beyond themselves), and perhaps also in Joel (although there it may be a literal army that is compared to a swarm of locusts), here in Revelation they symbolize demonic spirits unleashed throughout the earth.

Let's take each element one at a time:

- Their appearance was "like horses prepared for battle" (Rev. 9:7; cf. Jer. 51:27).
- On their "heads were what looked like crowns of gold" (Rev. 9:7), a likely reference to their sovereign authority to afflict the non-Christian world.
- "Their faces were like human faces" (9:7), perhaps pointing to their intelligence.
- They had hair like "women's hair" (9:8). In the Old Testament, long and disheveled hair had at least three meanings: (1) it was a sign of uncleanness for people with leprosy (Lev. 13:45); (2) it was a sign of mourning (Lev. 10:6; 21:10); and (3) it was part of the sacrificial protocol for a woman accused of adultery (Num. 5:18).
- Their teeth were like "lions' teeth" (Rev. 9:8). The "teeth of a lion" is a

proverbial expression for something irresistibly and fatally destructive (cf. Job 4:10; Ps. 58:6).

- They had "breastplates like breastplates of iron" (Rev. 9:9), pointing to their invulnerability.
- The sound of their wings "was like the noise of many chariots, with horses rushing into battle" (9:9). This is strikingly similar to Joel 2:4–5.
- They have "tails and stings like scorpions" (Rev. 9:10), a vivid way to portray the torment they inflict on the souls of mankind.
- "They have as king over them the angel of the bottomless pit [abyss]" (9:11). This is either the devil himself or his representative.

As we look across the vast expanse of human history since the first coming of Christ, and in anticipation of his second coming, we see the concrete and all-too-real effects of God's wrath against human sin, idolatry, immorality, and unbelief: widespread famine, devastating tornadoes, floods, infectious diseases, war, psychological and emotional torment, pollution of our natural resources, and the list could go on seemingly without end. And to what purpose? To warn mankind that God will not ignore the defilement of his glory or the calloused disregard for his mercy and longsuffering.

Yet in the midst of this earthly carnage and demonic assault, God's children are kept safe and secure, having been "sealed" by the indwelling presence of the Holy Spirit. We may well suffer at the hands of the unbelieving world. Persecution, slander, imprisonment, even martyrdom may come our way. But we will never endure the wrath of God, for Jesus has satisfied God's justice in our place on the cross.

THE PURPOSE OF THE COMING OF THE SON OF GOD

Let's reexamine 1 John 3:8: "The reason the Son of God appeared was to destroy the works of the devil."

Yes, Jesus came to live a sinless life, the life that you and I should have lived but are unable to do so perfectly. But in order to live this sinless life, Jesus had to successfully resist the temptation of Satan and defeat the enemy's efforts to undermine that obedience. Yes,

Jesus came "to take away sins" (1 John 3:5) and did so by dying in our place on the cross. But it was by means of the cross, as Paul says in Colossians 2:15, that Jesus "disarmed the rulers and authorities [Satan and his demons] and put them to open shame, by triumphing over them in him [or better still, in or through "it," that is, through the cross]." And, of course, it was by rising again from the dead that Jesus overcame and defeated the power of death and guaranteed for us that we too will one day be raised to an entirely new life in a new and glorified body. The author of Hebrews tells us that by dying and rising again, Jesus destroyed the one who has the power of death, that is, the devil, and delivered all those who through fear of death were subject to lifelong slavery (Heb. 2:14–15).

So I hope you can now see that God the Father sent God the Son in the power of God the Spirit to defeat and overthrow and ultimately destroy Satan and all his works. And that, I suggest, is also the primary emphasis or theme of the book of Revelation. And nowhere do we see this with greater clarity in Revelation than here in Revelation 9:13–19. So let's turn our attention to John's vision of the sixth and seventh trumpet judgments, for in them we find a graphic and highly symbolic description of the activity of Satan in the earth and the ultimate triumph of Jesus Christ and his kingdom.

The Sixth Trumpet Judgment of Revelation 9:13–21

We read in Revelation 9:14 that "four angels" have been bound (*deō*; cf. 20:2) "at the great river Euphrates," apparently restrained against their will. This would strongly suggest that these "four angels" are demons (cf. 9:1–3). It may be that what we read here is a rescinding of the command given back in 7:1–3 where "four angels standing at the four corners of the earth" were restrained from doing damage in the earth until the people of God had been sealed and made secure in their relationship with God.

In the time of John's writing, the Euphrates was the eastern border of the Roman Empire, beyond which were terrifying and greatly feared horsemen of the Parthian Empire. But the Jewish people viewed the Euphrates as the northern frontier of Palestine, across which "Assyrian, Babylonian, and Persian invaders had come to impose their pagan sovereignty on the people of God. All the scriptural warnings about a foe from the north, therefore, find their echo in John's blood-curdling vision."[1]

These demonic invaders are coming at God's appointed time: They had been "prepared for the hour, the day, the month, and the year." This clearly reminds us that contrary to what some may think, and contrary to all appearances, *God is in complete control not only of what Satan and demons are allowed to do but also the precise time when they have been ordained by God to do it.* Their aim is to kill a third of mankind. Is this numerically literal, such that precisely 33.3 percent of humanity are killed? Or is it John's way of describing a preliminary, partial judgment that will only later, at the end of history, reach its consummation? I think it is the latter.

A Massive Demonic Army Unleashed

Although it isn't explicitly stated, it appears from verses 16–19 that these four "angels" have power over a massive demonic army of horsemen. The number of mounted troops is "twice ten thousand times ten thousand" or 200,000,000 (in all likelihood, symbolic of an incalculable number, an innumerable, indefinite group; see Gen. 24:60; Lev. 26:8; Num. 10:35–36; Deut. 32:30; 33:2, 17; Dan. 7:10). It seems clear from what we saw in Revelation 9:1–11 and from the description of these horsemen that we are dealing with a symbolic portrayal of demonic hosts, not human soldiers.

Again, let's take each descriptive item in turn. In doing so, however, we must be careful not to let our concern for the particular elements of their makeup obscure the overall visceral impact that John intends. In other words, John's point in piling up these monstrous metaphors is to underscore "that the demons are ferocious and dreadful beings that afflict people in a fierce, appalling, and devastating manner."[2]

---

1 G. B. Caird, *The Revelation of St. John the Divine* (New York: Harper & Row Publishers, 1966), 122. On this, see especially Isaiah 5:26–29; 7:20; 8:7–8; 14:29–31; Jeremiah 1:14–15; 4:6–13; 6:1, 22–23; 10:22; 13:20; Ezekiel 38:6, 15; 39:2; Joel 2:1–11, 20–25; as well as Isaiah 14:31; Jeremiah 25:9, 26; 46–47; 46:4, 22–23; 50:41–42; Ezekiel 26:7–11.

2 G. K. Beale, *The Book of Revelation: A Commentary on the Greek Text* (Grand Rapids: Eerdmans, 1999), 510.

- The riders of the horses (and perhaps the horses themselves) had "breastplates the color of fire and of sapphire (or hyacinth) and of sulfur" (9:17).
- The heads of the horses "were like lions' heads" (9:17). Again, this points to their fierceness.
- Out of the mouths of the horses came "fire and smoke and sulfur" (9:17). Elsewhere in Revelation "fire and brimstone" or "fire and sulfur" are descriptive of scenes of the final judgment of unbelievers (14:10; 21:8) and of the dragon, the beast, and the false prophet (19:20; 20:10). See also "fire, sulfur, smoke" in several Old Testament texts relating to judgment (Gen. 19:24, 28; Deut. 29:23; 2 Sam. 22:9; Isa. 34:9–10; Ezek. 38:22).
- In verse 19 the power of the horses is said to be in their tails, "for their tails are like serpents with heads." John likens their tails to serpents, the heads of which are the source of the harm inflicted. That these are demonic armies is thus confirmed, for elsewhere in Revelation the "serpent" (*ophis*) is always a reference to Satan (12:9, 14–15; 20:2). This reference to the serpent-like tail of the horses may specifically allude to their deception of unbelievers, for "the sweeping of the Serpent's 'tail' [in Rev. 12] is symbolic of his [Satan's] deception of the angels whom he caused to fall."[3]

Again, the four angels who were bound at the river Euphrates, who are then released, employ this massive demonic army to kill one-third of mankind (9:15), utilizing the "fire and smoke and sulfur" that proceeded out of their mouths (9:18). The similarities with the destruction of Sodom and Gomorrah are obvious (Gen. 19:24, 28). Note that these three elements are now called "three plagues" (Rev. 9:18).

Whereas the demons, portrayed as locusts, in Revelation 9:5 were not permitted to kill anyone, but only to torment, this demonic army from beyond the Euphrates *is* permitted to kill. Is this a literal, physical termination of human life, or is it figurative for spiritual or emotional or psychological "death"? The verb translated "kill" (*apokteinō*) generally refers to literal physical death in Revelation. That would seem to be confirmed by

---

3   Beale, *Revelation*, 514.

verse 20 ("the rest . . . who were not killed"). If that is the meaning here, John envisions this demonic host (under and subordinate to God's sovereignty) killing a sizeable number of earth dwellers (unbelievers), whether through illness (perhaps outbreaks of infectious diseases), accident, natural disaster, famine, suicide, etc.

In verse 19 these demonic horses/horsemen are said to "wound" or to do "harm" (*adikeō*), the same Greek word used in 9:3–4, 10 where demonic "locusts" torment, but do not kill, those who lack the seal of God (cf. also its use in 2:11; 7:3). Perhaps, then, the "wound/harm" here (v. 19) is not physical death but a variety of forms of spiritual and psychological torment and emotional anguish short of, but a prelude to, death itself.

Verse 20 does not explicitly say that the purpose of the demonic plagues was to induce or stir up repentance. Certainly such plagues serve as a warning, but one that goes unheeded. This highlights the hardness of heart of those who lack the seal of God on their foreheads. Michael Wilcock adds this insightful comment:

> The death-dealing horsemen of Trumpet 6 are not tanks and planes. Or not only tanks and planes. They are also cancers and road accidents and malnutrition and terrorist bombs and peaceful demises in nursing homes. Yet "the rest of mankind, who were not killed by these plagues," still do not repent of their idolatry, the centering of their lives on anything rather than God, or of the evils which inevitably flow from it. They hear of pollution, of inflation, of dwindling resources, of blind politicians, and will not admit that the first four Trumpets of God are sounding. In the end they themselves are affected by these troubles, and for one reason or another life becomes a torment: the locusts are out, Trumpet 5 is sounding, but they will not repent. Not even when the angels of the Euphrates rise to the summons of Trumpet 6, and the cavalry rides out to slay—by any kind of destruction, not necessarily war—a friend or a relative, a husband or a wife: not even in bereavement will they repent.[4]

Here we have a typical Old Testament list of idols according to their

---

4   Michael Wilcock, *The Message of Revelation: I Saw Heaven Opened* (Downers Grove, IL: InterVarsity Press, 1975), 99–100.

material composition: gold, silver, bronze, stone, and wood (see Dan. 5:4, 23; Ps. 115:4–7; 135:15–17; Deut. 4:28). John portrays the worship of idols, in whatever form that idolatry might take, as the "worship" of "demons." We should probably translate Revelation 9:20 "so as not to worship demons, that is, the idols . . ." On this he agrees with Paul (1 Cor. 10:20) as well as several Old Testament texts (Deut. 32:17; Ps. 96:5; 106:36–37), that all idolatry, whatever form it may assume, is ultimately energized by and representative of demonic activity. In Revelation 9:21 they are described as not repenting of yet additional sins, a list obviously derived from the Ten Commandments. These particular vices—murder, sorcery, sexual immorality, and theft—are often associated with idol worship in both the Old Testament and New Testament (Jer. 7:5–11; Hos. 3:1–4:2; Isa. 47:9–10; 48:5; Mic. 5:12–6:8; Rom. 1:24–29; Gal. 5:20; Eph. 5:5; Col. 3:5).

Revelation 12

Revelation 12 describes believers' triumph over Satan—but it also describes Satan's efforts to destroy the church. Here, we'll focus on the latter.

In Revelation 12:1–6 we read in highly symbolic language of Satan's attempt to kill the infant Jesus: "And the dragon stood before the woman who was about to give birth, so that when she bore her child he might devour it" (v. 4). Satan's tool for this task was, of course, the effort of King Herod to kill the Christ child by having every male two years old and under in Bethlehem killed (Matt. 2:16–18).

Satan's design for destroying the church takes the form of severe persecution and, on occasion, outright martyrdom. This was the point of Revelation 12:4, where he "swept down a third of the stars of heaven and cast them to the earth." Satan's attempt to bring down the church typically takes the form of launching against its members accusations of guilt (v. 10). But by virtue of the life, death, resurrection, and current intercessory ministry of Jesus at the right hand of the Father (see Rom. 8:31–34; 1 John 2:1–2), all such accusations fall flat and carry no weight in the courtroom of heaven.

Satan turns his attention to persecuting "the woman," the church, the bride of Christ (Rev. 12:13), and seeks "to make war on the rest of her offspring" (v. 17). We know this is a reference to Christians, as John further identifies them as "those who keep the commandments of God and hold to the testimony of Jesus" (v. 17). In this one verse we find the most precise and riveting explanation for virtually everything we see in our world today, whether that be the rise of militant Islamic fundamentalism, the angry atheism that has erupted in recent years, global persecution of the Church of Jesus Christ, rampant sexual immorality, and oppressive laws that seek to restrict what Christians can say and do, just to mention a few.

But we cannot stop with the final verse of chapter twelve. Look at its relationship to the first verse of chapter thirteen. We read that Satan "stood on the sand of the sea" (Rev. 12:17b). What an odd way to conclude a chapter! Odd indeed, until you realize what happens in Revelation 13:1–18. Satan stands on the shore in order that he might beckon forth from the sea the "beast" with "ten horns and seven heads, with ten diadems on its horns and blasphemous names on its heads" (13:1).

The Beast and the False Prophet: Satan's Henchmen

Who or what is this "beast" and what relevance does it have for us today? Many mistakenly think that the "beast" is *only* the end-time antichrist. He is surely that. But he is more. When you read the description of the beast in Revelation 13:2 and following, you discover that John has taken the four world kingdoms described in Daniel 7 and combined them in one composite figure: the beast from the sea. Now, this book is not an extended commentary on Revelation, so I must restrict my comments to the role that Satan and his demons play in the emergence of both the beast and the false prophet.

To put it simply, the beast is a symbol for the very real system of satanically inspired evil, and thus opposition to the kingdom of God, that throughout history has manifested itself in a variety of forms, whether political, economic, military, social, philosophical, or religious. Anything and anyone that seeks to oppress, persecute, or destroy the Church is the beast! What I'm saying, then, is that although the beast is very much involved in earthly events, the beast is also a transcultural, transtemporal symbol for all individual and collective satanically inspired opposition to Jesus and his people. It is anything and everything (whether a principle, a person, or a power) utilized by the enemy to deceive and destroy the influence and advance of the kingdom of God.

Thus, the beast at the time when John wrote Revelation was the Roman Empire. At another time, the beast was the Arian heresy in the fourth century that denied the deity of Jesus Christ. The beast is, at one time, the emperor Decius (a third-century persecutor of the church); at another, evolutionary Darwinism. The beast is the late medieval Roman Catholic papacy, modern Protestant liberalism, Marxism, the radical feminist movement, the Pelagian heresy of the fifth century, communism, Joseph Stalin, the seventeenth-century Enlightenment, eighteenth-century deism, *Roe v. Wade*, the state persecution of Christians in China and North Korea, militant atheism in the twenty-first century, and ISIS.

Each of these is, individually and on its own, the beast. All of these are, collectively and in unity, the beast. Will there also be a single *person* at the end of the age who embodies in consummate form all the characteristics of the many previous historical manifestations of the beast? If so, should we call this person the antichrist? Probably.

Therefore, I believe that Revelation 13:1–18 is temporally parallel with Revelation 12:6, 13–17 and explains in more detail the precise nature and extent of the dragon's (Satan's) persecution of the people of God. In fact, Revelation 13 describes the earthly governmental, political, economic, as well as individual, powers of the earth through whom Satan works. Though Satan has been defeated (12:7–12), he can still oppress the saints (12:12). And the primary way in which he exerts this nefarious influence and wages war against the seed of the woman (12:17) is through the activities and oppression of the beast. Here John narrates his vision of the dragon standing on the seashore, calling forth his agents through whom he will carry out his persecution of the people of God. The "war" the dragon is said to wage with the church (Rev. 12:17) is actually undertaken by his servants as portrayed in chapter 13. Note carefully how this is stated in verse 2b:

> And to it [that is, to the beast rising out of the sea] the dragon [Satan] gave his power and his throne and great authority.

Satan's Efforts to Undermine Belief in the Incarnation of the Son of God

Interestingly, the only place in the New Testament where the word "antichrist" appears is in the Johannine Epistles (1, 2, 3 John), not in Revelation. Nowhere in Revelation is the "beast" ever called "antichrist." In his first epistle, John emphatically states that we may know this is the last hour because of the existence and activity of many antichrists. He says: "Children, it is the last hour; and as you have heard that antichrist is coming, so now many antichrists have come. Therefore, we know that it is the last hour" (1 John 2:18). Note well that the entire period between the first and second comings of Jesus are the "last days." See Acts 2:17; 2 Timothy 3:1; Hebrews 1:2; 1 Peter 1:20 (cf. 1 Cor. 10:11).

Later, in 1 John 2:22, he writes: "Who is the liar but he who denies that Jesus is the Christ? This is the antichrist, he who denies the Father and the Son." The spirit of the antichrist, says John, is found in anyone who denies that Jesus is God come in the flesh (1 John 4:3). Again, in 2 John 7, he writes: "For many deceivers have gone out into the world, those who do not confess the coming of Jesus Christ in the flesh. Such a one is the deceiver and the antichrist." Thus, for John, "antichrist" is

- Anyone "who denies that Jesus is the Christ" (1 John 2:22)
- Anyone "who denies the Father and the Son" (1 John 2:22)
- "Every spirit that does not confess Jesus" (1 John 4:3)
- "Those who do not confess the coming of Jesus Christ in the flesh" (2 John 7)

The term "antichrist" is a combination of *anti* (against or instead of) and *christos* (Messiah, Christ). It is ambiguous whether the antichrist is merely one (or anyone) who opposes Christ as his adversary or enemy, or is also a specific person who seeks to take his place. Most have believed that antichrist is a lying pretender who portrays himself as Christ; he is a counterfeit or diabolical parody of Christ himself (see 2 Thess. 2:3–12).

Although John's readers have been told that the antichrist's appearance is yet future, *"even now"* many antichrists have already come. Paul wrote in 2 Thessalonians 2:7 that "the mystery of lawlessness is already at work." In 1 John 4:3 he points out that the spirit of antichrist is *"now," "already"* at work in the world. Most believe that what John means in 1 John 2:18 is that the "many antichrists" (those who in the first century were denying the incarnation of Jesus) are forerunners of the one still to come. Because they proclaim the same heresies he/it will proclaim and oppose Christ now as he/it will oppose him then, they are rightly called antichrists (especially in view of their denial of Christ in 1 John 2:22–23).

The antichrists of 1 John 2:18 are the false teachers against whom the epistle is directed. In 1 John 2:19 he indicates that at one time they were members of the community that professed faith in Christ. They were actively involved in the ministry of the church and until the moment of separation were hardly distinguishable from the rest of the Christian society. *The essence of antichrist, the height of the demonic heresy, and the lie "par excellence" is the denial that Jesus is the Christ* (1 John 2:22).

Some have argued that John's point is that there is no other "antichrist" than the "one" even then operative in his day or the "one" who takes up and perpetuates this heresy in subsequent history. In other words, *anyone in general* can be "antichrist," if he or she espouses this heresy, but *no one in particular*, whether in the first or the twenty-first centuries, is *the* antichrist as if there were only one to whom the others look forward. In other words, the "antichrist" who his readers were told was yet to come is now with them in the form of *anyone* who espouses the heretical denial of the incarnation of the Son of God.

But I'm not persuaded by this. I believe that the "spirit" of the future antichrist (Satan) was already present in the first century among those who denied that Jesus was God come in the flesh. That same "spirit" of antichrist exists today, but that does not mean there won't be a final, personal embodiment in one particular individual.

Satan's Greatest Ploy: Worship of the Beast (Rev. 13:4)

Perhaps the single greatest threat that Satan poses to this world is diverting the devotion and worship of people everywhere away from Jesus and to himself and the beast. Thus we read in Revelation 13:4,

> And they worshiped the dragon [Satan], for he had given his authority to the beast, and they worshiped the beast, saying, "Who is like the beast, and who can fight against it?"

This clearly refers to the devotion of the unbelieving world to anything and anyone other than Jesus. The power and influence of the beast, in whatever form it manifests itself, is grounds for their declaration concerning what they perceive to be the beast's incomparable authority: "Who is like the beast, and who can fight against it?" Indeed, this is the precise terminology found throughout the Old Testament that is applied to YHWH (see Exod. 8:10; 15:11; Deut. 3:24; Isa. 40:18, 25; 44:7; 46:5; Ps. 35:10; 71:19; 86:8; 89:8; 113:5; Mic. 7:18).

Thus, the beast makes "war on the saints" and seeks to "conquer them" (Rev. 13:7). These verses simply portray yet again what we see throughout Revelation: the beast's (Satan's) blasphemy of God and persecution of his people throughout the present Church age. The statement "to make war" (v. 7) doesn't necessarily mean that the beast organizes literal armed conflict with the church, but rather has in view the beast's hatred of the Church and his/its efforts to undermine everything the Church does and believes. Thus, when John says the beast will "conquer" the saints, he doesn't mean the people of God lose their faith in Christ, but that many of them suffer martyrdom at the hands of the beast and his cohorts.

Satan's Scheme to Sow the Seeds of False Teaching (Rev. 13:11–18)

There's a common perception that the primary goal of Satan and his demonic hordes is to indwell men and women and compel them to manifest physically in bizarre and off-putting ways. Undoubtedly they often do this. But Satan's principle aim is to undermine the life and vitality of the church by sowing the seeds of false doctrine. This comes primarily in the form of a denial that Jesus Christ is the Son of God in human flesh.

In his final two letters written not long before he was beheaded in Rome under orders from the Emperor Nero, the apostle Paul was clearly energized and concerned about the emergence of false teaching that he obviously believed would pose a great threat to the health and well-being of the church. In 1 Timothy 4:1 he wrote, "Now the Spirit expressly says that in later times some will depart from the faith by devoting themselves to deceitful spirits and teachings of demons." Later he exhorted his young protégé, Timothy, to keep a close watch on himself and especially "on the teaching" of biblical truth (1 Tim. 4:16).

In his final letter, written perhaps only days before his execution, he again said to Timothy: "Follow the pattern of the sound words that you have heard from me, in the faith and love that are in Christ Jesus. By the Holy Spirit who dwells within us, guard the good deposit entrusted to you" (2 Tim.

1:13–14). He again warned Timothy that "the time is coming when people will not endure sound teaching" but "will turn away from listening to the truth and wander off into myths" (2 Tim. 4:3–4). And it was the invasive and influential presence of false teachers that prompted Jude to say in his short epistle that we should "contend for the faith that was once for all delivered to the saints" (Jude 3).

False teaching, deceptive doctrines, and distortions of biblical truth are perhaps the greatest threat to the health and flourishing of the church in this present age. If you ask me for explicit biblical support for this notion, we need go no further than what we read here in Revelation 13:11–18.

The So-Called "False Prophet" (Rev. 13:11–15)

We read in verse 11 that John saw yet another beast, this one arising from the earth (cf. Dan. 7:17). Like the first beast, it too is a demonic parody of Jesus, for it has two horns "like a lamb" (v. 11b). Perhaps it has two horns instead of seven in order to mimic the two witnesses, the two lampstands, and the two olive trees of Revelation 11:3–4. There have been numerous suggestions as to the identity of this "earth beast."

Some argue that this refers to the Jewish religious system of the first century that conspired with the Roman state to suppress and persecute the early church. Others point to the Roman imperial priesthood that sought to enforce worship of Caesar as god. Many of the Protestant Reformers and Puritans believed this is descriptive of the priesthood of the Roman Catholic Church or perhaps even the pope himself. Most dispensationalists believe the "false prophet" is a literal individual living and working in conjunction with the antichrist at the end of the age

But I'm persuaded that John is describing, once again in highly figurative language, *the presence and influence of false teachers, particularly false prophets, throughout the course of church history* (see especially Matt. 7:15–23). This beast is later called "the false prophet" (Rev. 16:13; 19:20; 20:10), and together with the dragon (Satan) and the sea-beast, forms the unholy trinity of the abyss.

Thus, there is a sense in which just as the devil seeks to imitate and take the place of God the Father, and the beast imitates and seeks to usurp the role of God the Son, so the earth beast or the false prophet claims to fill the role of the Holy Spirit. Thus, we see in verse 12 that just as the true Holy

Spirit empowers and sustains our worship of Jesus Christ, the false prophet of Revelation 13 empowers and directs unbelievers to worship the beast.

False prophets and deceivers were prevalent throughout the early church as evidenced by the consistent apostolic (Peter, Paul, John) warning concerning their influence (see especially 1 John 4:1–6). The aim of false prophets is to mislead the people of God by diverting their devotion from Jesus to idols. They aim to make the claims of the first beast plausible and appealing and, as is especially the case in Revelation 2–3, to encourage ethical compromise with the culture's idolatrous and blasphemous institutions (cf. the Nicolaitans, the false apostles, Jezebel, etc., in Revelation 2–3). Thus the "false prophet" or land-beast stands in immediate opposition to the true prophets of Christ symbolized by the two witnesses in Revelation 11.

It is clearly the purpose of the false religious systems of the world, as energized and sustained by Satan himself, to seduce people into idolatry, into worshipping and devoting their lives to anything or anyone other than Jesus Christ.

So what does it mean when John says in Revelation 13:13 that the so-called "false prophet," this beast from the earth, "performs great signs, even making fire come down from heaven" and again in verses 14–15 says that he even enables the image of the beast to speak? Clearly, this (these) false prophet (prophets) tries to mimic the ministries of both Moses and Elijah. As you will recall, it was Elijah who called down fire from heaven to destroy the prophets of Baal. Even in Exodus (7:11), Pharaoh's court magicians, with their secret arts, performed many of the same "great signs" as did Moses (see also Matt. 7:22; 2 Thess. 2:9).

Jesus himself warned that "false christs and false prophets will arise and perform signs and wonders, to lead astray, if possible, the elect" (Mark 13:22). We know from numerous sources that the priests of some cults in John's day were experts in the magical arts and sleight of hand and were able to make it appear as if statues could talk and seemingly could produce thunder and lightning. Of course, we must never forget that most of what they do is energized by demonic spirits. The apostle Paul spoke of the coming "lawless one" as someone who by "the activity of Satan" would perform false signs and wonders (2 Thess. 2:9).

Revelation 13:13–15 describes vividly and in highly figurative terms the idolatrous aims of the false prophet. The picture is clearly drawn from Daniel

3 and the command that all should worship the image of Nebuchadnezzar. Perhaps also the command to engage in idolatrous worship of the beast alludes in part to the pressure placed on the populace and the churches in Asia Minor to give homage to the image of Caesar as god.

To say that "it was allowed to give breath" to the image of the beast "is a metaphorical way of affirming that the second beast was persuasive in demonstrating that the image of the first beast (e.g., of Caesar) represented the true deity."[5] With the story of Daniel's three friends still in mind, John portrays Christians of his day as being pressured by this latter-day Babylon (Rome) to worship the image of Caesar or the state (as inspired and energized by the dragon, from whom the state/beast receives its authority and power). Whereas the immediate idea in John's mind may well be the attempts by the imperial priesthood to seduce the people of God into worshipping the image of a Roman ruler, Alan Johnson reminds us that "the reality described is much larger and far more trans-historical than the mere worship of a bust of Caesar."[6] Using the well-known story of Nebuchadnezzar, "John describes the world-wide system of idolatry represented by the first beast and the false prophet(s) who promotes it. John describes this reality as a blasphemous and idolatrous system that produces a breach of the first two commandments (Exod. 20:3–5)."[7]

The Mark of the Beast (Rev. 13:16–18)

There is an issue that continues to inflame debate concerning the end times and contributes greatly to the overall hysteria that serves only to discredit the Christian community in the eyes of the world. I have in mind the belief by many that the "mark" of the beast is a literal tattoo, or perhaps a chip implant, or imprint of sorts, or perhaps some other physiological branding by which his/its followers are visually identified. The popular notion among many Christians (usually of the dispensational, futurist school of interpretation) is that some such designation, whether "the name of the beast" or "the number [666] of its name" (Rev. 13:17) will be forcibly imposed on people living in the final few years prior to the coming of Christ. If one wishes to

---

5 Beale, *Revelation*, 711.

6 Alan F. Johnson, *Revelation*, The Expositor's Bible Commentary, vol. 12 (Grand Rapids: Zondervan, 1981), 135.

7 Ibid.

buy or sell and thus survive in the days ahead, he or she must submit to this means of identification.

Needless to say, this interpretation is entirely based on a futurist reading of Revelation, such that what John describes pertains largely, if not solely, to that last generation of humanity alive on the earth just preceding the second coming of Christ. If, on the other hand, as I have argued, the book of Revelation largely portrays events that occur throughout the entire course of church history, this view is seriously undermined. As is clear from Revelation 7, we should understand the "mark" of the beast on the right hand or forehead of his/its followers to be a satanic parody (a religious rip-off, so to speak) of the "seal" that is placed on the foreheads of God's people (Rev. 7:3–8; 14:1; cf. 22:4).

That being said, I do not believe that the so-called "mark of the beast" is a literal, physical mark on the bodies of unbelievers, either on their forehead or their right hand. All through Revelation we see Satan making every effort to copy whatever God does. So, for example, the three persons of the Holy Trinity—Father, Son, and Holy Spirit—find their evil counterpart in Satan, the beast, and the false prophet. Just as Jesus died and rose again from the dead, the beast is portrayed as dying and rising to life again.

My point is simply that the so-called "mark" of the beast that unbelievers receive on their forehead or their right hand is a demonic rip-off, a depraved parody, a counterfeit imitation of the "mark" that believers receive on their foreheads. On four occasions the people of God are "sealed" on their foreheads (see Rev. 7:3; 9:4; 14:1; and 22:4). No one I know of believes that all Christians will literally and physically have the name of Jesus Christ and the name of the Father tattooed on their foreheads. This is simply a way of describing the fact that those who are born again and redeemed by the blood of Christ belong to him and to his Father and are preserved in faith by the indwelling Holy Spirit.

So when we read that the false prophet causes everyone who isn't a Christian to have the mark of the beast written on his or her forehead, we are to understand this as a sign they belong to the beast and are loyal to him and to Satan. This "mark" on their foreheads or on their right hand is simply Satan's way of mimicking the seal of God that is on the foreheads of God's people. If you have the name of Jesus and God the Father written on your forehead, it simply means they own you, you belong to them, you are loyal to the Lord God Almighty. But if you have "the name of the beast" (Rev.

13:17) written on your forehead, it signifies that he owns you, you belong to him, you are loyal to the antichrist. My point is that if you don't argue that the name of Jesus and God the Father is literally tattooed on the foreheads of Christians, you have no reason to argue that the name of the antichrist (or his number, 666) is literally tattooed on the foreheads of non-Christians.

Thus, it seems quite clear that the "mark" of the beast on his followers is the demonic counterpart and parody of the "seal" that is placed on the foreheads of the people of God (see 7:3–8; 14:1; 22:4). "Just as the seal and the divine name on believers connote God's ownership and spiritual protection of them, so the mark and Satanic name signify those who belong to the devil and will undergo perdition."[8] Since the seal or name on the believer is obviously invisible, symbolic of the indwelling presence of the Holy Spirit, it seems certain that the mark of the beast is likewise a symbolic way of describing the loyalty of his followers and his ownership of them.

As for the number 666, I encourage you to read the chapter in my book *Tough Topics 2*,[9] in which I interact with all the many interpretations. To be brief, virtually all other numbers in the book of Revelation are figurative or symbolic of some spiritual or theological reality. Thus, the number refers to the beast as *the archetype man* who falls short of perfection in every respect. Triple sixes are merely a contrast with the divine sevens in Revelation and signify incompleteness and imperfection. The number of deity is 777, and 666 falls short in every digit. Again, "three sixes are a parody of the divine trinity of three sevens. That is, though the beast attempts to mimic God, Christ, and the prophetic Spirit of truth, he falls short of succeeding."[10] Thus, the number does not identify the beast, but *describes* him. It refers to his *character*. It isn't designed to tell us who he is but what he is like.

Satan, Demons, and the Battle of Armageddon (Rev. 16:12–16)

In the Old Testament, God's deliverance of his people was achieved by the drying up of the Red Sea, which allowed them to escape Pharaoh's armies. A similar phenomenon later occurred with the Jordan River, allowing Israel

---

8   Beale, *Revelation*, 716.

9   Storms, *Tough Topics 2*, 341–51.

10 Beale, *Revelation*, 722.

to enter the promised land. It may then be that "the drying up of the river Euphrates to allow the kings of the east to cross over it is the typological antithesis" of these earlier deliverances.[11] The point is that whereas in these two Old Testament cases the water is dried up to make possible the deliverance of God's people from his enemies, in Revelation the water is dried up to facilitate the attack on God's people by his enemies.

On yet another occasion, God's judgment of historical Babylon in the sixth century BC was achieved by the diversion of the Euphrates River, which allowed the armies of Cyrus to enter the city and defeat it (see Isa. 11:15; 44:24–28; Jer. 50:33–38; 51:13, 36; an event corroborated by the secular historians Xenophon and Herodotus). God raised up Cyrus "from the east" (Isa. 41:2–4, 25–27; 46:11–13), "from the rising of the sun" (41:25), and used him to destroy Babylon. It seems clear that the language of Revelation 16:12–16 is based on this familiar Old Testament pattern that John now universalizes. That is to say, what happened to one nation (ancient Babylon) on a local and restricted geographical scale in the Old Testament was a type or foreshadowing of what will happen to all nations on a global and universal scale at the end of history.

The imagery of kings coming from the east, from the vicinity of the Euphrates, was standard Old Testament prophetic language for the enemies of Israel coming to invade and destroy. For those in the Roman Empire, the Euphrates River marked the boundary, on the other side of which was their bitter enemy, the Parthians. But for the Jewish people the Euphrates served as the boundary across which their enemies would come, namely the Assyrian, Babylonian, and Persian invaders.[12]

The "kings from the east" therefore does not refer to the armies of Red China. It was a standard expression among the Jewish people for anyone who sought to invade and conquer Israel. You will notice that in verse 14 John refers to "the kings of the whole world" who assemble to wage war against God's people. So, the "kings from the east" is simply his way of describing the

---

11 David E. Aune, *Revelation 6–16,* Word Biblical Commentary 52B (Nashville: Thomas Nelson, 1998), 891.
12 On this, see especially Isaiah 5:26–29; 7:20; 8:7–8; 14:29–31; Jeremiah 1:14–15; 4:6–13; 6:1, 22; 10:22; 13:20; Ezekiel 38:6, 15; 39:2; Joel 2:1–11, 20–25; as well as Isaiah 14:31; Jeremiah 25:9, 26; 46–47 (esp. 46:4, 22–23); 50:41–42; Ezekiel 26:7–11.

global conspiracy just before Christ's return in which Satan and his demons try to destroy the kingdom of the Lord Jesus Christ.

Whereas verse 12 summarizes the sixth bowl, verses 13–16 provide the details. Here again we see the unholy "trinity" of Satan, the beast, and the false prophet (called that for the first time here). Their deceptive influence is portrayed through the imagery of three unclean, obviously demonic spirits in the form or appearance of frogs, which obviously alludes to the frogs in the Exodus plague (8:1–15).

In ancient Jewish literature frogs were viewed not only as ceremonially unclean but also as agents of destruction. Beale suggests that "the frogs and their croaking represent the confusion brought about by deception."[13] That the frogs are metaphorical is seen from the fact that they "perform signs" (Rev. 16:14). In other words, these demonic spirits utilize supernatural phenomena to deceive and thereby influence humans to follow after the beast (cf. 13:11–18). The primary target of their deception is the kings of the earth, such as political leaders and authorities who align themselves with the principles of the beast in opposition to God.

This is a clear and unmistakable reminder once again that the oppression and persecution of Christians all around the globe is energized and driven by Satan and his demonic hosts. But these demonic spirits do more than merely persecute the church. They work to orchestrate a conspiracy among the kings and leaders of all nations designed to utterly destroy the people of God.

We see from verse 14 that they are described as gathering or assembling the kings and nations of the earth "for battle." But that translation isn't helpful. It is literally "for the war" (cf. 19:19; 20:8). The use of the definite article ("the") points to a well-known war, the final, end-of-history, eschatological war often prophesied in the Old Testament between God and his enemies (cf. Joel 2:11; Zeph. 1:14; Zech. 14:2–14).

Revelation 16:15 is a parenthetical exhortation addressed to believers to be vigilant lest they be caught unprepared on that great day. The picture is of a person who stays spiritually awake and alert, clothed in the righteous garments of Christ. For the image of physical nakedness as a symbol of spiritual shame often brought on by idolatry, see Revelation 3:18; 17:16 (cf. also Ezek.

---

13 Beale, *Revelation*, 832.

16:36; 23:29; Nah. 3:5; Isa. 20:4). This is God's counsel to us all: Don't buy into the deceptive lies of the world regarding peace, prosperity, and material success; don't listen to the false teachers who would have you believe that Christ won't return because he never rose from the dead in the first place. Be alert! Be watchful! For you don't know when the Master of the house will appear!

The place of this eschatological war is called Har-Magedon (Rev. 16:16). "Har" is the Hebrew word for "mountain." This poses a problem for those who believe a literal battle at the literal site is in view, insofar as there is no such place as the Mountain of Megiddo.

Megiddo was itself an ancient city and Canaanite stronghold located on a plain in the southwest region of the Valley of Jezreel or Esdraelon. Although situated on a tell (an artificial mound about seventy feet high), it can hardly be regarded as a mountain! The valley of Megiddo was the strategic site of several (200, by some estimates) significant battles in history (see Judg. 4:6–16; 5:19; 7; 1 Sam. 29:1; 31:1–7; 2 Kings 23:29–30; 2 Chron. 35:22–24). It makes sense that the vicinity would become a lasting symbol for the cosmic eschatological battle between good and evil. As Mounce accurately notes,

. . . geography is not the major concern. Wherever it takes place, Armageddon is symbolic of the final overthrow of all the forces of evil by the might and power of God. The great conflict between God and Satan, Christ and Antichrist, good and evil, that lies behind the perplexing course of history will in the end issue in a final struggle in which God will emerge victorious and take with him all who have placed their faith in him. This is Har-Megedon.[14]

To help you understand this, think about how we have come to use the words Gettysburg or Waterloo or Dunkirk to refer not simply to those specific battles but to any major time or event of great conflict, perhaps even a global war. Be it also noted that the plain around Megiddo was barely large enough for one army to occupy. It could hardly accommodate all the armies of the entire earth.

To put it simply, Armageddon is prophetic symbolism for the whole world in its collective defeat and judgment by Christ at his second coming.

14 Robert H. Mounce, *The Book of Revelation* (Grand Rapids: Eerdmans, 1998), 302.

The imagery of war, of kings and nations doing battle on an all-too-familiar battlefield (Megiddo), is used as a metaphor of the consummate, cosmic, and decisive defeat by Christ of all his enemies (Satan, beast, false prophet, and all who bear the mark of the beast) on that final day. That, by the way, is how human history as we now know it will come to an end. It won't be due to environmental catastrophes or a large meteorite or alien invasions, but by the decisive and dramatic re-entrance into history of the King of the Universe, Jesus Christ!

The Demonic in the Present Age

This examination of Revelation has yielded the following conclusions regarding what Satan and his demons are doing in this present age. If this doesn't alert and waken God's people to spiritual diligence, I don't know what will.

- They inflict extreme suffering on God's people (Rev. 2:9–10).
- They arrange for Christians to be imprisoned (Rev. 2:10).
- They cause some to suffer martyrdom for their faith (Rev. 2:10).
- They embed themselves in certain locations as a base of earthly operation (Rev. 2:13).
- They pervert prophetic ministry to seduce people into sexual immorality and idolatry (Rev. 2:20–22).
- They promote their own worldview, the so-called "deep things of Satan" (Rev. 2:24).
- They deceive certain Jews into thinking they are reconciled to God, when they are not (Rev. 2:9; 3:9).
- They torment unbelievers (Rev. 9:1–5).
- They intensify the suffering of unbelievers to the degree that they long to die (Rev. 9:6).
- They kill upwards of one-third of mankind (Rev. 9:15, 18).
- They stir up worship of themselves instead of God (Rev. 9:20).
- Their leader, Satan, continually accuses God's people of guilt that has been forgiven (Rev. 12:10).
- They seek to destroy the church by any means possible (Rev. 12:15–17).
- They empower false religion and idolatry and persuade people to worship Satan (Rev. 13:4).

- They blaspheme God (Rev. 13:5–6).
- They make war on the saints (Rev. 13:7).
- They persuade people to worship the beast (Rev. 13:12–15).
- They perform signs and wonders to deceive people (Rev. 13:13–14; 16:14).
- They compel allegiance to the beast by enforcing his mark on the right hand or forehead (Rev. 13:16–17).
- They assemble unbelievers to launch a global assault against Christ and his Church at Armageddon (Rev. 16:14–16).

Thus we see that demonic spirits will be unleashed in an unprecedented way at the end of the age to stir up and mobilize the leaders of all nations to unite their forces in an effort to crush the Church and to wipe Christianity from the face of the earth. But to no avail!

ANNA'S STORY

I was sexually harassed by an older cousin when I was around eleven years old. At the time, I didn't understand the magnitude of what was happening. However, in later years, I knew all too well the memory of what I had experienced and the way it left me feeling, both as a little girl and now as a woman.

This particular memory came into my mind one evening during inner healing and deliverance prayer ministry. I was asked to invite the Lord to show me a memory or perhaps a picture of what it was that he wanted to heal. I went into the meeting that night having no clue as to what the Lord would put upon my heart. And when the memory came to mind, I told my mentor that although I had a memory to share, I didn't see why it was being brought to my attention. This incident wasn't something I had felt needed any further discussion. In previous years, I told the Lord about the way the experience had made me feel. I felt I had already received healing from that moment of my life. However, the memory was there that night of prayer ministry. So, I mentioned it.

My mentor asked me to close my eyes and ask Jesus where he was, with me, in that moment. I couldn't. I had tried asking Jesus about where he was in other memories too, but I just couldn't wrap my mind around placing Jesus in my memories, not knowing where he truly was during those experiences. It felt fake, and I just couldn't go there. I told my mentor that although I knew Jesus was there, I didn't actually see him or know what he was doing or where he had been when this all happened. I mentioned that perhaps he was down the hall in another room or something. I just couldn't be sure.

After sitting and waiting, my mentor then asked if I perhaps needed to repent of feeling abandoned by the Father. At first, I felt hurt that I would be the one needing to seek repentance, but the Lord gently showed me that I had indeed felt betrayed and abandoned on that day as a little girl. So, I confessed and repented, asking the Lord to build my confidence in knowing he truly was with me, even in that hard moment. I asked him to forgive me for doubting him and his goodness and for thinking he had left me alone to handle the situation myself, as a young girl. I closed my eyes one more time, asking Jesus to show me where he was during the incident. And almost immediately, I saw him. I had a clear picture of him standing behind me, his arms wrapped around me. When I relayed the picture to my mentor, I began crying, knowing for certain the Lord had been with me all along. I now understand that Jesus has never been down the hall in another room, even in the most painful times of my life. He is always with me.

CHAPTER 7

Territorial Spirits

Has Satan assigned specific demons special responsibility, authority, and power over specific geographical and political areas?[1] Could the entrenched resistance to the gospel in some nations and cultures be due to the ruling presence of a demonic spirit (or spirits) placed there by Satan? If so, what is the responsibility of the Christian? Is there a unique form of spiritual warfare calling for special tactics when it comes to dealing with so-called "territorial spirits"?

Biblical Evidence for Territorial Spirits[2]

Several lines of evidence lead me to conclude that there *may* well be territorial spirits.[3] We know, for example, that Satan has organized his demonic

---

1   This chapter has been adapted from my book *Tough Topics*, 184–192, and is used here with permission. There are numerous books devoted to defending the notion of territorial spirits, among which are John Dawson, *Taking Our Cities for God: How to Break Spiritual Strongholds* (Altamonte Springs, FL: Creation House, 1989); and George Otis Jr., *The Last of the Giants* (Tarrytown, NY: Chosen, 1991). C. Peter Wagner has written extensively on this theme. See, "Territorial Spirits," in *Wrestling with Dark Angels*, ed. C. Peter Wagner and F. Douglas Pennoyer (Ventura: CA: Regal, 1990), 73–91; C. Peter Wagner, *Engaging the Enemy: How to Fight and Defeat Territorial Spirits* (Ventura, CA: Regal, 1991); C. Peter Wagner, *Confronting the Powers: How the New Testament Church Experienced the Power of Strategic-Level Spiritual Warfare* (Ventura, CA: Regal, 1996); and Rebecca Greenwood, *Authority to Tread: An Intercessor's Guide to Strategic-Level Spiritual Warfare* (Grand Rapids: Chosen, 2005).

2   The best overall treatment of this issue, albeit a critical and somewhat negative one, is provided by Chuck Lowe in his book, *Territorial Spirits and World Evangelisation: A Biblical, Historical and Missiological Critique of Strategic-Level Spiritual Warfare* (Fearn, Ross-Shire, UK: Christian Focus, 2001).

3   A close examination of the literature advocating the reality of territorial spirits, notes Lowe, indicates that

forces into a hierarchy. There is some form of rank, as indicated by the six-fold description in Paul's letters: *principalities, authorities, powers, dominions, thrones, world rulers.* Jesus himself indicated that demons differ both in their degree or depth of wickedness (Matt. 12:45) and their strength or power (Mark 9:29). Could this possibly be what determines their organizational position? We should also remember that Satan does not operate haphazardly. He has a plan, schemes, tactics, and a cosmic agenda (Eph. 6:11; 2 Cor. 2:11; 1 John 5:18–19).

The scenario described in Daniel 10 is perhaps the most explicit support for the idea of territorial or "nationalistic" spirits. The events of this chapter occur in "the third year of Cyrus king of Persia" (10:1). This would have been 535 BC, two years subsequent to the appearance of Gabriel in Daniel 9. Daniel himself would have been approximately eighty-five years old.

It was in this year that "a word was revealed to Daniel," a word that "was true" regarding "a great conflict" (10:1). Daniel did not take this lightly, but immediately began a season of personal preparation that entailed three weeks of "mourning" and a fast in which he "ate no delicacies, no meat or wine" (10:3). Our best estimate is that he began his partial fast on the third day of Nisan (March-April, the first month) and experienced his angelic visitation on the twenty-fourth day.

There is no explanation given why Daniel himself had not returned to Palestine with the first wave of former captives. Perhaps his age was a hindrance. Perhaps he was too important in government affairs to be spared. He may even have voluntarily chosen to remain behind, thinking that he could do more for the Jewish effort from his power base in Babylon. In any case, he takes three weeks off from his duties and seeks the Lord in prayer and fasting, somewhere in the vicinity of the Tigris River, which originated several hundred miles north of Babylon and flowed to the Persian Gulf (it passed within twenty miles of the capital city).

"territorial demons are purportedly assigned not only to geographical regions, but also to geopolitical institutions, such as nations or states; to topographical features, such as valleys, mountains or rivers; to ecological features, such as trees, streams and rocks; or to smaller physical objects, such as houses, temples or idols" (ibid., 19).

THE ANGEL IN DANIEL

Several things should be noted concerning the characteristics of this "angel." In Daniel 12:6 an angel is portrayed as being in the air above the Tigris; perhaps the same is true here (notice that Daniel "lifted up" his eyes and looked, 10:5). This "angel" took on the form and appearance of a man and was clothed in "linen" (v. 5). Both priests (Ex. 28:42; Lev. 6:10) and angels (Ezek. 9:2–3, 11; 10:2, 6–7; Luke 24:4) wore white linen, a symbol of purity (cf. Isa. 1:18; Dan. 11:35; 12:10). His waist was girded with a belt of the "gold from Uphaz" (Dan. 10:5). This may have been a linen belt embroidered with gold, or perhaps even gold links, indicating royalty or the power to judge. His body was like "beryl" (v. 6), also identified as "chrysolite," some form of gold-colored precious stone. His face looked like "lightning" (v. 6), a reference either to lightning "bolts" or simply the "brilliance" of his face (after all, how does a face look like "lightning"?). His eyes were like "flaming torches" (v. 6; cf. Rev. 1:14). Pause for a moment and try to envision a face of "lighting" surrounding eyes that look like torches on fire! His arms and feet were like "burnished bronze" (v. 6). The "sound of his words" were "like the sound of a multitude" (v. 6; cf. Rev. 10:3).

Who was this being? Some say it was once again the pre-incarnate Son of God, the same divine person who appeared in the furnace (Daniel 3) and in the lion's den (Daniel 6). If so, we must differentiate between this being and the "angel" who appears in Daniel 10:10ff. (see the similar descriptions in Ezek. 1:26–28 and Rev. 1:12–16). But we face a slight problem, for if this is God the Son, we must ask about the purpose of his appearance. Why would he appear only then to be replaced on the scene by an angel? It makes better sense if the being who terrifies Daniel in Daniel 10:5–9 is the same one who touches and teaches him in verses 10ff. Therefore, others insist that this was Gabriel who had earlier appeared to Daniel in chapter 9. One argument used against this view is that in chapter 9 Daniel was not afraid of Gabriel but here in chapter 10 he is terrified. But that may well be due to the form of his appearance (perhaps the description in verses 5–6 is designed precisely to explain why Daniel reacted differently). Or this may be yet another angel, similar to Gabriel and Michael in power and majesty (see esp. Rev. 10:1).

In response to his humility and prayer (Dan. 10:12), God sent this angel to Daniel. His arrival was delayed twenty-one days because he had been hindered by "the prince of the kingdom of Persia" (v. 13). Who or what is this "prince"? There are several reasons why this can't be a human prince. In the first place, he is able to resist this exalted angelic being, something no human could reasonably be said to do. Second, he is able to resist with such force that Michael had to be summoned for help (v. 13b). We should also note that the word "prince" is applied equally to Michael (the archangel). It would seem, then, that we are dealing here with a demonic spirit who engages in direct conflict with another angelic being. Since he sustains an ongoing relationship to the nation of Persia (v. 20), I conclude that "the prince of the kingdom of Persia" is a demonic being assigned by Satan to this nation as his special area of activity. His purpose was to provoke hindrance to God's will and kingdom there, especially among God's people under Persian rule.

We read in verse 13 that Gabriel had been "left there with the kings of Persia." One view is that the "kings" of Persia refers to the future rulers of that nation and that Gabriel successfully gained a position of influence over them in the place of the "prince (demon) of Persia" mentioned in verse 13a. Others contend that the "kings of Persia" were additional demonic spirits assigned by Satan to influence this nation that currently ruled the world. We read in verse 20 that, after his encounter with Daniel, Gabriel was to return to resume his battle with the prince of Persia. This indicates that whatever the nature of the "fight" in verse 13, Gabriel was not able to forever destroy or banish that "prince." In verse 20 we also read of the "prince of Greece." Might this indicate that there is *at least* one high ranking demon assigned to each country or nation, perhaps with lesser demons assigned to assist? Note well that, according to Daniel 10:13, 21; and 12:1, Michael is portrayed as the special guardian or protector over Israel.

This passage gives us some important insights into heavenly conflict, people's role in it, and how we see its effects.

First, Daniel is nowhere portrayed as praying to or commanding angels. His prayer is directed to God alone, who in turn, it would appear, commissions his angelic hosts to engage in the conflict.

However, Daniel's prayer *did* provoke a heavenly conflict. The fact that Daniel's three-week fast coincides with the three-week struggle between the "prince of Persia" and the unnamed angel "demonstrates a relationship between human intercession and what happens on a higher plane. Daniel's prayers appear to influence angels who play a significant role in shaping the destinies of nations."[4]

Does this suggest that the outcome of the heavenly conflict is *dependent* on the frequency or fervency of one's prayers on earth? Whatever answer one gives to that question, it is important to remember, as Clinton Arnold points out, that "Daniel had no idea of what was happening in the spiritual realm as he prayed. *There is no indication that Daniel was attempting to discern territorial spirits, pray against them, or cast them down.* In fact, Daniel only learned about what had happened in the angelic realm *after* the warring in heaven."[5]

We also see from this passage that the demonic hosts are engaged in warfare with the angelic hosts of heaven, the prize being the opportunity to manipulate earthly kings, nations, and people. Page explains:

These rebellious angels oppose the forces that support Israel, and the conflict between these two groups affects relationships between the nations with which they are allied. That is, the situation on earth reflects the situation in heaven. Presumably, the antagonism of the prince of Persia in the extraterrestrial realm manifested itself in the human opposition Israel encountered as she sought to rebuild the walls and temple of Jerusalem (Ezra 4). Later, Israel would find herself under the control of another foreign power, Greece, and the mention of the prince of Greece alludes to this.[6]

4   Page, *Powers of Evil*, 64.
5   Arnold, *Three Crucial Questions*, 162.
6   Page, *Powers of Evil*, 64.

The outcome of battles and struggles on earth clearly reflects the involvement of heaven. "The purposes of kings and nations," observes John Goldingay, "are more than merely the decisions of particular human beings. Something in the realm of the spirit lies behind them."[7] In other words, the unfolding events in human history are not determined solely by the will of man. Page explains:

> In particular, there are malevolent forces in the universe that exercise a baneful influence in the sociopolitical realm, especially where the people of God are concerned. Nevertheless, the power of these evil agencies is limited, for transcendent powers of goodness oppose them, and the faithful prayers of believers are also effective against them. However antagonistic the forces of evil may be towards the will of God, they cannot prevent it from being accomplished.[8]

In a word, there is more to historical conflict than meets the eye (see 2 Kings 6:15–17)! Arnold observes:

> The events of Daniel 10 took place in 535 BC. On the human plane, the Greek Empire did not surface to prominence until the rise of Alexander the Great, almost exactly two hundred years later. For the next two centuries, the Persian Empire remained the dominant power in the Ancient Near East. It is important, then, to observe that the text does not teach that Daniel, by his prayer, was able to bind, cast down, or evict the Persian prince—he remains powerfully influential for two hundred years. Of course, casting down a territorial ruler was not the objective of Daniel's prayer anyway.[9]

Interestingly, whereas in Daniel 10:13, 21 we see that Michael came to assist Gabriel, two years earlier (ca. 538 BC) Gabriel had to assist Michael. Why? Perhaps this is related to the return of the Jewish exiles to Palestine following the decree of Cyrus. If indeed this was a necessary prelude to the eventual appearance of the Messiah, Satan would be especially concerned

---

7   John E. Goldingay, *Daniel*, Word Biblical Commentary 30 (Dallas: Word, 1989), 312.

8   Page, *Powers of Evil*, 64.

9   Arnold, *Three Crucial Questions*, 155.

to do everything in his power to undermine the return and renewal of Israel. It was a little more than fifty years later that another attempt was made to exterminate God's people when Haman secured the approval of King Ahasuerus to wipe out the Jewish race. Although we read nothing in the book of Esther of a cosmic battle between angels and demonic forces, it seems likely that her success was the result of angelic support and strength.

Additional Biblical Support for Territorial Spirits

Several other texts hint at the idea of a territorial dimension among the demonic hosts. For instance, the Septuagint translation of Deuteronomy 32:7–8, as well as a scroll of Deuteronomy from Qumran, tells us that the Lord apportioned humanity into groupings ("fixed the borders of the peoples") "according to the number of *the sons of God*"—an obvious reference to the angelic hosts. If these translations are correct, as many Old Testament scholars believe, the implication would be that "the number of the nations of the earth is directly proportional to the number of angels. Certain groupings of angels are associated with particular countries and peoples."[10] Thus, administration over the various nations has been, in a manner of speaking, parceled out among a corresponding number of angelic powers.[11] If God originally made this assignment among the holy angels, it would not be out of keeping with Satan's character to copy and combat it.[12]

Mark 5:10 also hints at the notion of territorial demonic spirits. Here, "Legion" makes the strange request that Jesus not "send them out of the country." Why did they fear (and resist) being driven from that specific geographical locale? Could it be that they had been assigned to that region by Satan and feared his reprisal for failing to "keep their post"? An alternative view is that the demons make this request because they did not want Jesus to send them "into the abyss" (Luke 8:31).

Although 2 Corinthians 4:4 does not directly address our subject, we read there that "the god of this world [Satan] has blinded the minds of the unbelievers, to keep them from seeing the light of the gospel of the glory of

---

10 Arnold, *Three Crucial Questions*, 151.

11 Some believe the idea of nations having "patron angels" is found in Psalm 82 as well.

12 This is admittedly only speculative and by itself a weak foundation on which to build a case for territorial spirits.

Christ, who is the image of God." Why would not the blinding of individuals by Satan extend to nations, states, and cities as well?

In Revelation 2:13 Pergamum is described as "where Satan's throne is" and "where Satan dwells." As we saw in chapter 5, this city was infamous for its paganism, and several things may account for this description. Pergamum was the center for the imperial cult where a temple had been erected in honor of the divine Augustus and the goddess Roma. There was also a temple in Pergamum for Zeus, king of the Greek gods. The citizens of Pergamum worshipped Asclepius, the god of healing (portrayed or symbolized by the serpent = Satan). Perhaps Pergamum was the focal point of Satan's activity at this time, the home base, as it were, from which he directed his demonic hosts.

Ultimately, I see nothing in the Bible that precludes the possibility of "territorial spirits," and I see numerous texts that certainly imply their reality. The point is that some places, and hence people, are more intensely under the control or rule of demonic power than others because of an unusual concentration or presence of demonic activity.

What Do We Do Now?

If territorial spirits exist, what should we do about it? Is there a special strategy for spiritual warfare that we should embrace and pursue? Well, Scripture gives no indication that our responsibility in the presence of a territorial spirit would be any different from what it is in dealing with a routine demonic influence elsewhere. We are never instructed to identify and aggressively engage a territorial spirit. We are never commanded to confront or rebuke a territorial spirit, as if by that alone we can break whatever power or authority it might have over a geopolitical region.

Spiritual Mapping

Some argue that an appropriate strategy is what is called *spiritual mapping*. This is an attempt to look beyond and behind the natural, material, and cultural features of a city to the spiritual forces that give it shape and influence its character. I once heard George Otis say that it involves "superimposing our understanding of forces and events in the spiritual domain onto places and circumstances in the material world." In other words, it is an attempt to discover the doors through which Satan and his demonic hosts gained access into and influence over a geographical locale, a city, or a nation. This will supposedly reveal the moral or legal grounds on which the stronghold is built, as well as the demonic spirits who energize it. I've heard spiritual mapping compared to what an X-ray accomplishes in the effort to diagnose a physical problem. That is to say, spiritual mapping provides a supernatural image or photograph, so to speak, of Satan's strategy, location, and authority, as well as the most effective way to defeat him. With this knowledge, intercessors are, supposedly, better equipped to pray for the dismantling of the spiritual stronghold and to pursue other courses of action that will break the demonic influence and thereby open up opportunities for evangelization of the lost.

Perhaps the best definition of spiritual mapping comes from Rebecca Greenwood, who writes:

> Spiritual mapping is the practice of identifying the spiritual conditions at work in a given community, city, or nation. By gathering objective information (including key historical facts such as foundational history, locations of bloodshed, idolatrous practices, key historical leaders, broken covenants, and sexual immorality) and combining it with spiritual impressions (prophecy, revelation, words of knowledge, dreams, and visions), believers can prayerfully combine all of this information and draw a map that identifies the open doors between the spirit world and the material world. These open doors help determine our response as we enter into warfare prayer.[13]

Spiritual mapping is often, but not always, based on an active and aggressive approach to spiritual warfare known as *strategic-level spiritual warfare*. According to this view, the church is called to do more than simply stand firm, resist, and defend. The church is called to actively seek out, uncover, and confront the demonic powers that influence our corporate existence.[14]

Personally, I see nothing in Scripture that explicitly endorses spiritual

---

13 C. Peter Wagner and Rebecca Greenwood, "The Strategic-Level Deliverance Model," in Beilby and Eddy, *Understanding Spiritual Warfare: Four Views*, 183. See also C. Peter Wagner, *Breaking Strongholds in Your City: How to Use Spiritual Mapping to Make Your Prayers More Strategic, Effective and Targeted* (Ventura, CA: Regal, 1993).
14 If you are looking for a persuasive response to this perspective and a proposal for a biblically grounded approach to the issue, I can do no better than refer you to Lowe's book *Territorial Spirits and World Evangelisation*, especially pages 46–73, 130–151.

mapping, but neither do I see anything that would necessarily rule it out as altogether illegitimate. Perhaps the best and most biblical response to what we have learned about the reality of territorial spirits is simply to follow Paul's counsel in Ephesians 6 and adorn ourselves daily with the armor of God, and having done so, to stand firm.

Identificational Repentance

Yet another strategy some Christians promote for defeating territorial spirits is *identificational repentance*. This concept is based largely on Old Testament texts that describe the land being defiled or corrupted by the sins of Israel. The idea is that, in order to overcome or reverse this judgment, we today must in some way "identify" with the people of the past and "repent" for the sins they committed. George Otis describes this "repentance" in two stages: "(1) an acknowledgement that one's affinity group (clan, city, nation, or organization) has been guilty of a specific corporate sin before God and man, and (2) a prayerful petition that God will use personal repudiation of this sin as a redemptive beachhead from which to move into the larger community."[15] But note that Otis nowhere makes reference here to the biblical concept of repentance. Yes, we must acknowledge the sins of the past and repudiate them, committing ourselves through the power of the Spirit not to repeat them in our experience. But this is far and away different from saying that we can "repent" for the sins of our ancestors.

Repentance, by definition, is the acknowledgement (which typically entails deep sorrow and contrition), confession of, and turning from the sins that one has committed, both in terms of what one believes and how one behaves. That being the case, it is impossible that I can repent for sins I haven't committed. However, that isn't to say that the sins of others, whether those of our ancestors or our contemporaries, are irrelevant to us. So how do we respond to the sins of others? What is our responsibility?

First, we should acknowledge and confess such sins. We should acknowledge that our ancestors or our contemporaries with whom we are in some manner connected or related, have transgressed the law of God. Perhaps

---

15 George Otis, *Informed Intercession: Transforming Your Community through Spiritual Mapping and Strategic Prayer* (Ventura, CA: Renew, 1999), 251.

the most explicit example of this in the Bible is found in Nehemiah. There Nehemiah says:

> "O LORD God of heaven, the great and awesome God who keeps covenant and steadfast love with those who love him and keep his commandments, let your ear be attentive and your eyes open, to hear the prayer of your servant that I now pray before you day and night for the people of Israel your servants, confessing the sins of the people of Israel, which we have sinned against you. Even I and my father's house have sinned. We have acted very corruptly against you and have not kept the commandments, the statutes, and the rules that you commanded your servant Moses." (Neh. 1:5–7)

A similar prayer was spoken by Daniel during the time of the Babylonian Captivity (see Daniel 9:1–19). But note carefully that nowhere do either Daniel or Nehemiah "repent" for other people. They identify the sins of others. They declare that they and others in Israel have transgressed. They make no excuse for their sins. They both ask God to have mercy on themselves and the people of Israel. But that is not the same as "repenting" for the sins of others. They undoubtedly repented for their own sins by resolving to forsake their sinful ways and to obey God's revealed will. But one person can't do that in the place of another. Each individual must do this for himself or herself.

We must also remember that both Nehemiah and Daniel were living under the dictates of the Mosaic Covenant. The blessings and curses (see Deut. 28) that would come on the people of Israel for their obedience or rebellion are no longer applicable to any other geopolitical nation state. God does not enter into covenant with nations, but only with the "holy nation" of the Church of Jesus Christ, a distinctively multiethnic, spiritual body of believers (1 Peter 2:9). We must guard against the tendency (especially seen in the broader Pentecostal-charismatic world) to apply uniquely old covenant texts with its promises and warnings to those who now live under the terms of the New Covenant in Christ.

Thus, I might confess to God that "we" at Bridgeway Church here in Oklahoma City have in some manner turned away from God and that "we" are rightly under his discipline. I can declare the truth regarding our transgressions, renounce them, and cry out to God on behalf of the people as a whole. But I cannot repent for what anyone else has done, only for what I have done, and then pray that God's Spirit would awaken others to likewise repent of their own sins.

Second, we should also renounce, repudiate, and disavow the sins of our ancestors or our contemporaries with whom we are in close relationship. We should make it clear by confession and behavior that we want no part of that sort of wicked behavior, that we wish never to repeat such sinful activity, and that we choose to distance ourselves from the destructive consequences that follow upon the sinful behavior of our ancestors or contemporaries. But to renounce the sins of others is not the same as repenting for the sins of others.

Third, it's important to remember in all this that none of us is held guilty by God for the sins of our ancestors or contemporaries, unless of course we ourselves contributed to their sins by encouraging them to behave wickedly or by choosing to repeat in our own lives the sinful behavior of theirs. But God will not hold me guilty for the sins of my ancestors, nor will he punish or judge me for what they have done.

What then do we make of texts such as Exodus 20:5–6?

> "You shall not bow down to them or serve them, for I the LORD your God am a jealous God, visiting the iniquity of the fathers on the children to the third and the fourth generation of those who hate me, but showing steadfast love to thousands of those who love me and keep my commandments."

Note carefully that the visitation of the iniquity of one's ancestors on subsequent generations comes only upon "*those who hate me.*" It is only when we choose to repeat or copy or perpetuate the sins of our ancestors that we suffer divine judgment. Likewise, it is on those who love God and keep his commandments that steadfast love comes.

Along these lines, we must take into consideration Deuteronomy 24:16 (NASB)—"Fathers shall not be put to death for their sons, nor shall sons be put to death for their fathers; everyone shall be put to death for his own sin alone" (cf. Ezek. 18:2–4, 20). The point is this: If you do not hate God, this threat is not applicable to you.

ORIGINAL SIN

The original sin of Adam in the Garden was a unique situation in which Adam stood as the representative head of the entire human race. His transgression brought guilt and death on all his posterity. All of us suffer the consequences of his sin. The guilt of his transgression was imputed to us and, as David said, we are all "brought forth in iniquity" and "in sin" did our mothers conceive us (Ps. 51:5). As Paul said, "many died through one man's trespass" (Rom. 5:15). But nowhere in Scripture are we told to repent for Adam's sin. Rather, we are told to repent for our own sin that was ultimately due to that one original sin.

Fourth, is there any potentially damaging or damning relationship between the sins and iniquities of my ancestors and me? Yes. The sinful behavior and beliefs of previous generations tend to set in motion systems of thought, beliefs about what is right and wrong and true and false, and patterns of behavior that can be handed down from one generation to the next. Alcoholism, drug abuse, occultic practices, gambling and the financial devastation it brings, various forms of abuse (sexual, physical, emotional), and a host of other sinful activities can set in motion a lifestyle, a pattern of behavior, a mindset that can wreak havoc on subsequent generations.

Clinton Arnold perceptively points out that we should also consider the fact "that children tend to act out many of the same sinful patterns of behavior that their parents engaged in. Thus, when we read Old Testament historical books such as 1 and 2 Kings and 1 and 2 Chronicles, we find the kings of Israel typically following in the evil steps of their ancestors. The biblical writer often asserts in the narrative a line such as 'he committed all the sins his father had done before him' (1 Kings 15:3). These tendencies may not only be genetic and environmental, but may also have a spiritual root. This is particularly apparent when we investigate the allegiances to other gods that the kings of Israel repeatedly gave themselves to."[16] Arnold

---

16 Arnold, *Three Crucial Questions*, 119.

goes on to recommend that "the solution is to recognize the sinful tendencies and the past ungodly commitments, ties, and allegiances of one's family and to disavow them. It is especially important to note that this is not a repudiation of one's family, only a renunciation of the sinful patterns and connections."[17]

The apostle Peter spoke of something akin to this in 1 Peter 1:18–19 when he reminded his readers that

> . . . you were ransomed from *the futile ways inherited from your forefathers*, not with perishable things such as silver or gold, but with the precious blood of Christ, like that of a lamb without blemish or spot." (emphasis mine)

These "futile ways" were most likely habits, customs, ways of thinking and acting, etc., that his readers had "inherited" in the sense that they were passed down from the behavior of one generation into the behavior of another. Of course, no one is enslaved to the "futile ways" of one's ancestors. We can choose to repudiate the sinful beliefs and actions of our parents, grandparents, great-grandparents, etc. We can renounce the wicked ways of our ancestors and declare that by God's grace we choose to walk in obedience to God's will.

Sometimes this is a challenging task. You must be able to identify the ways in which the sinful behavior of your ancestors has affected you. You must be willing to sever the connection in the sense that you renounce such behavior and commit yourself to God to walk in a different way. But the guilt of their "futile ways" is not your guilt until such time as you yourself choose to walk in the same or similar "futile ways." You may well suffer the economic and physical and social devastation put in motion by your ancestors, but you are not held accountable by God for such until you choose to embrace that way of life and make it your own.

So, is it possible to identify with the sins of others in order that we might repent of them, and thereby defeat the demonic forces that were supposedly unleashed on the land as a result of their transgressions? No.

---

17 Ibid., 124.

ELLEN'S STORY

I started inner healing and deliverance ministry in the summer of 2018 and went in with the hopes that I would experience some level of physical healing after hearing many stories of what God had done for others. Whereas each week was stretching and growing, I was the most apprehensive about the session covering generational curses. It turned out to be one of the most powerful lessons of my life.

I had a traumatic week just a few months prior to entering this ministry that kicked off a severe reaction that caused my ears to swell and my arms and legs to be covered in hives. After a visit to the doctor, I was encouraged to eliminate gluten from my diet, which caused the reaction to diminish almost immediately. In the weeks following, I noticed that eating gluten would continue to cause my ears to swell and that the hives would return for a day or so.

During the time devoted to exploring generational curses, I was able to have significant conversations with my parents. We uncovered numerous cultural ties that had taken root in my heart as ungodly beliefs and false ideas concerning honor and shame, the role of women, and parent-child relationships. Both of my Korean parents are either first- or second-generation believers in their families, so it also stood to reason that most of our ancestors would have been steeped in Buddhism, Shintoism, shamanism, and other sorts of Asian practices.

My physical reaction during the trauma of that week was provoked when my mother received a surprising medical diagnosis that would eventually require surgery. It was not lost on my prayer facilitators and me that there could be a family tie that needed to be broken. It was before we met to break off generational curses that I noticed a shift. For the first time in months, I had a donut over July 4th weekend that did not cause any reaction whatsoever! I had never experienced physical healing in my own body on this level, and it felt surreal for a few weeks. I'm so grateful for the Lord's healing power and grace!

My life, both physically and spiritually, has been forever transformed by the gracious work of the Holy Spirit. I know I will never be the same from this day forward.

THE THREAT OF THE DEMONIC

CHAPTER 8

Demonic Wisdom, False Philosophies, and Deceptive Doctrines

We saw in the previous section how much of Satan's strategy in the present age is to sow the seeds of false doctrine, idolatry, blasphemy, and the denial of the person and work of Jesus Christ as God's incarnate Son. Numerous places in the New Testament describe this enemy's wicked scheme, including Paul's letter to the Colossians. It is here that we are introduced to the "elemental spirits of the world." We'll spend much of this chapter digging deeper into the concept of "elemental spirits" and the threat they pose to believers.

The Colossian Heresy

In his letter to the Colossian church, the apostle Paul issued this stringent warning to the Colossian believers (and to us):

> See to it that no one takes you captive by philosophy and empty deceit, according to human tradition, according to the elemental spirits of the world, and not according to Christ. For in him the whole fullness of deity dwells bodily, and you have been filled in him, who is the head of all rule and authority. (Col. 2:8–10)

New Testament scholars debate exactly what problem prompted Paul to write his letter to the Colossian believers. The so-called "Colossian heresy" probably consisted of an odd mix of Gnosticism, asceticism, and an inordinate emphasis on the importance of angels; some have contended there was also a Judaizing element in it.

This passage has also earned a fair share of misinterpretation. For instance, I've met a few people who believed this passage prohibited them from majoring in philosophy in college. "The idea of a 'Christian philosopher,'" said one, "is a contradiction in terms." Now, there are many reasons to switch majors in college, but this verse isn't one of them. Paul is not condemning all philosophy in this passage, as if the discipline is itself inherently dangerous. Paul is referring to one specific expression of philosophical thought that was a threat to the faith of the Colossians in the first century. A literal translation of this verse would read "*the* philosophy." This is a philosophical perspective characterized by "empty deceit." It is *deceitful*, as opposed to "the word of *truth*" (Col. 1:5). It is *empty*, as over against the glorious *riches* (Col. 1:27) and *treasures* (Col. 2:3) that are in Christ.

Philosophy is a helpful discipline designed to help us think through ultimate issues such as the existence of God, the meaning of life, the nature of good and evil, how we use language, and other tough topics. Philosophical reasoning that is subject to the final authority of Scripture can shed great light on our search for and understanding of truth. But Christians *do* need to be cautious about any form of philosophy that is "not according to Christ" (v. 8), That is to say, if it is in any way contrary to the revelation of God in Christ or diminishes his supremacy and glory, we should shun it. Let's dig deeper into this verse to understand the nature of the philosophy of which Paul speaks.

Verses 9–10 indicate that Paul was speaking of a particular philosophy that detracts from the centrality of Christ and undermines our confidence that he is sufficient to be and do all that we need. Note that Paul begins verse 9 with the word "for" or "because." Paul's point is that *because* all the fullness of the divine nature dwells in Christ, and because we have been made complete in him and in no other, we have no need for human reasoning that purports to give us something that Christ didn't provide. Any philosophy (or theology) that says, "Christ was necessary, but not sufficient; we have more. We have the 'fullness' of divine wisdom and power that isn't available merely in a relationship with Jesus Christ" is demonic and must be rejected.

The philosophy that Paul condemns is "according to human tradition"

(v. 8). In other words, it is earthly in origin. This is a philosophy that was conceived in the mind of man and did not come by means of divine revelation. It may well be compatible with and confirm human traditions and make sense when looked at from the perspective of this world, but it has nothing in it of God.

Third, and most important, this philosophy is according "to the elemental spirits of the world." (v. 20). There is considerable debate among scholars about the meaning of the word *stocheia*, here translated as "elemental spirits" (although observe that the word "spirits" is not in the original text). Generally speaking, there are four ways in which this term has been interpreted:

1. It refers to the letters of the alphabet and thus for the basic or foundational truths on which knowledge is built—in other words, these "elements" are the fundamental principles of learning.
2. When it is qualified by the phrase "of the world" (see Gal. 4:3), the "elements" refer to the physical properties ancients believed make up our world—earth, air, water, and fire.
3. The "elements" are heavenly bodies, stars, planets, meteors, etc.
4. The "elements of the world" refers "to the entirety of the old, fallen, and sinful world, which is destined for corruption (Col. 2:22) and destruction (2 Pet. 3:10)."[1] This would include material elements as well as spiritual elements: the devil (in the light of [Col.] 1:13), demonic spirit beings (in the light of [Col.] 2:10, 15 and Gal. 4:8–9), sinful humans, and application of outmoded aspects of the OT law.[2]

The view that I find most convincing is that Paul is using this term in reference to demonic spirits. This interpretation can also include the second and third above. Many in the ancient world worshipped the material creation, believing the elements that constitute the physical world were themselves animated by spirits or were in some sense "gods" to be venerated and served. The same may be said of the heavenly bodies. It was quite common for people in ancient times to regard the stars and planets as deities that influenced the affairs on earth. This is the basis for much of both ancient

---

1 G. K. Beale, *Colossians and Philemon* (Grand Rapids: Baker Academic, 2019), 242.
2 Ibid., 242–43.

and modern astrology. Even within old-covenant Judaism, angels were often associated with the hosts of heaven, all of which were called upon to worship the one true God, Yahweh (see Ps. 148:2–4). Given Paul's belief that standing behind every lifeless idol are demonic spirits (1 Cor. 10:20), we can easily see how these various interpretations can be combined.

Colossians is not the only letter where Paul refers to these elementary principles. The phrase also appears in Galatians 4:3–11, where, in Tom Schreiner's view,[3] it also refers to demonic spirits:

> In the same way we also, when we were children, were enslaved to *the elementary principles* of the world. But when the fullness of time had come, God sent forth his Son, born of woman, born under the law, to redeem those who were under the law, so that we might receive adoption as sons. And because you are sons, God has sent the Spirit of his Son into our hearts, crying, "Abba! Father!" So you are no longer a slave, but a son, and if a son, then an heir through God.
>
> Formerly, when you did not know God, you were enslaved to those that by nature are not gods. But now that you have come to know God, or rather to be known by God, how can you turn back again to the weak and worthless *elementary principles of the world*, whose slaves you want to be once more? You observe days and months and seasons and years! I am afraid I may have labored over you in vain. (italics mine)

Clinton Arnold comments regarding this passage,

> At one time they thought they were worshiping real gods and goddesses in their pagan worship, but they were soon to find out that these were mere idols—tools of the devil and his powers of darkness. The Galatians had appeared to have turned their backs on their pagan gods, but they were now tempted to add Jewish legal requirements to the pure gospel of Christ, which Paul had taught them. In Paul's mind this would be trading one form of slavery to the powers for another. . . . Both pagan religion and the Jewish

---

3 Thomas R. Schreiner, *Galatians*, Zondervan Exegetical Commentary on the New Testament (Grand Rapids: Zondervan, 2010), 268.

law surface here as two systems that Satan and his powers exploit to hold the unbeliever in captivity and re-enslave the believer.[4]

There are two additional statements by Paul that would appear to confirm the identification of "elements" with the work of Satan and his demons. In Ephesians 2:2 Paul describes the pre-Christian experience of Gentiles as subject to "the prince of the power of the air, the spirit that is now at work in the sons of disobedience." And in his defense before King Agrippa, Paul described his commission from the risen Christ as opening the eyes of the Gentiles "so that they may turn from darkness to light and from the power of Satan to God" (Acts 26:18). As Schreiner points out, "Seeing the 'elements' here as spiritual powers, as 'elemental spirits,' makes good sense in that the Galatians are returning to the gods they previously served. On the other hand, perhaps Paul is simply saying that they are subjecting themselves to the things of this world, though it seems more likely that demonic powers are in view."[5]

When we turn back to Colossians 2:8, we see that Paul believes all non-Christian philosophies and false teaching that divert people's focus away from the sufficiency of Jesus Christ are "according to" or "based upon" these "elemental spirits of the world." There is undeniably, then, a demonic component behind all anti-Christian, cultic, worldly philosophies that deny the truth of the gospel of God as revealed in the person and work of Christ. Thus, when we encounter such false teaching, such deceptive doctrine, we must treat it as far more insidious and dangerous than merely another harmless worldview or perspective on the nature of God and reality. All such belief systems are, as Paul elsewhere says, doctrines or "teachings of demons" (1 Tim. 4:1).

I find it most likely, then, that by this word *stoicheia*, Paul is referring to spiritual beings, demons, that were thought to be active within and exercising influence over the physical universe. In other words, this would be another way of referring to those spiritual beings Christ created and over which he exercises sovereign rule, as well as those demonic spirits that Paul will soon declare (Col. 2:15) were defeated by means of the cross.

---

4 Arnold, *Powers of Darkness*, 131–132.
5 Schreiner, *Galatians*, 278.

If this is the case, no wonder Paul warned the Colossians so strongly lest they be taken captive. There is demonic energy behind any philosophy, says the apostle, that undermines or detracts from or tries to supplement the work of our Lord Jesus Christ. He, and he alone, is truly enough! He is all we will ever need. The NASB makes this clear by translating the first half of Colossians 2:10 as, "in Him you have been made complete." There is fullness in only one: Jesus! In him, and therefore in no one else, you will find every resource, every truth, and all power.

Look at Colossians 2:3 where Paul declared that it is in Christ that we find all the treasures of wisdom and knowledge. Instead of "made complete," this word has also been translated "you have been filled" or even "fulfilled." The same verb is used to describe Christians as being "filled" with the "fruit of righteousness" (Phil. 1:11), "joy" and "peace" (Rom. 15:13), as well as "goodness" and "knowledge" (Rom. 15:14), not to mention the "Spirit" himself (Eph. 5:18)! The false teachers tried to convince the Colossians that the fullness they desired was unattainable in Christ alone. Paul responds by reminding them that everything they need to be complete, full, and fulfilled is in Jesus, and Jesus alone.

The Colossian heresy no longer exists in precisely the form it did in Paul's day. But there is still great relevance in his words of warning. We must be diligent, constantly on guard, and ever alert to those deceitful and ultimately destructive philosophies and theologies that to the slightest degree draw us away from reliance on Christ and his all-sufficient grace.

Any idea or system of thought that would suggest he is not supreme and sovereign or that he is not infinitely and exclusively worthy of our absolute devotion and adoration is demonic at its core. Beware, says the apostle, of any such philosophy. Identify it. Denounce it. Deliver others from its destructive clutches.

We need this warning from Paul today more than ever, as our world is permeated with deceitful doctrines and philosophical perspectives that aim to undermine our confidence in the all-sufficiency of Jesus Christ and the knowledge of God that is revealed to us in and through him alone. Paul is telling us in this text that such belief systems or worldviews that do not have the revelation of God in Christ at their center are the fruit of demonic activity. Demons are ever present to blind the minds of men and women to the truth of the gospel and divert their attention or focus away from Jesus and who he is.

Demons and Legalism

In Colossians 2:20–23 Paul again speaks of the activity of the demonic realm. This time the demonic realm isn't promoting false philosophy, but legalism—an approach to Christian living that robs the believer of freedom and joy and replaces it with regulations and rules not found in Scripture that ultimately are useless when it comes to curbing the impulses of our sinful flesh. Here is what Paul said:

> If with Christ you died to the elemental spirits of the world, why, as if you were still alive in the world, do you submit to regulations—"Do not handle, Do not taste, Do not touch" (referring to things that all perish as they are used)—according to human precepts and teachings? These have indeed an appearance of wisdom in promoting self-made religion and asceticism and severity to the body, but they are of no value in stopping the indulgence of the flesh. (Col. 2:20–23)

Paul is speaking of those who impose man-made rules concerning the body and one's behavior as a means for enhancing one's relationship with God. He speaks in particular of asceticism: the belief that if you add up enough physical negatives you will get a spiritual positive. Ascetics view the body as a thing to be punished, denied, even abused. They regard the body as evil and believe the only way to defeat it is to starve it of anything that might spark desire. They take steps to diminish the intake of food and drink to an irreducible minimum. Mere avoidance becomes the pathway to holiness.

Paul says that demons ("elemental spirits of the world") are behind all such legalistic attempts to live a God-honoring life. I doubt if many of you have viewed legalism as a serious threat to your relationship with Christ, but Paul clearly asserts that any attempt to curry favor with God based on an ascetic approach to Christian living is an approach that is demonically inspired and sustained. When we encounter attempts to promote such a perspective or people who seek to put people in bondage to extrabiblical rules and taboos, we must alert them to the demonic source of all such teaching and resist their efforts with the power of the Spirit and the true gospel of grace-filled living.

The Devil Disguised

We've seen thus far that Satan and the demonic powers are ever at work to spawn false doctrines and deceptive philosophies, as well as corrupt concepts of the Christian life, in order to undermine the spiritual vitality of believers and their single-minded devotion to Jesus. It should come as no surprise that Satan employs specific individuals to achieve this goal. They are variously known as false teachers or false prophets, but in 2 Corinthians Paul describes them as false apostles who disguise themselves and their teaching to make it appear that they are authorized ambassadors of Jesus himself.

Before departing from Ephesus, the apostle Paul gathered to himself the elders of the church and spoke words of encouragement, exhortation, and stern warning. The latter proved to be prophetic. "I know that after my departure," said Paul, "fierce wolves will come in among you, not sparing the flock; and from among your own selves will arise men speaking twisted things, to draw away the disciples after them" (Acts 20:29–30). It's simply stunning to think that "fierce wolves" will emerge from within the body of Christ—indeed from within that very group to whom has been given the sacred task of leading and teaching the people of God. Such people have no regard for the spiritual health of God's people. They have even less regard for the truth. They are utterly self-serving. In order to gain a following and increase their authority, they speak "twisted things" and undermine the confidence of God's people in the finality and sufficiency of the work of Christ. Paul's words proved to be prophetic, for we read in both of his letters to Timothy of the presence and destructive influence of false teachers in the church at Ephesus.

Paul also faced such a scenario in the church at Corinth. He wrote:

> For such men are false apostles, deceitful workmen, disguising themselves as apostles of Christ. And no wonder, for even Satan disguises himself as an angel of light. So it is no surprise if his servants, also, disguise themselves as servants of righteousness. Their end will correspond to their deeds. (2 Cor. 11:13–15)

These men claim to be genuine apostles (v. 13b), men who serve Christ and are deserving of the authority that exalted office entails. But Paul labels them "false apostles," impostors, intruders, interlopers who consciously serve themselves and unwittingly do the devil's dirty work.

They were false for reasons already articulated in 2 Corinthians. They preached "another Jesus" and a "different spirit" and a gospel "different" from the one Paul proclaimed (11:4). They are false because they failed in every respect to reflect the character of Christ (10:1; 13:4). They are false because they employed cunning and deceit to achieve their goals (11:13). They are false because Christ had not commissioned them, as he had Paul (1:1). They are false because they did not serve God's people but oppressed and abused them (11:20). They are false because they diluted the truth and peddled the gospel for personal gain (2:17). They are false because they trespassed on foreign ground, where Paul had been assigned to minister (10:14–16). They are false because, as "deceitful workmen" (11:13), they misrepresented themselves, as well as their motivation and goals, and ultimately labored to lead people away from the truth of the sufficiency of righteousness through faith in Christ alone.

The presence of such false apostles is dangerous and disappointing, but it is not a surprise. Satan, whose ministers they are (whether consciously or not), regularly disguises himself and his tactics, assuming the guise of an angel of light.

And don't think for a moment that the scenario that played itself out in the first century cannot occur again in ours. In fact, it does, often on a daily basis. Fierce wolves, touting their academic credentials or pastoral experience, maneuver their way into positions of power in the local church. They pass themselves off as "apostles of Christ" (2 Cor. 11:13b), duly called and commissioned by the risen Lord and invested with the spiritual authority to lead the church. They use all the right words, speaking often of "Jesus" and the "gospel" and the "Spirit," all while injecting into such terms heterodox definitions and drawing implications that undermine the faith of those whom they supposedly serve. They will often talk of "righteousness" (2 Cor. 11:15) and portray themselves as servants of what is good and godly. Soon, though, and ever so subtly, the "righteousness" on which they insist takes on a new shape, develops a different scent, and feels legalistic rather than liberating, ultimately sapping the confidence of God's people rather than strengthening it.

There's no indication that anything sinister is afoot; not initially, anyway.

They would never openly claim to be "servants" (2 Cor. 11:15) of Satan! They are his sworn enemies, or so they say. And, in all likelihood, they are altogether unaware of the ultimate source of their spiritual energy. They go about their ways, teaching "twisted things" and calling it truth (Acts 20:30), unwitting accomplices in Satan's diabolical strategy to destroy the body of Christ. The result, notes D. A. Carson,

> . . . is an entire network of leaders, nicely installed in the church, who actively work against the gospel in the name of the gospel, seduce the people to another Jesus in the name of Jesus, and in the name of greater Christian maturity instill a deadly triumphalism that renders impossible "sincere and pure devotion to Christ." (2 Cor. 11:3, 4)[6]

How do such people gain a foothold in the life of the church in our day? What has opened the door to their presence and insidious influence? One significant contributing factor, notes D. A. Carson, is the new definition given to the term "tolerance." He explains:

> The appeal to limitless toleration—not just toleration of the other chap's right to be wrong, but toleration pushed so far one can never say that anything or anyone is wrong—presupposes the greatest evil is to hold a strong conviction that certain things are true and their contraries are false.[7]

This ugly reality forces us to think more deeply about the nature of temptation and sin and how Satan's work in the human heart unfolds. Permit me to cite Carson at length. His words are worthy of your close attention:

> Most believers are not enticed into sin by the prospect of committing great evil. Far from it; they rationalize their way into committing evil by seeing in it some kind of good, or at very least by blocking out the evil dimensions. They cheat on their income tax, not because stealing and lying are gross sins, but because (they tell themselves) there is so much government waste,

---

6   Donald A. Carson, *From Triumphalism to Maturity: An Exposition of 2 Corinthians 10–13* (Grand Rapids: Baker, 1984), 100.
7   Ibid., 101.

because government takes more than its share, because everybody is doing it, and because no one will ever know. They gossip about neighbors and friends, not out of conscious disobedience to God, but because they feel they are passing on truth, the result of mature discernment. They nurture bitterness and hate against a spouse or a fellow believer, not because they hunger to ignore the unambiguous warnings in Scripture against bitterness and hate, but because they are persuaded their emotions are not evil after all, but simply justifiable instances of righteous indignation.

Exactly the same warped motives often prevail in their doctrinal judgments. Christians will be seduced into thinking there is no hell, not because they choose to be selective about what teachings of Jesus they will accept, but because they have heard some extrapolations on the theme of God's love that not only go beyond the biblical text but also deny some other part of Scripture. They will offer generous support of heretical teachers who appear on television, not because they love heresy, but because the scoundrels on the screen talk fluently of joy, peace, triumph, experience, and of some sort of Jesus—and who can be against such things?[8]

"Spiritual Strongholds"

In many treatments of spiritual warfare, one hears about so-called "spiritual strongholds" and the urgent need to dismantle or destroy them. The text typically cited in this regard is 2 Corinthians 10:4–6. Here is what the apostle Paul said:

> For the weapons of our warfare are not of the flesh but have divine power to destroy strongholds. We destroy arguments and every lofty opinion raised against the knowledge of God, and take every thought captive to obey Christ, being ready to punish every disobedience, when your obedience is complete.

What can our weapons do? They destroy "strongholds" or "fortresses" (NASB), vivid imagery indeed. Paul's use of this word recalls the ancient practice of building a massively fortified tower inside the walls of a city where its

---

8   Ibid., 103.

citizens might retreat to make their final defense. But to what does Paul's language actually refer? What are the literal "strongholds" that our divinely empowered weapons destroy? Verse 5 gives the answer.

First, they are "arguments" or "speculations" (NASB), by which Paul means the thoughts, plans, and intentions designed to justify one's calloused disbelief in God (cf. 2 Cor. 2:11; 4:4; Rom. 1:21; 1 Cor. 3:20). He is saying that our weapons "destroy the way people think, demolish their sinful thought patterns, the mental structures by which they live their lives in rebellion against God."[9]

Second, our weapons are effective in bringing down "every lofty opinion raised against the knowledge of God (or "every pretension that sets itself up against the kingdom of God," 2 Cor. 10:5 NIV). People will often appear humble in their appeal to intellectual doubt as a way of keeping God at arm's length. Others display what Carson calls "a supercilious and condescending cynicism" or claim "an intellectual independence that loves to debate theology without ever bending the knee in adoring worship."[10] But we have been graciously equipped by God with the necessary weaponry to overcome every arrogant claim, every haughty or prideful thought, every pompous act that forms a barrier to the knowledge of God. We are fully empowered to address every argument used to rationalize sin and to justify unbelief and to delay repentance.

Furthermore, our warfare is not merely aimed at dismantling and tearing down the sinful reasoning and rationalizations that are strongholds by which the mind fortifies itself against the gospel. It is actually *effective* in doing so! The gospel will always remain foolishness to some and a stumbling block to others, but to those "who are being saved it is the power of God" (1 Cor. 1:18), "to those who are called, both Jews and Greeks" (1 Cor. 1:24), the gospel of a crucified Christ is "the power of God and the wisdom of God" (1 Cor. 1:24b).

The ultimate aim, of course, is to "take every thought captive to obey Christ" (2 Cor. 10:5b). The picture is of "a military expedition into enemy territory, an expedition so effective that every plan of the enemy is thwarted,

---

9   Ibid., 47.

10   Ibid., 48.

every scheme foiled, every counter-offensive beaten."[11] Whatever ideas of the unbeliever hindered faith, whatever notions or plans were barriers to repentance, they are defeated, captured, and graciously transformed, to be brought under the authority of Christ and ultimately to acknowledge a new loyalty, a new allegiance.

Paul Barnett suggests that, given the context, the "weaponry" Paul has in mind might refer to "his disciplinary ministry to them at the time of the second [painful] visit and through the 'Severe Letter.'"[12] On this view, the "destruction of fortresses" and the "pulling down" of speculations refer to his victory over the person who wronged him (cf. 2 Cor. 2:6; 7:12) and those in the congregation who have undermined his apostolic authority. This interpretation, however, is generally regarded as too narrow and restricted to fully account for Paul's language.

So, what then are our weapons of warfare? What is it that Paul utilizes to bring about this triumphant result? Surely he would point to the same armaments he cited in Ephesians 6:13–18, such as truth, righteousness, unyielding proclamation of the gospel, faith, the glory of salvation, the Word of God, and persistent prayer. These may not seem formidable, especially when one considers the political power and financial resources available to those who stand in opposition. But they are enough. And they are effective.

There are two additional issues that need to be addressed.

First, some have misinterpreted and misapplied this text as speaking of cosmic-level spiritual warfare (territorial demons; for more on this, see chapter 6). "Strongholds" and every "lofty thing" (NASB) have been taken as referring to demonic spirits who have been assigned by Satan to specific territorial or geographic regions. We, then, according to this view, are called to identify, engage, and, as it were, pull them down (ostensibly through prayer, fasting, proclamation, etc.). But the enemies in view are *ideas and arguments and philosophies and excuses that are antithetical to the kingdom and glory of God*. This isn't to pass judgment on whether there are territorial spirits, but simply to point out that this isn't what Paul had in mind when he penned this passage.

---

11 Ibid., 50.

12 Paul Barnett, *The Second Epistle to the Corinthians*, New International Commentary on the New Testament (Grand Rapids: Eerdmans, 1997), 464.

Yet, again, it is worth asking: Who is behind these thoughts? Who inspires and energizes such anti-Christian arguments and philosophies? What gives them the force that they appear to exert on the human soul? We mustn't forget that it is "the prince of the power of the air" who is even now "at work in the sons of disobedience" (Eph. 2:2; cf. 4:17–19). We see in 2 Corinthians 4:4 how "the god of this world [Satan] has blinded the minds of the unbelievers, to keep them from seeing the light of the gospel of the glory of Christ." How are they blinded if not by being deceived with philosophical and religious lies? Paul even said that Christ had called him "to open their eyes, so that they may turn from darkness to light and from the power of Satan to God" (Acts 26:18). In describing the condition of the latter days, he spoke of "deceitful spirits and teachings of demons" (1 Tim. 4:1).

So, whereas there is no basis for finding any reference to so-called "territorial" spirits here in 2 Corinthians 10, there is certainly good reason to think that Paul's warfare and divinely empowered weaponry applied to his (and our) conflict with principalities and powers, rulers and authorities, the cosmic powers and spiritual forces of evil in heavenly places (Eph. 6:12) who so often confuse, harden, blind, and enslave those who are resistant to the gospel.

Second, contextually, Paul is talking about "strongholds" in the lives and minds of those in the Corinthian church who were resistant to his apostolic authority. But do ordinary Christians today have them too? Yes. Such intellectual, philosophical, and moral enemies to the knowledge of God don't automatically and altogether disappear when we get saved.

A good working definition of a "stronghold" is a mindset or a mental framework that is shaped by feelings of hopelessness. This distortion in our thinking serves to convince us that change is impossible, even though we know that the way we are living and thinking conflicts with what God has said in Scripture. What he had in view are negative patterns of thought that cripple our ability to obey God and thus breed feelings of guilt and despair. They are often burned into our minds either through repetition over time (such as occurs in an abusive relationship) or through a one-time traumatic experience, or even more commonly through the influence of false teaching and a skewed theology. In relation to this latter point, Clint Arnold believes that "the critical thrust of the passage is directed against christological heresy. . . . Therefore, in its original context, demolishing strongholds refers to changing wrong ideas about Christ in the minds of believers who have been influenced by demonically inspired teaching."[13]

Whatever the case, no matter the opposition, the good news is that we have access to powerful and efficacious resources, adequate to prevail over all resistance and to defeat every enemy (Rom. 12:1–2; Eph. 4:20–24). We must dedicate ourselves to thinking and meditating on whatever is true and honorable and just and pure and lovely and commendable and excellent and worthy of praise (Phil. 4:8), and entrust ourselves to the power of the Spirit, who can overcome the influence of every negative and destructive thought.

Recognizing Demonic Wisdom

Movies and TV shows portray Satan's influence on our lives in graphic, hair-raising ways. But it's often more subtle than that. If we're expecting Satan's influence to look like Hollywood-worthy demonic possessions, we'll often overlook his efforts to sow the seeds of such things as jealousy, selfish ambition, envy, vile behavior, and overall disorder. And yet that is precisely what James says is yet another expression of demonic influence. Here is the relevant passage:

> Who is wise and understanding among you? By his good conduct let him show his works in the meekness of wisdom. But if you have bitter jealousy and selfish ambition in your hearts, do not boast and be false to the truth. This is not the wisdom that comes down from above, but is earthly, unspiritual, demonic. For where jealousy and selfish ambition exist, there will be disorder and every vile practice. But the wisdom from above is first pure, then peaceable, gentle, open to reason, full of mercy and good fruits, impartial and sincere. And a harvest of righteousness is sown in peace by those who make peace. (James 3:13–18)

The first indication that you have yielded to the world's manner of interpreting reality and the demonic energy behind it is that you are consumed by

---

13 Arnold, *Three Crucial Questions about Spiritual Warfare*, 54–55. Tom White defines a "stronghold" as "an entrenched pattern of thought, an ideology, value, or behavior that is contrary to the word and will of God" (*Breaking Strongholds: How Spiritual Warfare Sets Captives Free* [Ann Arbor, MI: Servant, 1993], 24).

"bitter jealousy" that fuels and energizes "selfish ambition" (v. 14a). Instead of "bitter jealousy," the word "envy" is more likely. He has in mind the sort of person who is bitter and resentful of others because they have things or power or name recognition that he or she does not. This is the sort of "sour soul" that results in disdain and even hatred of other people. It's a perverse emotional energy that says: "You have what I ought to have, and because of that I don't like you anymore. Not only do I not like you, but I'm going to devote all my efforts to getting what you've got. And once I've got it, I'm going to flaunt it and make sure everyone knows that I've finally obtained what I ought to have had from the start."

James then explains that when this perverse energy takes hold of a man or woman, it leads invariably to "disorder and every vile practice" (v. 16). In other words, peace and propriety and a reasonable approach to life are cast aside, and chaos takes over. And the sort of heart that is given to such things will eventually find a way to justify every manner of evil and immorality and vile behavior.

And what is James's assessment of this sort of so-called "wisdom" that expresses itself in this way?

1. It is "earthly" (v. 15a). That is to say, this is the sort of wisdom or perspective on life that is altogether circumscribed or limited by the values and beliefs of this world. No appeal is made to anything transcendent or heavenly or supernatural. What man wants is the measure of what matters. What man enjoys is the measure of what is good. The revelation of God in Scripture simply plays no part in forming this person's worldview or value system.

2. It is "natural" (v. 15b). There isn't a great deal of difference between something being "earthly" and it being "natural." The point in both cases is that the mental and emotional energy that gives direction to life need look no further than the depraved and self-serving interests of a fallen and corrupt heart.

3. It is "demonic" (v. 15c).[14] James appears to be saying that the sort of "wisdom" that leads to bitter envy and selfish ambition and arrogant boasting is "demonic" in nature and origin. This is how demons think

---

14 It's fascinating to note that this is the only place in the New Testament where this particular word appears.

and behave. And they love nothing more than to seduce people into thinking and acting like they do. Don't ever forget that Paul talks about "teachings" or "doctrines of demons" in 1 Timothy 4:1. And here James says there is such a thing as "demonic wisdom" as well.

Demons have a strategy for this world, for your church, and for your life. The heart of this strategy is to lie to you and make it sound like the truth. They aim to convince you that following Jesus is stupid, anti-intellectual, "on the wrong side of history," and contrary to the prevailing winds of enlightened culture. Following Jesus will only rob you of sensual and sexual pleasures that you deserve to experience. Such "wisdom," says James, is demonic. Don't be duped by it!

And what, in the end, will result from this sort of earthly, natural, demonic wisdom? Two things are noted in particular. The first is what James calls "disorder" (v. 16), by which he means the disruption of God's will for how humans should live. Disregard for the revelation of God's will, confusion rather than clarity, chaos rather than purposeful action. Just stop and look around the world today, and what do you see at every turn? Disorder. Don't mistake what James means by "disorder" as denouncing genuine, godly fervor and excitement. They are not the same! "Disorder" is whatever steps outside the boundaries of God's revealed will for how we live and speak and worship. But within those boundaries there must always be freedom and joy and excitement and passion.

But not only disorder, says James, "every vile practice" (v. 16) is in some way justified and said to be within your rights and ought to be protected by law. After all, you have a right to do what feels good. You have a right to pursue your pleasure in whatever way fits your fancy. Nothing is under control. Everything is permissible. Such is the fruit of the "wisdom" of this world. And it is all, either directly or indirectly, provoked and sustained by the activity of Satan and his demonic hosts.

Sin is subtle. So, too, is Satan. But as Paul said before, "we are not ignorant of his designs" (2 Cor. 2:11). Though he may come to us as "an angel of light" (11:14) and his workers as "servants of righteousness" (v. 15), we have the mind of Christ. We have the infallible revelation of his Word. May God grant us his wisdom and insight into its truth and the discernment to judge rightly.

MARK'S STORY

When I first began receiving prayer ministry for inner healing at our church, my expectations that I would receive anything beneficial were minimal. I considered myself an emotionally strong and mature Christian with few debilitating spiritual issues.

The first teaching concerned forgiveness and repentance. I understood what the Bible teaches about forgiveness and felt like I did not harbor unforgiveness toward anyone. What I discovered through the teaching was that I had unforgiveness toward my family and sin in my heart that I had ignored or minimized. This unforgiveness and unrepentant sin had kept me separated from a richer relationship with God.

The second teaching concerned ungodly ties, which deals with things that you place above God. I came to realize that one of my most damaging ungodly ties related to personal time and entertainment. I had rationalized it to myself that after being at work for ten hours, and then spending four hours with family and home responsibilities, I deserved to sit and relax for a few hours. But instead of spending that time in relationship with God, I was immersed in entertainment options that did not edify my spirit. After receiving the teaching on ungodly ties, I have committed to listen to worship music in times I would normally listen to secular music, read books that lift up my spirit, and spend more time in prayer. I have focused on thinking about whatever is true, noble, right, pure, lovely, admirable, excellent, and praiseworthy (Philippians 4:8), and as a result, my temptation to sin has been drastically reduced.

The third teaching concerned generational patterns of sin. As family members die, any demonic spirits that have a stronghold in that person's life look for a new target. From Scripture, we see patterns of sin that were passed from father to son. From experience, I've seen the same. It is only through breaking generational patterns of sin that we receive freedom from demonic attacks that would come against us and our children.

The fourth teaching concerned word curses and inner vows. I realized that I had made inner vows with myself that seemed humanly reasonable, but compared with Scripture, were ungodly.

The fifth teaching concerned ungodly beliefs. This section was very impactful for me. I came to realize that my experience does not necessarily equate to truth. The only truth in the world must be judged against what the Bible teaches, and just because I have experienced things that seem to be true, these "truths" must be judged against Scripture. Now, before I accept something as true, I compare it to Scripture to ensure that my thoughts are in line with the Word.

The sixth teaching concerned inner hurts, which deal with how we internalize things that have wounded us. Inner hurts can hinder our relationship with God and open up opportunities for demonic attacks against us.

The final teaching concerned deliverance, which is a culmination of identifying demonic strongholds in our lives, and then taking authority through the blood of Jesus over these demons and removing them from our lives, and then asking God to fill that void in our lives with his Spirit.

This teaching was incredibly valuable to me. I have come to see that the only way to effectively fight temptation is to understand God's ultimate worth, and desire to experience his glory more than I desire to experience whatever sinful behavior that would take the place of God's glory. I have never been closer to God in my life. The level of temptation to sin for me has been reduced by 90 percent.

Inner healing is not something to be taken lightly. I was told when I started in this prayer ministry that the enemy does not want Christians to draw closer to God, and there was a possibility that I would be attacked physically as well as spiritually. About the time I began receiving prayer, two spots that resembled warts came up on my stomach. Around the time we were going through generational sins, one of the spots became infected and spread down to my groin. I was in as much discomfort as I have ever experienced. I developed a fever and could not warm up with two layers of clothes, two blankets, and a heating pad. The shaking was so bad that I could not rest.

My wife prayed with me and had two words from God. The first was "heart of ice," which we took to mean a lack of compassion. I had previously seen my lack of compassion as an area in which I needed to become more Christlike. The other word was that "I was not standing on my feet and that my pelvic girdle was under attack," which we took to mean that I needed to take authority over our family and bind any demonic attacks on my line concerning sexual purity. As soon as we prayed against these demonic spirits, my shaking stopped, and I was able to rest. My son has experienced intense eczema on his legs for his entire life, and we realized that around the time we prayed for compassion and spiritual authority, his eczema went away. We are now two months removed and his legs are still clear.

While the shaking stopped, the infection continued to spread, and the next day I went to Urgent Care and received two rounds of antibiotics. I reacted badly to one antibiotic, and by the evening, I became unresponsive, so my wife called 911. It took so long for them to show up that, by the time they arrived, I had regained alertness. I did end up going to the Emergency Room, and after a few days, things went back to normal. The spots on my stomach went away after I was healed.

Within a month of this, I developed the worst sore throat I have ever experienced. My throat swelled, and it became very painful to talk or swallow. After a few days, the pain became so bad I was hardly able to get out of bed. My children prayed for me, and again, my wife had a word that this issue related to compassion. I prayed for God to increase my compassion, and immediately my throat was less painful and I was able to function. Several days later, I asked four men to pray for me, and I soon felt a physical release in my throat. I have experienced healing, but always over time. This was the first time in my life that I had an immediate healing. I was incredibly encouraged, and spent the day telling everyone I could about the healing. I am convinced that God allows things like this so we are encouraged after we experience healing.

As I see brokenness or separation from God with fellow believers, I desire for them to experience the freedom I have encountered through the inner healing ministry. For me, the cost was great, but the reward was infinitely greater. I cannot express to people how grateful I am to the believers who led me through the ministry, and to my church for putting the structure in place that allows people to intimately know God.

CHAPTER 9

Open Doors to Demonization and
Spiritual Oppression

One of the more difficult lessons for a Christian to learn is that protection against demonic attack is *not automatic*. Simply being a child of God does not guarantee that we can waltz through life insulated from demonic influence and invulnerable to the schemes and strategies of the enemy. The implements and weaponry of a soldier are not for decoration. They are to be utilized in fighting a war. So as we prepare to engage in spiritual warfare, the first questions we need to consider are "What does it mean to be 'demonized'?" and "Do Christians ever come under the influence of demonic powers?"

What Does It Mean to Be Demonized?

First, we need to define our terms.

The New Testament describes demonic influence in four ways. First, there is the Greek term *daimonizomai*, which appears thirteen times in the New Testament (all in the Gospels). The KJV always translates this word as "demon possession" (see Matt. 4:24; 8:16, 28, 33; 9:32; 12:22; 15:22; Mark 1:32; 5:15, 18; Luke 8:36; John 10:21 [the latter being a disparaging remark concerning Jesus]). However, I prefer the translation "demonization" for a few reasons:

- The Bible never once talks about *demon possession*. This phrase was popularized by its appearance in the King James Version, although it had appeared in other English versions prior to the 1611 edition.[1]

- I believe the emotional impact of the phrase detracts from an objective discussion of the subject. It is difficult for many to dissociate the concept of demon possession from scenes in the movie *The Exorcist*.
- The term "possession" implies ownership, and it is questionable to say that Satan or a demon owns anything.

In every case of where we see the term "demonization," it involves someone under the influence or control, in varying degrees, of an *indwelling* evil spirit. The New Testament writers never use the word "demonization" to describe someone who is merely oppressed, harassed, attacked, or tempted by a demon. In every case, it refers to a demon either entering, dwelling in, or being cast out of the person.[2] Hence, to be "demonized," in the strict sense of that term, is to be *inhabited* by a demon with varying degrees of influence or control.

Sixteen times the New Testament writers refer to a person who "has" a demon:

- It is twice used of John the Baptist by his accusers (Matt. 11:18; Luke 7:33).
- Six times the enemies of Jesus use it about him (Mark 3:30; John 7:20; 8:48, 49, 52; 10:20).
- Eight times it describes someone under the influence of a demonic spirit (Mark 5:15; 7:25; 9:17; Luke 4:33; 8:27; Acts 8:7; 16:16; 19:13).

Hence to "have" a demon is to be "demonized" or inhabited by a demon (see especially John 10:20–21).

On two occasions (Mark 1:23; 5:2) we find reference to someone who is "with" (Greek, *en*) a demon or spirit. To say there is a person "with" a demon is to say he "has" a demon, which is to say he is "demonized" or that he is indwelt by a demon.

---

1   Arnold, *Three Crucial Questions*, 205 n. 11.

2   Matthew 4:24 and 15:22 at first appear to be exceptions to this rule, but the parallel passages in Mark 1:32–34 and 7:24–30 indicate otherwise.

Finally, in Acts 5:16 (KJV) we find reference to a person being "vexed" by or with an unclean spirit.

According to this overview of New Testament terminology, if a demon indwells or inhabits a person, it is a case of demonization. Merely to be tempted, harassed, afflicted, or oppressed by a demon is not demonization. *Demonization always entails indwelling.*

A CASE STUDY: MATTHEW 12:43–45

In Matthew 12:43–45, Jesus uses the case of demonization and deliverance to describe the generation of unbelief to which he is speaking.

> "When the unclean spirit has gone out of a person, it passes through waterless places seeking rest, but finds none. Then it says, 'I will return to my house from which I came.' And when it comes, it finds the house empty, swept, and put in order. Then it goes and brings with it seven other spirits more evil than itself, and they enter and dwell there, and the last state of that person is worse than the first. So also will it be with this evil generation." (Matt. 12:43–45)

It is as if he says: "Let me describe what you Pharisees are like, indeed, what this entire generation is like. You are like a man who in some way is delivered of demonic influence. You put your life in order; you reform your ways; you clean up your act; you become morally respectable. But you are still spiritually dead and your house is empty because I don't live there. So, when that demonic influence comes back, he returns with seven of his cohorts and makes the latter situation worse than the former!"

The phrase "waterless places" probably refers to desolate, barren places, uninhabited by people, like the deserted cities where demons are found in the Old Testament (Isa. 13:21; 34:14; see Rev. 18:2). Jesus uses this image to describe how a demon, once expelled, returns "home" when unable to find someone else to indwell.

His point is that external reformation without internal regeneration is deceitfully dangerous. Beware of a morally reformed but spiritually Christ-less life. Any so-called "repentance" that does not lead to a new and wholehearted allegiance to Jesus leaves a void that a demon will exploit. In other words, neutrality towards Jesus can be deadly.

We aren't told how this man was delivered of the demonic inhabitation. If the demon were able to leave at will and return at will, it might explain the apparent success of pagan rituals of exorcism. In this case, demons could voluntarily depart for the purpose of deception. Or Jesus may be assuming that a valid deliverance has occurred (see vv. 22–28). In any case, it is important to remember that not everyone who was healed or delivered by Jesus became a believer in him. In the absence of commitment to Christ, they are always susceptible to renewed invasion.

There is no indication that this person does anything willful or deliberate that would invite a renewed infestation of demons. The mere absence of the indwelling Christ makes him susceptible to indwelling demons.

Description of Demonization

The New Testament provides us with few examples of demonization from which we can determine the symptoms of demonization. Additionally, we must be cautious before drawing generalizations from the New Testament examples and applying them to every other possible instance. The Bible nowhere claims to provide us with an exhaustive, encyclopedic list of every expression of demonic invasion. It is only reasonable to assume that the symptoms will vary on a broad spectrum depending on any number of factors:

- how the person came to be demonized—the legal and moral grounds on which the demon took up residence in the person;
- how many demons are involved (cf. Mark 5);
- what kind of demons are involved and the extent of their wickedness (see Matt. 12:44–45);

- the power of the demon(s) involved (Mark 9:29);
- the purpose for their indwelling;
- the degree of complicity on the part of the person indwelt;
- the permission of God.

Here are ten characteristics of the more extreme cases of demonization in the New Testament:

1. Projection of a new personality in the victim; often the virtual eclipse of the victim's personality by that of the demon.
2. Extraordinary physical strength (Mark 5:3–4; Acts 19:13–16). This may be due to supernatural enhancement of the person by the demon or utilization of something such as adrenalin that could conceivably occur under circumstances other than demonization. It is possible that both options come into play, although the cases in Mark 5 and Acts 19 can hardly be explained by adrenalin. If possible, avoid physically engaging a severely demonized person, such as the demoniac in Mark 5. Some have argued that Jesus himself never laid hands on the demonized, but the account in Luke 4:40–41 would indicate otherwise.
3. Fits of rage or extremely violent behavior (see Mark 5:4b; Matt. 8:28; see also Saul's attempt to kill David in 1 Sam. 19:8–10; cf. 1 Kings 18:28).
4. Vocal tirades and screaming (Mark 5:5a), which often becomes both obscene and blasphemous.
5. Self-destructive behavior (Mark 5:5b, 13; Matt. 17:14–20).
6. Antisocial behavior, often designed to humiliate the victim (Luke 8:27).
7. Physical disease, disability, or deformity (Matt. 9:32–34; Luke 13:10–17).[3]
8. An alien voice speaking through the vocal cords of the victim (Mark 5:7, 9; Acts 19).
9. Resistance to spiritual things, such as repentance (Mark 5:7).

---

3 This does not mean all disease is caused by demonic influence nor that all those who are demonized have a disease or disability as a result.

10. Possible clairvoyance. In Mark 5:7 the demonized man knew immediately, evidently without prior information, who Jesus was (cf. Acts 16:16).

There is no reason to conclude that these are the only symptoms or that every case of demonization will manifest all of these ten. For instance, there is no indication that the many demonized people brought to Jesus in Matthew 4:24 were in the extreme condition of the man we read about in Mark 5. In fact, the so-called Gadarene (or Gerasene) demoniac in Mark 5 may have been described in detail precisely because his case was so unique and extreme. The purpose of portraying his deliverance at length is to demonstrate that not even the worst-case scenario is beyond the power of the Lord Jesus Christ.

Open Doors to Demonic Intrusion

Having examined the nature of at least this one case of extreme demonization, we must now take note of why or how this phenomenon occurs. Under what circumstances or for what cause might a person experience demonic oppression, even to the point of demonization? We first need to distinguish between *voluntary* and *involuntary* demonization.

Involuntary demonization entails the many things that Scripture commands us to do that we, for whatever reason, fail to fulfill. It isn't that one little inadvertent slip-up will lead to demonization, but rather that *persistent and unrepentant* refusal to do what the Bible says to do may open the door. Here I have in mind such things as our failure or refusal to resist the devil (Jas. 4:7; 1 Pet. 5:9). Satan is not compelled to flee from us if we don't resist him. Similarly, the failure or refusal to wear or make use of the *armor of God* (Eph. 6) or our neglect in putting on Jesus (Rom. 13:14) may open the door to demonic invasion. Jesus appears to suggest that if we wish to be guarded against the wiles of the enemy, we must pray for divine protection (Matt. 6:13).

When we think of voluntary demonization, on the other hand, we think of things we willfully or deliberately do or practices that are an open door for the enemy's activity. I'm talking about the various forms of occultic activity (Deut. 18:9–14), such as astrology, palm reading, any form of fortune telling (reading tea leaves, using a crystal ball, etc.), Ouija board, tarot cards, witchcraft, sorcery, magic (not sleight of hand or illusion, but appealing to supernatural powers to effect miraculous events), table lifting, Dungeons & Dragons, automatic writing, seances, incantations, good luck charms, amulets, water-witching or dowsing, pendulum, etc. It is quite common to discover that those who have come under demonic influence have at one time or other indulged in one or more of these practices.

Idolatry is also incredibly dangerous, as numerous texts make clear (see Deut. 7:25; Acts 19:18–19; Lev. 17:7; Deut. 32:17; Ps. 106:34–39; 1 Cor. 10:19–21). Timothy Warner reminds us that

> When objects are made for occult purposes, or when people look to an object with the anticipation that it has power, demons will meet their expectation quite apart from any qualities inherent in the object itself. Or, in other cases, a person engaging in occult practices may invite demons to empower an object, and in this way the demons may become associated with that object.[4]

Willful, unrepentant, and unresolved sin can also increase our vulnerability to demonic intrusion (1 Tim. 3:7; 1 Peter 5:8; 2 Cor. 2:11; and especially Eph. 4:26–27). Believing demonic lies or heresy (1 Tim. 4:1; Rev. 2:24) is yet another avenue for demonic activity.

One thing in particular to which I want to devote considerable time is what can happen when we make inner vows or oaths that establish an experiential barrier between us and God. This next example is particularly personal, as you will soon discover.

But first, let me briefly explain what I mean by an "inner vow." Often there are certain ungodly or unbiblical beliefs we have embraced during the course of our lives, frequently in the aftermath of some personal trauma. For example, many who struggle to believe God truly loves them will make an inner vow such as, "I will never trust God with my life." In this way they think they have protected themselves from the pain of disappointment should God not "come through" for them in a particular hour of need or great crisis. As

---

4 Timothy M. Warner, *Spiritual Warfare: Victory over the Powers of this Dark World* (Wheaton, IL: Crossway, 1991), 94.

in the case just cited, words such as "never" and "always" sneak into one's vocabulary. Now consider this example from my own marriage.

A Demonic Intruder Strikes Close to Home

Ann and I were married at the end of our junior year at the University of Oklahoma. In May of 2020 we celebrated our forty-eighth wedding anniversary. Immediately after our graduation in May of 1973 we loaded up our belongings and made the short journey south to Dallas where I was soon to begin my preparation for ministry at Dallas Theological Seminary.

The first three years of marriage were wonderful and largely uneventful. But something happened in 1975 that threatened to unravel everything we worked and prayed to achieve. What makes it so odd is that I was totally oblivious to the incident for another eighteen years. For our third anniversary, I had secured a reservation for us at our favorite restaurant and then an evening at a local hotel. What happened next is indicative of how incredibly selfish and naïve I was at this early stage in our relationship. As we walked into the hotel room, I immediately turned on the TV and sat down to watch a baseball game. Ann stood silently glaring at me, incredulous that I could be so insensitive to her needs and her value to me as a wife. I have to confess that I was entirely unaware of what I had just done and the signal that I had inadvertently sent to her. Needless to say, the rest of the evening did not go well!

In the immediate aftermath of that disastrous night, Ann heard a voice in her head. The message was not reassuring. "God hasn't made you happy, Sam hasn't made you happy, come with me and I'll make you happy." From the moment she heard this invitation, Ann could see in her mind's eye the image of a hand, the index finger beckoning as if to say, "Come to me, this way, and I'll do for you what neither God nor your husband can do." As a result of the emotional devastation that my sinful insensitivity had provoked, Ann made an inner vow. She didn't know what to call it at the time, but there was a decisive moment when she resolved in her heart never to trust or be vulnerable with me or God ever again.

Ann never told me about how my actions had affected her. She never mentioned vowing in her heart not to entrust her soul to me or to God. For the next eighteen years I lived in ignorance of the entire event. She never said a word about the voice that echoed in her mind every day: "God hasn't made you happy, Sam hasn't made you happy, come with me, I'll make you happy." The voice was a constant torment to her soul, together with the daily temptation to abandon our marriage and indulge herself in whatever sin she was being led to believe would bring her the satisfaction and joy I hadn't provided.

It's important to understand that, in spite of this experience, we had a reasonably good and stable marriage. We genuinely loved each other and had been blessed with two wonderful daughters. But Ann was plagued almost daily with the consequences of the inner vow she had made. As I will explain later on, the truth found in Ephesians 4:26–27 was playing itself out in her life. There Paul writes:

> Be angry and do not sin; do not let the sun go down on your anger, and give no opportunity to the devil.

The word translated "opportunity" is *topos*, which can also be rendered place or location. Some English versions translate it as "foothold." What's important is that the failure to repent and extend forgiveness can, much like unresolved anger, open a door into our lives and provide the enemy with a base of operation. Whether or not this entails demonization and the actual intrusion and subsequent indwelling presence of a demonic spirit is something I'll address later in this book. What we do know is that by making this inner vow, Ann had opened her heart to demonic influence, and the enemy seized the "opportunity" to intensify her distrust.

The next eighteen years proved to be an ever-increasing hell on earth for my wife. She found herself in a daily conflict with the voice in her head promising her the happiness she was now convinced neither God nor I could provide. In the final few years of this conflict, the battle turned perverse. It's important to know that my wife has been the most faithful spouse any man could ever hope for. But the battle in her mind was driving her to the brink of self-destruction. She would later tell me of the perverse sexual images that would, without warning, race through her mind. The nightmares that included all manner of deviant behavior tormented her. The worst thing of all is that she would often have such ideas and images flash before her on Sunday mornings, as I was preaching. Her only thought was, "How can I be a Christian and a pastor's wife and experience these thoughts?" The "flaming darts of the evil one" (Eph. 6:16) rained down on her with incessant regularity.

At this stage in her spiritual journey, Ann was largely unaware of the realities of spiritual warfare. She knew that something was seriously wrong, but she never quite understood that her inner vow made many years earlier had opened the door into her soul for the enemy to establish a foothold in her life and in our marriage. She felt helpless to do anything about the war raging in her heart. Suicide seemed to her the only escape.

By this time, it was the spring of 1993. A young seminary student and now close friend who pastors a church here in Oklahoma City, Brock Bingaman, called me one day. Brock had never called before. He was in the midst of his studies at Trinity Evangelical Divinity School in Deerfield, Illinois. I knew Brock's family and was aware that he was a prophetically gifted young man, but I had never seen his gift in operation until that day.

Brock told me that on the previous night he had a dream in which I figured prominently. I won't go into detail with all that was involved, as I've told this story in my book *Convergence: Spiritual Journeys of a Charismatic Calvinist*. There were five scenes in the dream, but only one concerns us here. Brock told of seeing a lady sitting in a rocking chair in our home, swaying back and forth, praying fervently for God either to deliver her from her torment or to take her home to heaven. He couldn't see her face and never suggested that the lady was my wife. When I relayed the content of the dream to Ann, she knew instantly that she was the lady. She said nothing to that effect, and since the image didn't pertain to me, I quickly dismissed it from my mind. But the experience of the lady in Brock's dream was precisely Ann's experience on numerous occasions in our home, late at night. I should also mention that Brock felt confident in the dream that the lady's prayer would be answered with a wonderful deliverance.

Fast forward with me several months later to the summer of 1993. We were in Kansas City attending the annual Passion for Jesus conference hosted by what was then Metro Vineyard Fellowship, a megachurch pastored by Mike Bickle. In the late spring of that same year, Mike had extended an invitation for me to join his pastoral staff and serve as president of the in-house Bible school, Grace Training Center. Ann and I were fairly certain that this was God's leading, but we hadn't quite made up our minds. At least not until that night at the conference.

On the second night of the event, as Mike was preparing to continue his message on Psalm 2, he suddenly stopped. "God doesn't want me to preach right now. I have a strong sense that I trust is from the Lord that we are supposed to pray for some people that God wants to heal and deliver." Mike closed his Bible (he concluded his message on the following night) and called up on stage David Ruis, the worship leader at Metro Vineyard, and John Paul Jackson, a prophetically gifted man whom I had met two and a half years earlier at a large conference in Anaheim, California. I've told the story in detail in other places, so, to put it briefly, God had used John Paul in January 1991 in a powerful way in my life, speaking prophetically into circumstances I was facing. Here he was again, about to prophesy a transformation in Ann that would forever change our marriage and ministry.

Both Mike and John Paul discerned that the Lord wanted to minister to those in the audience who were oppressed by and in bondage to a spirit that evoked the fear of failing God. They asked for anyone to stand who wanted healing and deliverance from a spirit of failure and the shame it brings. There were approximately 2,000 people in attendance, and around fifty of them stood to their feet. My wife was among them.

To say I was shocked wouldn't remotely capture the essence of my reaction. To be honest, I was somewhat embarrassed. After all, I was a pastor and a leader. My pride led me to think that my stature in the church and value as a husband were dependent on my wife and me being free from any such spiritual struggles. How wrong I was!

As the worship team sang, several ladies neither Ann nor I had ever seen before laid hands on her and began singing in tongues. What I saw happening before my eyes was the spiritual transformation of my wife of twenty-one years. Intense sensations began in her temples and then gradually coursed throughout her body. She struggled to remain standing as the ladies lovingly continued their ministry to her. At one point, Ann reached up and patted their hands and said, "I'm okay. That's enough," all the while saying to herself, "But I'm a pastor's wife. I'm supposed to be okay." Thank God, the ladies knew better. "No," they said, "let's stay with this a while longer and see what God will do."

For all those many years, Ann had lived with what she now calls a hole in her soul filled with black goo. It crippled her relationship with the Lord. It adversely affected her intimacy with me. It daily tormented her with guilt and frustration and shame.

And then, without warning, it happened. As the ladies prayed and sang in the Spirit over Ann, the cleansing power of the Holy Spirit was released in her body and the invisible black goo came out. I know it sounds strange, but that's the only way Ann knows how to explain it. The ugly mass began to explode upward from her toes through her heart and out her mouth. The tears flowed as she was carried into a new revelation of Christ's love for her. The deep, dark hole was suddenly filled with the light of forgiveness and freedom and cleanness.

At that very moment, Ann herself had a vision she would never have anticipated. She saw herself as a pure, spotless bride in a radiant and gloriously white wedding gown, walking down the aisle as her groom, the Lord Jesus himself, waited at the altar. David Ruis began singing a song ("It Is Done") that he had received from the Lord only the day before. David didn't know Ann, but it was as if the lyrics were just for her, proclaiming her redemption through Christ.

It wasn't until the next day that we finally got around to unpacking what had happened the night before. Ann had to leave the conference early to return home and help our daughter get ready for cheerleading camp. We were heading to the airport in the car, trying to make sense of what had happened, when Ann suddenly grasped her head, placed her hands over her ears, and said:

"It's gone! It's gone!"

"What's gone?" I asked.

"The voice is gone," she said. "The voice that I've heard and fought against every day for years is gone!"

It's important to remember that up until that moment I had no idea of what I had done eighteen years earlier that had so deeply wounded my wife. She had kept it hidden within, never telling anyone of the inner vow or the tormenting voice that had quite literally haunted her all those years. But she suddenly felt the freedom to tell me everything. Needless to say, I was devastated by my own selfish sin and immediately asked her for forgiveness. "Yes," she said, "of course I forgive you."

What a change it has made. Our marriage isn't perfect, but it's great. Our relationship, spiritually and physically, is now on an entirely different plane. Yes, we do believe it was a demonic being, a tormenting spirit oppressing Ann for all those many years. No, we're not ashamed to talk about *deliverance*. Oh, what a glorious word! Set free by the mercy and cleansing grace of Jesus!

Praise God! I got a new wife. Together we got a new marriage! But I'm getting ahead of myself.

It was then that a look of fear and apprehension came over her face. "Oh no," she gasped.

"What?" I asked.

"I'm afraid it will be there waiting for me."

"What will?"

"That demon that I've been listening to and fighting with all these many years. I'm afraid it will be back home waiting for me to return."

I honestly didn't know what to make of this. Ann wasn't the only one who was new to the reality of spiritual warfare. But we were on our way to an understanding that largely accounts for why this book was written.

A Generational Spirit?

It was Thursday night, and the next day Ann was scheduled to drive our first-born daughter, Melanie, to Oklahoma City for her departure to cheerleading camp. I was still in Kansas City at the conference. They were up late, packing, when Ann noticed that Melanie was extraordinarily jumpy and nervous before bed, but she insisted that everything was okay. The next day as they were driving to Oklahoma City, Melanie said: "Mom, something happened last night. I didn't tell you then because I didn't think you'd believe me. But when I went downstairs to the dining room, I saw a man sitting on our love seat."

In our dining room was a large armoire, in the middle of which was a beveled mirror. "I saw his reflection in the mirror," Melanie explained, "and turned to look. He was sitting with his legs crossed. He had a scarf wrapped around his neck and sat with his chin in his hand. When I looked at him, he extended his hand, as if to invite me forward, waving his finger in a beckoning manner!"

In case you are wondering, no, we had not told Melanie anything about Ann's experience in Kansas City or the visual image in her mind that she had faced every day for those eighteen years of a demonic being wooing her to come, waving his finger, inviting her to come closer.

Ann was stunned and tried her best to find something positive in the experience.

"Melanie, do you think it was Jesus or an angel?"

"Oh, no, Mom," she said. "It was evil. I got scared and ran back upstairs."

Most of you don't know Melanie and need to understand that she is not the sort of person to be duped or easily deceived. She had never had any experience remotely similar to this before. Nothing had prepared her or created expectations in her mind that something of that nature might occur. She was as stable and mature as any fourteen-year-old I know. Although I had personally been on a spiritual journey, exploring the power and gifts of the Holy Spirit, neither one of our daughters had any idea of what was happening in my life, or in Ann's. My point is that Melanie was not in any way prepped or primed to fabricate this sort of experience.

What did she see? First of all, understand that she did not experience a vision. She saw this "man" with her physical eyes. Another surprising thing about his/its appearance is that it was the middle of July in southern Oklahoma, with temperatures still near 90 degrees even that late at night. And yet the "man" not only wore a winter scarf around his neck but also a large, heavy winter coat.

You can do with this what you wish, but Ann and I are convinced we know who and what it was. The "spirit" from which Ann had been so powerfully delivered, the "spirit" whose presence "back home" Ann was fearful would be waiting for her, was attempting to jump, as it were, to the next generation in our family line. We thank God that he gave Melanie the maturity and discernment to see the evil in this being and refuse it a place in her life.

The point of this story isn't sensationalism. We have no desire to stir up unbiblical speculation or to argue that every struggle in every person's life is due to some demonic presence. But we are convinced that this was precisely the case when it came to Ann and Melanie. There are numerous things that we do or fail to do that may well provide an open door, opportunity, foothold, place, or whatever else you wish to call it for the demonic to intrude into our lives. In Ann's case, it was the inner vow that she had made that May evening in 1975, a vow that she sinfully kept and nurtured for over eighteen years.

Ann's deliverance wasn't loud or violent or disruptive, as deliverance can so often be. But it wasn't for that reason any less real or life changing. And it can be the same for you. If you are tormented by unwanted voices, accusations, temptations, or perverse images that are impressed upon your mind, often at the most unusual times, you can be set free!

There is one more critically important factor that needs to be mentioned. Ann's deliverance did not occur "out of the blue," so to speak, or without cause. For the previous three to four years before that night in July of 1993, she had been on a spiritual journey of repentance and pursuing God. A significant contributing factor that we believe culminated in her being set free was Ann's growing awareness of God's love for her as his spiritual daughter. Over the course of the preceding three or four years, Ann, together with me and a dozen or so others in our church in Ardmore, Oklahoma, had been traveling up to Oklahoma City on the first Friday night of every month to participate in a worship service led by Dennis Jernigan.

Dennis was the worship leader at Western Hills Church in Oklahoma City. What he called the "Night of Praise" would typically last anywhere from three to four hours, with only one short break halfway through the event. That may sound a bit excessive for those of you accustomed to, at most, fifteen minutes of singing on Sunday morning. But it was in those services that God enlarged our hearts to embrace him, freely and fully, without regard for what people might think. The music and message of Dennis Jernigan contributed immeasurably to our growth as Christians. It was Dennis, in fact, who first made us aware of Zephaniah 3:17 and the shocking discovery that God loves his children so much that he *sings* over us.[5]

It was largely through what the Holy Spirit did in Ann's heart, by means of Jernigan's music, that gradually led her to open herself up to God once again. She began to realize what she had been missing, and that God was genuinely worthy of her trust. She and I both began to feel the freedom to *enjoy God*. We actually *felt* his presence. We actually *felt* his enjoyment of us in our enjoyment of him (cf. Zeph. 3:17). Ann in particular began to sense a *power* and *spiritual intensity* that at first was a bit frightening.

The simple fact was that God visited us in worship! As Ann drew near to God, he drew near to her (James 4:8). She began to experience an *intimacy* and *warmth of relationship* with God that reminded us both of Paul's prayer for the Ephesians:

> For this reason I bow my knees before the Father, from whom every family in heaven and on earth is named, that according to the riches of his glory he may grant you to be strengthened with power through his Spirit in your inner being, so that Christ may dwell in your hearts through faith—that

---

5 This is the theme of my book *The Singing God* (Lake Mary, FL: Charisma House, 2013).

> you, being rooted and grounded in love, may have strength to comprehend
> with all the saints what is the breadth and length and height and depth,
> and to know the love of Christ that surpasses knowledge, that you may be
> filled with all the fullness of God. (Ephesians 3:14–19)

This marvelous truth was the soil, so to speak, in which the Spirit sowed the seeds of conviction, repentance, forgiveness, and freedom that eventually bore the fruit of deliverance in Ann's life.

Involuntary Demonization

Some insist that there is no such thing as involuntary demonization. They insist that no demon can gain access or a foothold apart from the willful, voluntary complicity of the individual. But Scripture suggests otherwise.

Exodus 20:4–6: Consequences of Ancestors' Sinful Behavior

One widespread belief, especially among charismatic Christians, is that demonization can occur as a result of what is called *ancestral sin* and the activity of what are known as *generational spirits*. Those who believe in ancestral sin often appeal to Exodus 20:4–6.[6]

> "You shall not make for yourself a carved image, or any likeness of anything
> that is in heaven above, or that is in the earth beneath, or that is in the
> water under the earth. You shall not bow down to them or serve them, for
> I the LORD your God am a jealous God, visiting the iniquity of the fathers
> on the children to the third and the fourth generation of those who hate
> me, but showing steadfast love to thousands of those who love me and keep
> my commandments."

This text says nothing explicit about the passing down or generational transference of demonic spirits. The threat articulated here is the judgment of God, not the perpetuation of a demonic presence in a family line. The text also says that "*those who hate me*" are subject to this punishment. Nothing is said about innocent victims of ancestral rebellion.

---

6   I briefly discussed this text earlier in chapter 8.

We must take into consideration Deuteronomy 24:16: "Fathers shall not be put to death because of their children, nor shall children be put to death because of their fathers. Each one shall be put to death for his own sin" (cf. Ezek. 18:2–4, 20). The point is this: If you do not "hate" God, this threat is not applicable to you. We should also note that divine blessing or the experience of "steadfast love" does not extend automatically to the children of godly people, but only to "thousands of those who love me and keep my commandments."

Finally, the emphasis in the Exodus passage is on God's mercy, not his wrath. The point is that whereas the effects of disobedience last for some time, the effects of loving God are far more extensive ("to thousands"). My conclusion is that this passage in Exodus cannot be used directly to prove the reality of intergenerational spirits. What it does imply, however, is that the sinful behavior of one generation can have lingering and disastrous consequences on subsequent members of that family line. You cannot be held morally accountable before God for the sins of your father or mother, but you can be made (involuntarily) to suffer from the social, economic, and spiritual consequences of their sin.

Generational Spirits

While Exodus 20:4–6 doesn't necessarily provide evidence for generational spirits, other passages do—specifically, two cases from the Gospel of Mark.

The first is in Mark 7:24–30 and concerns the Syrophoenician woman "whose little daughter had an unclean spirit" (v. 25). After a brief interaction, Jesus told the woman that "the demon has left your daughter" (v. 29). When she arrived back home, she "found the child lying in bed and the demon gone" (v. 30). We can't be certain of the age of this girl, but she is described in verse 25 as the woman's "little daughter." The Greek *thugatrion* is the diminutive form of the standard word for daughter. Although it could point to her being quite young, it is also possible that this is merely a term of endearment, descriptive of the affection the mother had for her. In verse 30 she is described as a *paidion*, a "child." The implications from these two terms is that she was still a small child, perhaps even an infant.

There is a similar case in Mark 9:14–29 where a man was seeking help for his "son" who had "a spirit that makes him mute" (v. 17). The term "son" doesn't help us determine the age of this boy, but when Jesus asks his father,

"How long has this been happening to him?" (v. 21), he answers, "from child-hood" (*paidiothen*). It would be evasive to think that this refers to anything other than the boy's infancy.

In these two instances, a serious case of demonization had occurred in someone who was clearly too young to have done anything willfully or unrepentantly to warrant demonic attack. Surely neither was demonized for having spilled his or her milk! Nevertheless, for some reason that is not explicitly stated, both the young girl and boy had become demonized. How could this have happened? Are these not two undeniable instances of what we might call "involuntary" demonization? If so, we must determine how the demon gained access to their lives.

With regard to the incident in Mark 9, Clint Arnold argues that "the demonization was ... not the result of the boy's own sin or his choice to give his allegiance to false gods. The spirits were passed on to him from some other source, the most likely of which would be his family."[7] The mother in Mark 7 was a Gentile, an indication perhaps that she was raised in a culture given to idolatrous practices. In each case, we might suppose, for example, that the boy's grandfather or the girl's grandmother was demonized as the result of their involvement in idolatry or sexual perversion. When this grandfather or grandmother dies, what happens to the demon? Where does it go? Is it possible that the demon might assert a legal claim or "moral rights," so to speak, to this individual's posterity? We can't be dogmatic, insofar as the text is silent concerning the cause of the demonization. But some transmission of a demonic spirit embedded in the family line is as cogent an explanation as any.

Curses

One often also hears of an appeal to someone being cursed, and that some-how led a person to being demonized. One of the problems in discussing *curses* is the failure of most people to define precisely what is meant by the term. Although curses were most often verbalized, biblical curses have little if anything to do with modern profanity. Rather, to curse is to call down or send forth, from a supernatural source, calamity, trouble, chronic harm, or some other form of adversity upon another person or object. It is to speak

---

7 Arnold, *Three Crucial Questions*, 119.

evil of another person (hence, malediction or imprecation) with a view to inflicting injury (both physical and spiritual).[8]

Another problem in discussing curses is the misapplication of certain biblical texts. For example, appeal is often made to Galatians 3:13—"Christ redeemed us from the curse of the law by becoming a curse for us—for it is written, 'Cursed is everyone who is hanged on a tree.'" The problem is that this text and the Old Testament passages on which it is based all refer to *divine judgment* or the *penal consequences* of sin, not demonic attack. Leviticus 26 and Deuteronomy 27–28 are devoted to articulating the grounds on which God will "curse" as well as "bless" a person. Clearly, to be the recipient of a curse in this context means you come under divine judgment. God sends calamity or disaster or punishment in one form or another because of disobedience. Likewise, to be the recipient of a blessing is to experience his favor, his bounty, prosperity, and the like. When Jesus is said to have redeemed us from the curse by becoming a curse for us, the meaning is that he has suffered, in our place, the righteous wrath of God that we justly deserved. Therefore, Christians are no longer subject or vulnerable to a "curse" in that sense of the term.

In Joshua 6:26 and 9:23, a curse is pronounced by Joshua on both Jericho and Gibeon. But again, in both cases this appears to be a calling down of *divine* judgment, not demonic harm. In 1 Samuel 17:43, we see that pagan people in ancient times (in this case, Goliath) believed that curses (calamity) were the work of their gods. Spoken curses were thought to possess a power that derived from whatever deity they served. A curse was thought to trigger the release of malevolent spiritual energy toward the person or the object being cursed (see 2 Samuel 16:5–12).

The question remains: Does the Bible speak about demonic curses? Do we read in Scripture of anyone invoking or calling down or sending forth a demonic being to bring pain and problems, harassment and harm, to another person? This would appear to be what the Moabite king Balak asked Balaam to do regarding Israel. God himself forbids Balaam from cursing Israel: "you shall not curse the people, for they are blessed" (Num. 22:12). Although no mention is made of demonic spirits being involved, it is reasonable to think

8   Douglas Stuart, in *The Anchor Bible Dictionary*, says, "to curse is to predict, wish, pray for, or cause trouble or disaster on a person or thing" (New York: Doubleday, 1992), 1:1218.

that they would have been the instrument of bringing calamity on Israel had Balaam carried through with this task. As far as I can tell, there is no New Testament example of a demonic curse, although there are numerous New Testament instances of a curse as an expression of divine judgment for sin.

Proverbs 26:2 is especially instructive: "Like a fluttering sparrow or a darting swallow, an undeserved curse does not come to rest" (NIV). This seems to suggest that a curse is not effectual in itself. If it is undeserved, its impact is undermined. It would seem that a curse is, in itself, incapable of leading to demonization apart from the moral complicity of the person involved.

KARLA'S STORY

Reading has always been a tremendous challenge for me. My parents worked to find help for me, but at that time, there were limited resources. An educational tester believed I had a form of dyslexia.

My junior high history teacher made us read passages from our textbook to the class. I dreaded my turn because a girl in my class found great delight in jumping in as soon as I paused or mispronounced a word to mockingly correct me in front of everyone. I pronounced sugar with a "s" not "sh" sound one day, and of course everyone had a good laugh at my expense. This would go on with minimal intervention from the teacher until my passage was done, and of course my humiliation was complete. To be fair, she did this to anyone who struggled.

In high school all my church and school friends were very good students. The majority have pursued careers in medicine, engineering, accounting, and math. I felt like such a misfit, so unintelligent, and like the weak link. I even cheated a few times in my math and biology classes because I wanted to feel smart and to get great grades like my friends. While it briefly felt good to talk to my friends about how well I had done on my biology exam and for them to think I was smart too, it was short lived. I knew the truth, and I was overwhelmed with shame.

My mom began reading my textbooks to me in high school, and things began to improve a bit. It was not until college that I learned my eyes were not working together. This would explain why it always felt like I was bouncing down a bumpy road when I was reading. I would lose my place often, and it took abnormally long for me to read. I was able to do some vision therapy, and it helped some, but reading was still hard. But I was so determined to do things right this time, to prove I was smart, to not fail, and to be an excellent student even if I had to muscle my way through each word. At this time, I also determined not to fall into a religion. I took my vow with me through college, graduate school, and even toward completing a PhD. I didn't fail, but there were many missed opportunities and creative risks I did not take. I was too busy not failing.

God blessed me with two wonderful boys. Then I realized another level of reading frustration and difficulty. I struggled to read simple children's books aloud with them. It was choppy and difficult. My parents had both read to us growing up, creating wonderful memories. My struggle to carry on this special tradition with my little family was frustrating. I remember once when I was bumbling through a simple story, my husband said, "I had no idea how difficult it was for you to read."

I do not recall at any point asking the Lord to heal my eyes or to help me read. However, through some forgiveness teaching I was going through with two ladies from our church, the Holy Spirit gently instructed me that although I thought of myself as a forgiving person, what I really was doing was stuffing the mocking voices and public humiliation from the comments directed at me, and then going on as if nothing had happened. I was stuffing the shame of my failure and clawing forward. To help me commit to a lifestyle of freedom, these ladies shared some teaching and prayers with me. We would meet regularly for ministry and prayer, and I would read the prayers out loud as confessions of my sin and unforgiveness. I would also speak blessings for the people who had hurt and offended me. Some of the forgiveness prayers were for people who had teased me in school about my poor reading.

You can imagine how difficult the sessions were for me. I had to read the prayers out loud the majority of the time. But I truly felt the prayers were coming from a longing to be in close relationship with the Lord. Even thought it was difficult, I stumbled through the prayers. After meeting for several weeks, I looked up at the two ladies in the middle of a prayer and said, "Have you two noticed that I am not stumbling through these prayers anymore?" I wish you could have seen their faces! They were beaming and giggling and said, "We have! We were just waiting for you to notice it before we said anything!" It blew my mind because I realized how personal God is to me. He cares about every detail of my life, including my eyes. I had just accepted my difficulty with reading as my fate. My whole life I had been clawing through my studies, but my personal God, the Creator of the Universe, wants to heal every aspect of me.

The shame has lifted. Now I can read. For the first time, I really enjoy reading all kinds of stories to my boys. God is using this healing to bless me and my children. He is very good and loving from generation to generation.

CHAPTER 10

Can a Christian Be Demonized?

I find it strangely intriguing that of all the thorny topics addressed in this book, the one presently under consideration often provokes more heat and contention than all the others. So let's jump directly into the fray! Can a Christian be demonized? Can a Christian be indwelt by a demonic spirit? Scholarly opinions on this topic can be divided into three categories:

1. Yes/No—a believer can be demonized, but in a somewhat modified or restricted sense.
2. No—a Christian cannot be inhabited or indwelt by a demonic spirit.
3. Yes—a Christian can be indwelt by a demonic spirit.[1]

Let's explore each of these lines of thought in greater depth.

Arguments for a Modified Demonization of Christians

Several authors suggest that a believer can be demonized, but in a somewhat modified or restricted sense. Based on the doctrine of *trichotomy*, according to which a person is composed of three faculties (body, soul, and spirit), they affirm that a demon can inhabit a Christian's soul and body, but not his spirit. The body is one's physical constitution. The soul is comprised of one's mind, emotions, and will. The spirit is that element or faculty that relates to

---

1   Much of this chapter has been adapted from my book *Tough Topics*, 166–83, and is used here with permission.

God and at regeneration is born anew, sealed, and permanently indwelt by the Holy Spirit.

Although this view has become increasingly popular, I find it lacking in several ways. First, there is no explicit evidence for this in Scripture. Nowhere in the Bible do we read of a demon indwelling a person's "soul" or "body" but being excluded from the "spirit." Furthermore, this view is based on the validity of trichotomy (1 Thess. 5:23), a doubtful doctrine (see Mark 12:30). Man is dichotomous: He is both material and immaterial, both physical and spiritual, the latter often called the soul and at other times the spirit. On numerous occasions in Scripture "spirit" and "soul" are used interchangeably, as simply different names for the same immaterial dimension of our constitution, thus prohibiting us from drawing rigid distinctions between the two.[2]

I would also argue that the whole person is renewed by the Holy Spirit, not just one faculty or element within that person (2 Cor. 5:17). To restrict a demon to a person's soul and body, excluded from his spirit, is to suggest

---

2   Among the many Old Testament texts in which "soul" refers to the center of our spiritual life and our relationship with God, indeed the source from which flow godly love and the worship of God, are Deuteronomy 6:4–5; Song of Solomon 1:7; Psalms 63:1; 86:4; 139:14. Thus, throughout the Old Testament the "soul" is most often used to refer to the entire personality: love, joy, sorrow, understanding, longing, delight, devotion, etc., are all functions of the soul. There is nothing that would suggest that the "soul" is somehow separate from or inferior to the "spirit" or not just as engaged with God and devoted to serving him, loving him, and enjoying him. We see the same in the New Testament. See, for example, Matthew 11:22; 2 Corinthians 1:23; Ephesians 6:6; Colossians 3:2; 1 Thessalonians 2:8; Hebrews 6:19; 12:3; 10:39; 1 Peter 1:22; 2:11; 2 Peter 2:8 (be aware that in many English translations the words "heart" and "mind" are used to translate the Greek word for "soul" [*psychē*]). Texts in which "soul" and "spirit" are used interchangeably include Luke 1:46–47 and Philippians 1:27. We see the same in the experience of Jesus (cf. Mark 8:12 and John 13:21 with John 12:27 and Matt. 26:38). Similarly, joy is the experience or expression of, or is centered in, both the "spirit" (Ps. 32:2; 34:18; 51:10, 12, 17; Prov. 11:13; 16:19; Isa. 57: 15; Ezek. 11:19; 18:31; 36:26) and the "soul" (Ps. 42:1–6; 63:5; 103:1, 2; 116:7; 130:6; Isa. 26:9). The various terms point to a variety of exercises, functions, or activities of any particular person, but not to separate or divisible faculties. Thus we might summarize by saying that the "soul" is the whole immaterial being of a man or woman. When the "soul" engages with God, it is frequently spoken of as the "spirit," but on several occasions the "soul" itself engages, communes with, and worships and loves God. When the "soul" is viewed in its capacity to think and reason, it is called the "mind." When the "soul" functions in its volitional capacity or its power to make choices, it is called the "will." When the "soul" feels or experiences intense passions or longings, it is called the "affections" or "emotions" or the more vivid "kidneys" or "bowels of compassion," or the like. And when the "soul" is spoken of comprehensively, inclusive of all the above as the center of our innermost being, it is frequently called the "heart." But we must remember that all of these functions and terms are by and large interchangeable. The "heart" also thinks and loves and serves, as does the "soul," the "mind," and the "affections." We engage with God and experience intimacy and communion with him not only in our "spirit" but also with our "will" and our "emotions."

that there is a rigid, spatial compartmentalization of our beings. But *where* is the soul in the body? *Where* is the spirit? These are biblically illegitimate questions. It is an attempt to apply physical categories to spiritual realities.

Clinton Arnold offers a slightly different interpretation. Without drawing a distinction between soul and spirit, he refers to "the core of the person, the center of his or her being, his or her ultimate nature and identity."[3] It is this within each person that undergoes a radical, indeed supernatural, transformation in the new birth. He explains:

> At the center of this person's being now lies a desire for God and a passion to please him in every respect. This is the place of the Holy Spirit's dwelling. No evil spirit can enter here or cause the Holy Spirit to flee. To extend the image of the temple, we might say that this is the inviolable "holy of holies."[4]

Here again we see an attempt to restrict the access of a demonic spirit to certain *places* or *spiritual regions* within the individual. Does Arnold's model successfully avoid the weaknesses and criticisms of the trichotomist theory noted above? I don't think so.

Arguments against the Demonization of Christians

Those who insist that a Christian cannot be inhabited or indwelt by a demonic spirit appeal to several lines of evidence. Let's look at each one in turn.

Satan's Defeat

They begin by pointing to those biblical *texts that describe the defeat of Satan*, specifically John 12:31; 16:11; Colossians 2:14–15; Hebrews 2:14–15; and 1 John 3:8. The argument is that if Satan has been judged, stripped, and his work destroyed (1 John 3:8), how can he or his demons indwell a believer?

But these passages do not by themselves settle the issue. It is true that Jesus has "bound" (Matt. 12:25–29) the strong man (Satan), but it is equally the case that Satan can exert a significant influence in the lives of believers (Matt. 16:23; Acts 5:3; 1 Pet. 5:8). Jesus has defeated the devil (John 12:31;

3   Arnold, *Three Crucial Questions*, 85.
4   Ibid., 84.

16:11), but he must also continue to pray that God would guard us against the attacks of the evil one (John 17:15). On one hand, all demonic powers have been subjected to the lordship of Jesus and placed beneath his feet (Eph. 1:19–22). But, on the other hand, Paul warns us that our struggle is still against principalities and powers and the forces of this present darkness (Eph. 6:10–13). We have been delivered from Satan's domain, and Jesus has triumphed over the demonic (Col. 1:13; 2:14–15), but Satan can still hinder Paul's missionary efforts (1 Thess. 2:18). My point is simply that the reality of Satan's defeat does not eliminate his activity and influence in the present age.

The Promise of Divine Protection

Proponents of this view also appeal to *texts that describe the promise of divine protection*. Yes, Jesus instructed us to pray for deliverance from the evil one (Matt. 6:13), but this is clearly dependent (and not automatic) on our prayer for it. What happens if we do *not* pray? No one can snatch us from the hand of our heavenly Father (John 10:28–29), but if a demon could indwell a believer, wouldn't that mean our security is in doubt? No, because this text simply asserts the same truth we find in Romans 8:35–39, namely, that nothing, not even a demon, can separate us from the love and life we have in God. It says nothing about the possibility of demonization.

I'm grateful, as I'm sure you are, that Jesus prayed in John 17:15 that the Father would guard us against the enemy. But this text cannot mean that Jesus wanted the Father to make us utterly invulnerable to demonic attack. Indeed, it was after this prayer that Jesus told Peter of Satan's request to "sift" him like wheat. This prayer is more likely for our eternal preservation, or it may be that the fulfillment or answer to it is dependent on our availing ourselves of the Father's protection (Eph. 6).

Paul prays in 2 Thessalonians 3:3 that we would be "kept" or "protected" from Satan. But again, we must ask: Kept or protected from *what* regarding the enemy, and on what, if any, conditions? This promise of protection does not rule out attack or temptation from the enemy (see 1 Thess. 2:18; 2 Cor. 12:7; 1 Pet. 5:8). Therefore, either this is a promise pertaining to the eternal preservation of the believer (no matter how vicious the attack, no matter how bad life gets, Satan can't separate you from God), or it is a promise conditioned upon the obedient response of the believer. Fred Dickason explains:

This promise, then, is for those who walk in obedience to the Lord. Satan will not be able to take them unaware and render them weak, unfaithful, and unproductive in Christian life and service. It is a great promise for the obedient and watchful Christian, but is not a blanket protection promised to all. It does not promise that no Christian will ever be attacked or seriously affected by demonic forces. It does not address the matter of demonization.[5]

One of the most encouraging texts in the New Testament is 1 John 4:4, where the apostle assures us that greater is he who is in us (Jesus Christ) than he who is in the world (Satan). But this text does not mean that all Christians are always automatically guaranteed to never be deceived by error. It does mean that we *need not* ever be deceived, for the Holy Spirit is more powerful than Satan.

Satan Cannot "Touch" Us

I often hear reference made to 1 John 5:18 and the assurance that the enemy cannot touch the believer. The argument is made that it makes little sense to say, on the one hand, that the evil one cannot "touch" a Christian, and yet, on the other hand, that the evil one could conceivably indwell a Christian. But let's think about this more closely. For one thing, we can't press the term "touch" to exclude the attack and influence of Satan, for according to 1 Peter 5:8 it is possible to be "devoured" by the devil! We should also consider Revelation 2:10, where Jesus himself says that Satan can imprison and even kill the Christian. Thus, whatever "touch" means, it does not suggest that all Christians are automatically insulated against demonic attack. Also, to "touch" a believer may mean to rob him or her of salvation. If so, then Satan cannot "grasp so as to destroy" the spiritual life of the believer. Finally, it may well be that the promise is conditional, perhaps suspended on the fulfillment of 1 John 5:21.

Clearly, no Christian can be swallowed up by Satan or robbed of the salvation, life, and love of the Father. The Christian cannot be owned by Satan, nor separated from the love of God in Christ. But none of these texts explicitly rules out the possibility of demonization. The promises of protection

---

5   C. Fred Dickason, *Demon Possession & the Christian* (Chicago: Moody Press, 1987), 91.

are of two sorts: either a promise pertaining to the security of the believer's salvation, or a promise dependent on the believer's taking advantage of the resources supplied by the Spirit.

The Indwelling Presence of the Holy Spirit

Another line of argumentation is based on *texts that describe the indwelling presence of the Holy Spirit*. The argument is this: A demon cannot enter and dwell within a believer because the Holy Spirit lives there. Since the Spirit is greater and more powerful than any demon, there is no possibility that a demon would be granted access into a Christian's heart.

But I must again ask, Is this protection against demonic invasion automatic? What if the believer grieves the Holy Spirit through repeated and unrepentant sin? What if the believer fails to faithfully and prayerfully put on the armor of God (Eph. 6)? Several texts are relevant to this issue.

In Psalm 5:4 we read, "For you are not a God who delights in wickedness; evil may not dwell with you." Does this text really mean to suggest that God cannot dwell alongside an evil spirit inside a person? Observe that the two lines of verse 4 are in synonymous parallelism, that is, "evil may not dwell with you" is simply another way of saying that God does not delight in wickedness. The point is not that God cannot be in close spatial proximity to evil. We must not forget that the *omnipresent* God is in close spatial proximity to *everything*! The point of the passage is simply that God detests evil and has no fellowship with it.

Matthew 12:43–45 is a famous passage that needs to be cited in full. Jesus says, "When the unclean spirit has gone out of a person, it passes through waterless places seeking rest, but finds none. Then it says, 'I will return to my house from which I came.' And when it comes, it finds the house empty, swept, and put in order. Then it goes and brings with it seven other spirits more evil than itself, and they enter and dwell there, and the last state of that person is worse than the first. So also will it be with this evil generation." The argument is that if the house *is* occupied (presumably by Jesus or the Holy Spirit), demons can't enter. But does this mean that the person himself cannot "open the door" to intrusion by a demon through willful, unrepentant sin or idolatry? Also, the text does not say what the demon would have done had he found his previous home occupied. It does not say that *that* in itself would have prevented his re-entry. It may well have made re-entry more difficult, but not necessarily impossible.

In 1 Corinthians 10:21 Paul warns Christians, "You cannot drink the cup of the Lord and the cup of demons. You cannot partake of the table of the Lord and the table of demons." But the "cannot" in Paul's language refers to a moral, not a metaphysical, impossibility. If I say to a Christian who is contemplating committing adultery, "But you *cannot* do that!" I don't mean that it is physically impossible for him to commit adultery, but that it is *morally or spiritually incompatible* with his being a Christian. In other words, you can't expect to enjoy close intimacy with Christ and simultaneously give yourself to the influence of demons. It is a moral and spiritual contradiction to affirm your love for God while you simultaneously expose yourself to the influence of demons by participating in activities they energize. In fact, far from ruling out the possibility of a Christian "participating" in or "fellowshipping" with demons, Paul warns us to be careful of that very thing.

Two texts in the Corinthian letters describe Christians as the "temple" of the Holy Spirit in whom he dwells and of the danger in being "unequally yoked" with unbelievers and of seeking "fellowship" with darkness (1 Cor. 3:16–17; 2 Cor. 6:14–16). The argument from these texts at first glance seems persuasive: Surely a Christian cannot simultaneously be both the temple of God and the temple of a demon!

But Paul is not referring (in 2 Cor. 6) to the physical impossibility of a Christian being "yoked" in "fellowship" with evil or with an unbeliever. The fact is, we know it happens all the time, unfortunately. Rather, he is denouncing the *moral or spiritual incongruity* of such fellowship. The temple of God has no moral or spiritual harmony with idols. Therefore, avoid all such entangling alliances.

The argument from 1 Corinthians 3 is based on the idea that a demon indwelling a Christian is a "spatial" and "spiritual" impossibility. As for the former, it is argued that there is "not enough room" for both the Holy Spirit and a demonic being to coexist in the same human body. It would be too crowded! But this is to think of spiritual beings in physical terms. I could as easily ask, How can the Holy Spirit and the human spirit both indwell the same body? Wouldn't that be just as "crowded"? Mary Magdalene at one time had seven demons inhabiting her (Luke 8:2). The man in Mark 5 was inhabited by a "legion" (about six thousand) of demons—enough, at any rate, to enter and destroy two thousand pigs. And if the presence of the Holy Spirit "crowds out" demons, then demons couldn't exist *anywhere* because the Holy Spirit exists *everywhere*.

The second argument is that this would be a "spiritual" impossibility. That is to say, How can the *Holy* Spirit inhabit the same body with an *unholy* demon? But again, we must remember that the Holy Spirit in a certain sense "inhabits" everything and everyone in the universe, even unbelievers (of course, in the case of the latter, he does not indwell them in a saving or sanctifying way). The Holy Spirit is, after all, omnipresent. He dwells everywhere! You may also recall from the book of Job that Satan had access to the presence of God, indicating that the issue is not one of spatial proximity but of *personal relationship*. The Holy Spirit and demons are in close proximity when *outside* the human body, so why could they not be in close proximity while *inside* one? Finally, the Holy Spirit indwells the Christian even though the latter still has a sinful nature or sinful flesh. In other words, if the *Holy* Spirit can inhabit the same body with *unholy* human sin, why could he not inhabit the same body with an *unholy* demon?

It strikes me that the force of this argument appears to be more emotional than biblical. The idea of the Holy Spirit and a demon living inside a believer is *too close, too intimate*. The thought of it is emotionally provocative and scandalous; it violates our sense of spiritual propriety. The *feeling* is that God simply wouldn't allow it. His love for his own is too great to let demonic influence get that far. But we must always keep in mind that the only criterion for making a decision on an issue such as this is not what *seems* or *feels* proper to us, but what the Scripture explicitly asserts.

Other Arguments

There are a number of other arguments that I should mention. For example, I've been asked, "How can a Christian who is *possessed* by Christ be *possessed* by a demon?" But in this question, the word "possessed" is being used in two entirely different senses. To say that one is "possessed" by a demon (although that in itself is an unbiblical term) is to say that the Christian is severely influenced by the spirit. To say that one is "possessed" by Christ is to say he or she is owned by the Lord and purchased with the blood of Jesus (1 Cor. 6).

Another goes like this: "How can a Christian who is *in Christ* have a demon *in him or her*?" Again, words are being used here in a way that provokes an emotional response but lacks theological substance. To be "in Christ" refers to eternal salvation, whereas to say a demon is "in a believer" refers to influence or powers of persuasion.

Perhaps you've heard it said that the internal struggle of the Christian is portrayed in the New Testament as between the Holy Spirit and the flesh, not the Holy Spirit and a demon. However, in the first place, this is an argument from silence. Or to put it another way, what biblical text *denies* or *precludes* the Holy Spirit from fighting against an indwelling demon? Also, if a Christian yields to the flesh and grieves the Holy Spirit, wouldn't this open the door to demonic presence? Finally, Ephesians 6 says that our primary struggle *is* against the demonic. Although there is no explicit reference to this being an *internal* battle, there is nothing here that precludes it being an internal battle (especially if we fail to employ the full armor).

Arguments Supporting the Demonization of Christians

We've looked closely at most, if not all, of the arguments used to prove that a Christian cannot be demonized. My conclusion is that none of these texts or the conclusions drawn from them conclusively make the case. We now turn our attention to texts that may suggest a Christian can be indwelt by a demonic spirit.

The Reality of Demonic Activity and Attack

We begin with those passages that describe *the reality of demonic activity and attack*. Most of these texts fail to prove the thesis that a Christian can be demonized because they fail to say anything about the *location* of the activity relative to the individual. For example, 2 Corinthians 2:11 asserts that Satan has a strategy to bring division to the body of Christ. No one would deny that Satan seeks to divide and disrupt, to exploit disagreements, or to intensify unforgiveness, but nothing is said here explicitly about demonization.

Second Corinthians 11:3–4 speaks of the danger that the Corinthian believers might "receive" a "different spirit" from the one they had earlier accepted. What does "spirit" mean? Is this a demonic being, or could it be an attitude, an influence, or a principle? And what does "receive" mean? Is it invasion and subsequent inhabitation, or perhaps tolerance or attentiveness? The most likely explanation is that the Corinthians were tolerating the presence and influence of false teachers who were energized by demons.

We are all familiar with 2 Corinthians 12:7–8, where Paul's thorn in the flesh came to him through a "messenger of Satan." Although God used a demonic being to keep Paul humble, no one would wish to conclude that he was demonized! If he were, would he have rejoiced in its effects (vv. 9–10)?

Ephesians 4:26–27 is a far more important passage, for here we see what might happen should the devil exploit the relational strains and tension that develop in the Christian community. Page is correct to point out "that the devil is not credited with producing anger; that is, its source is apparently to be found within the person himself or herself. Nevertheless, anger can provide the devil with an opportunity to wreak havoc in the life of the individual and the community."[6] It seems reasonable that Satan's activity in this regard would extend to the other sins mentioned in the immediately subsequent context: stealing, unwholesome speech, bitterness, wrath, clamor, slander, malice, and unforgiveness (see vv. 28–32).

Clinton Arnold points to Paul's use of the term *topos*, translated "foothold" or "opportunity" (v. 27). He argues that this word is often used in the New Testament for "inhabited space" (cf. Luke 2:7; 4:37; 14:9; John 14:2–3). Even more to the point, says Arnold, are passages that illustrate the use of *topos* to refer to the inhabiting space of an evil spirit, such as Luke 11:24 and Revelation 12:7–8. Thus he concludes that "the most natural way to interpret the use of *topos* in Eph. 4:27 is the idea of inhabitable space. Paul is thus calling these believers to vigilance and moral purity so that they do not relinquish a base of operations to demonic spirits."[7]

Everyone is familiar with Ephesians 6:10–18 and Paul's passionate exhortation that we put on the full armor of God to prepare ourselves for the onslaught of demonic attack. What happens to the believer who does *not* stand in the strength of Christ, who does *not* put on the full armor of God, who does *not* therefore "stand firm" (v. 13)?

There are a handful of passages that speak of Satanic and demonic attack. First Thessalonians 2:18 says that "Satan hindered" Paul from making a desired visit to Thessalonica. The apostle describes the danger of a believer falling into "a snare of the devil." Does this entail demonization? There's no way to know. The language itself neither implies nor precludes the possibility. Characteristic of "later times" is that people will come under the influence of demonic doctrine, perhaps even a form of "mind control." Paul speaks of

---

6 Page, *Powers of Evil*, 188–89.
7 Arnold, *Three Crucial Questions*, 88.

them as "devoting themselves to deceitful spirits and teachings of demons" (1 Tim. 4:1). But does this entail or require inhabitation? And does he have in mind born-again Christians, or only professing believers who in fact know nothing of the saving grace of Jesus?

Paul describes some as escaping from "the snare of the devil, after being captured by him to do his will" (2 Tim. 2:26). But these would appear to be unbelievers whom Paul hopes and prays will come to saving faith through Timothy's ministry. But what happens when a demonized person comes to saving faith? Does the Holy Spirit's activity in regenerating such a person automatically result in deliverance or exorcism of the indwelling demon? No text of which I am aware ever answers that question.

As we saw earlier, James refers to a form of "wisdom" that is "earthly, unspiritual, demonic" (James 3:15) and evidently envisions the possibility that a believer might act on the basis of it. But does this entail demonization? More explicit still is Peter's exhortation that we be watchful in view of the fact that "your adversary the devil prowls around like a roaring lion, seeking someone to devour" (1 Pet. 5:8). His counsel is that we humble ourselves (v. 6) and cast all our anxieties on God and remain sober and alert. It seems reasonable to conclude that if we do *not* humble ourselves, if we do *not* cast our cares on him, if we are *not* sober and alert, we may well be *devoured* by the devil. "Devour" means to swallow up (Matt. 23:24; 1 Cor. 15:54; 2 Cor. 2:7; 5:4; Heb. 11:29; Rev. 12:16). Nothing, however, is said explicitly about how or from where this "devouring" takes place. I would think that if given the opportunity, Satan or demons can make a serious encroachment on the life of a believer; simply being a Christian does not automatically insulate you from this sort of potentially devastating attack. On the other hand, if we "resist" the devil (v. 9), we are assured of victory.

And a passage we looked at earlier, 1 John 4:1–4, would be relevant to this debate only if some of the false teachers in whom the spirit of antichrist operated were Christians. This, however, is highly unlikely.

The Experience of Certain Individuals in the Bible

We turn next to texts where the experience of particular individuals is described. *Balaam* (Num. 22–24) is often mentioned. But was Balaam a believer? Whatever the answer, nothing is said here about an indwelling demonic presence in his life. The case of *Saul* is more intriguing. Was he a believer? Probably so (1 Sam. 10:9). Because of his rebellion and sin, he came under demonic attack (1 Sam. 16:14–23; 18:10–11; 19:9). However, the evil spirit is said to come "upon/on" him, not "into/in" him. Does the fact that this happened prior to Pentecost have any bearing on how we interpret it? Most helpful of all is the story of *the woman bent double* (Luke 13:10–17). Her condition has been identified by some as ankylosing spondylitis, which produces fusion of the vertebrae. But was she a believer? She "glorified" God immediately on being delivered (v. 13) and is called "a daughter of Abraham" (v. 16; cf. Luke 19:9). The latter may simply mean she was Jewish. Was she demonized? The NASB reads, "had a sickness caused by a spirit," whereas it literally reads, "she had a spirit of sickness (or of infirmity)," which is similar to the language of demonization ("to have a spirit"; see also v. 16). Others have argued, however, that this narrative reads more like a simple healing than an exorcism. But even if so, that doesn't answer the question of whether or not the demon indwelt her.

I would be remiss if I didn't mention the story of *Ananias and Sapphira* (Acts 5). Certainly they were both believers. It seems unlikely that the example of their deaths would have any relevance for the church if they were not (cf. v. 11). Were they demonized? Satan is said to have "filled" their hearts (v. 3). This verb "filled" is the same one used in Ephesians 5:18 for being "filled" with the Holy Spirit. But with what did he fill them? Did Satan fill them with himself to indwell them? Or did Satan fill their hearts with the temptation or idea or notion to hold back the money? At minimum, this is the case of a believer coming under powerful Satanic influence. Notwithstanding Satan's influence, *they* were responsible for their sin. *They* were disciplined with death (see vv. 4b, 9—"you"). The point is that they could have said no to Satan's influence.

The case of the man in 1 Corinthians 5 who had been discovered having sexual relations with his stepmother is often mentioned in this debate. Paul counsels that he be delivered "to Satan for the destruction of the flesh" (1 Cor. 5:5). This probably refers to his excommunication or expulsion from the fellowship of the church. To "deliver to Satan" refers to turning him out into the world, back into the domain of Satan. "Destruction of the flesh" does not refer to physical death, but to the anticipated effect of his expulsion, namely, the mortification or crucifixion of his carnal appetites so that he may be saved on the day of Christ. So here we see yet another example of Satan intending one thing in a particular action (no doubt he wanted only to ruin this man) while God intended something entirely different (salvation).

"Communion" with Demons

First Corinthians 10:14–22 is a special case that probably comes as close as any text to providing us with the explicit evidence we need to draw a firm conclusion on this debate. There Paul urgently warns the Corinthians against participating in pagan feasts and then turning to the fellowship of the Lord's Supper in the meeting of the local church. Clearly, the apostle thought it possible for a Christian to become a "participant," "sharer," or "partner" with demons. The word he uses here is *koinōnia*, typically used to describe fellowship or communion with a person or thing. It is the same word used in verse 16 for our sharing in or participating with or entering into fellowship with Christ at his table! What does this mean? Is he referring merely to "agreement with" or the "holding of a common purpose with" Christ and/or a demon? Is it merely a description of external attendance at a pagan feast? Or does Paul have in mind a more active sharing of an internal spiritual bond, link, or fellowship with a demon? His point seems to be that when you sit to worship at the table of the Lord, or conversely, in the presence of idols, you open yourself to the power and influence of one or the other. There is a sharing of an intimate spiritual experience, an association of sorts, a relationship that is personal and powerful. But does it entail inhabitation by a demon?

Conclusion

Clinton Arnold responds to those who think it is significant that no text explicitly describes a case of a Christian being demonized:

> Although the Epistles do not use the terms *demonization* or *have a demon* to describe the experience of a Christian, the concept is nevertheless present. The ideas of demonic inhabitation and control are clearly a part of the biblical teaching on what demons can do to saints. To limit ourselves to the same Greek words that the Gospels use to describe the phenomena of demonic influence could cause us to miss the same concept expressed in different terms. No one, for instance, questions the validity of making disciples as part of the church's mission. Yet the term *disciple* (*mathētēs*)

never appears in the New Testament after the Book of Acts. It would be quite erroneous to conclude that the concept of discipleship died out early in the history of the church. What has happened is that Paul, Peter, John, and other New Testament authors have made use of a variety of other terms to describe the same reality.[8]

It would seem, then, that the debate reduces the question to the *location* of demonic spirits relative to the believer, rather than to their *influence*. In other words, all must concede that Christians can be attacked, tempted, oppressed, devoured, and led into grievous sin. Satan can fill our hearts to lie, he can exploit our anger, he can deceive our minds with false doctrine. The question, then, is this: Does all this take place from outside our minds, spirits, bodies, or could it arise from a demon indwelling us?

The New Testament does not supply an unequivocal, indisputable answer to our question. Nothing precludes the demonization of a believer. Nor does any text explicitly affirm it or provide us with an undeniable example of a believer who was indwelt by a demon. So of what *practical* significance is the question? In other words, will the location of the demonic spirit affect how I pray for and minister to the person who is under attack? Will I use different words, different prayers, or different portions of Scripture? I'm inclined to agree with Thomas White when he says, "Whether a demon buffets me from a mile away, the corner of the room, sitting on my shoulder, whispering in my ear, or clinging to my corruptible flesh, the result is the same."[9]

Or is it, in fact, the same? Is it necessary for a demon to be spatially "inside" a person's mind to infuse or to suggest words and thoughts, or for that person to hear voices not their own? In the case of Peter (Matt. 16), Satan put the thought into his mind without indwelling him. People often report hearing voices inside their heads—not audibly, but ideas, words, images springing into mind involuntarily. They have the sense that the source is not themselves. Must a demon be *inside* for this to happen?

If I were to tell you that a Christian can be demonized, you might be frightened. But if I tell you that a Christian can be hit by a passing car, you don't get scared; you simply take steps to stay out of traffic! You don't walk

---

8 Arnold, *Three Crucial Questions*, 92–93.

9 Thomas B. White, *The Believer's Guide to Spiritual Warfare* (Ann Arbor, MI: Servant, 1990), 44.

into the middle of a busy street. You don't live in constant worry or fear simply because it is *possible* to get hit by a car. And if the car jumps the curb and chases after you, you only need to run inside the building for protection. Likewise, if it were possible for a Christian to be demonized, do not be afraid. Rather, follow the steps outlined in Scripture, employ the protection made available by the Holy Spirit, and if you get chased anyway, seek refuge and protection in Christ Jesus.

There is one final question to be asked: What place or level of authority should we give to the testimony and experience of other Christians in deciding this issue? In other words, what am I to conclude, if anything, from personal experience in having prayed for and ministered to people who I have great confidence are Christians and who give every indication of being demonized? Those who are dogmatically assured that a Christian cannot be demonized would not be impressed by any examples I might describe. For them, in each case there are two options, not three. Either the person is self-deluded and has deceived others into thinking he or she is born again, or the demonic activity was not from within but from without. The possibility that the person is both born again and inhabited by a demonic spirit is simply not entertained.

So I will simply end with this tentative, guarded conclusion: Yes, in the final analysis, my opinion is that a Christian can be demonized.

BETHANY'S STORY

Before I started inner healing and deliverance, I would find myself in deep, dark, depressed places. This would lead me to a place where suicide seemed to be the only reasonable escape. My emotions would lead me into a deep trench. I would get horribly wound up and stuck in that place. I would have this urge and desire to escape, whether through leaving my family or ending my life. I was so reactive that I would just go off the handle when my husband or my kids would say something to me. My brain and emotions were overwhelmed or felt muddled.

Since going through inner healing and deliverance sessions, I can tell the Holy Spirit has broken off so many things. I have definitely noticed that

I do not stay in those dark places very long. I see the fruit of inner healing in the way that I respond. I am able to have more control over my emotions and thoughts. I'm able to stop myself. I've been able to receive the Father's forgiveness a little faster than before. I am able to identify the enemy's lies more quickly. I no longer walk in as much confusion, pain, and hurt. There is clarity and definitely more peace.

The most encouraging piece is that when I do mess up, I don't stay stuck in it. I'm no longer enslaved to the lies that say, "I'm a failure," "I'm a bad mother," or "I want to run away." I'm fast at noticing the lies and faster at saying, "No, I rebuke you in Jesus's name." Praise God for his liberating grace and power!

CHAPTER 11

Other Inroads to Oppression and Demonization

Shame, Unforgiveness, and Word Curses

Satan will exploit every opportunity possible to attack the believer and undermine her confidence in the sufficiency of Christ and the goodness of God. Three of the more insidious inroads by which Satan gains a "foothold" (Eph. 4:27) in the life of a Christian are shame, unforgiveness, and word curses. These three issues don't always lead to demonization, but they are often the means by which the enemy sows the seeds of doubt and fear, and in countless other ways paralyzes the child of God in her relationship with the Lord and anesthetizes her heart to the love and delight that God has in his own.

Shame

Shame has everything to do with spiritual warfare.[1] I'm not suggesting there is a "*spirit* of shame," as if a particular demon concentrates its activity on those who struggle with this debilitating experience.[2] But we must not forget that Satan is "the accuser" of our brothers and sisters in Christ. He is the

---

1 An extremely helpful treatment of the issue of shame and how to gain freedom is provided by Christine Caine in her book, *Unashamed: Drop the Baggage, Pick up Your Freedom, Fulfill Your Destiny* (Grand Rapids: Zondervan, 2016).

2 But we can't altogether dismiss this as a possibility. Although the Bible doesn't explicitly speak of a "spirit of shame" we can know with a reasonable degree of certainty that demons will take advantage of any spiritual weakness, be it shame or unforgiveness or unresolved anger or lust or any other failure on our part to fully embrace who we are in Christ and to trust wholly in his goodness.

"slanderer" who aims to persuade each of us that we are not who God says we are, and that God is not who he claims to be. Whether or not Satan and his demons are the primary cause of shame in the human soul isn't immediately relevant. But from what we've seen in Scripture, it appears more likely that the enemy will often exploit the opportunity by reminding you of virtually every sin you've committed, reinforcing the painful conviction that you are now beyond recovery, hopelessly helpless, a stain on the public face of the church, and of little to no value to God or to others.

When someone is paralyzed and oppressed by a deep-seated sense of personal shame, it can provide a "foothold," "opportunity," "place," or entry point (Eph. 4:26–27) for the enemy to exert an inordinate destructive influence on the soul of a person. If Satan's most spiritually lethal weapon is to undermine one's sense of identity as a blood-bought, adopted child of God, it makes sense that he would seize on shame and do everything in his power to intensify its crippling presence in our hearts. So, with this in mind, we turn our attention to what the Bible says about shame and how the Holy Spirit brings freedom and healing.

What Is Shame?

It's actually easier to identify the *effects* of shame than it is to define its *essence*. Shame is a painful emotion caused by a consciousness of guilt, failure, or impropriety that often results in the paralyzing conviction or belief that one is worthless, of no value to others or to God, unacceptable, and altogether deserving of disdain and rejection.

Shame can lead to a variety of emotions and actions. It leads to feelings of being not just unqualified but *disqualified* from anything meaningful. People enslaved to shame are constantly apologizing to others for who they are. They feel small, flawed, never good enough. They live under the crippling fear of never measuring up, of never pleasing those whose love and respect they desire. This often results in efforts to work harder to compensate for feeling less than everyone else.

Shame has innumerable effects on the human soul. Those in shame have a tendency to hide and to create walls of protection to hide their true selves. They are terrified that if they are truly seen and known, they will be rejected by others. So they put on a false face and adopt a personality or certain traits they think others will find acceptable. They are led to be less than they could be, less than they are, and they deliberately stifle whatever strengths they have. They say to themselves, "Don't ever be vulnerable. It's dangerous."

As you can see, *shame and guilt are not the same thing*, but the difference between guilt and shame is a very fine line. Guilt is the objective reality of being liable to punishment because of something we've done. Shame is the subjective feeling of being worthless because of who we are. It's the difference between *making* a mistake and *being* a mistake. Feeling guilt when we sin is a good, godly, and healthy response that makes us run to God and seek his forgiveness. But feeling shame when we sin is a bad and destructive response that compels us to run *from* him for fear of his disdain and contempt.

Be assured that perhaps the most devastating effect of lingering and deep-seated shame is the open door it provides to the enemy to oppress and accuse you.

The Ugly Reality of Shame in the Soul

One of the more amazing stories of healing in the New Testament is found in Mark 5:25–34. It concerns the woman who had suffered from a discharge of blood for over twelve years. She had spent virtually every dollar she had on doctors and other remedies, hoping to be set free from this debilitating condition. But we are told in Mark 5:26b that she "was no better but rather grew worse."

What made matters even more distressing was that, because of this condition, she was regarded as ceremonially unclean. In Leviticus 15:19–30 we read that everything she touched or that even inadvertently touched her was regarded as unclean and thus would be prohibited from engaging in temple worship or other religious activities in Israel. She would have been isolated and ostracized from her family and community.

One day she must have heard people talking about Jesus. Perhaps a glimmer of hope rose up in her heart. When she got the news that Jesus was in her community, she made up her mind that no matter what it might cost her, she would find him and seek him for healing. I don't know where or how she got such incredible faith, but she was convinced that she didn't need to talk to Jesus or have him lay hands on her or pray for her. All that was needed, she said to herself, was to touch him. "If I touch even his garments, I will be made well" (Mark 5:28). So she quietly sneaked up behind him, reached out, and touched the edge of his garment. Instantly she was healed. She felt it in her body, and Jesus felt it in his. Here is how Mark describes it:

And Jesus, perceiving in himself that power had gone out from him, immediately turned about in the crowd and said, "Who touched my garments?" And his disciples said to him, "You see the crowd pressing around you, and yet you say, 'Who touched me?'" And he looked around to see who had done it. But the woman, knowing what had happened to her, came in fear and trembling and fell down before him and told him the whole truth. And he said to her, "Daughter, your faith has made you well; go in peace, and be healed of your disease." (Mark 5:30–34)

Did you hear what Jesus said to her? There are three things, each of which is remarkable in its own right. First, he told her she was healed of her disease. Can you imagine what that must have felt like to her? After twelve long years of physical suffering and social rejection and intense feelings of shame and an untold amount of money spent and lost on trying to find a cure, she was instantly healed!

Second, he told her to go in peace. It's as if he said, "I know you've lived in fear for the past twelve years. You've watched as people ran from you lest they touch you and incur ceremonial defilement. You've lain awake at night filled with anxiety and doubt and worry that perhaps you were going to have to live the rest of your life in this condition. But I say to you, be at peace! Let not your heart be troubled! Rejoice that you are now healed of this horrible affliction."

But the third thing he said may be the most important of all. Did you hear how he spoke of her? He called her "*daughter*"! It strikes me as significant that he didn't call her "woman" or "lady" or any other label of designation. He called her "daughter," clearly a term of affection and endearment. Something has happened here that goes far beyond her physical healing. Jesus didn't just give her a new body. He gave her a *new identity*. "You're part of my family now. You're a true child of God. You are accepted just as you are."

Jesus clearly did more than alleviate physical suffering. He lifted her out of shame. One can only imagine the self-contempt she felt in her soul. One can only imagine her feelings of worthlessness, of being a nuisance, the pain of being constantly avoided and shunned. She had no place in society, much less in the kingdom of God. She was devoid of any sense of personal dignity or value. But Jesus changed all that with a single word: "Daughter!" Of all those in the crowd who were pressing in on him, touching him, shoving him, and demanding that he do something miraculous for them, Jesus singled out this one woman and with a simple touch transformed her life for now and eternity!

When I think of this woman in Mark 5, I can't help but think of the lady in Luke 7. She was a former prostitute. She wasn't ostracized and shunned because of a physical affliction, but because of a moral flaw. She undoubtedly felt as worthless and ashamed of who she was as this woman in Mark 5. But Jesus recognized her repentance as she bathed his feet with her tears and wiped them dry with her hair and then anointed them with oil. Jesus didn't recoil from being touched by her any more than he did when he was touched by the woman in Mark 5. They didn't render him unclean by touching him. Instead, by touching him in faith, he rendered them clean, whole, and accepted.

What was the common denominator in the lives of these two women? I'm convinced it was *shame*. I'm certainly not suggesting that this is a struggle only for women. Men live mired in shame no less so than their female counterparts. *Shame does not discriminate based on gender.* It is an equal opportunity offender.

If you and I had lived when Jesus did and had encountered either or both of these women on the street, I can assure you of their physical posture. They would both have rushed by, dropping their heads, diverting their eyes, not wanting to feel the shame of making visual contact with you. At least, that is what they would have done before they met Jesus.

That is why I so greatly appreciate how King David put it in Psalm 3. David was being ridiculed and persecuted and mocked by his enemies, primarily when he was forced to hide in the wilderness. His son, Absalom, had usurped the throne and betrayed David. According to 2 Samuel 15:6, "Absalom stole the hearts of the men of Israel." One can well imagine how ashamed David must have felt. It was worse than simple embarrassment. He was humiliated. His competency as king was now in question. His name was being defamed throughout the land. And yet here is what David said:

> But you, O LORD, are a shield about me,
>> my glory, and *the lifter of my head*. (Psalm 3:3, emphasis mine)

David was mired in shame. He undoubtedly began to question his calling, his competency, his value both as a man and as a leader. He quite literally hung his head in shame. But he is confident that God will elevate his face and restore his hope.

When people are shy or unsure of themselves, perhaps due to some insecurity or recent failure, they rarely look up or make eye contact. Their aim is to pass by without being noticed. They hug the wall lest a personal encounter expose their shame. Their deep feelings of inadequacy lead to withdrawal and silence. The last thing they want is to see or be seen. Fixing their eyes on the floor is safety for their soul. Embarrassment always expresses itself in a physical posture that is guarded and cautious.

Absalom's treachery inflicted a depth of humiliation on David that the human soul was never built to endure. It was emotionally crippling and threatened to destroy David's credibility and his confidence as a man after God's own heart. Some of you know exactly how David felt. In your case it may have been a stinging defeat, an embarrassing failure, or perhaps a public humiliation that you fear has forever destroyed your usefulness or your value to God or a place in his purposes. It's a devastating feeling.

It might even be the rebellion of a child, as in the case of David. For some it's the demise of a business venture into which you poured every ounce of energy and income. Or it might be something less catastrophic, but no less painful, such as a failed attempt at public ministry or an embarrassing misstep that left you feeling exposed and unprotected. In David's case, despite this crushing blow at the hands of his son, his faith in God never wavered, or at least not enough to throw him into utter despair. There was always and only One who was able to restore his strength, straighten his body, and give him reason to hold his head high.

This isn't arrogance or presumption or fleshly defiance, but humble, wholehearted assurance that God can do for us what we can't do for ourselves. People often say, "I just can't bear to look anyone in the face after this." But God will make you able! He is the Lord who "makes poor and makes rich; he brings low and he exalts. He raises up the poor from the dust; he lifts the needy from the ash heap to make them sit with princes and inherit a seat of honor" (1 Sam. 2:7–8).

Deliverance from Shame

Breaking free from shame is almost always a process, but it begins with a miraculous breakthrough. One can be enabled by the Spirit to see the lie of shame and the truth of forgiveness, but there is often a lifetime of behaviors and attitudes that must be progressively brought into alignment with the truth of who we are in Christ.

I want us to explore the only lasting and meaningful cure for shame. It comes from embracing in your heart the simple truth that your value and identity are not determined by what others have said *to* you, *about* you, or perpetrated *against* you. Your value and identity are determined by who you are as an image-bearer and by what Christ has done on your behalf. Let's examine how shame is portrayed in Scripture.

Types of Shame

First, we must be careful to differentiate between justifiable, deserved, and well-placed shame, on the one hand, and illegitimate, undeserved, and misplaced shame, on the other. When our actions, attitudes, or words bring dishonor to God, we justifiably and deservedly should feel ashamed. However, there are other actions, attitudes, or words for which we should not feel ashamed, even though they may expose us to ridicule, public exposure, and embarrassment.

Scripture contains several references to misplaced or unjustifiable shame. Here are four examples:

1. **"For I am not ashamed of the gospel, for it is the power of God for salvation to everyone who believes, to the Jew first and also to the Greek" (Rom. 1:16).** We should feel bold and courageous when we proclaim the gospel. If people mock us and mistreat us because of our vocal and visible declaration of the gospel, we should not feel any shame. After all, the gospel is the power of God to save human souls. The non-Christian world may think we are weak and silly, but the gospel is powerful and true.

2. **"Therefore do not be ashamed of the testimony about our Lord, nor of me his prisoner, but share in suffering for the gospel by the power of God" (2 Tim. 1:8).** If you feel shame when the gospel is made known or when you are identified and linked with someone who is suffering for having made it known, you are experiencing misplaced or unjustifiable shame. Christ is honored and praised when we boldly speak of him and willingly suffer for him.

3. **"Yet if anyone suffers as a Christian, let him not be ashamed, but let him glorify God in that name" (1 Pet. 4:16).** Being maligned and mistreated solely because of your commitment to Christ is no cause for shame. In fact, it serves to glorify God. Thus, shame is not determined based on how we are regarded in the minds of other people, but rather based on whether or not our actions bring honor and glory to God.

4. **"Then they left the presence of the council, rejoicing that they were counted worthy to suffer dishonor [shame] for the name" (Acts 5:41).** To be arrested, stripped, beaten, and exposed to public ridicule is a shameful experience. But the apostles did not retaliate. They willingly embraced the feeling of shame because it ultimately honored God.

The Bible also speaks of behaviors or beliefs that ought to induce shame in a person's heart. Consider these examples:

- "For whoever is ashamed of me and of my words in this adulterous and sinful generation, of him will the Son of Man also be ashamed when he comes in the glory of his Father with the holy angels" (Mark 8:38). In other words, when we refuse to obey the exhortation of Jesus to be humble and meek because we fear people will laugh at us for it, we should feel ashamed. When we fail to strive to live a life free of sexual immorality and the world congratulates us for not yielding to an "outdated" view on morality, we should feel shame.

- "I say this to your shame. Can it be that there is no one among you wise enough to settle a dispute between the brothers, but brother goes to law against brother, and that before unbelievers?" (1 Cor. 6:5–6) and "Wake up from your drunken stupor, as is right, and do not go on sinning. For some have no knowledge of God. I say this to your shame" (1 Cor. 15:34). In both cases their behavior is bringing disrepute on God. They have dishonored him and thus should justifiably feel shame.

- "But what fruit were you getting at that time from the things of which you are now ashamed?" (Rom. 6:21).

- "If anyone does not obey what we say in this letter, take note of that person, and have nothing to do with him, that he may be ashamed" (2 Thess. 3:14).

Breaking the Power of Shame

There are several things that help break the power of shame, deliver us from its paralyzing grip, and undermine Satan's efforts to use it to diminish our effectiveness in the church and in daily Christian living.

We must first wage war against the lies that bring shame by fighting for faith in the forgiveness of God. In other words, belief in the truth of the gospel is the power to overcome shame.

The prostitute who anointed the feet of Jesus with ointment and wet them with her tears had reason to be ashamed. She was a sinner and an outcast. But Jesus pronounced that her sins were forgiven and told her to "go in peace" (Luke 7:36–50). Jesus overcame her shame by promising that her sins were forgiven and that she could now live in peace. She no longer had to awaken each day with the emotional turmoil her sin had unleashed in her heart. The persistent fear and disruptive chaos that had for so long held a grip on her mind and heart were over. She could have chosen to believe the condemnation and judgment of the other guests and remained mired in shame. Or she could choose to believe that Jesus had truly forgiven all her sins. The way to wage war against the unbelief that we are not truly forgiven is to trust the promise of Christ.

The solution to sin in our culture is to celebrate it, brag about it, or join in a public parade to declare your pride in it. Thus, people tend to cope with the pain and weight of guilt by simply declaring that the behavior in question isn't bad after all. It's actually quite good and will contribute to a sense of identity and community. As someone said, "By denying sin, they attempt to take away its sting."

But the solution for shame isn't celebration or denial, but forgiveness. The message of Scripture is that you are probably far worse than even you can imagine, but that you are far more loved than you could ever possibly conceive. You can't solve your struggle with shame. Only Jesus can. And God's immeasurable and inconceivable love for you was demonstrated and put on display by sending his Son Jesus to endure the judgment you deserved.

Some of you think that the solution to your shame is to try harder, do more, obey with greater intensity. Sometimes you are tempted to create even more rules and commands that are not found in the Bible, and by legalistically abiding by them all, you hope to suppress or diminish or perhaps even destroy your feelings of inadequacy and shame and worthlessness. No!

The solution is found in only one place: the cross of Christ, where Jesus took your shame upon himself and endured the judgment of God that you and I deserved.

We also overcome the crippling power of shame when the Holy Spirit strengthens us to trust and experience the reality of God's immeasurable love for us in Christ.

> For this reason I bow my knees before the Father, from whom every family in heaven and on earth is named, that according to the riches of his glory he may grant you to be strengthened with power through his Spirit in your inner being, so that Christ may dwell in your hearts through faith—that you, being rooted and grounded in love, may have strength to comprehend with all the saints what is the breadth and length and height and depth, and to know the love of Christ that surpasses knowledge, that you may be filled with all the fullness of God. (Eph. 3:14–20)

The Holy Spirit is directly responsible for making possible our experience of feeling and rejoicing in the love God has for us in Christ. We break free from shame when the Holy Spirit awakens us to the glorious and majestic truth that we are truly the children of God.

> For you did not receive the spirit of slavery to fall back into fear, but you have received the Spirit of adoption as sons, by whom we cry, "Abba! Father!" The Spirit himself bears witness with our spirit that we are children of God. (Rom. 8:15–16)

> But when the fullness of time had come, God sent forth his Son, born of woman, born under the law, to redeem those who were under the law, so that we might receive adoption as sons. And because you are sons, God has sent the Spirit of his Son into our hearts, crying, "Abba! Father!" So you are no longer a slave, but a son, and if a son, then an heir through God. (Gal. 4:4–7)

Notice that in both texts the experiential, felt assurance of our adoption as the children of God is the direct result of the work of the Holy Spirit in our hearts.

We win in the war against shame when, by the power of the Spirit, we turn our hearts to the unbreakable promise of Christ that nothing can separate us from his love.

> But I am not ashamed, for I know whom I have believed, and I am convinced that he is able to guard until that day what has been entrusted to me. Follow the pattern of the sound words that you have heard from me, in the faith and love that are in Christ Jesus. By the Holy Spirit who dwells within us, guard the good deposit entrusted to you. (2 Tim. 1:12b–14)

Here we see that Paul overcomes the tendency to be ashamed by trusting the truth of God's promise to guard him. It is "by the Holy Spirit" that we find the strength to guard the good deposit of the gospel. "The battle against misplaced shame," says Piper, "is the battle against unbelief in the promises of God."[3] As Paul elsewhere says, "everyone who believes in him will not be put to shame" (Rom. 10:11).

When we are made to feel shame for something that we didn't do, we conquer its power by entrusting our souls and eternal welfare to the truth and justice of God.

> But with me it is a very small thing that I should be judged by you or by any human court. In fact, I do not even judge myself. For I am not aware of anything against myself, but I am not thereby acquitted. It is the Lord who judges me. Therefore do not pronounce judgment before the time, before the Lord comes, who will bring to light the things now hidden in darkness and will disclose the purposes of the heart. Then each one will receive his commendation from God. (1 Cor. 4:3–5)

In other words, notwithstanding the barrage of unjustified judgments that people may heap upon you, notwithstanding the baseless criticisms hurled in your direction, the promise of God on which you can rely is that in the end you will be vindicated. God will make the truth known on that final day, and you will never be put to shame!

---

3   John Piper, "Battling the Unbelief of Misplaced Shame," Desiring God, October 2, 1988, sermon, www.desiringgod .org/messages/battling-the-unbelief-of-misplaced-shame.

We overcome the enslaving power of shame by confidently believing that God's promises of a glorious and more satisfying inheritance are true.

> By faith Moses, when he was grown up, refused to be called the son of Pharaoh's daughter, choosing rather to be mistreated with the people of God than to enjoy the fleeting pleasures of sin. He considered the reproach [or shame] of Christ greater wealth than the treasures of Egypt, for he was looking to the reward. (Heb. 11:24–26)

The "reproach of Christ" likely means the public disdain, rejection, and shame that one experiences from unbelievers for having prized Christ above all earthly praise, possessions, or promotion. He strengthened his soul to endure undeserved shame by fixing his faith on the promises yet to come.

The Holy Spirit: The Power That Conquers Shame

If only the Holy Spirit can break the bonds of shame, here is how we must pray:

- Ask the Spirit to bring into conscious awareness the cause(s) of shame. What specific incidents in your past are the reason you now feel shame? Ask the Spirit to bring light and insight into what happened, when, and by whom.
- Ask the Spirit to awaken you to the realities of the gospel and strengthen your faith in the truth of all that God has done for us in Christ to secure for us the complete and comprehensive forgiveness of sins.
- Ask the Spirit to awaken you to who you are as an adopted child of God (Rom. 8:15–16; Gal. 4:4–7).
- Ask the Spirit to break the stranglehold the enemy has exerted on you. Satan wants to undermine your intimacy with Christ by convincing you that Christ would never want fellowship with someone who has done the things you've done. Satan wants to paralyze your usefulness to the church and to others by convincing you that you are an embarrassment and a reproach. Thus, we must pray that the Spirit would silence the voice of the enemy that has led you to believe that you are beyond the hope of God's love and forgiveness.
- Ask the Spirit to indelibly imprint on your heart the deep and abiding

conviction that God rejoices over you and sings over you in delight (Zeph. 3:17).

- Ask the Spirit to shine the light of truth into your heart and dispel the darkness of lies.
- Ask the Spirit to quicken your heart to feel the love of Christ (Eph. 3:14–21).
- Ask the Spirit to bring to mind any sins committed that led to bondage and shame.
- Ask the Spirit to enable you to repent honestly, openly, and thoroughly.
- Ask the Spirit to enable you to openly confess your sins to others.

Here is yet another prayer I trust will help you break free from your enslavement to shame and denounce the lies the enemy has used to keep you in his grip.

Father, I confess to you the shame I have held in my heart specifically as a result of _____. Through the power of the Holy Spirit, I choose now to repent of holding on to the shame and release it into your hands. I repent from and release to you all the sinful emotions of _____ that are connected to the shame that I've held in my heart. I break all agreements with the kingdom of darkness and ask by the blood of Jesus Christ that you would cleanse and wash away all the damaging effects of my shame regarding _____. I take my rightful authority as a child of God and command all shame about _____ to go in Jesus's name. Jesus, you said that you came despising the shame of the cross for me (Heb. 12:2). I ask that you replace my shame with the new identity that says I am _____. Holy Spirit, empower me to live in the new identity I have through Jesus's shed blood on the cross.

The Paralyzing, Crippling Power of Unforgiveness[4]

Virtually every counselor with whom I have spoken says that most of the ground that Satan gains in a Christian's life is the result of unforgiveness. The

---

4   Two of the better books on the nature of forgiveness are Jay E. Adams, *From Forgiven to Forgiving* (Wheaton, IL: Victor, 1989); and Chris Brauns, *Unpacking Forgiveness: Biblical Answers for Complex Questions and Deep Wounds*

willful refusal to forgive, together with the incessant nurturing in one's heart of bitterness, anger, and resentment toward the offending party, often leads to severe cases of both spiritual oppression and demonization. It isn't hard to figure out why, once we realize that unforgiveness breeds every manner of sin, unkindness, and even despair.

Forgiving others rarely seems to make sense. It feels profoundly counter-intuitive to human nature. Most often it grates on our souls like fingernails on a chalkboard. But we can't afford to ignore this crucial matter or to diso-bey the unmistakable command of Scripture to forgive one another "as God in Christ forgave" us (Eph. 4:32; Col. 3:13).

One thing I've learned over the years is that people typically refuse to for-give others or even to consider praying about the possibility of doing so because they have distorted, utterly unbiblical, and unrealistic concepts of what for-giveness entails. Once I've had the opportunity to explain what forgiveness is, as well as clarify misconceptions that have built up in their thinking about what forgiveness does and does not require of them, people are often far more inclined to deal with this problem in a way that can bring true reconciliation and healing. That isn't to say that people will always readily forgive once they have a biblical perspective on the matter, but it certainly helps.

Let's look at five myths about forgiveness—five lies many of us have embraced about what it means to forgive another person. Then we will examine five truths about forgiveness, or five essential elements apart from which true forgiveness will never take place.

Five Myths about Forgiveness
Myth 1: Forgiveness is forgetting.

How many times have well-meaning friends said to you, "Oh, come on, just forgive and forget"? It's a nice saying, and sounds so simple and easy, but it is also highly misleading and, to be frank, impossible. Why?

First of all, God does not forget. When Jeremiah 31:34 says "For I will forgive their iniquity, and I will remember their sin no more," the prophet is using a metaphorical word picture designed to emphasize God's gracious determination and resolve not to hold us liable for our sin. If God could

---

(Wheaton, IL: Crossway, 2008). Much of what follows on the subject of forgiveness is adapted from my book *Tough Topics 2*, 309–27, and is used here with permission.

literally "forget" it would undermine the truth of his omniscience. God always has and always will know all things. However, God *has* canceled the debt and will never demand payment. He *has* promised never to use our sin against us or to treat us as if the reality of our sin were present in his mind. As Jay Adams put it, God's promise not to remember means he will bury our sins "and not exhume the bones to beat you over the head with them. [God declares] I will never use these sins against you."[5]

"Forgive and forget" is also psychologically impossible. As soon as you make up your mind to forget something, you can be assured that it is the one thing that will linger at the forefront of your conscious thinking. We all forget things, but we do it unintentionally over the course of time. Life and experience and old age work to erase certain things from our memory, but that is rarely if ever the case with sins committed against us and the wounds we have suffered.

To think that forgiving demands forgetting can be emotionally devastating. Let's suppose that Jane succeeds for two months in forgetting Sally's betrayal of her. She's getting along well and hasn't given a second thought to Sally's sin. Then Jane is told that Sally did the same thing to Mary and she immediately remembers the offense she herself endured. She is suddenly riddled with guilt for having failed to forget. What she thought she had forever put out of her mind now comes rushing back involuntarily and she feels like an utter failure for not having "truly" forgiven her friend. Worse still, she now feels like a hypocrite for having promised to forget only to once again feel anger and resentment toward Sally. Not only is Jane emotionally devastated, she now realizes how impossible it is to literally forget something so painful. This makes her extremely reluctant ever to forgive anyone again, knowing in her heart that she is incapable of forgetting.

Myth 2: Forgiving someone means you no longer feel the pain of their offense.

In most cases, the only way you can stop hurting is to stop feeling, and the only way you can stop feeling is to die emotionally. But passionless robots can neither truly love God or others. This may be the primary reason people are reluctant to forgive. They know they can't stop feeling the sting of the sin

---

5 Adams, *From Forgiven to Forgiving*, 18. This is the best book I've read on the subject, and I am greatly dependent on this book in what follows.

against them and they don't want to be insincere by saying they forgive when deep down inside they know they didn't.

Let's suppose that Bill discovers that his wife Susan has had an affair. The agony and deep feelings of betrayal are intense. Although Bill seeks extensive counseling, he eventually separates from his wife for a season. Upon their reconciliation, he forgives her but is under the assumption that for him to do so means he must never again feel the pain of her adultery. Then one evening he sees Susan smiling and talking to another man at church. Although it was nothing more than innocent friendliness, the anguish and suspicion of her betrayal comes rushing back into his soul. He berates himself and questions his own sincerity: "What's the matter with me that I can't get over this?" Bill has to learn that the pain of his wife's adultery will probably never entirely dissipate, but that doesn't mean he hasn't truly forgiven her.

Myth 3: Forgiving someone who has sinned against you means you cease longing for justice.

Be certain of this: vengeance is not a bad thing. If it were, God would himself be in a bit of trouble, for as Paul tells us, "Beloved, never avenge yourselves, but leave it to the wrath of God, for it is written, 'Vengeance is mine, I will repay, says the Lord'" (Rom. 12:19). To long for justice is legitimate, but to seek it for yourself is not. Let God deal with the offender in his own way at the appropriate time. He's much better at it than you or I.

Forgiveness does not mean you are to ignore that a wrong was done or that you deny that a sin was committed. Forgiveness does not mean that you close your eyes to moral atrocity and pretend that it didn't hurt or that it really doesn't matter whether or not the offending person is called to account for his or her offense. Neither are you being asked to diminish the gravity of the offense, or to tell others, "Oh, think nothing of it; it really wasn't that big of a deal after all." Forgiveness simply means that you determine in your heart to let God be the avenger. He is the judge, not you.

Often we refuse to forgive others because we mistakenly think that to do so is to minimize their sin. "And that's not fair! He really hurt me. If I forgive, who's going to care for me and take up my cause and nurse my wounds?" God is. We must never buy into the lie that to forgive means that sin is being whitewashed or ignored or that the perpetrator is not being held accountable for his or her actions. It simply means we consciously choose to let God be the one who determines the appropriate course of action in dealing justly with the offending person.

Myth 4: Forgiveness means you make it easy for the offender to hurt you again.

Forgiveness does not mean you become a helpless and passive doormat for their continual sin. They may hurt you again. That is their decision. But you must set boundaries on your relationship with them. The fact that you establish rules to govern how and to what extent you interact with this person in the future does not mean you have failed to sincerely and truly forgive them. True love never aids and abets the sin of another. The offender may himself be offended that you set parameters on your friendship to prevent them from doing additional harm. They may even say, "How dare you? This just proves that you didn't mean it when you said you forgave me." Don't buy into their manipulation.

Myth 5: Forgiveness is a one-time, climactic event.

Forgiveness is most often a lifelong process. However, forgiveness has to begin at some point. There will undoubtedly be a moment, an act, when you decisively choose to forgive. It may well be highly emotional and spiritually intense and bring immediate relief; a sense of release and freedom. But that doesn't necessarily mean you'll never need to do it again. You may need every day to reaffirm to yourself your forgiveness of another. Each time you see the person, you may need to say, "Self, remember that you forgave _____!"

Five Truths about Forgiveness

As I noted earlier, the apostle Paul said in Ephesians 4:32 that we are to forgive "as" God in Christ forgave us. The word "as" points to two things: We are to forgive because God forgave us, but we are also to forgive in the same manner that he forgave us. So, how did God in Christ forgive us? This leads us to the five truths about forgiveness.

Truth 1: God in Christ forgave us by absorbing in himself the destructive and painful consequences of our sin against him.

Jackie Pullinger is a missionary and church-planter in Hong Kong who tells her remarkable life story in her autobiography *Chasing the Dragon*.[6] In the early years of Jackie's ministry, she met a young man named Ah Ping who had joined the Triads (gangs that controlled crime in Hong Kong) when he was only twelve years old. He soon came to be supported financially by a fourteen-year-old prostitute. When Jackie showed up and began to reach out in mercy and kindness to Ah Ping and his associates, he told her in no uncertain terms: "You'd better go. Just get out of here. We're no good. Go find some people who will appreciate what you're doing and be grateful for your kindness. We will only hurt you and exploit you and kick you around. Why do you stay? Why do you care?"

Jackie responded, "I stay because that's what Jesus did for me. I didn't want him either. But he didn't wait until I got good and wanted him. He died for me while I was his hateful enemy. He loved me and forgave me. He loves you too."

"No way," shouted Ah Ping. "Nobody could love us like that. We rape and fight and steal and stab. Nobody could love us."

Jackie explained how Jesus didn't love what they did, but that he still loved sinners and was willing to forgive them. Ah Ping was shattered. He sat down on the street corner and received Christ as his savior. Not long after his conversion, Ah Ping was attacked by a gang of youths and was beaten mercilessly with bats. When his friends vowed revenge, Ah Ping said, "No. I'm a Christian now and I don't want you to fight back." Ah Ping was transformed and made ready to forgive his enemies by his realization that Jesus Christ had absorbed in himself the consequences of Ah Ping's sins.

Forgiveness is deciding to live with the painful consequences of another person's sin. You are going to have to live with it anyway, so you might as well do it without the bitterness and rancor and hatred that threaten to destroy your soul.

Truth 2: God forgave us in Christ by canceling the debt we owed him. That is to say, we are no longer held liable for our sins or in any way made to pay for them.

The way we cancel the debt of one who has sinned against us is by promising not to bring it up to the offender, to others, or to ourselves. We joyfully resolve

---

6 Jackie Pullinger, with Andrew Quicke, *Chasing the Dragon: One Woman's Struggle Against the Darkness of Hong Kong's Drug Dens* (Ann Arbor, MI: Servant, 2006).

never to throw the sin back into the face of the one who committed it. We promise never to hold it over their head, using it to manipulate and shame them. And we promise never to bring it up to others in an attempt to justify ourselves or to undermine their reputation. And lastly, we promise never to bring it up to ourselves as grounds for self-pity or to justify our resentment of the person who hurt us.

Truth 3: Forgiving others as God has forgiven us means we resolve to revoke revenge.

As noted earlier, this doesn't mean you cease desiring that justice be served. It does mean you refuse, by God's grace, to let the anger and pain energize an agenda to exact payment from that person, whether that payment be emotional, relational, physical, or financial. It also means you refuse to use your past suffering to justify present sin.

Truth 4: Forgiving others as God has forgiven us means that we determine to do good to them rather than evil (see especially Rom. 12:17–21).

This may entail doing simple acts of kindness, like greeting them warmly, from the heart, or providing a meal when they are sick, or other routine acts of compassion or mercy. What will it accomplish? It will both surprise and shame them. Usually a person deliberately sins against you with the expectation that you will respond in like fashion. If you do, it justifies in their mind their initial sin against you. The last thing they expect is sustained kindness and strength. Thus when evil is met with goodness it disarms them; they are stunned with incredulity and often left breathless. When you return good for evil it serves to render the offender powerless. Hopefully, this will open a door in your relationship that will lead to a genuine life change.

Responding this way also shames him. I'm not talking about a bad sense of shame, as if you are seeking to humiliate him. Rather, your hope is to expose his heart's condition, to lay bare his motivation, and to enable him to see the wickedness of his deed. Responding to evil with good compels the offender to look at himself rather than at you. When the light of your kindness shines back in the face of his darkness, the latter is exposed for being what it really is. The shame he feels on being "found out" will either harden or soften his heart (depending on how he/she chooses to respond).

Truth 5: God forgave us in Christ by reconciling us to himself, by restoring the relationship that our sin had shattered.

Often we avoid forgiveness because we want to avoid conflict. Going to the offender and saying, "I forgive you," carries the potential for an explosion. They may even deny having sinned against us. But true forgiveness pursues relationship and restoration. True forgiveness is not satisfied with simply canceling the debt. It longs to love again.

It's important to remember two things here. First, the offending person may refuse your overtures of kindness and resist any efforts on your part to reconcile. But that's ultimately out of your control. As Paul said in Romans 12:18, your responsibility is to do whatever you can within your power to be at peace. If they refuse to be at peace with you, the fault is theirs. You will at least have fulfilled your responsibility before God. Second, often times when the reconciliation or restoration is successful, the relationship never fully returns to what it was before the offense was committed. Trust and confidence and delight in another person take a long time to fully recover from a serious sin, and sometimes never fully recover at all. But even if it doesn't, that doesn't mean you haven't fully forgiven them.

Of course, none of this will make sense to someone who has not experienced and received and tasted the joy of the forgiveness of God in Christ Jesus. If we do not forgive as the Scriptures command, perhaps the problem is with our ignorance of what God has done for us in Christ. That is why the key to forgiveness is the cross.

A Prayer of Forgiveness

It isn't enough to know what forgiveness is and is not. One must actually forgive! You have to take decisive action and freely and consciously forgive those who have sinned against you. When you do, the enemy loses his grip on your life. His authority is broken. His legal and moral claim to adversely influence your life is canceled.

> *Father, I confess the unforgiveness I have toward* _____ *specifically for the offense of* _____. *By your grace and through the power of the Holy Spirit, I choose with my own will to forgive her/him and release them into your hands. I repent from and release to you all the sinful emotions of* _____

that go along with the unforgiveness I've held in my heart toward her/ him. I am asking for my unforgiveness to be washed away in the blood of Christ and to be completely cleansed from all of its damaging effects. Your Word also says to pray for those who persecute you and bless those who curse you (Matt. 5:44; Luke 6:28). I want to pray for _____ that your Truth may be revealed to her/ him and that you bless her/him in order that she/he may become the child of God you desire.

Word Curses

The phrase "word curses" refers to the many ways in which Satan may seize an opportunity to harass and oppress the believer. Most of us have been unwilling recipients of word curses, even though we were unaware of what was being said to or about us and the long-term consequences of such utterances. The reason why many of you will more readily dismiss this potential inroad for the enemy's influence in your life is that you simply refused to believe what was said. You recognized it for the lie that it was. You stood firmly in your identity in Christ and were determined not to embrace any such curse as truth.

So what are some examples of a word curse? I've spoken with numerous individuals, both male and female, who were raised in highly dysfunctional homes where they were belittled and ridiculed by one or both parents. They've shared numerous instances where they were told such things as:

- "You're a tremendous disappointment to me. I doubt if you'll ever amount to much in life."
- "Why can't you be like your brother/sister? You're such a failure!"
- "You're so stupid!"
- "There's no way you're going to succeed later on if you keep screwing things up now. Why can't you get your act together?"
- "Neither your father nor I wanted you in the first place. You've been nothing but a burden on this family since day one."
- "It would be nice if I could brag on you. But that will never happen. If you could only be as successful in sports as your friend, Bobby."
- "I hope you never have children when you grow up. You'd make such a lousy parent."

Then there are word curses we speak over and to ourselves. Or if we never actually articulate them in so many words, they are lies that we believe to be true. Things like:

- "I can't speak in front of people. I always make a fool of myself."
- "God could never love someone like me. I'm a perpetual screw-up."
- "We'll always be poor. I'll never be able to make enough money to support a family."
- "I'm so ugly. No one will ever love me the way others are loved."
- "I'm too dumb to make it through college, so what's the use in wasting so much time and money in trying?"

The problem comes when such curses become embedded in our minds and we make critical decisions in life based on the misguided notion that they are true. Satan loves nothing more than to exploit these lies and reinforce in our thinking that we are useless to God, an embarrassment to the church, and of no benefit to anyone at all. Over time, we end up failing to seize opportunities for success and pursuing otherwise important relationships because of the tape that runs repeatedly in our heads that if we try, we'll just make a mess of it all and suffer public humiliation. All in all, I'm better off not trying in the first place.

As counter-intuitive as it may sound, Paul gave us clear guidance on how to respond to those who use their words to pronounce a curse on us: "Bless those who persecute you; bless and do not curse them" (Rom. 12:14). He probably based his exhortation on the words of Jesus in the Sermon on the Mount: "Blessed are you when others revile you and persecute you and utter all kinds of evil against you falsely on my account" (Matt. 5:11).

We are empowered to respond as these texts tell us only if we are confident and secure in our new identity in Christ. Spend time alone with the Lord and make this prayer your own.

I forgive those who cursed me with the spoken word by saying _____. I repent of cursing myself with the spoken word by saying _____. I repent for receiving this curse and giving it a place in my life. I ask you to forgive me, Lord, for believing these lies instead of believing the truth of who you say I am as your blood-bought child. I receive your forgiveness. I renounce and break the legal rights/power of this curse in my life based on the shed blood of Jesus Christ and his finished work on the cross. I trust in the power of the cross to cancel all false and misleading judgments against me. In the name of Jesus Christ and by the authority he has entrusted to me, I command every demonic voice to be silent. I forbid any attempt by Satan and his hosts to undermine or diminish my joy in knowing who I am in Jesus Christ. In the place of any and all word curses I proclaim the blessings of God over my life, who says of me in his Word that I am

_____.

KATHY'S STORY

During a marriage counseling session, the topic of inadequacy came up. The counselor pointed out that it seemed I had been struggling with a spirit of comparison. As we talked through this topic, the Lord brought a childhood memory to mind. When I was nine years old, I was invited to the lake with a school friend named Jill (name changed) for a weekend. There were other families at the lake house that week, and most were friends that Jill had grown up with.

One day while we were out on the boat just outside of the dock, Jill and I were joined by another girlfriend and a boy we all found cute and giggled over. We three girls were sitting on one of the benches in the boat, side by side, and the boy was standing in front of us. He said, "Hey, you gals are sitting in order of how pretty you are." Just in case any one of us girls should misunderstand, he clarified that I was sitting on the least pretty end of that bench. I remember immediately feeling embarrassed and self-conscious of the fact that I wore thick glasses and a retainer to correct my crooked teeth. I remembered taking my glasses off and hiding them behind me and wanting to hide.

As I recounted this memory to the counselor and my husband, I began to sob. I realized that I had gone into hiding that day as I set in motion a horrible pattern of comparing myself to others around me and hiding when I didn't measure up in beauty, intelligence, and outgoingness. I had partnered with the word curse that was spoken over me that day and had carried it into my adult life. It was even affecting my marriage. The counselor directed me to ask Jesus where he was in that memory, and I very quickly saw him sitting next to me at the very end of the boat bench with his arm around my shoulder, and he whispered in my ear, "I say you are the most beautiful girl I've ever seen." Hearing this and sensing his presence brought about sobbing again, but this time it wasn't because of pain of the memory, but because of the release of healing.

The counselor directed me to give the words of comparison a picture. He said, "What does the spirit of comparison look like in that memory now?" I immediately saw it as a green, slimy algae that covered not just me but all three of us girls sitting on that bench. I was directed to ask Jesus how he would take care of the slime, and I pictured him grabbing the Shop-Vac out of the covered boat dock, and he started vacuuming all the slime off of me and the other girls. This brought me to laughter, to think of Jesus using a Shop-Vac to clean up the mess that was spoken over me some thirty-five years earlier. Comparison is like a green, slimy algae that had been eating away at my identity for way too long!

But now I know and feel the beauty of freedom from such a word curse. The Holy Spirit has set me free from ungodly and destructive comparisons. The only opinion that matters now is that of Jesus.

CHAPTER 12

The Tempter's Tactics

S atan goes by many names and descriptive titles, but none so perfectly captures the wickedness of our adversary as does the label, "the tempter."[1] Of all the many sinister schemes of Satan and his demons, their attempt to lead us into sin and idolatry may well be the most threatening to the vitality of our relationship with God. I wish it were otherwise. Would that we might be free of the relentless assault of the enemy! But Satan is by nature and by choice a deceiver and a seducer who is hell-bent on devouring anyone who dares to fall in love with the Son of God.[2]

No one was more entranced by the beauty of the Father than the Son. No one was more single-minded in his spiritual focus than Jesus. Yet, notwithstanding Satan's decisive defeat in the wilderness, we read in Luke 4:13 that he only departed from Jesus "until an opportune time." If Satan's attack against our Lord was interminable, we should hardly expect less.

The focus of Satan's efforts is always the same: to deceive us into believing that the passing pleasures of sin are more satisfying than obedience. But there is great diversity and insidious ingenuity in the way he goes about this task. Wisdom demands that we become familiar with his tactics.

---

1 Twice Satan is described this way, once when he tried to tempt Jesus in the wilderness (Matt. 4:3) and yet again when Paul spoke of the enemy's efforts to tempt the Thessalonians (1 Thess. 3:5).

2 This treatment of temptation first appeared in my book *Pleasures Evermore: The Life-Changing Power of Enjoying God* (Colorado Springs, CO: NavPress, 2000).

SATAN HAS A STRATEGY

It strikes some as odd to say that Satan has a strategy. They mistakenly conclude that because our enemy is sinful, he must be equally stupid. Such reasoning has been the downfall of many in the body of Christ. He does not act haphazardly or without a goal in view. In 2 Corinthians 2:11 the apostle issues a warning so that "we would not be outwitted by Satan, for we are not ignorant of his designs." The word translated "outwitted" means to cheat or defraud someone by deception. Satan had a clear vision, an agenda, if you will, for the situation in Corinth. To think that he acts randomly and aimlessly is precisely what he wants.

Much the same idea is found in Ephesians 6:11 where Paul again speaks of satanic "schemes." Here he uses the Greek word *methodia*, from which we derive our English word "method." He has in mind cunning and wily stratagems (cf. Eph. 4:14) carefully crafted to devour unsuspecting Christians. Would it surprise you to know that Satan is operative in the formation and spread of value systems in our society, that he influences institutions, organizations, philosophical movements, political, social, and economic systems? Rest assured that Satan sets his goals and then utilizes and exploits the most effective means, while avoiding all obstacles, to reach his diabolical end.

On the flip side, the fact that Satan has plans and purposes to which he devotes his considerable and perverted prowess must not lead us to grant him a place of equality with God either in terms of prominence or power. It's a simple matter of logic: Satan is an angel. All angels were created (Col. 1:16; John 1:1–3). Therefore, Satan was created. He is, therefore, *God's devil*. Satan is *not* the equal and opposite power of God (contra *dualism*). He is not eternal. His power is not infinite. He does not possess divine attributes. In sum, he is no match for God! If anything, Satan is the equal and opposite power of the archangel Michael, but not of God.

Four Truths about Temptation

Let me begin by stating four fundamental truths about temptation. These principles are foundational to our battle to stay satisfied with God.

Truth 1: God tests our faith, but he never tempts it (Jas. 1:13).

The purpose of divine testing is to sanctify and strengthen. The purpose of satanic tempting is to deceive and destroy. Evil neither exists in the heart of God nor is he its author. It most assuredly exists in our hearts, and we are its author.

Truth 2: Temptation almost always begins in the flesh (Jas. 1:14).

Our flesh sets fire to sin. Satan simply fans the flames. Satan is generally powerless until we first say yes to sin. He exploits our sinful decisions, most often by intensifying the course of action we have already chosen.

Paul makes this point in Ephesians 4:26–27. He exhorts us, "Be angry and do not sin; do not let the sun go down on your anger; and give no opportunity to the devil." Satan is not credited with nor blamed for creating the anger in the first place. We are responsible for it. Satan's response is to use this and other such sins to gain access to our lives and to expand and intensify our chosen course of behavior.

Luke 22:31

Some might think that Luke 22:31 is an exception to this rule. Jesus tells Peter that "Satan demanded to have you, that he might sift you like wheat." By the way, it should be noted that Satan evidently obtained permission to tempt *all* of the disciples. When Jesus said "you," he employed the plural form of the pronoun, thereby including the other ten as well (Judas had already departed). There is no indication that Peter had planned on denying Jesus or that his "flesh" was in any way inclined to do so. Jesus seems to attribute what is about to happen to the devil.

Satan's intent in "sifting" Peter was obviously malicious. He wanted to destroy Peter by inciting him to deny Jesus. But God's intent in permitting Satan to do it was altogether different. Clearly, Satan is unable to act outside the parameters established by the will of God. He must first ask permission of God. God's purposes with Peter were to instruct him, humble him, perhaps discipline him, and certainly to use him as an example to others of both human arrogance and the possibility of forgiveness and restoration.

We cannot easily say "Satan did it" or "God did it." In cases such as this, both are true (with the understanding that God's will is sovereign, supreme, and overriding), but their respective goals are clearly opposite.

The Thorn in the Flesh

Yet another example of this is Paul's experience with his so-called thorn in the flesh. Following his translation into the third heaven, and in order to prevent him from falling into pride, Paul "was given" this thorn. There has been endless speculation concerning the nature of this "thorn," but that is not my concern here. Of greatest importance is its purpose, namely, "to keep me from becoming conceited" (2 Cor. 12:7).

What was the source of this "thorn"? The subject is left unexpressed: there "was given me" (v. 7a). Most commentators recognize this as an example of what is called "the divine passive" in which God is the unidentified cause or hidden agent that accounts for certain events in human experience. It is a conventional use of the passive voice to avoid mentioning the divine name. Had Paul wanted to say that Satan was the ultimate source, he probably would not have used the Greek verb *didōmi*, the word typically employed to indicate that God had bestowed some favor (cf. Gal. 3:21; Eph.3:8; 5:19; 1 Tim. 4:14). There were numerous Greek verbs available to express the idea that Satan was its origin (*epitithēmi*, "lay upon" [Luke 10:30; 23:26; Acts 16:23]; *ballō*, "cast" [Rev. 2:24]; or *epiballō*, "put on" [1 Cor. 7:35]).

That God is the ultimate source of the thorn is also evident from its purpose, namely, to prevent Paul from being puffed up in pride. Satan would have loved nothing more than for Paul to feel elated, elite, and arrogant as a result of his experience. Whatever Satan's role in the thorn may have been, you can rest assured it wasn't his design that Paul be kept humble!

But if the thorn was from God, why does Paul say it was "a messenger [literally, 'angel'] of Satan"? We must remember that God often uses the devil to accomplish his purposes (cf. Job; 1 Cor. 5:5). Although Satan and God work at cross purposes, they can both desire the same event to occur while hoping to accomplish antithetical results. Satan wanted to see Jesus crucified, as did God the Father (Isa. 53:10; Acts 2:23; 4:27–28), but for different reasons. The same is true in the case of Job. What Satan had hoped would destroy Job (or at least provoke him to blasphemy), God used to strengthen him.

The same is true here, as it was also in the case of Peter noted above. Although we can't be sure, it seems likely that the demon was not acting consciously in the service of God. Most likely, by God's secret and sovereign providence, this demonic spirit was dispatched to Paul, intent on oppressing and thereby hindering (or even destroying) his ministry. The *divine design*, however, was to keep Paul from sinful pride and to utilize this affliction to accomplish a higher spiritual good (cf. 2 Cor. 12:9–10). Thus, we see that Satan's intent is always to seduce, destroy, and undermine our confidence in God's goodness, while God can make use of the same experience to sanctify us and build into us the virtues and godliness of Jesus himself.

Truth 3: Temptation, in and of itself, is not sin.

The knowledge that temptation itself is not a sin is critically important, especially for those who suffer from an overly sensitive and tender conscience. Jesus was repeatedly tempted (Heb. 2:17–18; 4:15; Matt. 4), but he was sinless. We must resist thinking that we are sub-Christian or sub-spiritual simply because we are frequently tempted. It was the great reformer Martin Luther who first said, "You can't prevent the birds from flying over your head, but you can keep them from building a nest in your hair." His point is that a temptation only becomes a sin when you acquiesce to it, or, as it were, "fondle" it and "enjoy" it.

Truth 4: The source of temptation often comes by appealing to what is good.

The fourth foundational truth pertains to the source of a temptation's strength. Temptation is often strong because it comes in the form of an enticement to satisfy legitimate needs through illegitimate means. Satan's strategy with Jesus in the wilderness is a clear example of this. Bread is not evil, nor is the desire to alleviate hunger by eating—especially after you've fasted for forty days. Divine protection is a valid promise in Scripture (Ps. 91). Authority over the kingdoms of the world is something God promised the Son long ago (cf. Ps. 2). The temptation, therefore, was aimed at seducing Jesus into achieving divinely approved ends by sinful and illegitimate means. Temptation is often strongest when relief or satisfaction seems to dress itself in the very sin Satan is suggesting.

The strength of temptation also comes from a tendency to push virtues to such an extreme that they become vices. For example, it is all too easy for the joy of eating to become gluttony, or for the blessing of rest to become sloth, or for the peace of quietness to become noncommunication, or for industriousness to become greed, or for liberty to be turned into an excuse for licentiousness. We all know what it's like for pleasure to become sensuality, or for self-care to become selfishness, or for self-respect to become conceit, or for wise caution to become cynicism and unbelief, or for righteous anger to become unrighteous rage, or for the joy of sex to become immorality, or for conscientiousness to become perfectionism.

The story of Ananias and Sapphira in Acts 5 is a case in point. It wasn't through some overt and terrible act of human depravity, but through an act of religious devotion, that Satan brings about the downfall of this couple. This frightening story of instantaneous execution all began with an act of generosity.

Another instance in which Satan seeks to exploit the otherwise good intentions of the church is described in 2 Corinthians 2:10–11. Certain people in Corinth, ostensibly to maintain the purity of the church, were reluctant to forgive and restore the wayward, but now repentant, brother. This harshness would give Satan an opportunity to crush the repentant sinner's spirit and drive him to despair, most likely resulting in his being forever cut off from the church.

Or consider how Satan employs this tactic when it comes to sexual relations in marriage (1 Cor. 7:5). Paul approves of married couples' decision to refrain from sexual relations to devote themselves to prayer, but only for a season. To abstain entirely for a prolonged period of time exposes oneself to unnecessary temptation to satisfy one's sexual desires outside the bonds of marriage. Again, we see here an example of how the enemy takes an otherwise godly intention and exploits it for his own nefarious purposes.

Seven Tactics of Temptation

Satan has a strategy. The following is certainly not an exhaustive list of his schemes, but it's a good start.

1. Satan likes to tempt us when our faith is fresh.

He targets recently converted Christians who are less prepared to know how to resist his seductive suggestions. This is precisely Paul's grounds for warning against the premature promotion of a new Christian in 1 Timothy 3:6. An elder, says Paul, must not be "a recent convert, or he may become puffed up with conceit and fall into the condemnation of the devil." The latter phrase is most likely a reference to the judgment to which Satan himself has been subjected. This isn't to suggest that older, more mature believers are exempt, for according to 1 Timothy 3:7, Satan is able to exploit any blemish on the reputation of any Christian leader.

2. Satan likes to tempt us when our faith feels strongest—when we think we are invulnerable to sin.

If we are convinced that we have it under control, we become less diligent. We must remember the wisdom of Oswald Chambers who is ascribed to have said, "An unguarded strength is a double weakness."[3]

3. Satan likes to tempt us when we are in an alien environment.

Gordon MacDonald explains: "In the environs of home life with family and friends, there is a schedule of routines, a set of support systems, and a way of doing things, all of which lends encouragement to responsible living and, conversely restraint against irresponsible living. Virtually all of these external systems fall away when a person is hundreds of miles from home."[4]

Certainly, our desire is that our internal resistance to the temptation of sin, nourished and sustained by our fascination and joy with the beauty of God in Christ, would be adequate in such circumstances. But when the external boundaries that often unconsciously govern our behavior are removed or are expanded, we soon discover the depth (or shallowness) of maturity in our souls.

4. Satan also likes to tempt us when our faith is being tested in the fires of affliction.

When we are tired, burnt out, persecuted, or feeling excluded and ignored, Satan makes his play. His most common tactic is to suggest that God isn't fair, that he is treating us unjustly, from which platform Satan then launches his seductive appeal that we need no longer obey. Physical pain or relational and financial loss, when combined with the silence of heaven, serve only to

---

3   See www.inspiringquotes.us/author/9496-oswald-chambers/page:6.

4   Gordon MacDonald, *Rebuilding your Broken World* (Nashville: Oliver Nelson, 1988), 100.

intensify the appeal of temptation. This is nowhere better seen than in the experience of Job, a story that is crucial to understanding our response to God when tempted in the midst of the worst imaginable tragedies.

TEMPTATION IN JOB

Almost immediately after offering a sacrifice on behalf of his children (Job 1:5), Job hears the stunning news of their demise. He is first told of the destruction of his servants and his livestock. With hardly a moment to catch his breath, word comes that his children have been killed. But Job refuses to yield to the temptation to curse God. Indeed, "in all this Job did not sin or charge God with wrong" (v. 22).

The tempter persists in his skepticism about Job's sincerity. "It really wasn't much of a test," Satan snarls. "It was superficial at best. There are still too many restrictions." Satan's argument is that the experiment, cruel though it was, has not yielded a conclusive result because the terms by which it was carried out were not rigorous enough. His accusation is stinging. His manner of addressing the Almighty is insolent: "As long as you give him health and life, he remains loyal. Let me touch his *body* and we'll see how long he loves you!"

Satan doesn't waste a moment's time. As Job sat in sorrow, trying to cope with his indescribable loss, the enemy strikes with vicious cruelty (2:7–10). The extent of Satan's attack on Job is revealed not only here but elsewhere in the book. Some suggest Job suffered from leprosy. Whatever his "loathsome sores" were, you can be certain it was agonizing. The disease covered his body (2:7) and led to intolerable itching (2:8; he was probably scraping pus from the sores). His appearance was disfigured (2:12; 19:19). He suffered from loss of appetite (3:24a), depression (3:24b–26; 7:16), and sleeplessness (7:4). When he did sleep, he had recurring nightmares (7:14). He suffered from festering sores and broken skin (7:5), scabs that blackened and peeled (30:30), high fevers (30:30), excessive weeping and burning of the eyes (16:16), putrid-smelling breath (19:17), an emaciated body (17:7; 19:20), and chronic pain (30:17). It seems only appropriate that he would take up residence on a dung heap or ash heap where dogs scavenged for food among the corpses and refuse.

Most people come to the concluding five chapters of Job with great anticipation. The time has finally come for God to speak. Let's begin by noting what God does *not* say to Job.

First of all, there is no condemnation of Job, no reversal of the divine verdict on his character that was given in chapters one and two. God does not agree with the assessment of Bildad, Zophar, Eliphaz, or Elihu. He says nothing that would lead us to believe that Job's suffering was the direct result of Job's sin.

Second, there are no apologies. As Larry Crabb put it, "Job apparently expected God would listen to what he had to say, pull slowly on his beard, and reply, 'Job, thanks for sharing your perspective on things. You've got a point. Frankly, I really hadn't seen things quite the way you see them. Look, I've made a bit of an error but I'll straighten it all out right away.'"[5] Not!

Third, there are no compliments. After all Job had endured so that God might prove his point to the devil, one might have expected to hear something like this: "Job, bless your heart! You have no idea how proud I am of you. It really means a lot to me that you've persevered so valiantly. You exceeded all my expectations. We really showed that devil, didn't we!" God says nothing to Job that one might think would be appropriate for someone who had suffered so much. There are no words of encouragement or consolation, no words of how much good his experience will accomplish in the lives of others who face tragedy and the temptation it brings. There are no words of praise for his having stood his ground when the barrage of arguments came from his friends.

Perhaps the most shocking thing of all is that there are no explanations. At the very least you would expect God to lay it all out in black and white before Job. But nowhere do we find something like this: "Job, let me begin by explaining to you how this whole thing came about in the first place. You see, one day Satan came to me

---

5   Larry Crabb, *Inside Out* (Colorado Springs, CO: NavPress, 1988), 146.

and insisted that the only reason you worship me is because I treat you so well. I couldn't let him get away with that. I had to prove him wrong, and, well . . . the rest is history, as they say!"

Amazingly, there is no discussion of the problem of evil, of divine justice, of human sin, or any such thing. In fact, God supplies *no answers* at all to any of the questions raised. Instead, *it is God who asks the questions!* It isn't God who appears on the witness stand to undergo cross-examination in order to make sense of what has occurred. It is *Job*, of all people, who is cross-examined. More than seventy times God asks Job an unanswerable question.

For thirty-five chapters Job has been crying out, "God, put yourself in my place for a while!" God now responds and says, "No, Job, *you* put yourself in *my* place! Until you can offer lessons on how to make the sun rise each day or give commands to the lightning or design a peacock, don't pass judgment on how I run my world." In other words, God says, "Until you know a little more about running the physical universe, don't tell me how to run the moral universe. How do you expect to understand the complexities of my dealings with mankind when you can't even understand the simplicity of my dealings with nature?"

Instead of dealing with the complexities of temptation and human tragedy, God loudly asserts his absolute sovereignty over all of creation. He knows and controls every square inch of the universe, whether animate or inanimate. No snowflake or drop of rain escapes his providence. Every force of nature and every living thing within it are subject to his purposes. Such being the case with God's relation to nature, it stands to reason that he cares even more for those created in his image. It now seems ludicrous that a mere creature like Job would demand explanations from God. If Job cannot comprehend or control creation, what makes him think he can comprehend God's control of mankind?

Why, then, does God often decline to provide us with answers about his dealings with us, our sufferings, and the temptations that arise from them? I'm not sure, but perhaps it is because explanations might not help us. We ask "Why? Why?" on the assumption that if we had a reasonable answer, we could handle it better, be less bitter, and respond more humbly and submissively. But would we? Perhaps God keeps us ignorant because we are incapable of comprehending the answer. God has told us: "For as the heavens are higher than the earth, so are my ways higher than your ways and my thoughts than your thoughts" (Isa. 55:9; cf. Eccl. 11:5).

Perhaps God keeps us ignorant because ignorance is the most fertile soil in which faith can grow. In other words, ignorance in the midst of temptation compels us to do one of two things: either abandon God altogether or trust him all the more fervently.

In one sense, God *did* answer Job's questions. If God is truly such a majestic and sovereign being who rules every molecule with magnificent precision and purpose, then what he has done or allowed in the case of Job *must* make perfect sense. Also, it is important to remember that there is something more important than knowing why God does what he does, namely, learning to cling to him in faith when everything else threatens to destroy your soul.

The cynical among us might argue that, in the end, when all was said and done, it was easy for Job to resist temptation and to bow faithfully beneath God's sovereign purposes. After all, God restored everything he lost, and then some (Job 42:10–17). "No wonder he kept his mouth shut. Look at what it got him!" But these people overlook one important point: "Job spoke his contrite words [40:3–5] *before* any of his losses had been restored. He was *still* sitting in a pile of rubble, naked, covered with sores, and it was in *those* circumstances that he learned to praise God. Only one thing had changed: God had given Job a glimpse of the big picture. I have a hunch that God could have said anything—could, in fact, have read from the Yellow Pages—and produced the same stunning effect on Job. What he said was not nearly so important as the mere fact of his appearance. God spectacularly answered Job's biggest question: Is anybody out there? Once Job caught sight of the unseen world, all his urgent questions faded away."[6]

---

6 Ibid., 240.

Job's case was both unusual and exceptional. But that in no way detracts from what it tells us about Satan's tactics. He is as relentless as he is sadistic. He hits below the belt and kicks his victim while he's down. We, too, will be sorely tempted in times of physical distress to curse God and die. Job wavered, but he didn't break. God help us!

5. Satan especially likes to tempt us immediately following both spiritual highs and spiritual lows.

Periods of emotional elation and physical prosperity can sometimes lead to complacency, pride, and a false sense of security. When they do, we're easy targets for the enemy's arrows. The same thing happens during the doldrums when we find ourselves wondering if God even cares. We become bitter and despondent, and sin suddenly seems the reasonable thing to do.

6. Satan likes to tempt us by putting his thoughts into our minds and then blame us for having them.

This is perhaps Satan's most effective tactic. William Gurnall explains:

When thoughts or inclinations contrary to the will and ways of God creep in, many dear Christians mistake these miserable orphans for their own children, and take upon themselves the full responsibility for these carnal passions. So deftly does the devil slip his own thoughts into the saints' bosom that by the time they begin to whimper, he is already out of sight. And the Christian, seeing no one but himself at home, supposes these misbegotten notions are his own. So he bears the shame himself, and Satan has accomplished his purpose.[7]

The title "devil" (*diabolos*) literally means "slanderer" or "accuser" (see 1 Sam. 29:4; 1 Kings 11:14). It is the devil's aim to defame (Luke 4:2, 13; Rev. 12:9, 12). He is a constant source of false and malicious reports. Sometimes he slanders and utters lies to God about you (Rev. 12:10), bent on disrupting

---

7   William Gurnall, *The Christian in Complete Armour* (Carlisle, PA: Banner of Truth Trust, 1991), 262.

your relationship with the Father. But to no avail, thanks to the incessant intercession of Jesus on your behalf (1 John 2:2; Rom. 8:33–39).

When lying to God about you doesn't work, he lies to you about God. He does everything in his power to convince you that God isn't good, that he can't be trusted, that he's holding out on you, that he won't be there when you need him most (Gen. 3; Matt. 4). And if that weren't enough, he lies to you about yourself (Eph. 6:16), seducing you into believing you aren't what God says you are and that you will never be what God has promised you'll be.

7. Satan launches his accusations as if they were from the Holy Spirit.

Satan couches his terms and chooses his opportunities in such a way that we might easily mistake his voice for that of God. So how do we distinguish between satanic accusation and divine conviction? Among other things, the former comes in the shape of condemnation that breeds feelings of hopelessness. We are told our sin has put us beyond the hope of grace and the power of forgiveness. Satan's accusations are devoid of any reference to the sufficiency of the cross. Divine conviction for sin, on the other hand, comes with a reminder of the sufficiency and finality of Christ's shed blood, together with a promise of hope and the joy of forgiveness.

Four Tactics for Resisting Temptation

There are numerous ways to prepare ourselves for demonic enticement, but I want to focus on four in particular.

1. Cultivate in your heart a fascination and joy in the all-consuming beauty and all-sufficient majesty of God.

This is the first and perhaps most important tactic for facing temptation. When our hearts beat with perpetual fascination and our thoughts are filled with the beauty and splendor and adequacy of God, little room is left for the devil to gain a foothold (see Phil. 4:8).

When I received a desperate phone call from a friend whose sister was taking steps to abandon her family, my advice took the following form.

Jerry, your sister has to have a powerful *reason* to stay with her family. Right now, she doesn't believe she has one. She has rationalized her decision in such a way that she can live with her conscience. All that matters or makes sense to her right now is the hunger in her heart to experience something that neither her husband nor kids nor any amount of "religious activity" (which is how she thinks of Christianity) can give her. She's right! They *can't* give it to her. She's ignorant of the joy, peace, affirmation, and forgiveness that the child of God is offered. That's really what her hunger is for. She just doesn't know it yet. She desperately needs to hear and see what you've tasted in Jesus. Point her in the direction of him, whose love for her can transform those boring and lifeless daily routines into real joy. Let the aroma of the sweet-smelling fragrance of the knowledge and love of Jesus pass under her nose. Then pray that she'll catch a "whiff" of it and change directions.

2. Know yourself.

Ask the question often: "If I were the devil, where would I attack me?" In other words, be quick to identify your weaknesses, your vulnerable spots, areas where you've failed before, and take extraordinary steps to protect yourself in the future. If you are susceptible to the effects of alcohol, don't toy with a casual drink. If your fantasies are easily fueled by visual images, stay away from R-rated movies.

3. Deal radically with sin.

In the words of Jesus, "If your right eye causes you to sin, tear it out and throw it away. For it is better that you lose one of your members than that your whole body be thrown into hell" (Matt. 5:29). In the next verse he makes the same point about one's right hand.

Jesus was primarily concerned with those who thought their moral obligation was only skin-deep. Take murder, for example. As long as they refrained from literally spilling blood, they believed they had behaved righteously. They ignored the anger and malicious hatred of the heart that are the source of murderous deeds. The same was true of adultery. Lust was irrelevant. It was a matter of the heart over which the court of Moses had no jurisdiction. Again, so long as the sexual *act* was avoided, the sexual *attitude* was irrelevant.

But Jesus says otherwise. In Matthew 5:21–26 he pointed out that the prohibition of murder includes the angry thought and the insulting word.

Now in 5:27–30 he extends this principle to adultery: not just the physical act but the lustful look and the covetous heart must be curbed.

His point is that we must deal drastically with sin. "We must not pamper it, flirt with it, enjoy nibbling a little of it around the edges. We are to hate it, crush it, dig it out."[8] In the case of adulterous lust, if your eye leads you astray, "tear it out."

THE HEART, NOT THE BODY

It's one thing to say we need to deal radically with sin, but is Jesus recommending self-mutilation as the answer? A closer look at the context will lead us to what Jesus really meant.

Consider John and his relationship with Mary, his administrative assistant. John has always been stirred by Mary's beauty, but recently his gaze has turned to lust. There is no sin in merely looking. In fact, to acknowledge and compliment natural beauty is good. But looking to lust, looking to fantasize an affair, looking to mentally gratify a sexual urge is another thing altogether.

Taking Jesus's words literally, John proceeds to cut out his right eye. Thinking that the problem is solved, he returns to work after a period of rehabilitation only to find that now his *left* eye has lusted as well! So he cuts it out too. He now comes to work with a seeing-eye dog. He's not as efficient at his job, but he's convinced that he's been obedient to Christ and is beyond lusting after Mary. But then he hears her voice, and illicit desire rages yet again in his heart. So he lops off both his ears! He again returns to work, not a pretty sight, to say the least. Confident that it won't happen again, he walks by her desk . . . and smells her perfume! Lust rages once more. So he cuts off his nose. Not even that solves his problem, for as he gropes through the office in his self-inflicted blindness, his hands accidentally brush up against Mary's body, and his flesh is stirred yet again. So he (somehow?) cuts off his hands. It is only then that John realizes he still has a mind, and Mary's memory lingers vividly.

8 Donald A. Carson, *The Sermon on the Mount* (Grand Rapids: Baker, 1978), 44.

The problem is not with our body parts or our physical senses. The problem is with a corrupt and deceitful heart. Our external members are but the instruments we employ to gratify the lust that emerges from within. What our Lord was advocating, therefore, "was not a literal physical self-maiming, but a ruthless moral self-denial. Not mutilation but mortification is the path of holiness he taught."[9]

Stott advises believers:

Behave as if you had actually plucked out your eyes and flung them away, and were now blind and so *could* not see the objects which previously caused you to sin. Again, if your hand or foot causes you to sin, because temptation comes to you through your hands (things you do) or your feet (places you visit), then cut them off. That is: don't do it! Don't go! Behave as if you had actually cut off your hands and feet, and had flung them away, and were now crippled and so *could* not do the things or visit the places which previously caused you to sin."[10]

And as you do so, fix your mind on things above. Focus your heart on the promise of a superior pleasure in Christ. Ponder the joy of that river of delights that never runs dry.

4. Confront and conquer temptation at the beginning, not at the end.

The best and most effective tactic against temptation is to deal with it from a position of *strength*, before it has an opportunity to weaken you. Better to take steps up front to eliminate temptation altogether (if possible) than to deal with it later when your defenses are down.

I've found this principle to be especially helpful when I'm on the road. Although I don't travel nearly as often as I used to, there was a time when my ministry required it. I'm no different from any other man, whether a pastor

9   John R. W. Stott, *Christian Counter-Culture: The Message of the Sermon on the Mount* (Downers Grove, IL: InterVarsity Press, 1978), 89.
10 Ibid.

or lawyer or salesman or computer technician. I know what it is like to walk into a lonely hotel room, alone, away from home, devoid of the normal domestic restraints that I so easily take for granted.

So I made a deal with myself. Before I ever walk into a hotel room, I insist that the desk clerk black out all adult movies that might otherwise be available on a pay-per-view basis. Why do it *before* I check in? Because I'm a man of flesh, just like you. It's incomparably easier to say no before I'm in a position to say yes. Once I'm in that room and the only thing that stands between me and sin is the touch of a dial, my defenses weaken. My resolve to say no isn't nearly as strong as it was fifteen minutes earlier. My inclination to rationalize purchasing an inappropriate movie intensifies with each passing moment. If I am to defeat temptation, I must do everything I can to eliminate it before it launches its assault. I need to defuse its power when I'm in a position to do so instead of arrogantly assuming that if I feel strong now, I'll feel just as strong later.

An Invitation to Death

Make no mistake. There is a tempter whose sole design is to lure you into the embrace of fleeting pleasures and transient sins. His voice is soothing. His promises sound reasonable. But in the end is death. It is only with Jesus that you can walk down "the path of life" (Ps. 16:11). It is only in his presence that "fullness of joy" and "pleasures forevermore" may be found.

> The *pleasures* of loving and obeying, loving and adoring, blessing and praising the Infinite Being, the Best of Beings, the Eternal Jehovah; the *pleasures* of trusting in Jesus Christ, in contemplating his beauties, excellencies, and glories; in contemplating his love to mankind and to us, in contemplating his infinite goodness and astonishing loving-kindness; the *pleasures* of the communion of the Holy Ghost in conversing with God, the maker and governor of the world; the *pleasure* that results from the doing of our duty, in acting worthily and excellently. These, these are the *pleasures* that are worthy of so noble a creature as man is.[11]

---

11 Jonathan Edwards, "Christian Happiness," in *The Works of Jonathan Edwards: Sermons and Discourses 1720–1723*, vol. 10, ed. Wilson H. Kimnach (New Haven: Yale University Press, 1992), 305–06 (emphasis mine).

To what is it, then, that you are invited when you are invited to say no to temptation? "You are invited to the excellent and noble satisfactions of religion; you are invited to such a happiness as is the happiness of angels, and happiness that will be able to satisfy your desires. Be persuaded, then, to taste and see how good it is; keep no longer groveling in the dirt and feeding on husks with hogs."[12]

JANICE'S STORY

I used to hear voices that sounded something like this: "You don't belong here. Someone else could do this better. You should sit down. What you have to say isn't important. God's not going to use you. You don't know what you're doing."

I should clarify that these weren't audible voices I was hearing. They were subliminal, subconscious voices always floating around in the recesses of my mind. They were so familiar I assumed they were true. I assumed they were just a part of me and my personality. But I was wrong.

While going through an inner healing and deliverance ministry at my church, God began to pull back the curtain on that voice. He revealed to me the many lies of the enemy that I had been unknowingly subscribing to and believing. Lies that sounded like my own voice in my own head. I began to realize that the accusing voice in my head wasn't telling me the truth.

So I repented of believing those lies. I repented of agreeing with the father of lies who wants to destroy me. Then I ran into the arms of a Father who is always trustworthy and safe. I commanded all the demons associated with these voices to go in the name of Jesus. Almost instantly, I noticed a difference. My mind felt quieter and more at peace. I began realizing I wasn't hearing those accusing voices anymore. I felt the warmth of God's love and his delight in me. I heard a different voice. This voice said things like, "I have chosen you. I have equipped you. You have a special role to fulfill in My Church. I want to use you to bless others. I love you no matter what, all the time."

---

12 Ibid., 305.

This was the voice of my God. This is the voice I can hear clearly now because he delivered me from the oppression of the enemy. I now feel more sure of God's love and power in me than I ever have in my whole life. I do not second-guess his love for me. I know that I can stand confidently before him and others because of the love and sacrifice of Christ.

All praise be to him, forever and ever, Amen!

PART 3

RESPONDING TO THE DEMONIC

CHAPTER 13

The Defeat of the Devil and the Demonic

As Hitler's armies rolled across Europe, and the Japanese attacked America, dominating the Pacific theater of the war, there was considerable uncertainty about who would emerge victorious, especially in the early years of World War II. Often, when we are in the midst of the battle, our hearts are prone to fear and anxiety as we wrestle with an uncertain future. But no such fear or anxiety should exist in the hearts of God's children when it comes to our conflict with Satan and his demonic hordes. The conclusion of our war with the enemy has already been settled and sealed.

There is a time known not only to God but also to the demonic forces themselves when their predetermined demise will occur. Consider what the spirits cried after Jesus expelled them from the two demonized men in the country of the Gadarenes (Matt. 8:28): "What have you to do with us, O Son of God? Have you come here to torment us *before the time*?" (Matt. 8:29; emphasis mine). The demons' eventual demise is not in question or in doubt. It will happen. We also see this in several other texts (emphases mine):

> Then he will say to those on his left, "Depart from me, you cursed, into the eternal fire *prepared for the devil and his angels*." (Matt. 25:41)

> For if God did not spare angels when they sinned, but cast them into hell and committed them to chains of gloomy darkness to be kept *until the judgment* ... (2 Pet. 2:4)

> And the angels who did not stay within their own position of authority, but left their proper dwelling, he has kept in eternal chains under gloomy darkness *until the judgment of the great day.* (Jude 6)

> And the devil who had deceived them was thrown into the lake of fire and sulfur where the beast and the false prophet were, and they will be tormented day and night forever and ever. (Rev. 20:10)

The key to victory in spiritual warfare is in knowing both *what Jesus Christ has done for you* and *what he has done to Satan.* Christians too often live in fear of what they think the devil might do, but can't, and in ignorance of what they themselves can do, but don't. Defeat is thus the result of failing to reckon with and act upon the devil's dethronement and the believer's enthronement. Although we must fight and resist the devil, let us never forget that we engage a defeated foe.

Jesus Destroys the Works of the Devil

The apostle John spoke directly to this point when he said that "the reason the Son of God appeared was to destroy the works of the devil" (1 John 3:8). The word "destroy" means to loose, to unbind, to unravel, or to dissolve. Hence, Satan's works are conceived as chains that bind us, which Jesus now breaks. His works have a coherence, an interconnectedness, being somehow intertwined, as if a tapestry of sorts. Jesus came to undo and dissolve the enemy's efforts. The coming of Jesus "was concerned with unpicking the net of evil in which the devil has always attempted to trap human beings. In the process, the apparently interlocking and inescapable activities of Satan are disclosed as insubstantial."[1]

In an earlier chapter, we explored how Satan works by enticing people to sin, inflicting disease and death, seducing people into theological error, provoking hatred and chaos, producing injustice and oppression, and blinding the minds of unbelievers lest they believe the gospel. It is these and countless other "works" that Jesus came to destroy. So, how does he do it? How has he already done it?

---

1   Stephen S. Smalley, *1, 2, 3 John,* Word Biblical Commentary 51 (Waco: Word, 1984), 170.

Battling Satan: The Temptation in the Desert

We should first consider the earthly life and ministry of Jesus, specifically his encounter with Satan in the wilderness (Matt. 4:1–11). It's important to remember that whereas the temptation in the desert marks an important victory for Jesus (and us), it is merely the first battle in a continuous campaign of spiritual conflict. Two things confirm this. First, Jesus issues the command, "Be gone, Satan!" (Matt. 4:10), yet is forced to issue the same command once again when Peter becomes his unwitting tool: "Get behind me, Satan!" (Matt. 16:23). The Greek verb used in Matthew 16:23 is the same that we find in Matthew 4:10 (*hupage*). Evidently, even when Jesus commanded Satan to depart, it wasn't necessarily a once-for-all event that never needed to be repeated. Second, according to Luke 4:13, after Jesus issued this command, Satan "departed from him *until an opportune time*" (emphasis mine). No matter how often Satan is banished from our presence, he will not be permanently and eternally eliminated from our spiritual experience until he is finally cast into the lake of fire.

Binding Satan: Acts of Deliverance

Jesus also conquered the enemy in each instance of deliverance. Perhaps the most vivid example of this is found in Matthew 12:22–29 where Jesus healed a demonized man who was blind and mute. In response to the Pharisees' accusation that he performed this miracle by the power of demons, Jesus said:

> "But if it is by the Spirit of God that I cast out demons, then the kingdom of God has come upon you. Or how can someone enter a strong man's house and plunder his goods, unless he first binds the strong man? Then indeed he may plunder his house." (Matt. 12:28–29; cf. Luke 11:21–22)

Satan is the "strong man," his "home" is this present evil age, and his "goods" are the men and women under his influence. With the coming of Jesus, the kingdom of God has arrived and has invaded the kingdom of darkness. The devil's power has been broken and his captives set free.

Observe that Jesus first ties up or "binds" the strong man before he plunders his house. As Sydney Page notes, "the analogy of tying up/overpowering the strong man naturally suggests that the exorcisms were preceded by a decisive victory over Satan. A number of scholars have found just such a victory in the temptation of Jesus in the desert. This first encounter Jesus had with Satan came at a critical juncture in Jesus's life (after his messianic investiture at his baptism and prior to his public ministry), and Jesus emerged from the contest as the victor. Others, finding this connection to be overly subtle, suggest that the exorcisms themselves constitute the occasion of Satan's defeat."[2] Because of Christ's victory in the desert temptation, Satan cannot hinder Jesus from bringing the blessings of the kingdom (deliverance, freedom, forgiveness) to those formerly under his power.

We must remember, however, that although Jesus bound Satan, Satan is still active. In other words, to "bind" the devil is not so absolute as to restrict all his activity. As is clear from Matthew 16:23 and elsewhere, Satan, though in some sense "bound," continues to operate.

Defeating Satan: The Cross and Resurrection

The primary way in which Jesus defeated the devil and his demons was through the cross and resurrection. We should never forget that Satan's principal goal is to thwart God's principal goal. God's principal goal is to glorify himself. Insofar as the cross of Christ glorified God, it defeated Satan.

The Cross Glorified God

We must remember that sin belittles God's glory. This has special relevance in the centuries preceding the cross, during which God "passed over" sin, giving the appearance that his glory was of little worth (see esp. Rom. 3:23–26; John 12:27–28; 13:31; 17:1–4). John Piper explains:

> Therefore, all his pain and shame and humiliation and dishonor served to magnify the Father's glory, because they showed how infinitely valuable God's glory is, that such a loss should be suffered to demonstrate its worth. When we look at the wracking pain and death of the perfectly innocent and infinitely worthy Son of God on the cross, and hear that He endured it all so that the glory of his Father, desecrated by sinners, might be restored, then we know that God has *not* denied the value of his own glory; he has *not*

> been untrue to himself; he has *not* ceased to uphold his honor and display his glory; he *is* just—*and* the justifier of the ungodly.[3]

In other words, "the depth of the Son's suffering was the measure of his love for the Father's glory."[4] Thus, when Jesus died as God's judgment against sin, against that which belittles God's glory, Satan's principal goal was thwarted. Satan had come to vitiate God's glory. Jesus has come to vindicate it. In this regard, we also take note of Jesus's statement in John 16:11 that "the ruler of this world is judged," a proleptic reference to the impact of the cross on Satan. The verb "judged" (*krinō*) is in the perfect tense, perhaps better rendered "has been judged," "indicating an action that, from the readers' standpoint, is past but has ongoing results. The verdict on Satan is in. He has been found guilty and is now awaiting the execution of his sentence."[5] Here again we see that although Satan has been judged, his influence does not come to an end. Later, in the upper room discourse, Jesus speaks of the continuing assault that comes from the enemy (John 17:15).

The Cross Freed Humanity from the Penalty of Sin

A secondary goal of Satan is to keep men and women in their sin, under its penalty, held in bondage to its power, suffering mental and emotional defeat from its guilty accusations. Insofar as Christ's death secured redemption from sin and forgiveness of its guilt, Satan has suffered defeat. Especially instructive on this point is Colossians 2:13–15:

> And you, who were dead in your trespasses and the uncircumcision of your flesh, God made alive together with him, having forgiven us all our trespasses, by canceling the record of debt that stood against us with its legal demands. This he set aside, nailing it to the cross. He disarmed the rulers and authorities and put them to open shame, by triumphing over them in him.

---

3   John Piper, *The Pleasures of God: Meditations on God's Delight in Being God* (Colorado Springs, CO: Multnomah Books, 2012), 149–150.

4   Ibid., 163.

5   Page, *Powers of Evil*, 130.

The translation "record of debt" reflects terminology often used with reference to an IOU, that is to say, a signed acknowledgement of indebtedness. It is something similar to our promissory note today, in which the debtor signs a document that binds the individual to pay the full amount by a certain date. Without using the same terminology, Paul nevertheless makes the same point in Philemon 17–19, where he says, "So if you consider me your partner, receive him [Onesimus] as you would receive me. If he has wronged you at all, or owes you anything, charge that to my account. I, Paul, write this with my own hand: I will repay it . . ." In other words, Paul was giving Philemon an IOU signed with his own hand, in which he obligated himself to pay in full whatever Onesimus might have owed.

The "spiritual promissory note" Paul speaks of in Colossians 2:14 may have been the Mosaic Law with its "commandments and ordinances" (Eph. 2:15). In that case, Paul's point would be that the Jewish people were indebted to obey it in full. In the case of Gentiles, their conscience bound them to keep the moral law (cf. Rom. 2:14–16).

Note that Paul not only says this "record of debt" was "against" us, insofar as we are guilty for having failed to pay it, but that it also poses a very real threat to us (the NASB brings this across with its phrase, "which was hostile to us"; Col 2:14). The threat consists of the penalty that we incur for having failed to pay it in full. The penalty for nonpayment is not just a bad credit record. Not the repossession of our property. Not merely imprisonment. The penalty was death!

The passage clearly implies that some connection exists between the demonic hosts and the certificate of debt that is against us, such that the cancellation of the latter defeats the former. Page explains the nature of this connection:

> Perhaps, the powers exercised their influence over humanity through legal regulations, that is, by promoting the view that the way to please God is to conform to a set of religious and ethical rules. If this is the case, the disarming of the powers could relate to their losing their power to enslave people to a life of constant striving to reach perfection by following prescribed religious rituals and a strict code of conduct. Another possibility is that the powers were seen as sharing Satan's role as accuser (see Job 1:9–11; Zech. 3:1; Rev. 12:10). On this view, Christ's death on the cross deprived the

powers of their ability to demand a guilty verdict and its accompanying penalty for humanity. Since forgiveness is prominent in the immediate context, the latter explanation is preferable.[6]

Here again is the glorious good news of the gospel of God's grace in Jesus Christ. The way God forgave us all our trespasses (v. 13b) was "by canceling" our indebtedness to him. The word translated "canceling" has the sense of blotting out or erasing. God has wiped clean the slate! "I, I am he," declares the Lord, "who blots out your transgressions for my own sake, and I will not remember your sins" (Isaiah 43:25).

But God didn't simply tear up the note, so to speak, and throw it away. The infinitely righteous One cannot pretend that our indebtedness never existed. Instead, he canceled the IOU of our spiritual obligation by nailing it to the cross. Some see here an allusion to the ancient practice of affixing to the cross an inscription of the crimes for which the person was being executed. If so, then God nails the accusation against us to the cross of Christ. In any case, it is critical that we know there was no magic wand that waved off our guilt and made it disappear. God's justice and holiness are at stake here, no less so than our eternal destiny. That is why the payment must be made in full. We were buried beneath a mountain of spiritual bankruptcy. But God took that signed confession of indebtedness that stood as a perpetual witness against us and canceled it in the death of Christ.

We are no longer in default on the debt because Jesus paid it all! Whatever we owed, he paid. Whatever penalty we incurred, he endured. Well did the hymn writer declare:

> My sin, oh the bliss of this glorious thought,
> my sin not in part but the whole,
> was nailed to the cross and I bear it no more
> Praise the Lord! Praise the Lord! O my soul.[7]

Thus, we see that the forces of darkness have been dealt a fatal blow at the cross of Christ. This glorious truth must govern our faith and undergird

---

6   Page, *Powers of Evil*, 253.

7   Horatio Gates Spafford and Philip Paul Bliss, "It Is Well" (1873). Public domain.

all encounters with the enemy. You will never engage in spiritual warfare in a way that both honors Christ and encourages his people until you are energized by the truth that "he who is in you is greater than he who is in the world" (1 John 4:4b). The words of Jesus to the seventy-two disciples are as true today of you and me as they were then to them: "Behold, I have given you authority to tread on serpents and scorpions, and over all the power of the enemy, and nothing shall hurt you" (Luke 10:19).

The Cross Disarmed the Enemy

In Colossians 2:15 (NIV), Paul writes, "And having disarmed the powers and authorities, he made a public spectacle of them, triumphing over them by the cross." What Paul describes here was invisible to those standing at the foot of the cross. No one could see this remarkable phenomenon with their physical eyes. All they beheld at the moment of Christ's death was the crucifixion of a man on a Roman gibbet. But the apostle assures us that in his death a great and glorious victory was achieved.

In that cross the enemy of your soul was disrobed and disarmed. By means of that obscene instrument of execution, the accuser of the brethren was put to open and public shame. It was at Calvary that our Lord triumphed over every demonic entity. Like those who witnessed this event two millennia ago, we also must accept it by faith, on the authority of Scripture.

We must also take note of who the "he" is in verse 15 who is responsible for this remarkable triumph. Is the subject of this "disarming" God the Father, our Lord Jesus Christ, or perhaps, in some sense, both of them? In verses 13–14 God the Father was clearly the subject of the saving action described, and it is most likely that such is the case here again in verse 15.

However, many years ago J. B. Lightfoot proposed an interpretation of this text that is not only fascinating and instructive but would also suggest that we view Jesus himself as the one who performed or achieved this "disarming" or "disrobing" of the rulers and authorities. But before we look at Lightfoot's theory, we need to be clear on who Paul has in mind when he refers to "rulers and authorities."

Some have argued that by "rulers and authorities," Paul is referring to holy, elect angels who in the Old Testament were portrayed as mediators of the Mosaic Law. Thus, by means of the cross, God has stripped himself of the mediatorial ministry of angels, making a public display of them as inferior to Christ who alone is the mediator between God and man. This is highly unlikely, though, given the violent terms employed: "disarm," "strip away," "publicly display," as well as "triumph over." Most are agreed, therefore, that the "rulers and authorities" are fallen angelic hosts, whom we know as the devil and his demons. In fact, the terms Paul uses to describe them ("rulers and authorities") are standard vocabulary in the New Testament for demonic beings (see Eph. 1:20–21; 3:10; 6:10–20; Rom. 8:38).

What precisely, then, is meant in saying that God "disarmed" the demonic hosts? The only other place in the New Testament where this verb is used is in Colossians 3:9, where Paul describes Christians as those who have "put off" the old self, which is to say, they have "laid aside" or "stripped themselves" of the old self as if it were a garment to be discarded. Lightfoot contended that Paul's point is that whereas the powers of evil constantly attacked our Lord, assailing him throughout the course of his earthly ministry, by means of his atoning death, Jesus "stripped" them from himself much as one would disrobe and cast aside an old and filthy garment.

Perhaps an illustration will help. In ancient mythology, Hercules once permitted his wife Deianira to be carried across a flooded stream by a centaur named Nessus. The centaur provoked Hercules by his rudeness and was subsequently shot with a poison arrow. As Nessus lay dying, he told Deianira to save his blood as a love charm. Later, when Hercules fell in love with Iole, Deianira dipped a robe in the blood of Nessus and sent it to her husband. When Hercules put it on, the poison began to eat away his flesh. In agony, he begged his friends to burn his body to end the ordeal.

Thus wrote Bishop Lightfoot: "The powers of evil which had clung like a Nessus robe about His [Christ's] humanity, were torn off and cast aside forever."[8] The demonic powers beset our Lord at every turn of his life and shrouded, as it were, his person with their poisonous hostility, much as the Nessus robe did the body of Hercules. But whereas the mythological hero was defeated by death, our Lord was victorious by it. In his crucifixion he stripped the forces of evil from himself as one would a tattered and ragged robe.

Lightfoot's is a vivid and instructive interpretation, but an unlikely one. Whereas the translation "disrobed" is a better rendering of this word than "disarmed," in Colossians, God the Father, in effect, "stripped" the demons of

---

8   J. B. Lightfoot, *Saint Paul's Epistles to the Colossians and to Philemon* (Grand Rapids: Zondervan, 1976 [1879]), 190.

their power and authority. They have thus been disarmed and defeated and are unworthy of either our honor or fear.

More than that, God has put them to open shame or made a public spectacle of them. This is a bit unusual, insofar as we humans cannot see or witness such an exposure of these spiritual beings. In what sense, then, were they put to open shame or made a public spectacle? There are two ways of answering this question. On the one hand, Paul may be referring to a display or spectacle visible only to the spiritual realm itself. In other words, it is before both the holy angels as well as the unholy, fallen hosts that this triumph was made known. In Ephesians 3:10, Paul says that it is through the church that the wisdom of God is being "made known to the rulers and authorities in the heavenly places." Clearly, it is important to God's purposes that the demonic realm see or be aware of his wisdom as it is revealed in the salvation and ministry of the church on earth. Perhaps, then, the disrobing or disarming of the demonic hosts is made public to the unseen world of angels and demons alike as part of God's design to glorify himself in the salvation of sinners. On the other hand, we may be guilty of pressing Paul's language beyond its proper bounds. It would seem he is making use of a common image in his day to make a theological point. In other words, our problem may be that we are expecting some literal manifestation of a truth that is described in obviously metaphorical terms.

The verse actually says that he "put them to open shame, *by triumphing over them* in him" (emphasis mine). In other words, the way in which the rulers and authorities were put to open shame was by being subject to the "triumphal procession" of God in Christ. The word translated "triumphing" (used elsewhere in the New Testament only in 2 Cor. 2:14) was descriptive of a Roman general parading his captives behind him as the spoil and booty of war, all of which was designed to humiliate them and bring public attention to their subjugation.

Thus, Paul's point here may simply be that God's defeat of the demonic hosts is like that of an earthly military commander's triumph over and public display of his enemies. We are not to look for some specific time or event or way in which this "open shame" of the demonic hosts was made known or visible. Rather, we are to rest assured and rejoice in the promise that our spiritual enemies were as thoroughly defeated and stripped of their dignity and power as were those physical enemies who unsuccessfully opposed and were eventually conquered by a Roman general and his army.

But surely the most stunning statement of all is the final phrase of Colossians 2:15. It was "in" or "through" or "by" the cross that this victory was achieved. The ESV renders it, "in him," as if referring to Christ. This is certainly possible, but I think it more likely that the antecedent in view is the "cross" of verse 14, to which God is said to have nailed our sins.

Amazing! The very instrument that to all eyes appeared to seal Christ's doom was his tool of triumph! In a marvelous twist of divine irony, the cross, the emblem of disgrace and death by which the demonic hosts thought they had defeated Christ, is turned on them and becomes the instrument of their humiliating demise.

As our Lord "was suspended there," wrote F. F. Bruce, "bound hand and foot to the wood in apparent weakness, [the rulers and authorities] imagined they had him at their mercy, and flung themselves upon him with hostile intent. But, far from suffering their assault without resistance, he grappled with them and mastered them, stripping them of all the armor in which they trusted, and held them aloft in his outstretched hands, displaying to the universe their helplessness and his own unvanquished strength. . . . But now they are dethroned and incapacitated, and the shameful tree has become the victor's triumphal chariot, before which his captives are driven in humiliating procession, the involuntary and impotent confessors of his superior might."[9]

John Calvin put it best: "For there is no tribunal so magnificent, no throne so stately, no show of triumph so distinguished, no chariot so elevated, as is the gibbet on which Christ has subdued death and the devil, nay more, has utterly trodden them under His feet."[10] The bottom line is this: Spiritual authority is in the name of Christ, the balance of power rests with us, and the ultimate outcome has been settled in our favor. We do not fear those who've suffered a decisive defeat, but our faith is in God. Therefore, we stand firm, resisting the enemy with the assurance that he will flee.

And this glorious truth that was confirmed by the resurrection was the Father's "Amen!" to the Son's "It is finished!" By raising Jesus from the dead and exalting him to the right hand of the majesty on high, God the Father

9   F. F. Bruce, *The Epistles to the Colossians, to Philemon, and to the Ephesians* (Grand Rapids: Eerdmans, 1984), 111.

10   John Calvin, *The Epistles of Paul the Apostle to the Galatians, Ephesians, Philippians and Colossians*, trans. T. H. L. Parker (Grand Rapids: Eerdmans, 1972), 336.

ratified, confirmed, and openly proclaimed the sufficiency of the cross. (See Rom. 5:8–11; 1 Cor. 15:16–17; Eph. 1:18–23; Col. 2:10; 1 Pet. 3:22; Rev. 1:17–18.)

Revelation 12 and the Defeat of the Devil

Another crucially important statement concerning the defeat of the devil is found in Revelation 12:1–11.

> And a great sign appeared in heaven: a woman clothed with the sun, with the moon under her feet, and on her head a crown of twelve stars. She was pregnant and was crying out in birth pains and the agony of giving birth. And another sign appeared in heaven: behold, a great red dragon, with seven heads and ten horns, and on his heads seven diadems. His tail swept down a third of the stars of heaven and cast them to the earth. And the dragon stood before the woman who was about to give birth, so that when she bore her child he might devour it. She gave birth to a male child, one who is to rule all the nations with a rod of iron, but her child was caught up to God and to his throne, and the woman fled into the wilderness, where she has a place prepared by God, in which she is to be nourished for 1,260 days.
>
> Now war arose in heaven, Michael and his angels fighting against the dragon. And the dragon and his angels fought back, but he was defeated, and there was no longer any place for them in heaven. And the great dragon was thrown down, that ancient serpent, who is called the devil and Satan, the deceiver of the whole world—he was thrown down to the earth, and his angels were thrown down with him. And I heard a loud voice in heaven, saying, "Now the salvation and the power and the kingdom of our God and the authority of his Christ have come, for the accuser of our brothers has been thrown down, who accuses them day and night before our God. And they have conquered him by the blood of the Lamb and by the word of their testimony, for they loved not their lives even unto death."

Contrary to what most of you have probably been led to believe, the "stars of heaven" in Revelation 12:4 that Satan throws to the earth are probably not those in the angelic host who fall with him in some pre-temporal rebellion and subsequently constitute the demonic hosts of which we read in both the Old Testament and New Testament. There are two reasons for this.

The time of this event described in verse 4 is immediately before the birth of Jesus, whereas most believe that the angelic rebellion occurred prior to creation. Second, it seems reasonable that the "stars" of verse 4 that are swept down by Satan must be related to the "stars" of verse 1, which are found in the crown of the woman. Thus the "stars" of verse 4 are not to be identified with the dragon's "angels" in verses 7–8. Instead, Revelation 12:4 is probably describing the persecution of God's people by Satan, perhaps even their martyrdom.

What is far more important for our purposes is the second half of verse 4, where we read of Satan's determination to kill Jesus upon his birth. Surely this has in view the barbaric and heartless command from King Herod that all the male infants in Bethlehem, two years and younger, be killed (Matt. 2:16–18). I don't want to minimize the horror of this event, but people have often believed that this was a mass slaughter, when in fact the population of Bethlehem in those days would have allowed for, at most, two dozen young boys to be the victims of Herod's wrath.

Revelation 12:5 provides us with a synopsis or snapshot of Christ's entire life. Such abbreviations are not uncommon in the New Testament (cf. John 3:13; 8:14; 13:3; 16:5, 28; Rom. 1:3–4; 1 Tim. 3:16; see also Rev. 1:5, 17–18; 2:8). His being "caught up to God and to his throne" in verse 5b is not protection from death but a reference to the resurrection and ascension of Jesus. The reference to Jesus ruling all the nations with a rod of iron is an allusion to the prophecy of Psalm 2:7–9 and indicates that, whereas this will be consummated at the end of the age (see Rev. 19:15), an inaugurated fulfillment has already begun (see Rev. 2:26–28). Jesus has *already* received the authority spoken of in the Psalm and is now ruling the nations from his heavenly throne, but he has *not yet* manifested that authority in its fullness.

War in Heaven and Victory on Earth (Rev. 12:7–11)

Revelation 12:7–11 is introduced by John to explain why the woman (the church) had to flee into the wilderness (vv. 1–6). The reason why Satan's fury is now unleashed against the Church of Jesus Christ *on earth* is because he has lost his place and position *in heaven*; his power has been curtailed.

What kind of "war" does John have in mind? What kind of "weapons" might have been employed, if at all? Was there some sort of contact, appropriate to spiritual beings, that occurred? Could such war have resulted in some form of injury to the combatants, even death? Or is the use of the terminology of "war" simply a metaphor designed to paint a theological picture? If so, what is that picture?

So, when did (or when will) this expulsion of Satan and his demons from heaven occur? Three answers have figured prominently among evangelicals. According to dispensationalists who read Revelation as applying almost exclusively to the future, it will occur just before or during the so-called seven-year "great tribulation" period. Others say it is timeless. No specific moment in history is in view. It is simply a highly symbolic description of Satan's downfall. I, on the other hand, believe it is because of the incarnation, life, death, and resurrection of Jesus in the first century that this defeat of the devil occurs, and indeed, has already occurred. Michael and his angels are given the task of expelling Satan consequent to the victory of Jesus *at the time of his first coming* (we see a whisper of this event in the words of Jesus in Luke 10:18). Christians carry on this victory over Satan (Rev. 12:11) as they stand on the achievements of the cross and boldly proclaim the authority of Jesus's name.

In other words, the victory of Jesus Christ over sin and death provoked this war. Michael and his angels are here portrayed as enforcing the results of Christ's victory on his enemies, namely Satan and his demons. Michael and his angels win because Christ won. Satan's accusations no longer have any legal or moral force following his defeat at the cross. This, I believe, is the meaning of his being "thrown down" and there no longer being "any place for them in heaven."

This is not a description of a literal or spatial or geographical change in the devil's dwelling place. Rather, we should understand that this is John's way of describing the glorious fact that Satan's power was broken through Christ's atoning sacrifice on the cross and his bodily resurrection. The result is that Satan can no longer successfully bring accusations against God's people. Prior to the cross, the accusations and slander of Satan had legal force, for the sin of those against whom he spoke had not been fully expiated. But now, subsequent to the cross, "there is therefore now no condemnation for those that are in Christ Jesus" (Rom. 8:1). Whatever ongoing work of accusation Satan may attempt is countered by the intercessory ministry of Jesus (Rom. 8:33–34; Heb. 7:25; 1 John 2:1–2).

According to verse 10, the fact that Satan has been defeated, that the atoning death and resurrection of Jesus have stripped him of his legal right to accuse the brethren,[11] is evidence that the kingdom of God and the authority of Christ have been inaugurated. Thus, Revelation 12:10 does not merely anticipate the final and consummate coming of God's kingdom but celebrates the presence of the kingdom in the here and now. Verse 11 thus reassures the people of God, then and now, that suffering and even martyrdom at the hands of the devil is *not defeat for them, but for him!* It is an ironic victory, but a victory nonetheless. Verse 11 declares that followers of Christ "triumphed over" Satan. By what means did they overcome him? John answers this question by mentioning three things in particular:

1. The blood of the Lamb
2. The word of their testimony
3. By not loving their lives "even unto death"

Let's explore each of these powerful means of overcoming the devil in more depth.

Conquered by the Blood of the Lamb

John first declares that they conquered Satan "by the blood of the Lamb" (v. 11a). This is done when we stand on the truth of Romans 8:1, that there is no condemnation for those in Christ Jesus. It is done when we proclaim the truth of Colossians 2:13–15 and Christ's triumph over Satan and his forces by means of his cross. It is done when we declare and trust in the truth that the cross/resurrection of Jesus has secured for us the presence and power of the Holy Spirit. Thus, the phrase "the blood of the Lamb" is simply a way of referring to Jesus in his capacity as Lord and Savior, the one who triumphed over sin and death.

Simply put, Satan's only hope for victory in your life is the presence of unforgiven sin. But Christ's blood cleanses us from the condemning power of that guilt incurred by our sin (1 John 1:7), and thus forever removes any and all grounds on which Satan might have a legal basis for launching his attack.

Conquered by the Word of Their Testimony

John next states that they conquered Satan "by the word of their testimony." This starts with the confident proclamation of our identity in Christ. One of Satan's

---

11 See the discussion of Satan's names and roles in chapter 3.

primary weapons is the *lie*. He is committed to deceiving you into believing you *are not* what, in fact, *you are*, and that you *cannot do* what, in fact, *you can*. Satan will try to persuade you that you are a failure, a fool, of no use to God or other Christians, worthless, an embarrassment to Christ, that you are wasting your time to confess your sins (God won't listen), that you are inferior to other believers, destined always to fall short of their successes, that you are a hopeless victim of your past and helpless to change your future, that you are a pathetic excuse for a Christian, that you are owned by Satan, that you are now what you will always be (there's no hope for improvement), that you are stupid and beyond the reach of prayer, etc. You must respond to such deceitful, destructive slander by remembering and standing firmly on the truth of 2 Corinthians 5:17; Ephesians 2:1–7; 5:8; and 1 John 3:1–3.

The "word" of our "testimony" is also expressed when we engage in heartfelt, passionate worship of the Son of God. The power to repel the enemy, the authority to overcome, is *not* to be found in the physical elements of music per se. Volume, melody, and rhythm have no inherent spiritual power. Power to repel and overcome the enemy resides in the truth of what is sung or played and the heart of the singer or player.

The devil pays no attention to decibels or sweat or physical gestures. But he is compelled to submit to the proclamation of truth, the presence of the Spirit, and the authenticity and intensity of heart devotion to Jesus. Intimacy in worship (God's love and ours), together with our adoration, declaration of God's power, grace, kindness, justice, etc., as well as the affirmation of our commitment to Christ, do more to repel the enemy than anything. That is warfare worship. Nothing will do more to drive away demons than the intensity of intimacy with Jesus!

The "word" of our "testimony" is also expressed in *prayer*. This involves praying for ourselves and others to be given insight and understanding into who we are in Christ and what is ours through faith (Eph. 1). There are also prayers of resistance and rebuke of the enemy. This is a subject we'll explore in more detail when we come to Ephesians 6.

Conquered by Not Loving Their Lives "Even unto Death"

Finally, John says that they conquer Satan by not loving their lives "even unto death." What is being described in this little phrase is a value judgment, a prioritizing that affected every aspect of their lives. They loved Jesus more than their earthly welfare, more than earthly pleasures, more than earthly convenience, more than peace, prosperity, and comfort.

Here he means the willingness to give up good things for the sake of better things and to sacrifice all in life, even life itself, because life isn't the most valuable thing to us. They would rather die than yield one inch of their hearts to the world or Satan; no earthly pleasure was worth denying Jesus. No promise of peace or power was deemed of greater value than the value of remaining steadfast. We read in Hebrews 10:34 (NASB), "For you ... accepted joyfully the seizure of your property, knowing that you have for yourselves a better and lasting possession." They had refused to let anything in life get a grip on their hearts in such a way that it might diminish their devotion to Jesus. "Jesus is more valuable to us than anything life can offer. Jesus is greater treasure than life itself. We will gladly die before we renounce him!"

Satan has absolutely no chance of winning when he confronts a heart like that! Simple, unqualified, unconditional devotion to Jesus! That is why even in their death they overcame him (Rev. 2:10). *Satan only wins when we love our lives more than we love God*, when we allow our hearts to be captured by earthly comfort and find that we would do anything and everything to procure more, preserve what we have, promote it, make it comfortable, insulate it, etc. Too many of us love our lives illegitimately; there is a good and legal love of life (I'm not talking about that; celebrate life, enjoy it, etc.). This is an overprotective concern for personal comfort, convenience, peace, prosperity, and the resultant energy and lifestyle designed to perpetuate it. *Satan wins whenever we treasure anything more than Jesus.*

So, how does this perspective on life overcome the enemy? When you prioritize your life so that nothing means more to you than Jesus, you deprive Satan of any legal right to your heart or mind; you undermine and short circuit his power to influence your soul. How? If this (Rev. 12:11) is your life, what can he possibly latch hold of? What is there in your life to which he can affix himself? To what can he appeal in your soul that would give him a power base from which to operate?

The Church, the Dragon, and Divine Protection (Rev. 12:12–17)

Although he was decisively defeated at the cross of Christ, Satan's efforts to destroy the church will continue until the second coming of our Lord. John describes this figuratively in Revelation 12:12–17:

"Therefore, rejoice, O heavens and you who dwell in them! But woe to you, O earth and sea, for the devil has come down to you in great wrath, because he knows that his time is short!"

And when the dragon saw that he had been thrown down to the earth, he pursued the woman who had given birth to the male child. But the woman was given the two wings of the great eagle so that she might fly from the serpent into the wilderness, to the place where she is to be nourished for a time, and times, and half a time. The serpent poured water like a river out of his mouth after the woman, to sweep her away with a flood. But the earth came to the help of the woman, and the earth opened its mouth and swallowed the river that the dragon had poured from his mouth. Then the dragon became furious with the woman and went off to make war on the rest of her offspring, on those who keep the commandments of God and hold to the testimony of Jesus. And he stood on the sand of the sea.

Revelation 12:12–13 picks up where verse 6 left off. Having failed to destroy the "child" (Jesus), Satan turns his wrath and destructive attention to the Woman, that is, the people of God, the Church.

Verse 14 is a vivid and figurative portrayal of how God has taken steps to protect his people and preserve them against Satan's attacks during this present church age. John uses vivid imagery of water pouring forth from the serpent's mouth to drown the woman to describe the devil's persecution of the church. The imagery of an overflowing flood or torrential waves of water is used throughout the Old Testament in two primary ways:

1. It points to the persecution of God's people by his enemies (see 2 Sam. 22:5; Ps. 18:4, 16; 46:3; 66:12; 69:1–2, 14–15; 124:4–5; 144:7–8, 11; Isa. 43:2).
2. It is also used to portray the judgment that God brings against those who resist him (see Isa. 8:7–8; 17:12–13; Jer. 46:8; 47:2; 51:55; Hos. 5:10).

It may be that since the waters pour forth from the serpent's "mouth," the idea is particularly of Satan's attempt to destroy the church through deception and false teaching or false doctrine (see Rev. 2:14–16, 20–22; 3:15–17; Rom. 16:17–20; 1 Tim. 4:1; 5:15; 2 Tim. 2:23–26). Recall the numerous times in church history (past and present) where the rise of heresy threatened the purity (and even existence) of the church: Gnosticism and Marcionism in the second and third centuries, anti-Trinitarian Monarchianism in the third century, Arianism in the fourth century, Pelagianism in the fifth century, the various false teachings in Roman Catholicism throughout the middle ages, Socinianism in the sixteenth and seventeenth centuries, Deism in the seventeenth and eighteenth centuries, and the emergence of Darwinian evolution and religious liberalism in the nineteenth and twentieth centuries.

And do you remember how God's defeat of Pharaoh's armies at the Red Sea is portrayed? We read in Exodus 15:12, "You stretched out your right hand; [and] the earth swallowed them." Later in the wilderness, "the earth opened its mouth and swallowed" the families of Korah, Dathan, and Abiram because of their resistance to Moses's leadership (Deut. 11:5–6; see also Num. 16:12–14; Ps. 106:17).

The devil's fury and wrath are now directed at the "rest of her offspring." That's you and me. Satan hates you. He hates everything about the church, the people of God. He hates those "who keep the commandments of God and hold to the testimony of Jesus" (v. 17).

Guaranteed Victory

The Church, the people of God, have been engaged in a war with Satan for more than 2,000 years. It is a staggering testimony to the wickedness of our enemy that "he knows that his time is short" (12:12b) yet continues to assault, accuse, and do everything in his power to undermine our faith in Jesus. But we have been guaranteed victory, not because of our righteousness or spirituality, but because of the victory secured for us by Jesus, whose blood cleanses from all sin. Praise be to God!

REBEKAH'S STORY

My first encounter with deliverance happened before I even knew what the term meant. I grew up in a church where gifts of the Spirit, and consequently, spiritual warfare were not discussed. When I found myself as a young mom overcome with postpartum depression, anxiety, and OCD tendencies, I believed the Lord would be with me through my trials. And I clung to him knowing he was enough. But I had never dared to hope or to pray that God would rescue me from the paralyzing fear that was wreaking havoc on my relationships. Through short-term use of antidepressants and long-term counseling, I learned to cope with my symptoms.

Shortly after my husband and I began attending Bridgeway, Sam Storms began a sermon series on healing. For the first time, I had hope. I learned that not only was it okay to ask for healing, but that God wanted me to faithfully ask him. Even if the Lord never chose to heal me, I was overjoyed that he wanted me to ask for healing! Every Sunday, as members of the congregation prayed over those seeking physical or mental healing, I stood for prayer. The Lord did not choose to heal me, but I knew I would continue to ask him.

The last Sunday of the sermon series, Sam taught on demonic oppression. I listened to him describe how the enemy will frequently operate: how thoughts will come out of nowhere and how he will make you believe it's just how you are. I realized that what I had been experiencing all those years was demonic oppression! At the end of the sermon, I stood for prayer. Unlike previous Sundays, I did not tell the two women praying over me what I needed prayer for. Instead, they prayed silently while Sam prayed a prayer of deliverance over us.

As they were praying, I felt a rush of wind, like a warm spring breeze. I saw an image of a simple barn in a field. The wind was blowing from one end of it to the other, rustling its white curtains in the wind. I knew, as the Lord spoke to my heart, exactly what he was doing to my mind. He was cleaning out my mind and bringing refreshment to my thinking. As I started to weep, one of the ladies asked if I would share with them what I felt they should pray for. I told them my struggles with anxiety and OCD and what I had just seen and felt. I was even more overwhelmed by the Lord's power when one of the women shared that she had the impression to pray for the Lord to renew me like a cool breeze. And, the other lady had actually followed the Holy Spirit's prompting to blow on me! It was a day of rejoicing! I remember truly feeling a celebration of new life. It was like a birthday. I knew I was free!

As I prayed through and processed with the Lord, I understood that while I may have these predispositions or tendencies towards anxiety and OCD, I was not in bondage to them. I could choose to walk in the freedom the Lord had given or choose to follow my old habits. The enemy had taken real struggles and made me believe I had no choice. I now know that even though I may still have tendencies or impulses, I have a choice to walk in them or not. I understand not all mental health issues are demonic, and I want to be sensitive to those for whom it is a physiological issue. But, in my case, for various reasons (including the fact that my licensed counselor found my case/diagnoses confusing), I believe it was a demonic foothold the enemy had gained through certain life events. It has been several years since this moment of deliverance, and the Lord continues to give me more freedom and teach me to follow him and not fear. The Lord dramatically delivered me from this chokehold of the enemy, giving me freedom and hope. I will forever rejoice!

CHAPTER 14

Our Identity and Authority in Christ

One of Satan's primary weapons is the *lie*. He is committed to deceiving you into believing you *are not* what, in fact, *you are*, and that you *cannot do* what, in fact, *you can*. Why is this important to know? Because your personal identity or how you perceive yourself governs how you live. That is why Satan will try to persuade you that you are:

- a failure
- a fool
- of no use to God or other Christians
- worthless
- an embarrassment to Christ
- wasting your time to confess your sins (God won't listen)
- inferior to other believers
- destined always to fall short of their successes
- a hopeless victim of your past
- helpless to change your future
- a pathetic excuse for a Christian
- owned by Satan
- stupid
- beyond the reach of prayer

We must respond to such deceitful, destructive slander by remembering that we are a new creation in Christ (2 Cor. 5:17), that we have been forgiven by God's grace in Christ and are now seated with him in heavenly places

(Eph. 2:1–7; 5:8), and that we are the beloved children of God who are destined by grace to be wholly conformed to the image of Jesus Christ (1 John 3:1–3).

The Believer's Identity and Authority in Christ

Christians often try to excuse their inactivity or their feelings of spiritual impotence by pointing to Luke 9:1, where Jesus "called the twelve together and gave them power and authority over all demons." People will tell me, "I'm not an apostle. What reason do I have for believing I might have that kind of authority?" Well, the reason is Luke 10, where average, non-apostolic followers of Jesus are given the same authority over Satan and his forces.[1] In Luke 10:1 we read that "after this the Lord appointed seventy-two others and sent them on ahead of him, two by two, into every town and place where he himself was about to go." By "others," Luke means other than the Twelve, which is to say, non-apostolic disciples or followers of Jesus. We should read Luke 10:1 in contrast with Luke 9:1, where Jesus "called the twelve together and gave them power and authority over all demons."

Jesus sent them out "two by two" to provide mutual protection, encouragement, and support, and also to establish legal attestation and binding testimony to what might subsequently occur (see Deut. 17:6; 19:15). It would appear that the commissioning, authorizing, and empowering of the seventy-two (some texts put the number at seventy) is a prelude to the ministry of the larger body of Christ universal. As Susan Garrett explains, "Luke may have conceived of the mission by 'seventy (-two) others' as foreshadowing the period of the church, when not only the twelve but *many* sons and daughters would receive the Spirit of the Lord and prophesy, and would thereby be enabled to carry out Jesus' work."[2]

If we keep reading in Luke 10, we'll encounter an important passage when it comes to equipping and encouraging average Christian men and women to engage the enemy:

---

1 This treatment of Luke 10 is largely derived from my book *Practicing the Power: Welcoming the Gifts of the Holy Spirit in your Life* (Grand Rapids: Zondervan, 2017), 151–60, and is used here with permission.

2 Susan Garrett, *The Demise of the Devil: Magic and the Demonic in Luke's Writings* (Minneapolis: Fortress Press, 1989), 48.

The seventy-two returned with joy, saying, "Lord, even the demons are subject to us in your name!" And he said to them, "I saw Satan fall like lightning from heaven. Behold, I have given you authority to tread on serpents and scorpions, and over all the power of the enemy, and nothing shall hurt you. Nevertheless, do not rejoice in this, that the spirits are subject to you, but rejoice that your names are written in heaven." (Luke 10:17–20)

You can't escape the obvious excitement on the part of the seventy-two. Even the demons are subject to us in your name. Wow! It may be that they had no expectations for this outcome and were genuinely surprised by the effectiveness of the power they were given. But notice that they do not say the demons are "subject to us." Yes, they are "subject to us," but only in Christ's name. The authority and the power that produced results belonged to Christ. He, in turn, had imparted it to or invested it in them.

"I SAW SATAN FALL LIKE LIGHTNING"

What does Jesus mean when he says he "saw Satan fall like lightning?" It is unlikely that the "fall" (v. 18) of Satan referred to here is a reference to his original, pre-temporal, fall into sin, since Jesus's comment was in response to their report concerning the success they had experienced in casting out demons. As Sydney Page points out, "the context demands a reference to a fall that is the result of being defeated, not a fall that is the result of sinning."[3]

The verb used here for "saw" (*theōreō*) is not used elsewhere for visions Jesus had (although it is used to describe the visions that others experienced: see Acts 7:56; 9:7; 10:11). Whether or not Jesus experienced a vision or simply is using figurative language is unimportant. Of more significance is the nature and time of this "fall" of the enemy.

This could be a visionary experience in which Jesus "saw" the impending fall or demise of the devil, an event yet to be fulfilled (cf. Dan. 7:2, 4, 6, 7, 9, 11, 13). Perhaps Jesus was looking forward to the

3   Page, *Powers of Evil*, 109.

judgment Satan would incur by virtue of the atoning sacrifice of the cross and the subsequent resurrection of Jesus from the dead. Others see here a reference to Satan's "fall" that occurred because of his defeat in the wilderness when he failed in the tempting of Jesus. Still another possibility is that this "fall" is a reference to his defeat each time his house his plundered (Matt. 12:22–32) as a result of successful deliverance ministry. Whichever view is correct, Jesus does not intend to suggest that because of this "fall" from heaven Satan is no longer active or a threat. In Luke 10:19 he issues a promise that makes sense only if there are real dangers from which his disciples need to be protected.

Luke 10: Believers' Authority in Christ

This statement is key: "I have given you authority" (Luke 10:19a). Authority simply means delegated power—not only the responsibility, not only the prerogative, but also *the spiritual power to enforce compliance*. Authority is the right and power to act and speak as if Jesus himself were present (v. 16).

This is an incredibly important reminder of something I heard Neil Anderson say: "Spiritual warfare is not a horizontal tug of war but a vertical chain of command." We must never envision ourselves as operating on a level playing field with Satan and his demons. Alone and in the power of our own identity, we don't stand a chance against him. But in Christ and on the basis of who we are in him, and in light of the authority of the risen Lord that has been bequeathed to us, Satan and his demons are a defeated lot. They must obey us. Don't ever think of yourself as at one end of a rope and Satan at the other, both of you struggling to overpower the other. No! You are in Christ, who is over all. Satan is beneath you, in Christ's name.

Serpents and Scorpions

What are the "serpents" and "scorpions" mentioned in verse 19? They are not to be taken literally. They are, in all likelihood, a vivid way of describing demonic beings.

Serpents and scorpions were familiar sources of evil and pain in Palestinian life, and thus served to symbolize all kinds of adversity and affliction (see Num. 21:6–9; Deut. 8:15; Ps. 58:4; 140:3). The scorpion was also a means of divine chastisement in 1 Kings 12:11, 14 (see also Luke 11:11–12). Additionally, Satan is often portrayed as a serpent in Scripture (Gen. 3; 2 Cor. 11; Rev. 12 and 20). Hence, his domain is that of snakes and scorpions (see Ps. 91:12–13).

The "serpents and scorpions" of Luke10:19 are a reference to the "demons" of verse 17. Within verse 19 itself, "serpents and scorpions" are parallel to "all the power of the enemy," an undeniable reference to Satan and his hosts. In verse 20 Jesus again indicates clearly that "serpents and scorpions" are a reference to demonic "spirits" (see also Rev. 9:3, 5, 10).

And contrary to the way some have interpreted verse 20, it isn't wrong or sinful to rejoice in this authority over the demonic. If it were, Jesus would never have given such authority to his disciples in the first place. The point, rather, is that in comparison with being saved, such power is far less significant. Authority over the demonic spirits is great, but being saved, forgiven, and having one's name recorded in the book of life is greater!

Authority in Christ Today

Do we, the church, have the same authority Jesus granted the seventy-two in Luke 10? Or was this a temporary endowment?

We have even *greater* authority.

We need to remember that Jesus gave this commission and the authority and power it entailed to the seventy-two, not simply to the Twelve. Jesus's selection of seventy-two is surely in anticipation of the worldwide mission of the entire body of Christ. The seventy-two were not uniquely gifted or specially called people with high office or position in the body of Christ. They were ordinary followers of Jesus, just like you and me.

We must also keep in mind that we live and operate on *this* side of the cross, subsequent to the defeat of Satan. The authority and power of those seventy-two living prior to the cross can hardly be regarded as equivalent to ours, subsequent to the cross. Similarly, we live and operate on *this* side of Pentecost. That means we operate with the fullness of the indwelling power and presence of the Holy Spirit. They did not. We have received the fullness of divine authorization as stated in the Great Commission (Matt. 28:18–19). Plus, we have been raised up and seated with the exalted Lord, under whose feet all principalities and powers have been subjected (Eph. 1:19–2:7; Col. 2:9–10).

Finally, the *evidence* of authority is the *exercise* of authority. One need only read numerous texts of the authority and power operative in the early church, following the ascension of Jesus, to see confirmation of this point (see Acts 5:16; 8:7; 16:18; 19:12–16; 2 Cor. 10:3–4; Eph. 6:10–13; Jas. 4:7; 1 Pet. 5:8; 1 John 2:13–14).

The Exercise of Authority: Binding, Resisting, Rebuking

Is the verbal *rebuking* and *binding* of demonic spirits a legitimate biblical expression of our authority over the enemy? Those who say no are often heard to say, "Why not just pray, 'O God, please resist, rebuke, and bind this evil spirit for me'?" In other words, they insist that we should always defer to God.

But consider Ephesians 6:10–20, where we are called to stand firm and struggle against the enemy. We must avail ourselves of the power and weaponry secured for us by Christ's victory. Let us not forget that, as we've just seen in Luke 10, God has *delegated* his authority to us. It is not God's desire to settle all our spiritual disputes. He desires for us to utilize the authority he has invested in us. God wants us to share in and to enjoy the thrill of victory, just as Jesus was obviously pleased with the response of the seventy-two in Luke 10.

Furthermore, God is pleased to utilize us in the pursuit of his ends. He wants to involve us in the work of the kingdom. We are his representatives, spokespeople, and ambassadors in evangelism and ministry—and in spiritual warfare too. No one would ever think of saying, "O God, preach the gospel to the lost," "O God, teach the truth to your people," or "Lord, would you please visit the sick today as I'm simply too busy?" Rather, God desires to use us to proclaim the gospel, teach the principles of Scripture, and minister in mercy to those who are hurting. We have been entrusted with his authority, his power, and his gifts to minister to his people in his name and to participate in expanding his kingdom.

Binding and Resisting the Enemy

Is it biblical to *bind* and *resist* the enemy? We find the terminology of "binding" in three texts in Matthew:

- Matthew 12:29: Here it is Jesus who "bound" the devil, most likely a reference to his victory over him in the wilderness. Whereas Jesus is nowhere recorded as saying, "I bind you," he did bind, restrict, or inhibit the ability of the enemy to keep people in bondage.

- Matthew 16:19: Here we read of the "keys" (see Luke 11:52) granted to the leadership of the Church. These are likely a reference to the power to know, understand, and proclaim the terms of entrance into or exclusion from the kingdom of God. Whatever we "bind" (prohibit) or "loose" (allow) through the proclamation of the gospel will prove to be an earthly application or confirmation of what heaven has already decreed. We have been given authority to pronounce forgiveness or judgment, depending on a person's response to the truth (cf. John 20:23).

- Matthew 18:18: This passage speaks of church discipline and the decision of the church in adjudicating a dispute between two people. Here, to "bind" is to declare someone guilty. Those who are guilty remain under the condemnation of God as the penalty for sin. Conversely, to "loose" is to declare them innocent. The decision of the church on earth reflects the decision already made in heaven. That is to say, when we conform to biblical guidelines and accurately declare the terms on which membership and fellowship in the church are possible, our decisions will be an earthly expression of heaven's prior decree.

It would appear that nothing in these three texts gives explicit endorsement to the practice of saying, "Satan, I bind you in Jesus's name." However, before we dismiss this as unbiblical, we need to observe other explicit commands.

In Ephesians 6 we are told to "stand" (v. 11) against the schemes of the devil. We have also been equipped with spiritual armor, that we might "withstand" in the evil day (v. 13). More explicit still is the statement by James that we should "resist the devil," together with the assurance that, if we do, "he will flee from" us (Jas. 4:7). Likewise, Peter says, "Resist him," that is, our "adversary the devil" (1 Pet. 5:8–9). To "resist" means to stand against or to oppose, to set oneself against someone or something. To resist Satan or his demons thus means to employ the authority and power given us by God to restrict demonic activities, to restrain satanic efforts, to thwart the devil's plans. What does this mean, if not to "bind"? To "bind" means to inhibit or to restrain someone from an action or activity.

Therefore, on the one hand, it is true that neither Jesus nor anyone else in the New Testament ever says, "Satan (demon), I bind you." On the other hand, both Jesus and Christians do, in terms of practical and experiential impact, "bind" Satan and his demons. This is done primarily by the truth of God's Word spoken (Matt. 4:1–11) and moral resistance (Eph. 6:10–20). Thus, I conclude that whereas we should not appeal to any of the three texts cited above in Matthew's Gospel to support our practice, it is theologically permissible to use the terminology of "binding" when we "resist" the enemy.

However, I have often been in the presence of overzealous Christians who think that simply by saying aloud and with great emotional energy, "Satan, I bind you in the name of Jesus," the enemy is thereby rendered wholly and permanently incapacitated. Sadly, this more closely approximates presumption than it does a legitimate expression of our authority over the enemy. I can certainly "bind" or restrict or defeat the activity of Satan and demons in my own life. This comes by way of repentance and humble dependence on the Lord and the finality of his victory at the cross. But there does not appear to be any biblical basis for thinking that I, or any other Christian, can "bind" Satan's work of promoting abortion in our city or the proliferation of pornography or sex trafficking.

Can individual men and women be set free from Satan's grip in regard to any of these sinful practices? Yes, of course. But taking authority over the enemy in one's own life and resisting his nefarious schemes is one thing. Thinking that merely by speaking the words, "Satan, I bind you" or "I prohibit any demonic spirit from sowing the seeds of sin and perversion in our city," is something entirely different. As long as those who promote and participate in such wicked behavior continue to willfully engage in it and refuse to repent, there is little hope that our words alone will break the authority of the enemy in their lives.

Rebuking the Enemy

Is it biblical to *rebuke* the enemy? The term "rebuke" (*epitimaō*) is used frequently by Jesus in his encounters with demonic spirits (Matt. 17:18; Mark 1:25; 3:12; 9:25; Luke 4:35, 41; 9:42). The term functions as a word of command by which evil forces are brought into submission. Thus "it combines the idea of moral censure expressed by the word *rebuke* with the notion of the subjugation of demonic powers. Thus, *epitimaō* shows that Jesus has authority over the evil spirits and that they are powerless to resist his control."[4]

---

4 Page, *Powers of Evil*, 143.

In summary, consider Paul's deliverance of the slave girl in Acts 16:18—"And this she kept doing for many days. Paul, having become greatly annoyed, turned and said to the spirit, 'I command you in the name of Jesus Christ to come out of her.' And it came out that very hour." The apostle didn't say, "Evil spirit, I bind you," or "I rebuke you." But he *did*, in effect, both bind and rebuke the spirit when he said, "I command you in the name of Jesus Christ to come out of her." Paul's words were a rebuke that bound (restricted or restrained) the evil spirit's activity as it pertained to the girl. My contention in this chapter is that the same power and authority here exercised by Paul has been given to all Christians by the risen Lord.

ALLISON'S STORY

I definitely went into the inner healing ministry at our church unsure of what to expect. I suffered from debilitating anxiety that only got worse when I got married. Having another person to worry about brought issues to the surface that I had stuffed down for a long time. I struggled constantly with comparing myself to other people, which almost always resulted in me feeling inferior, unloved, and unimportant. I didn't realize then that I was walking in this victim mentality that made me feel like everything and everyone was out to hurt me. The enemy had been working through so many life circumstances to silence my voice and make me believe that my prayers were not heard and my voice didn't matter.

So, I started in this prayer ministry hoping that God would heal all these different parts of my heart that were hurting and broken. Every week I felt more and more freedom! Walking through forgiveness, breaking ungodly ties, and renouncing ungodly beliefs I'd held onto for years opened this door in my heart to hear the Father's voice telling me who I was and who he was more clearly than I'd heard in a long time.

After just a few weeks, I felt my anxiety leaving me. I was able to look at people from the past who had previously stirred up extremely negative emotions and feel real joy in watching them walk in relationship with Jesus. I felt confidence and boldness rise up in me, giving me the strength to speak up for myself and declare truth over my life and my family. I'm sleeping better, I'm hearing God better, I'm experiencing true freedom, and I am so incredibly grateful for the work the Holy Spirit has begun in me. I know he will continue working and will give me as much freedom as I am willing to ask for.

CHAPTER 15

Deliverance Ministry: Then and Now

D on't be frightened or put off by the word *deliverance*. Put out of your mind the movie by that name starring Burt Reynolds. Try not to think of those horrific scenes from *The Exorcist* or the histrionics of so-called "deliverance ministries" that you may have encountered. Deliverance is a beautiful term that points to the freedom from demonic oppression that Jesus died to secure for us. One of the disappointing features in so many treatments of spiritual warfare is the neglect of this truth. I sense that this is largely due to the desire to avoid being associated with those who've done a poor job of facilitating genuine freedom from enslavement to the enemy's tactics. I trust that what follows will serve to restore in your thinking a biblical understanding of this blessing and provide some practical steps you can take in helping others enter into the glorious fullness that is available to the child of God.

Are Christians Called to Engage in Deliverance Ministry?

The best place for us to begin our examination of deliverance ministry is with a reminder of what the seventy-two said to Jesus upon their return: "Lord, even the demons are subject to us in your name!" (Luke 10:17). Jesus, in turn, declared: "Behold, I have given you authority to tread on serpents and scorpions, and over all the power of the enemy, and nothing shall hurt you" (Luke 10:19). As noted in chapter 14, these were seventy-two ordinary followers of Jesus. They weren't apostles. They were just like you and me. Many today who deny the validity of deliverance ministry insist that it was a task assigned solely to the Twelve as a sign of their apostolic authority and the truth of the gospel message entrusted to them. This episode in Luke 10 says otherwise.

One author insists that "nowhere in Scripture are post-resurrection believers commanded or explicitly encouraged to attempt to cast out demons."[1] Of course, neither is there any text where post-resurrection believers are commanded *not* to cast out demons. Furthermore, why should it make any difference on which side of the resurrection one stands? If anything, we who live on this side of Pentecost, in whom the Holy Spirit permanently dwells, should operate in even greater levels of authority. We minister to the demonized subsequent to Satan's defeat at the cross and the empty tomb. And did not Jesus himself, on *this* side of his resurrection, instruct his followers to teach everyone "to observe all" he had commanded (Matt. 28:20)?

I sense that much of the justification for neglecting deliverance ministry is due to an illicit dispensationalism in which certain truths and practices reflected in the four Gospels are relegated to a past era that has little application to believers in the present church age. On what basis does the author cited above conclude that what we read in the Gospels is inapplicable to believers on the other side of the empty tomb? I recall a handful of my professors in seminary denying that much of the Sermon on the Mount was relevant and binding on us in the church of Jesus Christ. While I fully recognize that there is a progressive unfolding of divine revelation, especially in moving from the jurisdiction of one biblical covenant into another, one must provide considerable exegetical and theological justification for suggesting that we today are prohibited from casting out demons. I seriously doubt this author denies that people can be demonized in the present age. Did not the apostle Paul himself cast a demon out of a young girl in Acts 16:16–18? Was Paul in error in doing so? If not, why would we be?

If McKinley and others of his theological persuasion are correct, how are we to understand the numerous instances of deliverance in the book of Acts? We read of many who were "afflicted with unclean spirits" (Acts 5:16) being healed and set free. When the deacon (not an apostle!) Philip ministered in Samaria, "unclean spirits, crying out with a loud voice, came out of many who had them" (Acts 8:7). Why or by what means did they "come out"? Would it not

---

1   Mike McKinley, *Did the Devil Make Me Do It? And Other Questions about Satan, Demons and Evil Spirits* (London: Good Book Company, 2013), 45.

be reasonable to conclude that it happened when Philip commanded them to depart? People were obviously subject to demonization in the post-resurrection period of the early church, for "evil spirits came out of them" when they came in contact with handkerchiefs or aprons that had touched Paul's skin (Acts 19:12). Are we to think that, had any of these people come directly to Paul asking for help, he would have said to them: "I'm so sorry, but I'm not allowed to cast out demons in the name of Jesus Christ. That was only for the time before his resurrection. But here, take hold of my handkerchief and you'll be fine."

Let's consider another example. Although the New Testament contains instruction on the process of church discipline (see 1 Cor. 5; 2 Cor. 2:5–11), nowhere in any post-resurrection text are we commanded to follow the counsel of Jesus in Matthew 18:15–20 relative to how a sinning brother should be treated. Should we conclude that since this instruction is found only in a pre-resurrection passage that it has no bearing on church life today? And are we consigned only to Paul's instruction on divorce and remarriage in 1 Corinthians 7, since the teaching of Jesus in Matthew 5:31–32 and 19:3–12 was given prior to his resurrection from the dead? Are there not numerous other examples of ministry and principles of biblical truth found in the Gospels that we embrace today, even though there is no explicit post-resurrection text that repeats them?

McKinley does provide us with instruction on what he thinks the believer today is to do when faced with someone who is spiritually oppressed or demonized. He encourages us to use our spiritual gifts to discern where demonic influence may be at work (1 Cor. 12:10). But what good is that if we do not have the authority in the name of Jesus to drive the demons out? He also tells us to exercise faith in God through prayer and cites Matthew 17:20 and Mark 9:29 to justify doing so. And yet, interestingly, these are both pre-resurrection texts! Furthermore, what are we to pray for? Why should we not pray that the demon be cast out and the person set free? He also tells us to resist the devil, thus causing him to flee. But how do we "resist" him? Would it not be in the same way the first disciples did, namely, by commanding the demons to come out and never to return?

Although I disagree greatly with Greg Boyd's open theism and the way it affects his understanding of spiritual warfare, I must confess that he is spot on when he insists that we today must carry on the same ministry of deliverance as we see in the life and ministry of Jesus. He writes:

There is absolutely no reason to think that people today no longer suffer from demonic oppression or from demonically influenced afflictions. Nor is there any reason to think that Christians today are no longer called and empowered to follow the example of Jesus and the early church to manifest God's reign by freeing people from their oppression and afflictions. And as was the case with Jesus, every deliverance and healing we engage in today pushes back the kingdom of darkness and points to a coming kingdom in which there will be no more spiritual oppression, sickness, disease, or disability.[2]

My conclusion is that in the absence of either sound theological reasons or explicit biblical assertions telling us otherwise, we today are responsible to exercise the authority of the risen Christ and, in the power of the Holy Spirit, to drive out demons wherever they appear and in whomever they may be found.

Five Reasons Christians Avoid Deliverance Ministry

Many Christians today studiously avoid any form of deliverance ministry. I suspect that most who do so are frightened by the subject of spiritual warfare and feel ill-equipped to handle the sort of ugly and disruptive outbursts that often occur when the Holy Spirit confronts the realm of principalities and powers.

There is no escaping the fact that if you ever hope to encourage people in your local church to deal courageously and effectively with demonic activity, you need to educate them on why they feel so reticent to get involved in the first place. There are in fact several reasons why many Christians would prefer to ignore this subject. Here are a few.

1. Christians avoid deliverance ministry because they have been offended by those who have taken it to unbiblical and damaging extremes.

Make no mistake, the professing church has been damaged by the so-called "ministries" of men and women who argue that every sin is demonically induced. We hear them speak of the "spirit of nicotine" or the "spirit of greed"

---

2   Gregory Boyd, "The Ground-Level Deliverance Model," in Beilby and Eddy, *Understanding Spiritual Warfare: Four Views*, 154.

or the "spirit of anxiety." Virtually every moral weakness, addiction, or spiritual failure, together with every other grievous transgression is attributed by such folk not to the fleshly impulses of our selfish, fallen selves, but to some demon who is responsible for its presence and enslaving power in our lives. Can Satan or one of his demons aggravate and intensify our chosen acts of rebellion and unbelief? Yes. Can he cripple us with feelings of shame and guilt and blind us to the liberating grace of the cross of Christ? Yes. But no one can justifiably exonerate their bad behavior by insisting that "the devil made me do it!"

Lingering in the memory of some are those horrible scenes of a helpless man or woman being angrily berated by a deliverance expert or having a crucifix pressed painfully on their forehead. One thing I do know about the devil: he's not hard of hearing. Increased decibel levels spewed from the mouths of spiritual showmen accomplish nothing. Sadly, though, the image of such manipulative excess has turned off many from ever giving serious consideration to what can be done to serve and set free those who are genuinely and grievously afflicted by the demonic.

2. Christians avoid deliverance ministry because they wrongly believe that deliverance is a special ministry for special people with special spiritual gifts.

Whenever there is a manifestation of demonic activity, they instinctively turn to see if that especially "spiritual" person is available to deal with the problem. They feel inadequate and often excuse their withdrawal by insisting that they simply don't have that particular "spiritual gift." At the bottom of this hesitation is a failure to understand the full extent and efficacy of the authority given to all believers by Jesus himself (see the earlier discussion of Luke 10).

3. Christians avoid deliverance ministry because they're wrongly interpreting key Scripture

I've come across some Christians who avoid deliverance ministry because of a wrong interpretation of 2 Peter 2:10–11 and Jude 8–9. Peter speaks of holy angels who, "though greater in might and power, do not pronounce a blasphemous judgment against them [fallen angels/demons] before the Lord." Even more daunting to them is what we read in Jude:

> Yet in like manner these people also, relying on their dreams, defile the flesh, reject authority, and blaspheme the glorious ones. But when the archangel Michael, contending with the devil, was disputing about the body

> of Moses, he did not presume to pronounce a blasphemous judgment, but said, "The Lord rebuke you." (Jude 8–9)

But these texts do *not* mean that we, as Christians, are forbidden to rebuke, verbally resist, or pronounce judgment against demonic beings. Neither unbelievers (the "false teachers") nor even the holy angels have the authority we have received by virtue of our being in Christ. In Christ, with his authority, we both can and must resist and rebuke the enemy (see Luke 10:1–20; Acts 5:16; 8:7; 16:16–18; 19:12). Jude makes no attempt to extend to Christians the restriction placed on Michael.

4. Christians avoid deliverance ministry because they wrongly assume that Christians cannot be demonized.

I addressed this controversial issue in an earlier chapter. Let me simply remind you that every case of demonization described in the New Testament involves someone under the influence or control, in varying degrees, of an indwelling evil spirit.

Even if it should be proven that a Christian cannot be indwelt by a demonic spirit, all would concede that Christians can be oppressed, tormented, and in a variety of ways spiritually and mentally assaulted by the powers of darkness. In any case, regardless of where the demon might be, believers are often in need of deliverance and the freedom Christ died to obtain for them.

5. Christians avoid deliverance ministry because they are afraid of encountering the demonic.

Hollywood portrayals of ritual exorcism have not helped in this regard (think back to the film, *The Exorcist*). And, of course, Satan himself loves nothing more than to intimidate Christians with offensive images, sounds, and a variety of physical manifestations for which they feel altogether ill-equipped.

The Deliverance Ministry of Jesus

Some Christians do not believe that Jesus is a proper role model for us when it comes to dealing with the demonic. They regard him and the supernatural nature of his ministry as unique and not one that we can expect to see evident in our lives today. Whereas there are certainly aspects of Jesus's life and ministry that are unrepeatable, I see nothing in his response to the demonic that would suggest it was restricted to a mere three years in time. On the contrary, Jesus remains a model for ministry today.

There are numerous instances where Jesus encountered the demonized, one of the more helpful being Mark 5. As I look closely at this story, together with other examples in our Lord's ministry, I discern no fewer than seven elements in his approach to deliverance. Not all are employed in every instance, but each is important.

1. **Jesus secures the name of the demon or seeks to identify the spirit.** In the case of the man indwelt by a "Legion" of demons, Jesus asked him, "What is your name?" (Mark 5:9). Some people argue that Jesus does this because in the ancient world people believed that to know and speak someone's name was to gain spiritual authority over them. But Jesus already had this authority. Perhaps he did so to let observers know the full extent of demonic power he was confronting. Or it may simply have been to reveal to the man himself how serious his condition was. Either way, by asking for a name, Jesus makes known that this man was under the influence of a virtual army of demons: The word "Legion" referred to a contingent of Roman soldiers numbering upwards of 6,000.

2. **Jesus binds the spirit.** He prohibits it from engaging in some activity and thus curbs or breaks its power (see also Matt. 12:29).

3. **He rebukes the spirit.** He censures or warns or denounces the demon. We see this explicitly in Mark 1:25: "but Jesus rebuked him [the demon], saying, 'Be silent and come out of him'" (see also Matt 17:18; Mark 9:25; Luke 9:42). This sort of *rebuke* is not just a verbal reproof but a technical term for subjugation of the evil power.

4. **He silences the demon.** In Mark 1:34 we read that "he healed many who were sick with various diseases, and cast out many demons. And *he would not permit the demons to speak*, because they knew him" (emphasis mine). We don't know with certainty why he refused to let them speak, but Peter Davids cites three possible reasons:[3] (1) "'the

---

3   Peter H. Davids, *More Hard Sayings of the New Testament* (Downers Grove, IL: InterVarsity Press, 1991), 27.

teachers of the law' associated him with Beelzebub, 'the prince of demons' (3:22). Any tendency to show that he accepted the demonic would have given extra evidence to these opponents"; (2) "To accept the testimony of demons about himself would give a precedent to his followers to accept (or even seek) testimony of demons about other things. This would threaten to make Jesus' movement an occult movement"; (3) "Jesus' whole mission was a call to faith based on evidence, not on authoritative testimony.... Therefore the demons were short-circuiting Jesus' whole methodology. His command to them was a sharp 'Shut up!' His invitation to the crowd at their expulsion was, 'See and believe that the Kingdom of God has come."

5. **He would cast them out (see Mark 1:25; 7:29; Matt. 8:16).**
6. **He would refuse to let the spirit return.** We read in Mark 9:25: "And when Jesus saw that a crowd came running together, he rebuked the unclean spirit, saying to it, 'You mute and deaf spirit, I command you, come out of him and *never enter him again*" (emphasis mine). This implies that the recurrence of demonization after deliverance was a possibility and steps had to be taken to prevent such from happening. Evidently, often after being cast out from a person, a demon was free to return to the person or to enter someone else.
7. **He would, on occasion, send them into the abyss.** We read in Luke 8:31 that the demonic spirits themselves "begged him not to command them to depart into the abyss." If the "abyss" is likely the place from which demons originate, why would they fear returning there? Is it a place of imprisonment where they would be temporarily consigned, awaiting the final judgment? Or is it the place where they will finally be punished? Aside from its appearance here and in Romans 10:7, the word *abyssos* is found only in Revelation 9:1–2, 11; 11:7; 17:8; 20:1, 3. Jesus did not always consign exorcised demons to the abyss or to some place of permanent detention (Mark 9:25).

Prayer and Deliverance

In Mark 9, Jesus criticizes the disciples for their lack of faith in dealing with the demonized boy (vv. 19, 28–29). Evidently, the disciples' previous success in deliverance ministry had led them to believe that divine power was at their disposal to use as they saw fit, apart from constant reliance on God.

But this kind of demon, says Jesus (v. 29), can come out only by prayer. This is intriguing, insofar as *there is not a single instance of deliverance by prayer in the New Testament*. Deliverance elsewhere always occurs by the word of *command*. It is also interesting to note that deliverance from an indwelling spirit is never granted in response to the faith of the one who is demonized, although it is sometimes related to the faith of others.

We can conclude that, in particular cases where an especially powerful demon is involved, prayer may be needed. Page explains, "Mark focuses on the need for prayer because it clearly demonstrates that divine power is not under human control; it must always be asked for. Manifestations of the power of God, such as are needed when dealing with the forces of evil, come only in response to the attitude of trust and reliance upon God that is expressed in humble prayer."[4] Jesus doesn't specify precisely what should be asked for in prayer, but we can assume that it is for the power and presence of the Holy Spirit to enable us to do what we in our own power could never accomplish (see Luke 11:13).

Instantaneous Deliverance?

It surprises many to discover that even for Jesus, deliverance was not always instantaneous or without considerable resistance (see Mark 1:26; 5:8; 9:26). If this is difficult to grasp, consider the analogy of a parent and child. When my daughters were young and still in the home, and I would exercise parental authority and tell them to do something or to cease from some activity, it was not unusual for them to delay their obedience. They would resist complying with my command, using any number of tactics. Soon, though, they began to obey, but then hesitate. They stalled, made excuses, and insisted on arguing about whether or not it was right or necessary for them to obey me. They might try to distract me from the issue at hand by diverting my attention to something of equal or greater urgency. They moved slowly, hoping I'd forget. They might even play me off against Ann, telling me that she said it was okay. However, if I persisted in the exercise of my authority as their parent, they would eventually do as I said or suffer the consequences!

The point for spiritual warfare is this: Our approach should not be, "Speak the word of command in Jesus's name *and* it is done," which usually

---

4 Page, *Powers of Evil*, 164.

leads to frustration and disillusionment. Our approach should be, "Speak the word of command in Jesus's name *UNTIL* it is done."

A Simple Approach

We should also note that Jesus's approach was never ritualistic or mechanical or magical. He employed no elaborate religious formula. No incantations. No candles. No mood music playing in the background. No charms. No religious formulas. No chanting. No dancing. No cutting off of a chicken's head. He didn't have to shout or jump up and down. He didn't physically restrain the demonized man or press a cross against his forehead. He didn't use "holy" water or incense. He simply said: "Shut up! Get out!"

It is little wonder, then, that the people of his day were amazed by how Jesus dealt with deliverance (see Mark 1:27; Matt. 9:32–33). According to Matthew 8:16, Jesus "cast out the spirits with a word." Jesus never appealed to a higher authority when expelling demons, unlike Paul, for example, who cast out a demon from the slave girl in Acts 16 by appealing to "the name of Jesus Christ" (v. 18).

Encounters with the Demonic and Deliverance in the Book of Acts

Acts 19:13–17 offers a compelling story of the deliverance ministry in the early church:

> Then some of the itinerant Jewish exorcists undertook to invoke the name of the Lord Jesus over those who had evil spirits, saying, "I adjure you by the Jesus whom Paul proclaims." Seven sons of a Jewish high priest named Sceva were doing this. But the evil spirit answered them, "Jesus I know, and Paul I recognize, but who are you?" And the man in whom was the evil spirit leaped on them, mastered all of them and overpowered them, so that they fled out of that house naked and wounded. And this became known to all the residents of Ephesus, both Jews and Greeks. And fear fell upon them all, and the name of the Lord Jesus was extolled.

Acts 19:13 contains the earliest known occurrence in Greek literature of the word "exorcist" (*exorkistēs*) and the only occurrence of it in the New

Testament. Whereas here it is used of the Jewish "exorcists," it is never used of Christians engaged in deliverance ministry (perhaps because of its magical connotations).

Acts 19:12 indicates that Paul was engaging in a successful deliverance ministry in Ephesus. Although the connection is not explicit, it is instructive that Luke appears to link the presence of disease with that of demons as well as the healing from disease with the expulsion of demons. Also present in the vicinity of Ephesus were some itinerant exorcists. These were not Jewish Christians, otherwise they would have simply appealed to the name of Jesus as the one whom *they* preached. Any reference to Paul would have been unnecessary (v. 13). Also, the way the demon speaks of them indicates they were not true believers.

The demon is here portrayed as an intelligent being, able to converse openly and clearly with humans, to distinguish between Christian and non-Christian, between true faith and false profession. Also, this demon appears to have something of a sense of humor. He is, at minimum, quite sarcastic: "Jesus I know, and Paul I recognize, *but who [the heck] are you*?" (v. 15, my paraphrase!). The question is not for the purpose of learning their identity (names) or obtaining personal information about them. It is a case in which the demon challenges their right to use the name of Jesus. "I know Jesus. I must bow to his authority and obey. And I know Paul acts in Jesus's name. But who are you that I should obey what you say or pay any attention to your demands?"

As John Stott points out, "to be sure, there is power—saving and healing power—in the name of Jesus, as Luke has been at pains to illustrate (e.g., 3:6, 16; 4:10–12). But its efficacy is not mechanical, nor can people use it second-hand."[5] Christians, such as Paul, most certainly do have a right to the name of Jesus, and demons must obey.

This narrative demonstrates that demons are by nature violent and can infuse their victims with superhuman strength (v. 16). Although this does not mean we should never make physical contact with the demonized (Jesus certainly did; see Luke 4:40–41), it is certainly a cautionary note that we should

---

5   John Stott, *The Spirit, the Church and the World: The Message of Acts* (Downers Grove, IL: InterVarsity Press, 1990), 307.

never act presumptuously or carelessly when dealing with the supernatural power of the enemy.

Neil Anderson's Approach to Deliverance

Author Neil Anderson proposes a helpful approach to deliverance.[6] He advocates what he calls the *truth encounter* method of deliverance as opposed to the *power encounter*. A *truth encounter* requires that the demonized or oppressed individual personally renounce the enemy, repent of all known sin, affirm the truth, and submit to the Lordship of Jesus. No one else need be engaged in the process. It is a form of self-deliverance.

A *power encounter* occurs when you confront the demon directly and verbally command that it identify itself (name, function, point of entry, etc. [although this is not essential to the power encounter]) and cast it out (to the abyss, or to wherever Jesus sends it). Jesus employed the power encounter approach, as did Paul in Acts 16. Someone described this approach as follows: (1) *Expose* (discern and document that demonic activity is present), then (2) *Engage* (identify, name, function, point or ground of entry), and then (3) *Expel* (in the name and authority of Jesus).

Anderson rejects using a power encounter in deliverance for several reasons. First, he argues that conversing with demons is never advisable because demons are liars (John 8:44). My response is that certainly demons will try to lie, but they can be compelled to speak the truth when subjected to the authority of Christ (see Mark 1:24, where demons spoke the truth).

Second, he argues that the epistles are our guide to deliverance, not the Gospels or Acts. The epistles stress what we do for ourselves, not what others do for us. Anderson insists that he has not attempted to "cast out" a demon in years but has helped people find freedom in Christ by enabling them to resolve their personal and spiritual conflicts. He believes that success in attaining freedom is dependent on the cooperation of the person who is oppressed.

Unfortunately, Anderson gives no textual or reasonable theological

---

6 See especially, *The Bondage Breaker* (Eugene, OR: Harvest House, 2000); *Victory over the Darkness: Realize the Power of Your Identity in Christ* (Ventura, CA: Regal, 1990); and *Ministering the Steps to Freedom in Christ* (Ventura, CA: Gospel Light, 1998).

arguments for rejecting the Gospels and Acts as a pattern for deliverance. His position is probably the fruit of his dispensational approach to biblical interpretation. Also, while it is good for the individual to participate in deliverance, what about a child or someone who can't perceive the truth sufficiently to work through Anderson's Steps to Freedom? What if the bondage is so intense as to have crippled the person's ability and strength to work through the steps, or if a person is so thoroughly deceived that he or she doesn't believe the truth or effectiveness of the steps? What if the person has been blinded by the enemy (2 Cor. 4:4)? *Anderson's truth encounter is certainly good and helpful and ought to be employed whenever possible.* But in cases of severe demonic stronghold or intractable resistance, a direct power encounter may also be required.

Anderson asks the question, "If *you* expel or cast out a demon from someone, what is to prevent the demon from returning?" In other words, he says that without the involvement of the person, without the responsible activity and mental participation of the victim, the problem may disappear for a while only later to re-emerge. My response is that what prevents a demon from coming back is the same authority and power by which it was compelled to leave in the first place. In Mark 9 Jesus commanded, "never return." So, too, should we. Of course, the person can always re-open the door, but that should not prevent us from helping them get free.

Anderson's approach is cognitive, being a form of self-deliverance. We are not exorcists, says Anderson, but facilitators:

> In a truth encounter, I deal only with the person, and I do not bypass the person's mind. In that way people are free to make their own choices. There is never a loss of control as I facilitate the process of helping them assume their own responsibility before God. After all, it isn't what I say, do or believe that sets people free—it's what they renounce, confess, forsake, whom they forgive and the truth they affirm that sets them free. This "truth procedure" requires me to work with the whole person, dealing with body, soul and spirit.[7]

There is considerable wisdom and great practical value in this approach,

---

7   Neil Anderson, *Released from Bondage* (San Bernardino, CA: Here's Life, 1991), 17.

and I often make substantial use of it. But of course, in the final analysis, it isn't what "I" say, do, or renounce even in the power encounter, but what "I, *in the name and authority of Jesus*," say and do that brings deliverance. Let us also remember that there is no power inherent in truth. All power is in God. It is the God of truth who has power to set the captives free.

A Practical Model for Deliverance

We are now ready to articulate a model for deliverance ministry. This certainly isn't the only way to approach those who are severely oppressed, but I've found it helpful.

1. Pray for Discernment

I strongly endorse and highly recommend the value of having someone skilled in deliverance and gifted in discernment present with you. Those who are new in deliverance ministry often presumptuously and incorrectly connect demonic spirits with certain emotional and/or psychological symptoms and bizarre behaviors. Whereas we don't want to ignore demons if they are present, even greater damage can be done by assuming that they are the cause of a problem when they aren't.

SPIRITUAL GIFT OF DISCERNING OF SPIRITS

The spiritual gift of discerning of spirits[8] is most likely the ability to distinguish between works of the Holy Spirit and works of another spirit (demonic) or perhaps even the human spirit. Not all miracles or supernatural displays are produced by the Holy Spirit. Whereas all Christians are responsible to "test the spirits to see whether they are from God" (1 John 4:1), Paul has in mind a special ability that is fundamentally intuitive or subjective in nature (1 Cor. 12:10).

First John calls believers to test the spirits by evaluating their messages. In particular, do they confess that "Jesus Christ has come in the

8   For more on this, see my book *Understanding Spiritual Gifts: A Comprehensive Guide* (Grand Rapids: Zondervan, 2020).

flesh" (1 John 4:2)? This requires no special gifting. But the spiritual gift of distinguishing of spirits is probably a supernaturally enabled sense or feeling concerning the nature and source of the spirit. Some possible instances where this gift was in operation include:

- Acts 16:16–18, where Paul discerned that the power of a certain slave girl was in fact a demonic spirit.
- Acts 13:8–11, where Paul discerned that Elymas the magician was demonically energized in his attempt to oppose the presentation of the gospel.
- Acts 14:8–10, where again Paul discerned ("saw") that a man had faith to be healed.
- Acts 8:20–24, where Peter saw (not physically, but to perceive or sense) that Simon Magus was filled with bitterness and iniquity.
- John 1:47, where Jesus looked at Nathanael and described him as a man "in whom is no guile" (KJV).

Someone gifted with discerning of spirits is able to discern whether a problem in someone's life is demonic or merely the consequence of other emotional and psychological factors, or perhaps a complex combination of both. Often, people with this gift are also able to detect the presence of demonic spirits in a particular location.

Here are some important steps in the process of discernment:

- **Pray for the Holy Spirit to open your spiritual eyes and speak to you regarding the individual.** He may be pleased to reveal to you the cause of the oppression or what sins(s) might have occurred that gave the devil an "opportunity" or "foothold" (NIV; literally, a "place") in this person's life (Eph. 4:27a).
- **Pray with your eyes *open*.** The presence of a demonic spirit will often lead to physical, visible manifestations. If it does, don't react in disgust or surprise. Satan would love nothing more than to intimidate you into thinking that you are incompetent for the task of securing freedom for this individual.

- **Don't ever conclude that any case of demonic oppression or demonization is above your spiritual pay grade.** Simply take authority over the "spirit(s)" in Jesus's name. You may recall from the story in Mark 9 that when a father brought his demonized boy to Jesus for deliverance, the demon suddenly "convulsed the boy, and he fell on the ground and rolled about, foaming at the mouth" (Mark 9:20). Even after Jesus commanded the demon to "come out of him and never enter him again" (9:25b), the physical manifestations didn't immediately cease: "And after crying out and convulsing him terribly, it came out" (9:26a).
- **Learn (by experience) the signs and symptoms of oppression and demonization.** This will only come with time, as no two cases are always precisely the same. I've discovered that in most instances of serious demonization, the enemy will do everything possible to resist the truth of the gospel.

2. Instruct the Person

Take time to explain to the individual what you are doing and why. This will help alleviate their fears. Explain to them that *if* they have a demon, this does not mean they are dirty, more sinful than other Christians, sub-spiritual, or unloved of God. Instruct the person to cooperate with what is happening by constantly giving you feedback: what they are feeling, thinking, physical sensations, intrusive thoughts, violent or sinful impulses, etc.

3. Articulate Your Authority in Christ

Begin by verbally declaring the authority of Christ and his supremacy over all demonic spirits. I encourage either you or the person who is suffering to read Luke 10:17–20, Ephesians 1:15–23 (especially v. 21), and Colossians 2:9–15 aloud. These passages speak of how "all rule and authority and power and dominion" have been "put under" the feet of the risen and exalted Christ (Eph. 1:21–22). Direct, authoritative prayer and Bible reading should stir and agitate demonic spirits if they are present. Ask the person if he or she is hearing or feeling anything unusual when you read the Bible or speak of Jesus and his blood. If the answer is yes, take time to rebuke every spirit and command them to cease and desist from their efforts to block deliverance.

The afflicted person will often stutter, stumble, get distracted, complain of dizziness, or angrily refuse. Whenever one lady in my church was asked to read Ephesians 1:21–22 or Colossians 2:13–15, she would speak of how a mental "fog" of sorts suddenly engulfed her mind, clouding and jumbling her thinking, and essentially rendering her incapable of speaking the truth of God's Word. It remained for me to speak authoritatively to every demonic spirit hindering her from speaking what she knew to be true, before she was able to do so for herself.

4. Explore the Possibility of Causes Other Than Demonic

Never assume too quickly that the problem is demonically caused. Conduct an interview of sufficient depth that you explore the possibility of other potential sources for the problem, such as a physiological problem (Have they had a physical examination recently?), prescription medications (Are they on any?), other organic causes, stress, fatigue, circumstantial issues, relational dynamics, etc. Be aware of the fact that even if the presenting problem is caused by something other than a demonic spirit, the enemy can still aggravate, intensify, and exploit such factors.

5. Ask the Right Questions

Ask the person to give you a personal testimony of faith in Christ. Do they struggle in doing so? Are they able to affirm without agitation or hesitation their submission to the Lordship of Jesus? Ask the person if they experience any special hindrances when they engage in spiritual activities, such as praying, reading the Bible, worship, etc. Ask them if at any time he or she is feeling anger or hate toward you. Do they feel prompted to assault you either verbally or physically?

Determine as best you can if any behavior or beliefs of the person may have opened the door to demonic activity. Focus particularly on *family history* (any involvement of ancestors in the occult or unbiblical practices) and *personal sins* (idolatry, witchcraft, unforgiveness, sexual immorality, etc.). If something in particular is discovered, lead the person in a prayer of confession, repentance, and repudiation of whatever it is that may have led to demonic intrusion. In short, lead them in a prayer by which *they* close any doors that may have been opened.

6. Confront the Enemy

I have found the most effective strategy is to engage the person in eye-to-eye contact. Explain to them that though you will be looking at them, you will not be speaking to them. You will be addressing any demonic spirit that might be present (this is what Paul did in Acts 16:18).

Look directly into their eyes and say, "In the name of the Lord Jesus Christ and through the power of his shed blood and resurrection life, I take authority over any demonic spirit either present in or around _____ (name of person). In the name of the Lord Jesus Christ I command any and every demonic spirit to leave _____ (name of person) and never return."

You may find it necessary to repeat this prayer of command more than once. Demons are quite good at misdirection and will try to deceive you into thinking they have left when they are actually still present.

These commands and prayers for deliverance may take any number of forms. You may want to be specific in naming any sins that may have led to the problem. You may want to pray for the Holy Spirit to shine the light of revelation and truth into the person's heart and mind, dispelling all darkness and confusion. You may wish to pray prayers of protection over the person. Remember, the key is not in particular words or formulas, but in the simple, irresistible authority of the risen Christ in whose name you act.

If there is a demon present, you can usually expect some form of resistance or physical manifestation. Encourage the person to report to you any impressions, thoughts, emotional impulses, physical sensations, voices, etc., that occur in the course of your prayer.

7. Assessment

It's important to remember that demons will often hide quietly behind certain strongholds in a person's life, patterns of thought, and behavior that are so deeply ingrained that one assumes this is simply "who I am" or "how I was made." In this way demons are able to disguise their presence and deceive everyone into thinking that all is well. When this happens, there is a great need for extended, persevering prayer and seeking insight from the Spirit into the true state of the person's soul. Don't be quick to conclude your work is done. Wait on God to shine the light of truth into every situation.

In the final analysis, one of three things is most often true. It may be that the demon(s) really did leave. Its departure may be loud, violent, and visible, or silent, simple, and unseen. Don't be too quick to draw conclusions about whether it left based on how the person felt or reacted. If you suspect it might still be present, repeat the above procedures.

There is also the possibility that the demon(s) is still there. If it is still present, there are at least three possible reasons: (1) the person doesn't want it to go; (2) the demon(s) has moral grounds for staying; or (3) this is an especially powerful demon that requires more prayer, faith, fasting, and concentrated effort on the part of all involved (see Mark 9:28–29).

Finally, you may have to reckon with the fact that the demon was never there in the first place and that the nature and cause of the affliction (whether it be emotional or physical) is of a different order, calling for a different approach.

8. Concluding Prayer

Consider closing with a prayer such as this:

> *Father, I thank you that _____ (name of person) is your child, redeemed by the blood of Christ Jesus, forgiven and justified by faith in his name, and indwelled by the precious and powerful Holy Spirit. Guard him/her. Protect him/her. Surround your child with your angelic hosts. Fill him/her with a renewed sense of your love and the peace that surpasses all understanding.*

DAVID'S STORY

I am a worship pastor in Edmond, Oklahoma. I hit a significant wall about six months ago and reached out for help at Bridgeway Church after their Convergence Conference. Three years ago, I had an episode on stage leading worship that prevented me from finishing. I had what I would now call a panic attack in the middle of the service. I went to the ER and everything checked out with my heart. Ever since then, there has been this increased experience of fear and anxiety on stage. I had a hard time pressing through and was really fearful that it was going to happen again while I was leading worship. This developed over three years into full-blown social anxiety. Being present in crowded places like a football or basketball game would cause anxiety and "mini" episodes of panic attacks where I would lose my breath and have to call somebody or sit down and work myself through it. I had faith that God was with me during those times. I was working through it with the help of doctors and counseling, but I hadn't received any extended prayer ministry.

I grew weary of my job and started having significant doubt about my calling as a worship pastor. I struggled to be present and joyful with my family on the weekends. Friday and Saturday leading up to Sunday was such a struggle. Because of the anxiety, I was short, grumpy, and controlling. I was not fun to be around. I didn't like being around myself. I questioned and doubted my calling as a minister. I also had an underlying fear of illness and sickness that started at a young age. I even remember sitting in a classroom and being gripped by fear in kindergarten as I learned about death and dying. There were seasons of time that any ailment in my body would become a source of tremendous fear that I was dying. Could this be cancer?

Walking through forgiveness and ungodly beliefs were the most powerful sessions during this process. I was shocked that I had been living with unforgiveness in my heart as a pastor, as a minister, and as someone who has walked with Jesus for many years. I would have said that I was not harboring unforgiveness, but as I went through the exercise, I realized I truly was. Instead of confessing the unforgiveness, I asked myself What am I feeling? What are the emotions I'm having? Who are they towards? Why? Only then was I able to see what the offense was and against whom I was withholding forgiveness. To be perfectly honest, I was harboring unforgiveness toward other ministers, people I worked with, and even those in my family, as well as individuals in my past. One of the more surprising instances of unforgiveness in my heart was against my best friend. There was lingering hurt I needed to let go.

As I was trying to figure out whom to forgive, there were people coming to me to ask for my forgiveness. It was amazing to watch. On the day of my forgiveness session, I was running late because I was asked to give a ride to someone I worked with, against whom I was also harboring unforgiveness. She confessed to me things she had done that could have hurt me and asked for my forgiveness. It was an amazing display of God's desire

286 PART 3: RESPONDING TO THE DEMONIC

to set me free and to remove the bitterness in my heart.

As we prayed through the issue of generational patterns in my family line, I didn't think anything would come up. But the Lord graciously alerted me to issues of physical abuse, poor communication, infirmities, substance abuse, suicide, transgender issues, and sexual sins. The Lord lovingly spoke to me in numerous ways to help me address these matters. To replace broken relationships and divorce in my family line, I remember hearing the Lord say, "I want to replace that with relationships that bear good fruit." I saw a picture of an open book and God saying, "I want you to be an open book to your wife and the boys." I sensed that God wanted to give me a playful heart. I had a vision of being yoked with God, walking arm in arm in response to generational patterns of control and codependency. I had a vision of a giant ladder that descended down into those dark places of my life. I sensed the Lord saying that he was providing a way for me to climb out of it all.

During our time of prayer, I had a picture of two magnets replacing abandonment and rejection. God was saying to me, "I am connected to you like two magnets coming together. I will never abandon you, and we are always going to grow closer. We are going to be connected and inseparable." When it came to matters of physical infirmity, disease, and suicide, the Lord reminded me that he is the great physician. I had a picture of a medicine cabinet being cleared out and God standing in its place. I had a longstanding fear of medicine due to my family's multiple addictions throughout their lives. The Lord was telling me, "You don't have to be fearful of this anymore. I am with you."

When the time came to address ungodly beliefs that had controlled my life, I realized how much of my anxiety and fear was related to things I had falsely believed were true, such as, "I have to earn others' and God's love and affection by serving and helping them." I felt loved only when others served me. It was profoundly life-changing to realize that as a pastor I had believed that the only way I could feel loved was by loving others. In the place of this ungodly belief, I wrote down: "I love and serve others because God showed me his love by sending Jesus and the Holy Spirit. God's love in not earned. It's always available. It's always sufficient. God's love satisfies more than that of any man or woman."

Another of my many ungodly beliefs was that I need to be loved by others to be satisfied. Deliverance from such misunderstandings of God's Word didn't happen in an instant, but only as I spent time with Jesus and made certain that his words were abiding in me (John 15:7). I began to realize that God's love fully satisfies. As a pastor I knew that in my mind, but I wasn't walking in its truth. So, I soaked my soul in Scripture, such as Psalm 107:9, "For he satisfies the longing soul, and the hungry soul he fills with good things." Isaiah 58:11 declares that "the Lord will guide you continually and satisfy your desire in scorched places and make your bones strong; and you shall be like a watered garden, like a spring of water, whose waters do not fail." Jeremiah 31:25 spoke loudly to me: "For I will satisfy the weary soul, and every languishing soul I will replenish." In Psalm 16:11, David declared, "You make known to me the path of life; in your presence there is fullness of joy; at your right hand are pleasures forevermore."

I honestly believe that God healed me from the panic attacks, fear, and anxiety. As I walked through this process, I experienced increased joy and peace. Before walking through this time of prayer ministry, I was barely able to lead worship on a Sunday morning. I was experiencing panic attacks immediately before I would go on stage. I was desperately clinging to the Lord and asking him to deliver me and barely able to make it through a worship set. I would plead to God the whole time to keep me safe.

But as a result of the inner healing I received, I sensed all of the anxiety lifting. I remember experiencing for the first time this joy and peace while leading worship on a Sunday. No more anxiety or fear to paralyze me. It didn't happen all at once, but gradually over the next few weeks. My healing journey still continues. It feels so good to experience freedom from those fears that had plagued me for so long. God has delivered me, and I'm praising him for that. Now I have the tools to fight back should this ever try to creep back into my life.

Praise be to God for his incredible goodness!

CHAPTER 16

Who's Your Real Enemy? A Study of Ephesians 6

Best-selling author of *Knowing God*, J. I. Packer, once made the astute observation that "Satan, whose nature and purpose is always to spoil any good God produces, keeps pace with God in it."[1] This quotation is striking in its truth. Scripture shows us that Satan will make every effort to thwart, undermine, or distract us from the remarkable and miraculous things we've seen in our lives and in the life of the church. When we begin to see fresh spiritual and supernatural energy—when we see healings, when we see people come to faith, when we see more people begin to attend church— you can bet Satan is taking notice. And I'm here to tell you, without the slightest hint of melodrama or manipulation, Satan won't sit idly by without attempting to push back.

I don't know what his tactics will be. I don't presume to understand his ways perfectly. But the apostle Paul, in Ephesians 6:10–20, provides us with the clearest and most vivid description of what we're up against and how we must prepare ourselves for this fight:

> Finally, be strong in the Lord and in the strength of his might. Put on the whole armor of God, that you may be able to stand against the schemes of the devil. For we do not wrestle against flesh and blood, but against the rulers, against the authorities, against the cosmic powers over this present darkness, against the spiritual forces of evil in the heavenly places.

1 "Piety on Fire," in *Serving the People of God: The Collected Shorter Writings of J. I. Packer, vol. 2*, ed. Jim Lyster (Vancouver: Regent College, 2008), 104.

Therefore take up the whole armor of God, that you may be able to withstand in the evil day, and having done all, to stand firm. Stand therefore, having fastened on the belt of truth, and having put on the breastplate of righteousness, and, as shoes for your feet, having put on the readiness given by the gospel of peace. In all circumstances take up the shield of faith, with which you can extinguish all the flaming darts of the evil one; and take the helmet of salvation, and the sword of the Spirit, which is the word of God, praying at all times in the Spirit, with all prayer and supplication. To that end, keep alert with all perseverance, making supplication for all the saints, and also for me, that words may be given to me in opening my mouth boldly to proclaim the mystery of the gospel, for which I am an ambassador in chains, that I may declare it boldly, as I ought to speak.

The Context for Conflict

In Ephesians 4:1–6:9 the apostle provided us with a list of responsibilities for Christian living. The moral issues that he begins to address in 6:10 and following extend beyond simple questions of right and wrong, and thrusts us into the heart of a larger, indeed, *cosmic* battle in which our enemies are not primarily other human beings but spiritual beings of indescribable evil intent.

Many believe the imagery of "armor" came to Paul from his observation of the Roman soldier to whom he was chained (Eph. 6:20). Others think that the imagery of a soldier fully arrayed in battle armor is taken from Isaiah (11:4–5; 49:2; 52:7; 59:17), which describes the armor of God and his Messiah. These texts portray the Lord of Hosts as a warrior dressed for battle as he prepares to fight on behalf of his people. Two passages will make this clear:

> But with righteousness he shall judge the poor,
>> and decide with equity for the meek of the earth;
> and he shall strike the earth with the rod of his mouth,
>> and with the breath of his lips he shall kill the wicked.
> Righteousness shall be the belt of his waist,
>> and faithfulness the belt of his loins. (Isaiah 11:4–5)

He put on righteousness as a breastplate,

> and a helmet of salvation on his head;
> he put on garments of vengeance for clothing,
> and wrapped himself in zeal as a cloak. (Isaiah 59:17)

Thus the "full armor" that Paul will tell us to put on or with which we are to adorn ourselves is in fact God's own armor. And Paul's invitation is that we take it up and wear it even as God has worn it on our behalf. In other words, it is the armor of God not simply because he gives it, but because *he wears it!*[2]

Nine Vital Truths about the Urgency of Spiritual Warfare

The best way to approach Ephesians 6:10–20 is to break it down phrase by phrase, verse by verse. As we do so, we'll encounter nine truths.

1. Be Alert

Take note of the word with which it all begins, *"Finally."* It's as if Paul says: "Finally, after all I've said, after all the doctrine, the exhortations, the rebukes, the encouragement, here is one more thing. *I've saved it for last, not because it's least important, but because it's the greatest threat.* Something threatens to undermine and subvert everything we've talked about. So pay close attention!"

Some suggest that "finally" means "from now on" (cf. Gal. 6:17) or "for the remaining time," referring to the period between the first and second comings of Jesus. In other words, the idea is that from now on, at all times until Jesus comes, we are at war. Be alert! Be armed! There is never a truce or ceasefire. Satan takes no holidays. He observes no Sabbath rest. There may be times of greater and lesser intensity, but never a time to relax or let down your spiritual guard. In all likelihood, both ideas are present in this word.

2. Be Strong in the Lord

Paul goes on to command us to *"be strong in the Lord"* (Eph 6:10). The verb is best taken as a passive: "be strengthened" or "be made strong" by God

---

2   The various virtues and other items connected with these pieces of armor have already figured prominently in earlier portions of Ephesians: truth (1:13; 4:15, 21, 24, 25; 5:9), righteousness (4:24; 5:9), peace (1:2; 2:14–18; 4:3), the gospel (1:13; 3:6), the word of God (1:13; 5:26), salvation (1:13; 2:5, 8; 5:23), and faith (1:1, 13, 15, 19; 2:8; 3:12, 17; 4:5, 13).

(cf. 3:16). The phrase "in the Lord" is vital. Without it, the exhortation "be strong" would be both dangerous and useless. *Self-reliance in spiritual warfare is suicidal.* Believers do not strengthen themselves. Our strength must come from the Lord.

Spiritual warfare is opposite from earthly warfare. In an earthly army, an earthly general finds strength in his troops. Without them, he is just an individual. But in spiritual warfare, Christian troops find strength in their general—in God. We see this in Joshua 1:6–9, where the exhortation to "be strong and courageous" is grounded in the reassuring promise that "the LORD your God is with you wherever you go" (v. 9b). Consider these other examples of God's strength in the lives of his people:

- "And David was greatly distressed, for the people spoke of stoning him, because all the people were bitter in soul, each for his sons and daughters. But David strengthened himself in the LORD his God" (1 Sam. 30:6).
- "Listen, all Judah and inhabitants of Jerusalem and King Jehoshaphat: Thus says the LORD to you, 'Do not be afraid and do not be dismayed at this great horde, for the battle is not yours but God's'" (2 Chron. 20:15).
- "I love you, O LORD, my strength" (Ps. 18:1).
- "For who is God, but the LORD? And who is a rock, except our God?— the God who equipped me with strength, and made my way blameless" (Ps. 18:31–32).
- "For you equipped me with strength for the battle; you made those who rise against me sink under me" (Ps. 18:39).
- "The LORD is my strength and my shield; in him my heart trusts, and I am helped; my heart exults, and with my song I give thanks to him. The LORD is the strength of his people; he is the saving refuge of his anointed" (Ps. 28:7–8).
- "But I will sing of your strength; I will sing aloud of your steadfast love in the morning. For you have been to me a fortress and a refuge in the day of my distress. O my Strength, I will sing praises to you, for you, O God, are my fortress, the God who shows me steadfast love" (Ps. 59:16–17).
- "Awesome is God from his sanctuary; the God of Israel—he is the one who gives power and strength to his people. Blessed be God!" (Ps. 68:35).

- "Turn to me and be gracious to me; give your strength to your servant, and save the son of your maidservant" (Ps. 86:16).
- "The LORD is my strength and my song; he has become my salvation" (Ps. 118:14).
- "Blessed be the LORD, my rock, who trains my hands for war, and my fingers for battle; he is my steadfast love and my fortress, my stronghold and my deliverer, my shield and he in whom I take refuge, who subdues peoples under me" (Ps. 144:1–2).

The "strength" to which Paul refers in Ephesians 6:10 is none other than the "strength" he described in Ephesians 1:19–34: the power of God that raised Jesus from the dead and exalted him above all authority:

> And what is the immeasurable greatness of his power toward us who believe, according to the working of his great might that he worked in Christ when he raised him from the dead and seated him at his right hand in the heavenly places, far above all rule and authority and power and dominion, and above every name that is named, not only in this age but also in the one to come. And he put all things under his feet and gave him as head over all things to the church, which is his body, the fullness of him who fills all in all.

We find the same trio of Greek terms used in both Ephesians 1 and Ephesians 6: *dunamis*, *kratos*, and *ischus* (see Eph. 3:16; Col. 1:11, 29).

How might we obtain this strength, this power? There are multiple spiritual disciplines that serve as a pathway to the experience of God's power. It comes,

- through prayer;
- by fasting;
- by making certain that biblical truth is forever flowing in our spiritual veins;
- through the fellowship and encouragement of other Christians;
- through praise and worship and adoration;
- by drawing near to God;
- by partaking of the Lord's Supper;

- through the anointing and filling of the Holy Spirit;
- through the proper exercise of spiritual gifts (1 Cor. 12:7–11); and
- by adorning ourselves with the armor of God (Eph. 6).

3. Put on the Whole Armor of God

Paul then exhorts us to "put on the whole armor of God." We aren't born with the armor on—we must *put* it on. And once we put it on, we must never take off the armor, even if we think the hostilities have subsided. No, we must walk in it, work in it, sleep in it, eat in it. *It is never safe to disrobe.*

But talking about the armor, describing the armor, and declaring the importance of the armor is not enough. We must *use* it.

4. Stand Firm

We must put on the whole armor of God so that we *"may be able to stand"* or *"stand firm."* Paul repeats this goal for which we arm ourselves four times in this paragraph (Eph. 6:11, 13 [twice], and 14). Clearly he wants us to be immovable, steadfast, and unshaken by the enemies' attacks (see Eph. 4:14). We are to hold our position, to resist, to refuse to surrender ground to the enemy, to preserve and maintain what has already been won.

We must never forget that God has already won the decisive victory over the demonic realm through the life, death, and resurrection of Jesus. Paul calls us to stand on the truth of what Jesus has done and all that is ours in and through him. However, although the ultimate outcome has already been determined, we are still in a war with our enemy. Whereas we may suffer minor defeats or setbacks along the way, we must never be discouraged or disheartened, because Satan's final demise is as certain as is our ultimate victory.

5. Take a Stand against the Devil's Schemes

Paul calls us to take our stand against *"the schemes of the devil."* The word translated "schemes" is a rendering of the Greek term *methodeias*, from which we get the English word "methods." Paul is talking about Satan's wiles, tactics, stratagems, and secret agendas.

The plural of this word suggests that the devil's attacks "are constantly repeated or of incalculable variety."[3] What are they? Temptation, accusation,

---

3   O'Brien, *Letter to the Ephesians*, 463.

intimidation, humiliation, shame, division, and other such assaults against individual believers and the church corporately. Are all Satan's "methods" or "tactics" explicitly revealed in Scripture? Probably not. He is remarkably resourceful, and we must always be alert to any new plans he may hatch in his efforts to undermine our faith in God's goodness.

One especially important question we all should ask is this: If you were the devil, what tactics would you employ?

One of Satan's especially effective tactics during times of spiritual renewal and revival is not to promote explicit error, but to push Christians *beyond* truth. Satan will typically fail to prevent us from the pursuit of truth. As much as he may try, he rarely will succeed in driving us backwards into theological error. During seasons of renewal, you won't typically find Christians denying Christ's deity or bodily resurrection or salvation by grace. Satan devotes all his energy to push us in the direction of truth—but he doesn't stop there. *He pushes us beyond it into excess and fanaticism.*

Truth taken to an unbiblical and unhealthy extreme can be just as destructive as blatant error and falsehood. This is what has happened in virtually every revival in church history. Some examples of this might be:

- "Oh, isn't it wonderful that God has healed some! Surely, then, it must be his purpose to heal all." And when that doesn't happen, Satan accuses people of not having enough faith, accuses God of not caring enough for his children, and thereby undermines our confidence in his goodness.
- "Oh, isn't it wonderful that we are hearing God's voice in prophetic words and inward impressions of his Holy Spirit!" Yes, it is. But before you know it, people have abandoned their focus on Scripture and listening to God in his written Word, thinking it to be less exciting and less personal than getting a direct revelation from his Spirit.
- "Oh, isn't it wonderful to see how quickly and decisively God moves in power! He appears to accomplish in a short time what used to take us weeks, even months." And before you know it, people have abandoned the daily disciplines of prayer, Bible study, mutual encouragement, and the ordinary means of grace by which we are sanctified.
- "Oh, isn't it wonderful what happens in corporate worship and prayer! It only makes sense that we should cancel our small groups and other

activities and even minimize the preaching of God's Word so we might have more time to experience God's presence." And before you know it, the life of a local church is woefully out of balance, having taken what is good and truthful and life-changing and using that as an excuse to ignore the less sensational responsibilities the Bible requires of us.

- "Oh, God's grace is so amazing. He saves and delivers us apart from works we perform. It seems only right, then, that we stop encouraging people to repent of their sin and to pursue holiness lest they fall into the trap of legalism." And before you know it, the people of God are given over to licentiousness and immorality, appealing to the liberating effect of "God's amazing grace" to justify their behavior.

In each of these examples, Satan isn't trying to persuade us that we are wrong in emphasizing healing, prophetic words, powerful personal encounters, and life-changing supernatural experiences. He'll never succeed in pushing back on that effort. So instead, he takes what is right, good, and true, and pushes us faster and further than we should go, moving us beyond biblical boundaries into excess, fanaticism, and theological error.

So don't for a millisecond back down from embracing the good things God has done. Don't for a millisecond put the brakes on your wholehearted pursuit of God's power and presence. But be wise and discerning and careful that you do not let a good thing become the only thing, and in doing so fall into unbiblical and unbalanced fanaticism.

6. Wrestle

In Ephesians 6:12 Paul tells us with whom we wrestle. The Greek term translated "wrestle" (*palē*), used only here in the New Testament (and never in the Greek Old Testament), means to struggle or strive. We as Christians should never expect to coast, amble, or skip merrily along to paradise. We wrestle! We struggle! We wage war!

Why did Paul use a sporting term in a context pertaining to armor and military preparedness? Why didn't Paul use the term *strateia* ("warfare" in 2 Cor. 10:4; 1 Tim. 1:18) or *machē* ("fight" in 2 Cor. 7:5; 2 Tim. 2:23; Titus 3:9) or even *agōn* ("conflict," "struggle," or "fight"; Phil. 1:30; Col. 2:1)? Paul likely chose the image of wrestling because wrestling was an extremely popular event in the athletic games held in Asia Minor, particularly in Ephesus. Paul's readers would have been familiar with "the flesh-and-blood wrestling," but Paul reminds them that "the true struggle of believers is a spiritual power encounter which requires spiritual weaponry."[4]

Clinton Arnold points out another potential background for this terminology. Ephesus was famous for the magical arts, principal among which were the "Ephesian Letters" (*Ephesia grammata*).[5] These six magical terms/ names (*askion, kataskion, lix, tetrax, damnameneus,* and *aisia*) were alleged to possess power that would ward off evil spirits. People used them as either spoken charms or written amulets to obtain power and to protect them from harm. According to one popular story of the day, an Ephesian wrestler was unbeatable in the ancient Olympics because he wore the "Ephesian Letters" around his ankle. When officials discovered the letters and had them removed, the athlete proceeded to lose three consecutive matches.

Paul may have been alluding to this story with his use of the Greek word *palē*. So he was warning both the Ephesians and us today not to place our trust in magic. Don't trust in amulets, charms, tokens, or special words that you mistakenly believe carry supernatural power. Instead, trust in God and his power that comes to you when you faithfully adorn yourselves with the spiritual armor he has made available.

7. Know Who Your Enemy Isn't

Paul goes on to remind his readers, *"we do not wrestle against flesh and blood."* By "flesh and blood," Paul means people: human men and women (Matt. 16:17; Gal. 1:16; Heb. 2:14). Paul is not trying to deny that we have earthly and human antagonists. He's simply reminding us that beneath our daily, earthly struggles with people, institutions, and ideologies is an unseen spiritual battle. Satan lurks behind the efforts of our human enemies (see Matt. 16:23).

8. Know Who Your Enemy Is

According to Paul, our struggle, our battle, is "against the rulers, against the authorities, against the cosmic powers over this present darkness, against the spiritual forces of evil in the heavenly places." Paul uses a variety of terms to describe the enemy. Let's investigate each one further.

---

4   Clinton E. Arnold, *Power and Magic: The Concept of Power in Ephesians* (Grand Rapids: Baker, 1997), 117.
5   Ibid., 15–16.

- rulers/principalities (*archē*)—A ruler must have someone or something over which to exercise dominion (Eph. 1:21; 3:10; 6:12; Col. 1:16; 2:10; Rom. 8:38).
- authorities (*exousia*)—Again, authority, by definition, demands a subordinate (Eph. 1:21; 3:10; Col. 1:16).
- cosmic powers (*kosmokratōr*)—Used only in Ephesians 6:12; their realm as well as their character is referred to as "this present darkness," something from which believers have been delivered (see Eph. 5:8; Col. 1:13).
- spiritual forces (or spiritual hosts) of wickedness in the heavenly places—It may well be that this is not a separate class of cosmic powers but rather a general term for all the preceding spirits and an indication of their locality.

If all angels and demons are of the same type or rank or carry the same authority, why does Paul use such a variety of terms to describe them? It would also seem that with difference in rank comes difference in power, task, etc., although we must be careful of unhealthy speculation. Remember that our struggle is against *subjected powers* (see Ephesians 1:19–23). No matter how frightening or intimidating they may be, they have already been defeated and put under the feet of Christ (see Col. 2:15).[6]

9. Remember When This Takes Place

We must remember that all this takes place "*in the evil day.*" This phrase appears nowhere else in Paul's writings in precisely this form, although the phrase "the present evil age" is found in Galatians 1:4, and Paul said, "the

---

6 We should take brief note of a trend since World War II of identifying these "powers" not with personal spiritual beings such as demons, but with interior structures of society and thought: tradition, custom, laws, authority, religious systems, economic philosophies, political parties, governmental organizations, etc. This view is found primarily in the writings of Walter Wink (*Naming the Powers: The Language of Power in the New Testament* [Philadelphia: Fortress Press, 1984]; *Unmasking the Powers: The Invisible Forces That Determine Human Existence* [Philadelphia: Fortress Press, 1986]; and *Engaging the Powers: Discernment and Resistance in a World of Domination* [Philadelphia: Fortress Press, 1992]). This view cannot be supported by the evidence in Paul's writings. However, as O'Brien points out, "to reject the *identification* of the powers with human traditions and sociopolitical structures . . . is not to deny that these supernatural intelligences work through such agencies" (*Ephesians*, 469).

days are evil" in Ephesians 5:16. Commentators usually point to one of three explanations of this phrase (or a combination of them):

1. This phrase may be synonymous with the evil days of Ephesians 5:16 and thus refer to the whole of this present age between the two comings of Jesus.
2. This phrase may refer to a single day of unique tribulation just before the coming of Christ.
3. This phrase may point to critical times in a believer's life when demonic activity is especially intense and focused.

O'Brien is probably correct when he says that "the apostle is not only speaking of this present time between the two comings of Jesus, but is also alerting believers to the dangers of the devil's schemes on critical occasions in this present evil age. There may appear to be times of reprieve for Christians, but they must not be lulled into a false sense of security, thinking that the battle is over or that it is not especially difficult. They must always be prepared and put on the full armour of God, for the devil will attack when least expected."[7]

The Armor of God

The threat believers face in Satan is real and undeniable. Elsewhere, Paul calls believers to "Be sober-minded; be watchful. Your adversary the devil prowls around like a roaring lion, seeking someone to devour. Resist him, firm in your faith, knowing that the same kinds of suffering are being experienced by your brotherhood throughout the world" (1 Peter 5:8–9). So what can we as Christians do in the face of this threat? Are we helpless victims of Satan's power and purposes for this earth? By no means!

God has graciously provided for us everything we need to resist and overcome Satan and his demons. In fact, when we employ God's resources and power, we are assured of victory over all Satan's schemes. This is what we read in the second half of our passage, Ephesians 6:14–17. So let's turn our attention to the "armor" that God himself has provided for our protection.

---

7 O'Brien, *Ephesians*, 471–72.

The Belt of Truth

We begin with *the belt of truth* (v. 14a). The "belt" or "girdle" was not simply a strip of cloth around the waist or even a narrow belt to hold up one's pants. It was a leather apron that helped protect the lower part of the body. It had two additional functions: (1) it was used to hold the sheath for one's sword, and (2) one's tunic would be tucked into it whenever fighting or running (cf. 1 Pet. 1:13). In the Old Testament God is described as girded with might (Ps. 65:6) and also as girding the psalmist with strength for battle (Ps. 18:32, 39).

But what does Paul mean by "truth"? On the one hand, *Jesus* is the truth (John 1:14; 14:6; Eph. 4:21; see also Rom. 13:14). Thus we pray: "I put on the Lord Jesus Christ; I clothe myself with his character; I am filled with his power; I am committed to pursuing his praise; I cherish, prize, treasure, and adore him above all else." But the *Bible* is also the truth (2 Tim. 2:15). Successful spiritual warfare begins with the question: "Do I accept the Bible as God's Word, inspired, infallible, and inerrant, the sole authority for belief and practice?" The vast majority of people who are adversely influenced by the principalities and powers of which Paul speaks suffer precisely because of their ignorance of biblical truth.

The apostle Paul also speaks of the *church* as the pillar of truth (1 Tim. 3:14–15). The church provides protection, reinforcement of biblical virtues, encouragement, stability, guidance, etc. Paul may also be referring to the essential role of the objective truth of Christian *doctrine* (John 17:15–17; 2 Cor. 4:1–2; Eph. 4:14–15). Satan will always flourish in the midst of theological ignorance. "Truth" may also refer to *truthfulness* in our speech and behavior; the absence of duplicity, hypocrisy, lying, or deception (Eph. 4:25; 5:9); perhaps also the ideas of faithfulness and loyalty. There are two areas in particular in which demonic lies are most prevalent and powerful: lies about God (character and attributes) and lies about yourself (who you are, your identity and position in Christ, your authority and power). We must fight against Satan's deceptive ways by standing firmly on the "whole counsel of God" as revealed in Scripture.

The Breastplate of Righteousness

Paul next describes *the breastplate of righteousness* (Eph. 6:14b). The "breastplate" (*tho˘raka,* from which we get "thorax") usually extended from the base of the neck to the upper part of the thighs, covering what we would call the abdomen or trunk. So, is this righteousness "objective" or "subjective"? That is to say, does Paul have in mind the righteousness of Jesus Christ that has been imputed or reckoned to us when we first trusted in Christ for salvation? Or does he mean the experiential righteousness of godly living, day in and day out? Probably both, but with emphasis on the former. By objective righteousness, Paul would be referring to the breastplate of our justification, our righteous standing/position through faith in Christ, and our legal holiness (Phil. 3:3–8; 2 Cor. 5:21; Rom. 3:19–24). If the emphasis is on our subjective righteousness, the idea would be that the breastplate is our experiential holiness of life, our habitual obedience to all God has commanded (Eph. 4:24; 5:9).

The reason why the "breastplate of righteousness" is so important is that one of Satan's most common and effective strategies is to undermine your faith and create doubt in your heart by reminding you of how wicked you are and of how often you have failed as a Christian. Our response must always be to say: "No matter how badly I have sinned, God sees me as perfectly righteous in Jesus Christ. His righteousness has been imputed to me." In essence, you fight Satan's accusations by throwing back in his face the truth of what Paul wrote in Philippians 3:8–9:

> Indeed, I count everything as loss because of the surpassing worth of knowing Christ Jesus my Lord. For his sake I have suffered the loss of all things and count them as rubbish, in order that I may gain Christ and be found in him, not having a righteousness of my own that comes from the law, but that which comes through faith in Christ, the righteousness from God that depends on faith.

Shoes of the Gospel

We must also put on the *shoes of the gospel* (Eph. 6:15). This is a reference to the half-boot or military sandal worn by the Roman legionary. Hobnails or studs underneath provided stability. There are two possible ways of taking Paul's imagery. On the one hand, he may mean that we are to shod/fit our feet with preparation or readiness *for* making known the gospel of peace, that is, we are to be prepared and ready to proclaim the glorious gospel of peace (1 Pet. 3:15; Isa. 52:7; Rom. 10:13–15). The gospel is the power of God by which people are set free from Satan's captivity and tyranny (2 Cor. 4:3–4; Eph. 2:1–2; Acts 26:18). See especially Revelation 12:10–11.

But I'm inclined to follow the ESV translation of Ephesians 6:15, which suggests that our feet are to be fitted with "the readiness given by the gospel of peace." Thus, it isn't readiness to proclaim the gospel but *readiness that is produced in us by the gospel*. More specifically, the peace the gospel produces is to prepare us for Satan's attacks. As you know, the word "peace" in the New Testament can have either of two different points of reference. It may refer to "peace with God," in the sense that the enmity between us and him is put away through the death and resurrection of Jesus (Rom. 5:1–2; Col. 1:19–22). That is most likely what Paul has in mind. But it could also include "the peace of God" or the spiritual calm and tranquility that he imparts to us through the Holy Spirit (Phil. 4:6–7). Therefore, the reference is either to *the peace **in** the gospel,* which we proclaim or to *the peace **of** the gospel,* which we experience. Paradoxically, it is in the midst of spiritual *warfare* that we are called on to proclaim spiritual *peace*!

What a glorious gospel indeed, bringing peace with God, the end of all hostility and wrath and condemnation, at the same time as it imparts to us God's very peace, the joy and rest found in the heart of God himself.

The Shield of Faith

We must also take up *the shield of faith* (Eph. 6:16). The "shield" refers to an oblong device approximately four feet long and two feet wide. It was made of two layers of wood glued together and covered first with linen and then with hide. It was then bound on the top and bottom with iron. Its purpose was to defend against the incendiary missiles of the enemy: arrows dipped in pitch, set aflame, and launched. We are to employ the shield of faith "in all circumstances" or at "all times" or on every occasion when the enemy launches his attack.

What are the "flaming darts of the evil one"? Peter O'Brien believes they depict "in highly metaphorical language, every kind of attack launched by the devil and his hosts against the people of God."[8] I believe Paul's focus is somewhat narrower. My sense is that he has in mind the sudden and unexpected eruption in our minds of vile images and thoughts that shock and

---

8 O'Brien, *Ephesians*, 480.

surprise us (such that are obviously and undeniably contrary to our most basic desires). He also likely has in view words and pictures that disgust you and violate your God-given sense of propriety/morality leaping into your mind, such as blasphemous thoughts about Jesus; revolting images of sexual perversity; suicidal urges; compulsive thoughts of doing horribly violent things to family/friends; unaccountable impulses to rebel against God, against one's family, against one's church; subtle insinuations against God's character/goodness; or false feelings of guilt.

Frequently, people report these things occurring while reading the Bible (not newspapers or magazines), while praying, even while praising God. This aggravates feelings of personal guilt and worthlessness, insofar as such occasions are regarded as spiritual ("What kind of person am I that I would have such thoughts/fantasies at precisely the time I should be loving and worshipping God?").

People often ask, "How do I know the difference between the fiery missiles of the evil one and the sinful activity of my own flesh?" That's a challenging question to answer, if for no other reason than that it pertains to our subjective experiences. But in most instances our sinful and fleshly propensities are something with which we are already quite familiar. Satan's "flaming darts" (Eph. 6:16) most often strike us as strange, unprecedented, and virtually out of nowhere. They appear suddenly in our minds without warning or any sense about what may have provoked them. Furthermore, when the problem is our sinful flesh, the Holy Spirit will bring conviction of sin but without condemnation. This often painful, awakened awareness of our failure comes with the promise of forgiveness as the Spirit faithfully points us to the cross. Satan's flaming darts of damnation, on the other hand, produce only guilt and shame without any hope of freedom from their condemning power.

So, what, then, does Paul have in mind when he uses the word "faith"? There are at least three kinds of Christian faith described in the New Testament. There is *saving* faith (a product of the new birth); *sanctifying* faith (the fruit of the Holy Spirit), which comes in two forms: a) our faith/belief in the truth of God's Word (faith in the doctrines of the Bible) and b) faith in the trustworthiness/goodness of God himself; and *supernatural* faith (a spontaneous gift of the Holy Spirit). Paul probably has in mind the second of these: sanctifying faith (1 Pet. 5:8–9; 1 John 5:4). We might also refer to these three expressions of faith as converting faith, continuing faith, and charismatic faith.

But let's keep in mind several things about "faith." First, faith, in and of itself, does not protect us against Satan. Rather, it is the object/focus of our faith: God and his powerful presence in our lives (Prov. 30:5; Ps. 5:12; 2 Sam. 22:3). That being said, it is *we* who extinguish the fiery darts of the evil one through faith. *We* are active. Faith is something *we* do.

Also, faith functions as a shield of protection in several ways. Consider Hebrews 11:24–26 where we are told that it was Moses's faith in the glory of the coming Christ and the rewards of obedience that enabled him to say no to the temptations he encountered in Egypt. When Satan whispers, "God may have cared about you once before, long ago, but his interest in who you are is gone," you lift up the shield of faith and say, "*That is impossible!* God is immutable. He cannot change. His concern for me is eternal. What he has promised me he will fulfill."

Or when Satan whispers, "God doesn't love you anymore, not after you've failed him so many times," you lift up the shield of faith and say, "*That is impossible!* God's love for me can't cease to exist, for he demonstrated it when he gave his Son to suffer in my place." Or again, the shield of faith functions whenever we say to the enemy, "I'm going to believe God when he tells me that there is great gain in godliness, and therefore I will not fall prey to your seductive temptations." Simply put, the shield of faith functions each time we hold up the truth of the Scriptures under the onslaught of Satan's lies.

The Helmet of Salvation

Yet another piece of the armor God has provided is *the helmet of salvation* (Eph. 6:17a). The principal battleground in spiritual warfare is in the mind. Thus, we have need for a helmet of protection, a "spiritual hardhat" if you will. The helmet of the Roman soldier was made of iron or bronze with a sponge of some sort lining the inside. The "helmet of salvation" is most likely a reference to *the assurance of our salvation.* Satan knows he can gain a major strategic advantage over us if he can sow the seeds of doubt in our minds concerning our relationship with God. In every instance of serious and sustained demonic attack I have encountered, the individual was plagued with doubt concerning his or her salvation. To put on the "helmet of salvation," therefore, means to live in the knowledge and assurance of the truth expressed in Romans 8:1, 31–39, and Hebrews 13:5–6. There is nothing Satan can do to alter or undermine the fact that we are saved. As Paul said in Romans 8:38–39,

> For I am sure that neither death nor life, nor angels nor rulers, nor things present nor things to come, nor powers, nor height nor depth, nor anything else in all creation, will be able to separate us from the love of God in Christ Jesus our Lord.

But, what he *can* do is erode our assurance and confidence that we are saved. Our salvation, our standing with God, does not fluctuate or diminish with our success or failure in spiritual battles. But Satan is determined to convince us that it does. We also read in 1 Thessalonians 5:8–9 that our "helmet" is the "hope of salvation." In other words, this assurance of salvation is not simply a confidence *now* that I'm saved *now*, but also a confidence *now* that I *will be* saved later.

The Sword of the Spirit

The final piece of our armor is *the sword of the Spirit, which is the word of God* (Eph. 6:17b). The "sword" (*machaira*) refers to the short (twelve to fourteen inches), straight sword used in close combat. Another term, *romphaia*, refers to the long sword. Satan not only launches fiery missiles from afar, he also moves in close for hand-to-hand combat! Some argue that since the sword is our only offensive weapon, spiritual warfare is largely, if not exclusively, defensive. But the sword was the only offensive weapon a Roman soldier carried! The point of the armor was to prepare a soldier for fighting in battle, in whatever form that battle might be.

The Spirit is not himself the sword. The Word is the sword. This sword is "of the Spirit" in the sense that it is the Holy Spirit who gives power both to the written and spoken Word of God. This raises the question: What is the "word" of God in verse 17? The "word" here does not refer to the "Word" of John 1:1 (the *logos*)—it is not a reference to Jesus Christ. There are two terms in the New Testament for "word": *logos* and *rhēma*.

People have often insisted that *logos* always refers to the objective revelation of truth that ultimately became the written word of God (the Bible). *Logos*, therefore, refers to the general, collective body of truth we have in

Scripture. *Rhēma*, on the other hand, refers to a specific spoken word, an individual utterance, a declaration or saying. Thus, *logos* is the written Scriptures, whereas *rhēma* is the application of the written word to specific situations or circumstances, in accordance with the immediate need of the moment. In sum, the *logos* is the objective, written Word of God, whereas *rhēma* is the subjective Word of God that is given for each occasion as we encounter our enemy.

The problem with this is that the two terms are often used interchangeably in the New Testament. For example, in 1 Peter 1:25 *rhēma* is used instead of the expected *logos*. In Revelation 12:10–11 *logos* is used instead of the expected *rhēma*. *Logos* is frequently used with reference to individual, spoken utterances (Matt. 7:24; John 2:22; Eph. 4:29; 5:6, and especially Eph. 6:19). And *rhēma* can be used of the collective body of truths that comprise the gospel (Eph. 5:26). This is a healthy reminder that we should always be cautious about drawing theological conclusions based solely on an alleged distinction between terms.

Nevertheless, having said that, I do believe Paul is talking about *the spoken word of God* here in Ephesians 6:17. I have three reasons for this. First, there is no escaping the fact that in the majority of cases where *rhēma* is used in the New Testament it has in view individual spoken utterances or sayings. Second, Satan cannot read our thoughts or our minds, hence the need to speak aloud our resistance to his efforts. Why do I say this? I say it because no biblical text says he can read our minds. Satan is a creature and therefore has limitations. Satan is not God! Only God is omniscient.

Also, such knowledge is portrayed in the Bible as peculiar to God. Knowing the heart, mind, intents, thoughts, and motives of a person is an ability or prerogative reserved for God alone (Ps. 139:1–4, 23–24; 26:2; 7:9; Jer. 17:9–10; Rom. 8:27; 1 Cor. 4:5; 1 Thess. 2:4; Heb. 4:12–13). Finally, if Satan could always read our thoughts or know what was in our hearts, there would be no place within us of unassailable communion with God. Thus, we are to wage war and resist the enemy as Jesus did in Matthew 4, by speaking it aloud (the "word" Jesus spoke [the *rhēma* that proceeds out of God] was Scripture).

In summary, there are three primary ways in which we wield the sword of the Spirit. We proclaim the Word (as Jesus did; see also Rev. 12). We pray the Word (Eph. 6:18–19; Acts 6:4; John 15:7). And we praise with the Word (i.e., sing the Scriptures).

A Very Personal, Terrifying Incident

I've decided to share with you something about which I have remained largely silent over the years, an incident that I now believe was a concentrated "flaming dart" of the enemy against my life. It proved to be the most intense and overwhelming demonic attack I have personally experienced. It was in the early summer of 1993. Some two months earlier I had been offered a position as President of Grace Training Center at the church in Kansas City, known then as Metro Vineyard Fellowship. Mike Bickle, who currently leads the International House of Prayer in Kansas City, was the senior pastor and had invited me to join his staff. Mike encouraged me to come to Kansas City to solidify the details of this new position. I had already informed close friends and family in Ardmore, Oklahoma, where I was serving as pastor of Christ Community Church, that I fully intended to accept his offer.

I won't go into the details behind the policies Mike had put into practice for full-time pastors at the church. Let me simply say that I quickly learned that in order to make this move to Kansas City, I would have to take a 40 percent cut in salary. Throughout the course of my day with Mike, as I reflected more deeply on the implications of this move, a dark cloud of deep depression began to descend on my mind. To this day I find it difficult to explain. Never before in my life had I experienced even the slightest measure of depression. I'm not even sure depression is the most accurate term to describe what I suddenly felt. The words "despair" and "sheer terror" would be more appropriate.

As I met several of the staff members at the church and shared a meal with them, I struggled to focus as my mind was filled with countless irrational thoughts about what this move would entail. I slowly found myself persuaded that this would be the most damaging and regrettable decision of my life. Every reason not to go to Kansas City suddenly took on dire and seemingly destructive proportions. To move would destroy my church in Ardmore, my family, my reputation, my future success in ministry, and everything else I cherished. Of course, none of that was true, but no one could have convinced me otherwise that day.

Not long before I made this trip to Kansas City, I had watched the newly released film *The Firm*, starring Tom Cruise. Without rehearsing the plot, there is a scene in which Cruise is confronted by agents of the justice department who tell him that the law firm in Memphis he recently joined was the sole legal representation for the Mafia. Cruise is presented with two options. Either he agrees to betray client confidentiality, supply the government with the documents they demanded, and be disbarred, or he could refuse to cooperate and most likely end up in prison with the other attorneys of the firm. I tell you this story because of one comment made to Cruise by the justice department representative. "What are you saying?" Cruise asks. The justice department representative replies, "I'm saying that your life, as you know it, is over."

As I was being driven back to the airport for my return to Oklahoma, that line echoed over and over in my head. It was as if Satan took that phrase and repeatedly pounded it into my soul, signaling the end of any meaningful way to escape the dilemma I faced. "Sam," I said to myself, "you've put yourself in the worst possible situation. You can't return to the church in Ardmore. You've already disclosed to too many people that you are more than likely moving to Kansas City. But you can't move. There is no way you can live on the offered salary. Your life, as you know it, is over."

That may not strike you as especially devastating, but for me it felt like the end of the world. As we made our way to the airport, it suddenly dawned on me that the only way out of this mess was to commit suicide. Yes, I know that sounds extreme and irrational. Of course it was! But I know now that Satan was seeking to take my life. I found myself looking in the side-view mirror of the car, hoping to find the traffic to our right heavy and threatening. My hand was literally on the door handle as I prepared to open it and jump to my death. I struggle to this day to accurately describe what I was feeling. It was a strange mixture of depression, despair, hopelessness, and fear. Death seemed the only solution.

The only reason I didn't open that door and end my life was that God's grace intervened. The Holy Spirit stayed my hand. Never before nor since have I even remotely considered suicide. In fact, I struggled to understand how anyone could contemplate taking their own life. But now I knew what they felt. Now I knew the nearly irresistible urge to end it all. No amount of rational thought or carefully crafted reasons not to kill myself registered in my soul. By the mercy of God, we made it to the airport.

But the temptation didn't stop once we arrived. As I waited to board the plane, the same fear and despair engulfed me once again. I began to pray that God would cause the plane to crash and that I would be the only one who would die. It sounds silly, but when the enemy darkens your thinking and launches this sort of insidious attack, it all seems so reasonable. I paused long enough to call my wife on the phone to tell her what was happening. Neither of us can recall the content of our conversation, but she prayed fervently for me before she hung up. She immediately shared this with our fourteen-year-old daughter, Melanie, who spent the next hour or so praying for her daddy.

By the time I landed in Oklahoma City, the dark cloud had lifted. My reason returned to me. All thoughts of taking my life vanished. When I arrived back home in Ardmore, I discovered taped to my bedroom door a handwritten note from Melanie, telling me of her love and how she was praying for me. And yes, in case you were wondering, I accepted Mike's offer, and we made the move to Kansas City in August of 1993.

Perhaps only those of you who have battled depression and struggled with suicidal impulses can understand what I experienced. There is not the slightest doubt in my mind that a demon, or perhaps several, had set their sights on destroying my life. I have not encountered anything remotely similar to this in the years since that day in 1993. But at least now I can empathize with those who so often face this temptation. The reality of demonic attack and oppression hit home with indelible force that day. The fact of the matter is that I had everything to live for. Yet, under the barrage of Satan's "flaming darts" (Eph. 6:16), the only reasonable choice was to kill myself.

My primary motivation in writing this book is to alert others to the wicked schemes of our invisible enemy. I'll be honest. It wasn't easy writing about this incident. To this day I feel a measure of embarrassment confessing that I genuinely contemplated suicide for what in hindsight I now know to be frivolous reasons. But such is the force and deception of Satan's tactics. The apostle Paul told the Corinthians, "we are not ignorant of his [Satan's] designs" (2 Cor. 2:11). And my hope for you is that by reading this book you would not be ignorant of them either.

JONATHAN'S STORY

One afternoon, while at work, I unexpectedly began experiencing thoughts that I knew were not my own. The voice was somewhat familiar, but it had a new level of intensity.

"You are worthless and insignificant."

"Do you really think God has a grand purpose for your life?"

"The world is right about who you are, and not even Jesus can change that."

"You are a fool to believe that what God says about you is actually true. You have no power."

Though I was able to recognize the lies, the intensity of the onslaught enticed me to agree with what was being spoken to me. This continued for several hours as I entered a defeated state of mind, feeling powerless to break out of the attack. Upon returning home, my wife took one look at me and asked, "What happened to you?"

"I don't know," I replied, "but that can't happen again."

I pursued inner healing and deliverance prayer. While pursuing the freedom that God could bring to my life and learning how to deal with demonic attacks, I found myself constantly repenting of how low my expectations were. I was amazed by how much freedom Jesus could bring and how much he cared for the smallest details of my life and history. The concept of Jesus being a friend always felt a little distant to me until he started interceding in my life in a way that felt very much like a good friend would. It sounds like Christianity 101, but I found that when I truly obey all the commands Jesus gives, I receive the freedom, joy, and peace that Jesus promises. I was interested in spiritual warfare, but I was surprised to learn that it doesn't always look like what we expect. Hearing from the Holy Spirit took on a new intensity. Out of all my experiences during this extended time of prayer, two in particular stand out as profound.

First, a particular sort of ungodly music had been a stronghold in my life for years. The Lord slowly began breaking me of it six months before pursuing inner healing. After committing to fully breaking the ungodly tie during one session, the facilitators prayed a prayer over me specifically, and also for us as a group, to break all ungodly ties with music. Within a couple of days, the son of one of the facilitators who had been experiencing night terrors for years suddenly began sleeping peacefully through the night. It was later discovered that shortly after our session, a CD with music very similar to what had enslaved me had been removed from their house. The Holy Spirit extended the healing and freedom that was given to me to a young man who had been battling torment for years.

I've learned that what we consume or allow to enter our minds has a more profound effect on our spiritual well-being than we could ever imagine. The enemy would prefer that we downplay or trivialize what we consume. "It's not a big deal." "You're just being an alarmist." "You're not a little child, this is fine." But in reality, every word, every image, every exercise of our senses affects us spiritually. There is no neutral ground. I'm convinced that we often don't understand the gravity of what we are inviting into our lives on a daily basis and that many of the open doors for demonic activity are hiding in plain sight.

A second experience involved a particular belief I held about temptation. While engaging in a session on repentance, I was asked if a particular temptation was an issue for me. I described that it wasn't currently an issue, that I had dealt with it decisively years ago, and that I was committed to continuing the fight against that temptation for the rest of my life. Weeks later, we revisited the issue.

"Do you believe that you will always be tempted by this?"

"Well, yes," I replied, thinking that my belief aligned with Scripture.

"Is that a godly belief?"

"Well, I think so, but I've never really considered whether or not it was."

"Well, let's ask Jesus about it."

I repented. About a week later, I suddenly realized that the temptation was virtually nonexistent. "That's encouraging," I thought, not realizing the absence of that temptation would last for weeks and weeks, and then months and months, and continues to be largely absent today. Jesus displayed his power for me in a unique way that I never expected. Even though I had the wisdom and the tools to deal effectively with the temptation, the enemy kept me bound to it in a way that appeared to be spiritually virtuous on the surface but was actually enslaving. Jesus decided that, for me, even those hidden chains would be completely broken.

The gate of my mind is the front line of spiritual warfare. Once a front line is broken, damage is much harder to contain. If I can protect the front line first, I can prevent the chain reaction of destruction the enemy attempts to provoke. I do this by trying to be aware of every thought that crosses my mind and comparing the content of those thoughts to the truth of Scripture. If the thought doesn't agree, I resist it, renounce it, and replace it, to be obedient to Christ (2 Cor. 10:5). I've learned that I must believe Scripture is true over and above my experience. This idea used to seem foolish to me, that I was somehow denying reality and affirming what I *wanted* to be true, rather than making peace with what was actually true. However, the Holy Spirit revealed to me that it was prideful to believe that my perception of reality was somehow truer than God's reality. If my thoughts disagree with the promises or the truth of God, then I'm wrong!

I've learned the importance and significance of speaking my spiritual authority into the air. Making my intentions known out loud to the powers of darkness carries a unique power and influence. My authority as a believer is exercised in the spirit realm when I turn my intentions into words that carry into the physical realm. Upon speaking aloud my intentions to resist the powers of darkness, I often notice a unique shift in the atmosphere, and peace enters where disorder used to reign. As a mentor once suggested to me, tell the opposition out loud, "I see what you're doing, and I resist it."

I've learned that my knowledge of Scripture is paramount. If I am to be able to effectively discern between the Spirit of God and the voice of the enemy, I must be intimately familiar with what each of them sound like. Simply put, the Spirit of God sounds like the God of Scripture, and if I long to recognize his voice, I must be constantly immersed in his Word.

CHAPTER 17

Warfare Prayer

I'm often asked why spiritual warfare is even necessary. Wouldn't it have been easier for us if God had simply annihilated Satan from the start, or at least not have waited until the final judgment to cast him into the lake of fire (see Rev. 20:10)? That is the sort of question that haunts us and makes us wonder why God does the things he does, or why, when he does them, he chooses not to do them earlier! It's a question that may have entered your mind as you read this book, and it certainly deserves our serious consideration.

Related to this is the urgent plea in Scripture that we pray for ourselves and one another in the midst of this seemingly incessant spiritual conflict. What relationship does prayer sustain to our war with the enemy, and why does God regard it as essential to our growth in Christ and our victory over Satan and his demonic hosts? These are the issues we'll seek to address in this chapter.

The Question of Satan's Continued Existence

In Ephesians 6, Paul declares that our battle, our struggle, is not ultimately with other human beings but with rulers or principalities and authorities and cosmic powers—with Satan and his demonic hordes. He repeatedly exhorts us to stand firm by adorning ourselves with the armor of God (Eph. 6:14–17).

But why? Couldn't God simply dispense with all of this by immediately destroying Satan and all his demons? Why doesn't God just annihilate Satan and his demons immediately? He could certainly do so. After all, God is omnipotent, and Satan is only a creature. God made him, and God can certainly destroy him. Satan exists by virtue of God's sustaining power, as do we all. God upholds Satan in existence the same as he upholds us and all of creation.

We also know that God certainly has the right to destroy Satan. The moment Satan sinned he was subject to judgment. That Satan continues to exist doesn't mean God can't or that God shouldn't destroy him. He can, and he most assuredly has every right to do so.

Furthermore, not only is God able to remove Satan, not only does he have the right to remove Satan, we also know from Scripture that he *will* judge and remove Satan forever. We know that it is God's ultimate purpose to cast Satan and all his demons into the lake of fire. We know this from several texts. In Matthew 25:41, Jesus himself referred to "the eternal fire prepared for the devil and his angels" (see also Jude 6). And we read in Revelation 20:10 that Satan will eventually be cast into the lake of fire to be tormented forever.

So, it wouldn't be unjust for God to consign him there *now*. It wouldn't violate any principle of fair play or be inconsistent with what we read elsewhere in Scripture concerning Satan. There is nothing in the removal of Satan and his demons that would be contrary to God's character or his purpose for human history.

So why does he remain in place? Why does God permit him to continue hurling his "fiery darts" at Christians around the world? Wouldn't the Christian life be immeasurably easier if God were to eliminate Satan altogether? After all, in the Lord's Prayer we ask God not to lead us into temptation but to deliver us from the evil one—Satan. So if we are to successfully avoid temptation and be delivered from Satan, the simple solution would be for God to remove him altogether from the scene, right now. So why doesn't he?[1]

Is he giving Satan and demons time to repent? Are we to be patient with Satan's presence in hopes that he might come to his senses, turn from evil, and cry out for God's forgiving mercy? The answer to those questions is clear: no. Scripture consistently communicates that Satan and his demons are irredeemable. They cannot and will not repent. Jesus didn't die on the cross for angels, but only for men and women (see Heb. 2:14–18).

---

1 I was greatly aided in answering this question by John Piper and his book *Spectacular Sins: And Their Global Purpose in the Glory of Christ* (Wheaton, IL: Crossway, 2008), 31–51.

So why doesn't God eliminate Satan altogether, right now?

The Bible doesn't provide us with an explicit answer to this question. I wish it did, but it doesn't. So we are left to piecing together an answer that makes sense of Satan's ongoing existence and activity.

For God's Glory

Romans 11 is one passage that grounds our answer in who God is and what he is doing in human history. We read this in Romans 11:36: "For from him and through him and to him are all things. To him be glory forever. Amen." What this declaration by Paul tells us is that everything that exists exists because God caused it to exist. All things are "from him." And everything that continues to exist exists because God wills that it exist. All things are "through him." And most important of all, it tells us that everything that exists exists in order to glorify and magnify and make known the greatness of God. All things are "to him" or "for him," which is to say, they came into being and continue being so God might be honored and praised. And that certainly applies to Satan and his demons.

What this tells us is that God permits Satan and his demons to exist because in some way their existence and activity serves to bring greater glory to God than if God were to immediately judge them by casting them into the lake of fire. How can this be? Again, I don't have specific biblical texts, but I do believe that my answer is thoroughly biblical.

For example, God knows that when you and I are confronted with temptation and we turn to his grace and the empowering presence of the Holy Spirit to say no to what Satan and his demons are up to, it brings him more glory and honor than if we had never been tempted at all. God knows that our growth into spiritual maturity that comes when we battle Satan and resist his temptations and trust in God's mercy and forgiveness will produce more opportunities for God to be seen as kind and sufficient for all our needs than if Satan were nowhere present and not at all involved in our daily struggles.

Consider how the incarnation, life, death, and resurrection of Jesus more greatly magnify God because of Satan's presence than if Satan were absent. When the Son of God was conceived in the womb of Mary and became the man Christ Jesus, Satan turned all his efforts toward destroying him (see Rev. 12:3–6). But he failed. And in that failure God's greatness was magnified. When Jesus resisted Satan's temptations in the wilderness, the sustaining power of the Holy Spirit in him and the sufficiency of all the Father provided him were put on display more so than if Satan had never had the opportunity to tempt our Lord.

We saw earlier in Colossians 2:15 that when Jesus was nailed to a cross "he disarmed the rulers and authorities [the demonic hosts] and put them to open shame, by triumphing over them in him," or better still, "in" or "through it," that is, in and through the cross itself. In other words, Satan and his hosts evidently thought that by conspiring to nail Jesus to a cross they could defeat God's purposes. But Paul says that Jesus subjected himself to the temptations and taunting of Satan and eventually to the shame of crucifixion itself precisely because, in this way, his grace and glory in forgiving sinners could be put on display. The consistent testimony of the New Testament is that there is more glory that will come to God because of the suffering of Jesus than would have come had Jesus avoided the cross by immediately annihilating Satan and his demonic hordes.

Furthermore, when you and I are supremely satisfied in the goodness and beauty of God rather than in what Satan offers to us by way of temptation to sin, we more clearly demonstrate God's glory and greatness than if we had never been confronted by Satan at all. When you love and trust Jesus in spite of what Satan offers, God's glory shines more clearly than it would have had you never been confronted or tempted by the enemy.

If God were to destroy Satan and all demons right now, it would surely magnify and draw attention to his power. But God wants to do more than merely put his power on display. He is determined to magnify his superior beauty and transcendent worth and to show to all concerned that he is deserving of our trust and that he alone can satisfy our deepest desires. When God works in us to win our love and allegiance to Jesus as we resist and say no to the deceptive lies of the enemy, God is greatly glorified.

The Stages to Satan's Defeat

What all this means is that God is determined to defeat Satan in stages, progressively, rather than in one decisive act. This is God's strategy because it will serve to glorify his greatness and beauty more than any other approach.

- The *first* stage was the incarnation of the Son of God in human flesh. You may recall that according to Revelation 12, Satan made every effort to destroy Jesus at his birth. We know this because King Herod, Satan's accomplice, sought to kill all the newborn boys in Bethlehem.

- The *second* stage was when Jesus resisted Satan's temptations in the wilderness.
- The *third* stage was when Jesus cast out demons from those who had come under their oppressive influence.
- The *fourth* stage was when Jesus disarmed and humiliated the demonic hosts by his voluntary sufferings on the cross for sinners.
- The *fifth* stage is when he brings men and women to saving faith in himself. The apostle Paul said that the purpose of his mission to the Gentiles was "to open their eyes, so that they may turn . . . from the power of Satan to God" (Acts 26:18). In the absence of sin and guilt, Satan has no power or authority over us. By permitting Satan to exist until the end of time, he is compelled to watch as God's elect people turn to Christ for forgiveness and treasure him above anything Satan could ever provide. In other words, when by God's grace men and women turn to Jesus, it exposes the ugliness of Satan and highlights the beauty of Christ.
- The *sixth* stage is when we, by God's sustaining strength and by our use of the armor he has provided, resist Satan's temptations.
- The *seventh* and final stage is when God will put all of his attributes on display at the final judgment of Satan, when he is cast into the lake of fire forever and ever.

You might say, "But that is a very costly way of gaining glory and honor for himself. The sufferings of Jesus were a pretty steep price to pay for God to be glorified." Yes, but our great Triune God, Father, Son, and Holy Spirit, determined it was worth the cost. I can hear some of you saying to yourselves, "But Sam, you make it sound like *it's all about God*, that it's all about what makes *him* look good, that it's all about what serves more effectively to magnify *him* and *his* greatness." Well, yes! The God-centered answer is always the best and most biblical. That's what Romans 11:36 is all about.

Others of you might say, "But I don't agree with that approach. I don't think God should run the world in this way. I don't think God should make his own glory preeminent in his decision regarding Satan and demons." Well, personally, I would rather trust the wisdom of an infinitely wise and omniscient and good God than to trust the wisdom of a finite creature such as yourself, whose wisdom is stunted, whose heart has been corrupted by sin, and who obviously is very, very far from being omniscient.

So, what this means to you and me is that we need to be extraordinarily diligent to obey what Paul says in Ephesians 6, that we must take up arms against the devil and stand firm! Be glad in God, be satisfied with all that he is for you in Jesus, and say no to Satan and his demons—and in doing so show God to be immeasurably glorious and sufficient for all your needs.

Perseverance in Prayer

I believe there is yet another reason why God doesn't immediately destroy Satan, and that reason is found in Ephesians 6:18–20. The victory we achieve over the enemy will only come about by means of perseverance in prayer. In other words, it is only as we turn to God in prayer, over and over and over again, that we overcome Satan's seductions.

Why does God command us to pray? Why utilize prayer as the means for our victory in spiritual warfare? Couldn't God shut down the enemy without our asking him to give us strength, power, wisdom, and the incentive to stand firm in our faith? Yes. *But prayer magnifies him more.*

Prayer puts God on display as the only one worthy of our devotion and trust. When you are laid up, sick and helpless, and you need someone to clean your house and mow the grass and bring food to your kitchen so you can eat, and someone who cares about you answers your phone call for help and says, "Of course, I'd be delighted to help," who gets the glory? Not you. You're weak and helpless and all you did was to call for the assistance of another. The glory and praise go to the one who rushes to your side and, in generosity and kindness, provides you with all you need. That is why God wants us to pray during seasons of spiritual attack. It magnifies him as the one who comes to our aid. It honors him as the only one powerful enough to pull it off. It shines a light on his mercy and all-sufficiency to do for us what only he can do.

I think God ordains prayer during spiritual warfare for another reason: He wants us to *partner with him* in securing the victory. When, by God's grace, we stand firm by praying at all times, we gain far more joy and satisfaction than if we did nothing at all. God doesn't say to us, "Stand over there and do nothing." He says, "Come to me and ask for all the resources and spiritual strength needed to defeat your enemy." The principle here is that, except on rare occasions, God will not intervene to give you daily victory unless you ask him to. If Paul believed that God would give him strength, clarity, and courage to preach apart from the intercessory prayers of the Ephesian church, he would never have written verses 18–20!

Prayer is not the seventh piece of spiritual armor. Nor is it the way we wield the sword of the Spirit (which is the Word of God). Grammatically, both "praying" and "keeping alert" (v. 18) are connected with the verb "stand" all the way back in verse 14. In other words, prayer is what characterizes and permeates the whole of the Christian soldier's activity: "Take your stand, praying . . . Put on the belt of truth, praying . . . Put on the breastplate of righteousness, as you pray . . . ," etc. Prayer is the power behind the armor. Prayer is what makes the armor effective in battle. You will probably have little success in putting it on and standing firm if you fail to pray as Paul exhorts us to pray in verses 18–20.

The Four "All's" of Prayer

Paul uses the word "all" four times in Ephesians 6:18–20.

1. Pray with All Prayer and Supplication

He first tells us that we are to pray "with all prayer and supplication" (v. 18a). In other words, prayer is not monolithic. It is not all the same.

There is a wide variety of prayers that God calls upon us to employ. The different kinds/types of prayer available to us include silent prayer, audible prayer, public prayer, private prayer, both short and long prayers, prayer with fasting, prayer with feasting, prayer with praise, petition, intercession, rebuke, doctrinal praying, emotional praying, prayer in tongues, resisting-the-enemy prayers, prayers of thanksgiving, prayers of confession, prayer for healing, prayers for help, prayers for courage, etc. As prayer pertains specifically to spiritual warfare, consider six forms it may assume:

1. Prayer for Ourselves

There is, first of all, prayer for ourselves and others to be given insight and understanding into who we are in Christ and what is ours through faith (Eph. 1:15–23). Knowing who you are in Jesus, knowing what he has accomplished for you by his life, death, and resurrection, is a powerful weapon to use in your battle with the enemy. Satan will always lie to you about who you are. If he can undermine and sow seeds of doubt in your mind about what Christ has done in making you into a child of God, he can win.

2. Prayer of Resistance and Rebuke

Second, there are prayers of resistance and rebuke of the enemy. Tom White provides this example:

> Satan, I rebuke you in the authority of Jesus Christ. I declare your works in my life destroyed. Jesus triumphed over you in the wilderness, on the cross, and in the grave. His resurrection has sealed your fate. I triumph over you now in the strength of his name. I resist and rebuke your efforts to oppress, afflict, or deceive me. I remove from you the right to rob me of the joy and fruit of my salvation. Through the power of the blood of Calvary, I command all powers of darkness assigned to me, sent to me, or surrounding me now, to leave. Go where Jesus Christ orders you to go, never to return.[2]

3. Prayer for Protection

Third, there are prayers of protection in which we ask God to shield, guard, and support us. One such prayer may sound like this:

> Lord, I commend and entrust _____ into your watchful care. May your glory surround and protect him/her. May you drive away the enemy and deliver him/her from all evil and temptation and every attack of the evil one.

We are to pray alertly, "with all perseverance" (v. 18c). Simply put, never give up! Never quit! Pray without ceasing (1 Thess. 5:17)! Don't let physical exhaustion get the better of you. Don't be discouraged. Don't grow weary. Resist the temptation to think that God isn't listening, or worse still, that he doesn't care. Some cease to pray because they think their prayer is one that God simply won't answer. But that isn't true. The answer is often either yes, no, maybe, wait, or "I'm God, and I've got a better idea!"

Paul's aim in this exhortation is to encourage you to endure, no matter

---

2 White, *The Believer's Guide to Spiritual Warfare*, 116.

the cost. Quitting is so very, very easy. It takes no effort. It requires no resolve. No planning is needed. You just stop praying. Period. And one of the reasons we quit, aside from thinking that our prayers haven't been answered in the way we wanted, is that prayer is hard. It's a struggle. More than that, it's a war! There's a reason Paul concluded his teaching on spiritual warfare and our battle with Satan with this exhortation. When he tells us to "keep alert," he's reminding us that daydreaming, falling asleep, or simply yielding to the countless distractions that come our way require diligent focus and a commitment to persevere.

Staying "alert," as Paul puts it, is a strain on our souls. In his letter to the church in Rome, he appealed to them "by our Lord Jesus Christ and by the love of the Spirit, to *strive* together with me in your prayers to God on my behalf" (Rom. 15:30, emphasis mine). Yes, you must "strive" to pray. In Colossians 1:29 and 2:1 he used the language of "*toiling*" and "*struggling*."

We are so easily derailed from coming consistently to the throne of grace, thinking that other activities are more fruitful or essential. And perhaps the greatest obstacle to persevering at all times in prayer is the presumptuous and sinful belief that God will do for us apart from our prayers those things that he has promised to do for us only through prayers.

There is yet another important reason why Paul issued this exhortation to persevere in prayer at the conclusion of his discussion of spiritual warfare. It is because Satan and his demonic hosts persevere in their relentless assault against us. We must remain alert precisely because Satan is always on the alert for ways to undermine our confidence in God. When we fall asleep, we must never think that Satan does. Although we grow weary in prayer because of our physical finitude, no demon ever does. As spiritual beings, they are not distracted as we are. They do not grow weary or exhaust themselves in their efforts to bombard us with temptations. We must struggle and toil and never quit in our prayers because our enemy struggles, toils, and never quits in his diabolical efforts to lure us away from the heart of God.

If the enemy incessantly launches his fiery missiles against us, we must no less incessantly bring our requests and intercessory petitions to the throne of grace (Heb. 4:16). Paul knew that neither Satan nor his demons take a day off. They observe no sabbath rest. They know nothing of a spiritual cease fire. This reality alone should suffice to justify our obedience to the apostolic command that we pray "with all perseverance" (Eph. 6:18c).

4. Prayer over a Location

Fourth, there are prayers for the places where you go, stay, or live (especially when traveling or in a strange location). I will never forget when I first met Jack Taylor. I picked him up at the airport in Kansas City and took him to his hotel. He insisted I come with him to his room. He said he never takes up residence in a hotel room, no matter how short the stay, without praying. He asked me to get down on my knees with him and he prayed:

> Father in heaven, would you by your Spirit cleanse and purify this room. Whatever sins have been committed here, I ask that I be shielded from any and all defilement. Whatever evil spirits were invoked or may have taken up residence in this room, by the authority of Jesus Christ I command that they leave. If pornography was viewed in this room, or if adultery was committed in this room, I ask that you drive away all lingering spiritual influence that may have come as a result. In the name of Jesus, I pray. Amen!

Tom White gives us yet another prayer to use in your home or any other place where you may spend extended periods of time:

> Lord, I claim this place for your purposes. I stand on the truth of your Word: "The scepter of the wicked will not remain over the land allotted to the righteous" (Ps. 125:3). I believe you have given me this place. I dedicate it to you and ask you to fill it with your holy presence. I separate myself from any iniquity that has occurred here in past times. I apply the power of Jesus's blood to remove any desecration of God's name in this place. I ask you, in Jesus's authority, to set watching angels around this property for your purposes, protecting your servant from the work of the evil one.[3]

Finally, we are to pray for "all the saints" (Eph. 6:18c). Everywhere, for everyone. Out of sight, but never out of mind or heart. Observe Paul's need for this (vv. 19–20)! Paul generally closes his letters with a request for prayer for himself (see Rom. 15:30–32; Col. 4:3; 1 Thess. 5:25; 2 Thess. 3:1–2; see also

---

3   Ibid., 18–19.

2 Cor. 1:11; Phil. 1:19). "Like every nervous preacher, he desires 'the liberty of the Spirit to express it (i.e., the gospel) freely, clearly, and boldly."[4]

When Paul speaks of "all the saints" there's no reason to think that he had in mind only those in Ephesus. I say this because of how he describes his own prayer life in Colossians 1:3. "We always thank God, the Father of our Lord Jesus Christ, when we pray for you." Again, in verse 9 he writes, "And so, from the day we heard, we have not ceased to pray for you." This is significant because Paul had never met these people! There's no evidence that he had ever visited the town of Colossae. He didn't know their names and obviously wouldn't have been able to recognize their faces. It was Epaphras who had planted the church in that city (v. 7). But this was no hindrance to Paul's continued intercession on their behalf. And your lack of personal acquaintance with people in any particular city or local church should never become an excuse to stop praying for them.

5. Prayer for the Afflicted and Oppressed

Fifth, there is prayer for those afflicted and oppressed when you are ministering to them. A few things you might wish to pray are:

- that the demon(s) afflicting this person would be prevented from communicating with other demons or with Satan himself;
- that the Holy Spirit would confuse and weaken the grip that any and all demons might have on this person;
- that the person would be strengthened in his or her faith to understand his or her position and identity in Christ and to trust and obey the Word, even if feelings or experiences might be different from what Scripture says;
- that the person may be able to distinguish between his or her thoughts and feelings and the thoughts and feelings of demons; in other words, pray that the individual might have discernment to know the difference between his or her own ideas and those ideas suggested to them by the enemy;
- that God would protect and guide his child and set angelic forces at work to break up every scheme of the enemy.[5]

---

4 O'Brien, *Ephesians*, 487.

5 These five suggestions are adapted from Dickason, *Demon Possession & the Christian*, 255–56.

6. Prayer for Angelic Support

Sixth, there is prayer for angelic support, ministry, and protection. If that sounds weird to you, may I remind you that after Jesus had been tempted by the devil himself, we are told that "angels came and were ministering to him" (Matt. 4:11). We are told in Daniel 10:10–21 that an angel was "sent" (Dan. 10:11) to Daniel to give him understanding in God's purposes. The angel "touched" Daniel and "strengthened" him (Dan. 10:18). He told him, "fear not, peace be with you; be strong and of good courage" (Dan. 10:19). And Daniel responded by saying, "as he spoke to me, I was strengthened" (Dan. 10:19; see Acts 12:5–8).

DOES METHOD MATTER?

Don't be obsessed with "how" you pray. It betrays the assumption that prayer is a kind of religious formula or magical incantation that requires just the right words to prevail. People often think that the wrong words will anger God or frustrate him and provoke him to say no to their requests. Remember Romans 8:26–39.

2. Pray at All Times in the Spirit

Paul's second use of the word "all" in relation to prayer is found in his exhortation that we pray "at all times in the Spirit" (Eph. 6:18). I find it instructive that Paul used the same phrase, "in the Spirit," to describe his regular practice of praying in tongues (1 Cor. 14:14–19).[6] But whereas tongues is certainly included in what Paul meant here, there are numerous other ways in which we pray "in the Spirit." For example, we are to pray as the Holy Spirit prompts us. Listen to his voice. Be sensitive to his leading regarding what you should ask God to do. We are to pray in the strength and power the Holy Spirit supplies. Perhaps we should ask for a fresh infilling of the Spirit's presence before we pray. We are also to ask the Holy Spirit to remind us of truths in

---

6   For more on the gift of speaking and praying in tongues, see my book *The Language of Heaven: Crucial Questions about Speaking in Tongues* (Lake Mary, FL: Charisma House, 2019).

the Word relevant to the matter at hand. And we must always ask the Holy Spirit to cleanse our minds of sin and fill them with purity.

3. Pray with All Perseverance

As noted earlier, Paul exhorts us to pray alertly "with all perseverance" (Eph 6:18). The easiest thing about prayer is giving up. To pray without ceasing (1 Thess. 5:17) sounds exhausting, but with the Spirit's empowering presence to sustain us, it is within our reach. Yes, it is exhausting at times. Yes, we can easily get discouraged. But we must remember that God is attentive to every syllable we utter and every sigh of our hearts, no matter how we may feel or how weak or insipid our prayers may seem.

Praying against Satan and His Schemes

There is, admittedly, a lot we don't know or understand about prayer. How it is incorporated into the way a sovereign God providentially governs the universe remains largely a mystery. Why some prayers are answered swiftly, others slowly, and some not at all often baffles us. But this doesn't mean we are left in the dark when it comes to prayer.

We know, for example, that we are to pray to God the Father, in the name of God the Son, and through the sustaining power of God the Holy Spirit. We know that we are to come to the throne of grace "with confidence" so "that we may receive mercy and find grace to help in time of need" (Heb. 4:16). And Jesus himself reminded us that he delights in answering our prayers because in this way "the Father may be glorified in the Son" (John 14:13).

But other questions remain largely unanswered. The issue we are addressing in this chapter is how prayer factors into our obedience to the command that if we "resist" Satan "he will flee" from us (Jas. 4:7).

Of this we may be certain: at no time are we to pray *for*, or on behalf of, Satan. As noted above, Scripture repeatedly assures us that his eternal destiny in the lake of fire is sealed and irreversible. Neither Satan nor his demons are capable of repentance. Salvation has not been provided for them. Indeed, "it is not angels that he [Christ] helps, but he helps the offspring of Abraham" (Heb. 2:16). The cross is the instrument of Satan's defeat, not his redemption (Col. 2:13–15; Heb. 2:14–15).

Scripture is equally clear that we are not to pray *to* Satan. There is nothing he would do for us but evil, and it is to God alone that we bring our many requests. To petition Satan or to pray to him for his presence and power is what only those who honor him as "lord" would dare to do. So, how does prayer relate to Satan and the demonic hosts? In what ways should we pray against him?

Earlier in this book we saw that Satan does not act haphazardly or randomly. Several texts indicate that he operates on the basis of a carefully conceived strategy (see 2 Cor. 2:10–11; Eph. 6:11). If we are to pray effectively in our effort to resist Satan, we simply need to keep in the forefront of our thinking the many ways in which he seeks to disrupt the life of the local church and the ministries of God's people. I don't want to revisit what we've already discussed, so I will only list the many things that Scripture explicitly states are a part of his nefarious purposes.

Satan opposes the spread of the gospel at every turn (1 Thess. 2:18) and aims to induce spiritual blindness in those to whom the gospel is proclaimed (2 Cor. 4:4). Therefore, our prayers should be for the Spirit to facilitate the many details required for missionaries and evangelists to take the gospel to the unreached. At the same time, we should pray that God would shine in their hearts "the light of the knowledge of the glory of God in the face of Jesus Christ" (2 Cor. 4:6).

Satan can occasionally be the source of bodily sickness (Luke 13:10–17; Acts 10:38) and consistently induces the fear of death to keep people enslaved in spiritual darkness (Heb. 2:14). He sought to disrupt the early church by filling the heart of Ananias and Sapphira to lie about the monetary gift they had previously pledged to make (Acts 5:3). Perhaps his most wicked scheme was to make use of Peter himself to deter Jesus from going to the cross to secure our salvation (Matt. 16:21–23). Knowing that our enemy has these goals in view should inform how we pray and the specific requests we make of God.

As we hear on a daily basis of the severe persecution and even martyrdom of our brothers and sisters around the world, we need to be diligent to pray that the Spirit would restrain Satan's hand and especially that God would strengthen the faithful resolve of those who have put their lives at risk for the sake of the lost (1 Pet. 5:8–9; Rev. 2:10). Since Jesus himself prayed for our unity as the people of God (John 17:15, 20–21), we can be assured that Satan will do all he can to sow seeds of discord, mistrust, and division. We must therefore align ourselves with our Savior and seek God for the bonds of unity to deepen and overcome Satan's wicked intentions.

The apostle Paul makes clear in Ephesians 5 that the loving relationship of a husband and wife is illustrative of the gospel and the love Christ has for his bride. I can well imagine, then, that Satan will strive to create conflict and disloyalty in marriages. That alone should energize our intercession for our own marriages and those of others in our local churches.

We looked in some detail at how Satan will attempt to exploit our sinful behavior and especially our unforgiveness to gain a foothold in our lives (Eph. 4:26–27). To be alert to what our enemy might do and to pray fervently against his efforts is not borne of fear but faith in the supremacy of Christ and his designs for our lives (1 John 4:4).

Without wanting to be simplistic, ponder deeply the many exhortations in Scripture, the moral values that it upholds, the vision for life in the local church and in families, and know that Satan will strive to resist, undermine, oppose, and distort each and every one. That alone will be sufficient to guide and inform your prayer life. Knowing all that is good and godly will alert you to what our enemy is determined to destroy. Stand firm! Resist him! Pray without ceasing!

THE REST OF REBEKAH'S STORY

In the summer of 2019, I entered Bridgeway's inner healing and deliverance ministry. My primary motivation for going through the program was to be equipped to minister to others. The Lord had already rescued me from years of anxiety and OCD tendencies, and I was excited for an opportunity to see him bring freedom to others. I knew the Holy Spirit would continue to deepen my intimacy with him during this time, and I was hungry for whatever he had for me. As I filled out the intake form for the program, I was unable to define areas in which I needed profound inner healing or deliverance. In my limited awareness, I believed all major areas of bondage had already been eliminated from my life, and the Lord's work here would be one of a subtler refining. The only "issue" I identified upon starting the ministry was "a little indecisiveness."

As the weeks progressed and I systematically moved through prayer and confession in major areas of my life, I became aware that warfare was being waged in so many corners of my life. Week after week the Holy Spirit moved powerfully to bring the darkness that had been hiding in the corners of my life to light and drive out the foothold of the enemy. It was a time of deep spiritual renewal as I profoundly experienced the manifest presence of the Holy Spirit.

Over the course of the program I realized that the "minor" area of indecisiveness was not minor, but instead a pervasive symptom of serious spiritual bondage. It wasn't until I experienced freedom that I could see where I had been in bondage. One day, while on a date with my husband, I perused the menu and quickly gave the server my order. In that moment, I realized the extreme bondage the enemy previously held me in. Normally, ordering was a long angst-ridden process, frequently filled with last-minute changes. In that moment I realized I was actually enjoying eating out because I was no longer riddled with fear of "making the wrong decision."

There were many other moments that showed me the extent of the bondage I had lived under. At Christmas, I selected a couple of gift options for my in-laws and asked my husband to choose between the two. Normally, this would have been a lengthy, stressful process where I relied heavily upon my husband's input to aid me. Even at the gym I saw areas where I had lived in bondage. Burdened by the need to "get it right," I was usually the class member asking the coach to tell me the exact amount of weight to use. I laughed one day when I simply added more weight until it felt heavy enough. These examples may seem trivial, but my indecisiveness was so extreme that it had paralyzed me from functioning freely in even the most basic aspects of my life. I was riddled with doubt and confusion at almost every moment of my existence. My indecisiveness was an outward symptom of spiritual and demonic oppression robbing me of living in the freedom, abundance, and joy the Lord had already given me.

The enemy had remained undetected until prayer waged warfare and brought the imposter out of the shadows. My deliverance from indecisiveness did not happen in some grand moment of exorcism but was the result of progressive weeks of gentle prayer and confession and repentance. I cannot name the precise moment the Lord delivered me, but there were specific times when the Lord drove out cloudiness and spoke truth over me. As the Lord broke generational patterns of performance and unspoken rules in my life, I saw an image of a board game as the Lord told me, "God's rules are clear, and when we play by his rules, we are free to move autonomously about the board." I also saw myself floating in the pool on a sunny day, hearing the words "this is fun." I was learning the truth that I could rest in the Lord and no longer needed to perform. The Holy Spirit had broken the bonds of the enemy through the power of prayer.

I am no longer riddled by the anxiety of pleasing people, but instead I can live with the lightness and peace that come only from God. I am chosen, saved, and accepted by my heavenly Father. Therefore, I live to please him alone. Perfect love has driven out fear and shame. I am no longer a people pleaser; I am a daughter of God, my heavenly Father!

Conclusion

If you have closely read each chapter of this book and persevered to the end, I trust you have a deeper and clearer grasp of the nature of the spiritual battle that confronts every Christian, every day. I've done my best to avoid sensationalizing the reality of Satan and his demons, but their existence and activity simply cannot be denied, and are ignored only to the detriment of the individual believer. Every effort has been made to account for the biblical data in a way that will neither turn people away in fear nor lead them to minimize our spiritual enemies and the threat they pose.

But my primary design in this book is to bring to the reader's awareness the hope for deliverance and freedom. The many personal testimonies scattered throughout these pages were not fabricated. They are the stories of real people that I know, people like many of you, who often have been subjected to horrific mistreatment and have suffered oppressive demonic attack as a result. What I most want you to hear in this book isn't that Satan is wicked or that demonic assault is frequent, although both are true. I want you to hear that you don't have to continue your life enslaved to false beliefs. You don't have to recoil in anxiety over the existence of cosmic powers (Eph. 6:12). You don't have to remain in bondage to your past. There is no need for you to suffer from the constant barrage of fiery darts that the enemy rains down on your head. You can be free of the fear that plagues your daily life and torments you at night. You can truly walk in the peace that surpasses all understanding (Phil. 4:7).

My hope for those reading this book is that they would, by God's grace, enter into new dimensions of personal spiritual freedom, the kind that Jesus came to secure for us. My desire is that many of you would find it possible to experience what Peter refers to as "joy that is inexpressible and filled with glory" (1 Pet. 1:8). My aim in describing the defeat of our enemy was that you might no longer live each day in the grip of doubt and intimidation. My continual prayer is that you would come to understand and operate in the power of that authority that Christ himself has imparted to each of his followers (Luke 10:17–20). The emotional turmoil in which so many of you live each day need not continue! That distorted sense of personal identity that prevents you from enjoying and resting peacefully in what it means to be a blood-bought, redeemed, adopted child of God can undergo a glorious transformation today. Although Satan will do everything he can to prevent it, God wants you to know who you really are.

Yes, Satan is real. His intentions are perverse and wicked. But "the reason the Son of God appeared was to destroy the works of the devil" (1 John 3:8). This is your hope for a fresh start. This is the basis on which you can cut off the influence of all demonic forces and enter into the "abundant life" (John 10:10) that the Good Shepherd gave his life to secure for his sheep. Shame and self-loathing and the spiritual paralysis that so often results need not hold you down any longer. The same divine power and grace that have "delivered us from the domain of darkness and transferred us to the kingdom of his beloved Son" (Col. 1:13) are present to equip and empower us to gain daily victory over the temptations and sinister tactics of the enemy.

If I can leave you with one thought that I pray will exert a consuming and powerful influence on your life, it is the truth that "he who is in you is greater than he who is in the world" (1 John 4:4). Praise be to God for the victory we have in Jesus!

Select Bibliography

(The resources available on the subject of spiritual warfare are seemingly endless. This listing, therefore, is necessarily limited. Inclusion below does not imply my endorsement of everything they teach.)

Anderson, Neil. *The Bondage Breaker*. Rev. ed. Eugene: Harvest House, 2019.

_____. *Ministering the Steps to Freedom in Christ*. Grand Rapids: Baker, 1998.

_____. *Released from Bondage*. San Bernardino, CA: Here's Life, 1991.

_____. *Victory over the Darkness: Realizing the Power of Your Identity in Christ*. Rev. ed. Ventura, CA: Regal, 2020.

Arnold, Clinton E. *3 Crucial Questions about Spiritual Warfare*. Grand Rapids: Baker, 1997.

_____. *Power and Magic: The Concept of Power in Ephesians*. Grand Rapids: Baker, 1997.

_____. *Powers of Darkness: Principalities & Powers in Paul's Letters*. Downers Grove, IL: InterVarsity Press, 1992.

Beilby, James K., and Paul Rhodes Eddy, eds. *Understanding Spiritual Warfare: Four Views*. Grand Rapids: Baker, 2012.

Boyd, Gregory A. *God at War: The Bible & Spiritual Conflict*. Downers Grove, IL: InterVarsity Press, 1997.

Cole, Graham. *Against the Darkness: The Doctrine of Angels, Satan, and Demons*. Wheaton, IL: Crossway, 2019.

Cook III, William F., and Chuck Lawless. *Spiritual Warfare in the Storyline of Scripture: A Biblical, Theological, and Practical Approach*. Nashville: B & H Academic, 2019.

Cuneo, Michael W. *American Exorcism: Expelling Demons in the Land of Plenty*. New York: Doubleday, 2001.

Dickason, C. Fred. *Angels: Elect and Evil*. Chicago: Moody, 1995.

_____. *Demon Possession & the Christian*. Chicago: Moody, 1987.

Gilhooly, John R. *40 Questions About Angels, Demons, and Spiritual Warfare*. Grand Rapids: Kregel Academic, 2018.

Green, Michael. *I Believe in Satan's Downfall*. Grand Rapids: Eerdmans, 1981.

Heiser, Michael S. *Angels: What the Bible Really Says about God's Heavenly Host*. Bellingham, WA: Lexham, 2018.

_____. *Demons: What the Bible Really Says about the Powers of Darkness*. Bellingham, WA: Lexham, 2020.

_____. *The Unseen Realm: Recovering the Supernatural Worldview of the Bible*. Bellingham, WA: Lexham, 2015.

Hitchcock, Mark. *101 Answers to Questions about Satan, Demons, & Spiritual Warfare*. Eugene, OR: Harvest House, 2014.

Ingram, Chip. *The Invisible War: What Every Believer Needs to Know about Satan, Demons & Spiritual Warfare*. Grand Rapids: Baker, 2015.

Keener, Craig S. *Miracles: The Credibility of the New Testament Accounts*. 2 vol. Grand Rapids: Baker Academic, 2011.

Kolenda, Daniel. *Slaying Dragons: A Practical Guide to Spiritual Warfare*. Lake Mary, FL: Charisma House, 2019.

Lane, Anthony N. S., ed. *The Unseen World: Christian Reflections on Angels, Demons, and the Heavenly Realm*. Grand Rapids: Baker, 1996.

Lewis, C. S. *The Screwtape Letters*. New York: Collier Books, 1982.

Lowe, Chuck. *Territorial Spirits and World Evangelisation: A Biblical, Historical and Missiological Critique of Strategic-Level Spiritual Warfare*. Fearn, Ross-Shire, UK: Christian Focus Publications, 2001.

MacNutt, Francis. *Deliverance from Evil Spirits: A Practical Manual*. Grand Rapids: Chosen, 1995.

Mallone, George. *Arming for Spiritual Warfare: How Christians can Prepare to Fight the Enemy*. Downers Grove, IL: InterVarsity Press, 1991.

McCloud, Sean. *American Possessions: Fighting Demons in the Contemporary United States*. Oxford: Oxford University Press, 2015.

McKinley, Mike. *Did the Devil Make Me Do It? And Other Questions about Satan, Demons and Evil Spirits*. London: Good Book Company, 2013.

Montgomery, John Warwick, ed. *Demon Possession: A Medical, Historical, Anthropological and Theological Symposium.* Papers presented at the University of Notre Dame, January 8–11, 1975, under the auspices of the Christian Medical Association. Minneapolis: Bethany House, 1976.

Moreau, A. Scott, Tokunboh Adeyemo, David G. Burnett, L. Myers Bryant, and Hwa Yung, eds. *Deliver Us from Evil: An Uneasy Frontier in Christian Mission.* Monrovia, CA: World Vision International, 2002.

Murphy, Ed. *The Handbook for Spiritual Warfare.* Nashville: Thomas Nelson, 1992.

Noll, Stephen F. *Angels of Light, Powers of Darkness: Thinking Biblically about Angels, Satan & Principalities.* Downers Grove, IL: InterVarsity Press, 1998.

Oropeza, B. J. *99 Answers to Questions about Angels, Demons & Spiritual Warfare.* Downers Grove, IL: InterVarsity Press, 1997.

Page, Sydney H. T. *Powers of Evil: A Biblical Study of Satan and Demons.* Grand Rapids: Baker, 1995.

Powlison, David. *Power Encounters: Reclaiming Spiritual Warfare.* Grand Rapids: Baker, 1995.

Thomas, John Christopher. *The Devil, Disease and Deliverance: Origins of Illness in New Testament Thought.* Sheffield, UK: Sheffield Academic Press, 1998.

Wagner, C. Peter, and Douglas F. Pennoyer, eds. *Wrestling with Dark Angels: Toward a Deeper Understanding of the Supernatural Forces in Spiritual Warfare.* Ventura, CA: Regal, 1990.

Warner, Timothy M. *Spiritual Warfare: Victory over the Powers of this Dark World.* Wheaton, IL: Crossway, 1991.

White, Thomas B. *Breaking Strongholds: How Spiritual Warfare Sets Captives Free.* Ann Arbor, MI: Servant, 1993.

———. *The Believer's Guide to Spiritual Warfare.* Ann Arbor, MI: Servant, 1990.

Scripture Index

Subject Index

Abyss, 5, 62, 87–88, 91, 102, 119, 273, 277
angel(s)
  fallen, 45–46, 48, 59, 243, 270
  Gabriel, 61, 114, 115–16, 118
  good/holy, 46, 47, 51, 53, 61, 62, 64, 66, 119, 196, 244, 270–71
  in Daniel, 115–16
  Michael, 25, 61, 65–66, 116, 118, 214, 246, 248, 270–71
  occurrence of, in Bible, 45
Anderson, Neil, 259, 277–79
antichrist, 97–100, 102, 106, 109, 183–64
Arnold, Clinton, xi–xiii, 13–14, 16, 117, 118, 119, 125, 134–35, 144, 168, 175, 182, 185, 296
atheists, 7–8
authority
  believer's, 259, 260–61
  in Christ, 86, 256–65, 281
  of Satan, 9, 10, 48, 49, 297
Armageddon, 106–11

Barnett, Paul, 143

beast, the, 94, 97–98, 102, 103, 108
  mark of, 104–6
  worship of, 100–1, 103, 104
Beilby, James K., xix, 121, 269
believer's
  authority, 259, 260–61
  identity, 257–59
  triumph, 67, 92, 96
belt of truth, 289, 299, 318
biblical worldview, xvii, 16–17
binding Satan. *See* deliverance
blessings(s), 25, 123, 167, 169, 171, 218, 238, 266
Bliss, Philip Paul, 214
Boyd, Gregory A., 23, 27, 268, 269
breastplate of righteousness, 289, 299–300, 318
Bruce, F. F., 245

Caine, Christine, 189
Calvin, John, 160, 245
Carson, D. A., 140, 142
Christ
  authority in, 86, 256–65, 281
  being "in", 9–10, 13, 33, 66, 67, 74,

Understanding Spiritual Gifts

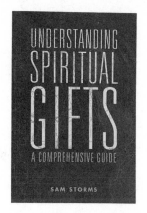

Author and pastor Sam Storms has spent several decades teaching on the topic of the spiritual gifts and equipping believers in the faithful practice of God's gifts. Yet there remains a great deal of confusion about the nature of the gifts and how they best function in the body of Christ. In this comprehensive guide to the spiritual gifts, Storms addresses the many bizarre and misleading interpretations that abound and confronts the tendency to downplay the urgency of spiritual gifts for Christian living and ministry. He explains how spiritual gifts, both the more miraculous and the somewhat mundane, are given to build up the body of Christ. God has graciously provided these "manifestations of the Spirit" so that believers might encourage, edify, strengthen, instruct, and console one another, all with a view to an ever-increasing, incremental transformation into the image of Jesus Christ.

Throughout this guide, Storms unpacks the glorious truth that there is a supernatural and divine energy or power that fills and indwells the body and soul of every born-again believer. God does not call upon us to speculate about the nature of this power or to embrace it as a mere idea. His desire is that we avail ourselves of it to partner with him in his purposes on earth. His desire is that we cry out to him, that he might intensify, expand, increase, and deepen the manifestation of this power through us in ever more demonstrative and tangible ways in our lives.

Understanding Spiritual Gifts is useful as a reference to address common questions about the gifts, but it also serves as a training manual for using and exercising the gifts in ministry. It is perfect for any individual or group who wants to grow in their understanding of the gifts for today.

Available in stores and online!

Practicing the Power

The Bible teaches us that we are to be filled with God's Spirit and that God's presence and grace is manifested among his people as they serve, love, and minister to one another. Yet some of the gifts that God offers to his people are not commonly seen in many churches today. Gifts of prophecy, healing, tongues, and other supernatural gifts of God seem to be absent, and many Christians are unsure how to cultivate an atmosphere where God's Spirit can work while remaining committed to the foundational truth of God's Word.

How can Christians pursue and implement the miraculous gifts of the Spirit without falling into fanatical excess and splitting the church in the process? In *Practicing the Power*, pastor and author Sam Storms offers practical steps to understanding and exercising spiritual gifts in a way that remains grounded in the Word and centered in the gospel.

With examples drawn from his forty years of ministry as a pastor and teacher, Storms offers a guidebook that can help pastors, elders, and church members understand what changes are needed to see God move in supernatural power and to guard against excess and abuse of the spiritual gifts. If you long to see God's Spirit move in your church and life, and are not sure why that is not happening or where to begin, this book is for you.

Available in stores and online!